D0205808

# Jews and the Military

# Jews and the Military

**A HISTORY**

Derek J. Penslar

PRINCETON UNIVERSITY PRESS

Princeton and Oxford

Copyright © 2013 by Princeton University Press

Published by Princeton University Press, 41 William Street, Princeton, New Jersey 08540

In the United Kingdom: Princeton University Press, 6 Oxford Street, Woodstock, Oxfordshire OX20 1TW

press.princeton.edu

JACKET ART: Arthur Szyk, cover drawing for 1941 United Palestine Appeal yearbook. Reproduced with the cooperation of The Arthur Szyk Society, Burlingame, CA. www.szyk.org

LIBRARY OF CONGRESS CATALOGING-IN-PUBLICATION DATA

Penslar, Derek Jonathan, author.

  Jews and the military : a history / Derek J. Penslar.
      pages cm
  Includes bibliographical references and index.
  ISBN 978-0-691-13887-9 (hardcover)
    1. Jewish soldiers—Europe—History—19th century.  2. Jewish soldiers—Europe—History—20th century.  3. Jews—Europe—History—19th century. 4.  Jews—Europe—History—20th century. 5. Jews—Cultural assimilation—Europe—History—19th century.  6. Jews—Cultural assimilation—Europe—History—20th century.  7. Jews—Europe—Identity.  I. Title.
    DS135.E83P45 2013
    355.0089'92404—dc23        2013000893

British Library Cataloging-in-Publication Data is available

This book has been composed in Minion and Univers

Printed on acid-free paper ∞

Printed in the United States of America

10  9  8  7  6  5  4  3  2  1

# CONTENTS

# ILLUSTRATIONS

# ACKNOWLEDGMENTS

I t takes a village to write a book. Over the years of this book's gestation many colleagues have steered me toward fascinating areas of inquiry and sources. Deepest thanks to Israel Bartal, Michael Berkowitz, David Biale, Pierre Birnbaum, Bernard Cooperman, Natalie Zemon Davis, Todd Endelman, David Engel, Leah Garrett, Matt Goldish, Rachel Greenblatt, Elliott Horowitz, Paula Hyman (z"l), Joy Jacoby, Jonathan Karp, Alexander Kaye, Rebecca Kobrin, Paul Lerner, Mark Mazower, Deborah Dash Moore, Sam Moyn, Yochanan Petrovsky-Shtern, Joseph Schatzmiller, Anita Shapira, Michael Silber, Michael Stanislawski, Adam Teller, Scott Ury, and Ruth Wisse. I have known David Sorkin since graduate school and Steven Zipperstein for almost as long; their advice, on this project and on all the previous ones, has always been invaluable and deeply appreciated. Special thanks to Richard Kravitz, an old and dear college friend, who gave me the idea for this book during a conversation almost a decade ago.

At the University of Toronto, Eric Jennings directed me to one of the book's most important archival sources, read portions of the book manuscript, and helped me maintain a global perspective. Jonathan Gribetz, who spent a year at Toronto on a postdoctoral fellowship before moving on to a faculty position at Rutgers, is a delightful colleague and a gently exacting reader. I am grateful to the students in my fourth-year undergraduate seminar, "Power and Identity in Jewish History," who read the draft manuscript and quickly overcame qualms about criticizing their professor. (One of those students, Arielle Lewis, prepared the bibliography and made innumerable library runs for me.) My Toronto colleagues Doris Bergen, Ritu Birla, Ivan Kalmar, Jeff Kopstein, Michael Marrus, and Anna Shternshis have been constant sources of support, intellectual exchange, and friendship. On the other side of the pond, my new colleagues at Oxford Abigail Green and David Rechter as well as François Guesnet at University College London critiqued the book manuscript with a sharp eye, sound judgment, and good humor.

It has been a great pleasure working with Princeton University Press. Thanks to my sponsoring editor Fred Appel, who showed enthusiasm for this project from the very start. The suggestions I received from Fred, the Press's anonymous readers, and my colleagues and students have helped me sharpen and clarify my arguments, cut redundant or extraneous material, and avoid embarrassing mistakes. Naturally, any remaining errors in fact or faulty judgments are entirely my responsibility.

Visiting professorships at Harvard in 2006 and Columbia in 2009, as well as a fellowship in 2008 from the University of Pennsylvania's Katz Center for Advanced Judaic Studies, offered stimulating intellectual environments and unparalleled library resources. Thanks to the Katz Center's director, David Ruderman, and to the directors of Jewish Studies at Harvard and Columbia, Shaye Cohen and Jeremy Dauber, for these opportunities. A fellowship from the National Endowment for the Humanities in 2009–10 allowed me to write the bulk of the book manuscript.

I thank the archivists and librarians of the Central Archive for the History of the Jewish People and the Central Zionist Archive in Jerusalem, the Haganah archive in Tel Aviv, the Service historique de l'armée territoriale, Service historique de la marine, and Archives Nationales in Paris, and the Imperial and Royal Military Archive in Vienna. I am particularly grateful for assistance and guidance provided by Sabine Hank of the Stiftung Neue Synagogue–Centrum Judaicum in Berlin and Michael Lax of the Archive of the Israel Defense Forces. I gathered much of the book's German-language material at New York City's Center for Jewish History, which has become over its short existence a scholars' paradise. Within the center I made particularly heavy use of the collections of the Leo Baeck Institute, whose staff members extended me every courtesy, as did the staff at the New York Public Library, the Library of Congress in Washington, D.C., the British Library, and the National and University Library in Jerusalem.

Portions of chapter 4 were previously published in "An Unlikely Internationalism: The Jewish Experience of War in Modern Europe," *The Journal of Modern Jewish Studies* VII, 3 (2008), 309–23. An early version of chapter 5 was published as "The German-Jewish Soldier: From

Participant to Victim," *German History* 29 (2011), 423–44. I thank both publications for allowing me to use this material.

Anne Lloyd sent me documents from the Harley Library archives at the University of Southampton, and Rivka Brot did the same from the Yad Vashem archive in Jerusalem. I relied upon Brendan Cook and Natalie Oeltjen for translations from eighteenth-century Latin, and upon Daniel Mahla and Sylwia Szymanska-Smolkin for translations of Polish material. Talia Penslar, in addition to critiquing the entire manuscript, provided a far more stirring translation of a sermon by Esdra Pontremoli than my workaday Italian could muster. At my suggestion, Yitzhak Lewis prepared a powerful translation of Shaul Tchernichovsky's poem "Bein Ha-metsarim," which I discuss and cite in part in chapter 4. I hope that he will someday publish it.

Daniel Heller, Sonya Issard, Tatjana Lichtenstein, Rafi Netz, Sophie Roberts, Dina Roginsky, and Daniel Rosenthal browsed and prepared photocopies from dozens of microformed periodicals. Samuel Biagetti and Simon Luling transcribed the faded and crabbed French handwriting of Captain Fernand Bernard, and Connie Aust did the same for scrawled German script from nineteenth-century L'viv.

My debt to my family is beyond words. Over the years that I worked on this book, my children Joshua and Talia matured from adolescents into independent adults. My wife of thirty years, Robin, is my closest friend and most unsparing critic. She has ridden the wave of four books with the inevitable swells and crashes, the good writing days and the bad. She remains my love and anchor, forever and always.

DECEMBER 2012
*Oxford and Toronto*

# Jews and the Military

# Introduction

At a Toronto synagogue some years ago I gave a talk on Jewish soldiers in modern armies. I began the talk by asking members of the audience how many of them had served in the military or had close relatives—fathers, brothers, uncles, grandfathers—who did the same. There were a few elderly veterans of the Second World War, and several who had served in Korea. People spoke of grandfathers who had fought for the German kaiser or the Russian tsar, or of fathers who had flown for the Royal Air Force, or of sons and daughters currently deployed in Afghanistan. After a few minutes of this conversation, an older man stood and announced, in an unmistakably Israeli accent, that he had fought in the Harel Brigade in Israel's War of Independence. The audience broke out in spontaneous applause.

Why did the audience applaud this gentleman and not any of the other veterans present? Was his military service more distinguished than theirs? Had be been braver, stronger, or more resourceful? It does not matter. It was not the man who received the adulation of the audience, but the cause for which he fought. Israel is inseparable from its military, in which many Jews throughout the diaspora continue to take a fierce pride. Israel casts a shadow over the millions of Jews who throughout modern times have served, as conscripts or volunteers, in the armed forces of their homelands.

From the beginnings of conscription in the late 1700s until the end of the Second World War, military service was of enormous concern to Jews throughout the world. Advocates for Jewish rights presented the Jewish soldier as proof that Jews were worthy of emancipation and social acceptance. For Jewish soldiers, as for all who serve, military life could be a torment but could also be thrilling and liberating, the most memorable experience of a young man's life. Two sets of historically contiguous events—the Holocaust and establishment of the state of Israel, on the one hand, and the 1967 Middle East war and the anti–Vietnam War movement, on the other—blotted the Jewish soldier out of Jewish collective memory. Europe's betrayal of its Jews made the century and a half of patriotic Jewish military service appear futile and misguided. The Israeli fighter assumed the role formerly held by the diaspora Jewish soldier as the epitome of Jewish masculinity and valor. Israel's lightning victory over its Arab foes in 1967 accelerated the lionization of the Israeli soldier and marginalization of his diaspora counterpart. At the same time, Jewish activists passionately opposed to American involvement in Vietnam condemned the army and wanted nothing to do with it. From the 1970s onward, Jewish historical writing in North America steadfastly neglected Jewish solders. Meanwhile, in Israel scholars usually considered the diaspora Jewish soldier to be too inconsequential for serious attention.

The Jewish soldier in the diaspora deserves to be rescued from oblivion and subjected to serious historical study. His presence or absence and the forms he takes throw new light both on the modern state's policies toward Jews and on changing Jewish attitudes toward state power and the use of force.

There is another, perhaps even more important, motive that has compelled me to write this book. It is impossible to understand the origins of Israel's military—one of the hallmarks of the Jewish state—without probing the history of the relationship between Jews and the use of armed force in modern times. The Zionist project aspired to create a new Jewish warrior on the soil of the Jews' ancient biblical homeland. Yet the course of an entire civilization cannot be changed in a generation or two. Intricate mixtures of continuity and rupture with the Jewish past have characterized all aspects of modern Israel—its politics, economics, social structure, and culture. There is no reason to assume that its military should be an exception to this rule.

Before the establishment of the state of Israel Jews had a long history of engagement with military power. Although Jews have frequently seen the military as something to be feared and avoided at all costs, there have been many situations in which Jews have had few qualms, and have even been enthusiastic, about military service and the waging of war. In modern states, Jewish valor was a function of emancipation and social acceptance: when Jews felt themselves to be part of the body politic, they willingly went forth to defend it. In rabbinic tradition, Jews are the children of Jacob, who is presented as meek and studious in contrast with his aggressive brother Esau. In historical reality, however, Jews have been Jacob and Esau and everything in between. It was not the Zionist project, but modernity as such, that introduced Jews to the ethical dilemmas of the use of force and challenged their historical self-representation as a people who shunned war.

The scope of this book spans Europe, the Middle East, and North America, and a period of some three hundred years, from the mid-seventeenth to the mid-twentieth centuries. In the 1600s, Jews in eastern and central Europe began to assume roles in urban defense. With the development of mass conscription from the late eighteenth to the early twentieth centuries, the military became a fact of life with which most Jewish males in Europe, the Ottoman Empire, and North America had to contend. Jews the world over had essential interests in the twentieth century's global conflicts, especially the 1948 Middle East war that secured the existence of the state of Israel. Israel itself is not the main focus of this book, but in the epilogue I discuss the relationship between the long sweep of diaspora Jewry's military involvement and the role of the army in Israeli society.

My sources are mostly printed: newspapers, books and pamphlets, statistical studies, rabbinic sermons, and works of fiction. In key sections, however, I make use of unpublished materials from the French and Austro-Hungarian military archives, the archive of the Israel Defense Force, and the archives of French- and German-Jewish philanthropic organizations that cared for Jewish veterans, war widows, and orphans. There is a vast body of scholarly literature on some of the themes covered in this book (e.g., German Jews in the First World War), which I synthesize, and I also draw upon a variety of useful, though widely scattered, scholarly works on the social history of Jews in the military.[1]

This book combines the methodologies of social and cultural history to explore both action and sensibility: how modern Jews came to be soldiers and what their experiences in service were like, as well as what they thought of those experiences and what the Jews back at home thought of their brethren in uniform. My methodology may be holistic, but I do not strive in this work for comprehensive coverage of Jewish conscription, volunteering, and soldiering throughout the world. A book that attempted such a project would be encyclopedic, whereas my framework is thematic. Each chapter posits a certain aspect of the Jewish encounter with the military and then examines a number of case studies that illustrate the phenomenon. I hope that the book's arguments will stimulate other scholars to think about the relationship between Jews and the military in those places and periods that I lacked the time or expertise to cover.

Despite its thematic structure, the book has a strong narrative component. It tells stories about individual Jewish soldiers, drawing on their service records and private writings, and about Jewish spiritual and lay leaders who saw the Jewish soldier as the embodiment of the struggle for emancipation—or the ultimate proof of emancipation's failure.

Throughout modern history, soldiers have been overwhelmingly male, and conversation about Jewish conscription has been inseparable from notions of masculinity. Classic antisemitic thinking associated Jewish men with physical weakness, cowardice, and an unwillingness to risk their lives for the peoples among whom they lived.[2] Modern patriotic thinking channeled masculine aggression against the nation's enemies by collapsing distinctions between the intimate sphere of the family (the loved ones whom any head of household would defend when threatened) and the imagined family of the nation.[3] Jewish patriotism, in turn, emphasized the historic courage of the Jews to stand up for their faith in the face of ceaseless persecution and their soldierly virility in antiquity, both within the ancient Hebrew homeland and in armies in the Greco-Roman world.

The association between citizenship and military service implicitly excluded women from full membership in the body politic, as they were not subject to conscription.[4] Women's advocates formulated alternative conceptions of citizenship defined in terms of maternal care for the nation via involvement in philanthropy and other forms of civil society. This alternative notion of citizenship was disseminated from the late nineteenth through mid-twentieth centuries by women's peace activist organizations, in which Jewish women were heavily involved.[5] These organizations were vocal, but their memberships were small, and in general Jewish women's philanthropic activity, like that of Christian bourgeois women, was patriotic and supportive of their countries' war efforts, and manifested in what one scholar has called a "voluntary ethic of care, which stressed collective community responsibility for the wounded soldiers, the veterans, and their families."[6]

The place of military history within the historical discipline as a whole has undergone massive shifts over the past 150 years. "In the nineteenth century," writes David Bell, "history was still preeminently a literary, narrative art, and the past offered no more dramatic or compelling subject than war. Such masters as Ranke, Macaulay, Michelet, and Parkman all gave it a major place in their works, took military science seriously, and put climactic battles at the heart of their stories."[7] These pioneer historians were all fervent nationalists. Nationalist historical scholarship is by definition literary, for it invents a nation by constructing a coherent narrative in which the willingness to fight as and for the collective is a paramount indication of national identity.

After World War II, academic historians sloughed off nationalist ideologies and so lost interest in the battlefield. They shunned telling stories in favor of analyzing underlying socioeconomic structures (in the language of the influential Annales school, "histoire événementielle" was replaced by the "longue durée"). The military, perceived as an extension of political elites, was neglected in the great wave of social history that began in the 1960s. The annals of war became the specialized province of military historians, whom academic historians have too often associated waspishly with amateur enthusiasts, battlefield tourists, and the popular fare aired on cable television's history channels. The first sign of war's return to the study of culture was the late Paul Fussel's landmark work of 1975, *The Great War and Modern Memory*. Since then scores of scholarly books have narrated the experience, commemoration, and collective memory of war. Somewhat more belatedly, the military has become the province of social historians who see in it a crucible of interaction and contestation between state and society.[8] Some scholarship on ethnic and religious minorities has taken up the theme of conscription as both a blessing and a curse, an opportunity for the improvement of a minority's social and political status yet also a source of oppression or segregation or, at the opposite extreme, enforced assimilation.[9]

Jewish historians have not ignored these developments altogether, but they have tended to focus their attention in a different direction. David Biale's provocative book *Power and Powerlessness in Jewish History* (1986) notes medieval Jewish society's respect for military competence and the many situations in which access to weapons reflected the Jews' integration into the feudal social order. Yet Biale does not treat the most obvious case of Jewish engagement with military power, as soldiers in modern armies. Modern history is replete with wars, and any one life span of even a half century would be witness to one or more major conflicts in addition to numerous revolutions and rebellions. Yet one would surmise from most Jewish historical writing that before the First World War Jews took up arms only sporadically and in small numbers. (We know far more about Jews as victims of pogroms than as participants in the tsar's army, although the latter vastly outnumbered the former.) A great deal has been written about the Jews in the First World War, but most attention has been paid to the persecution of Jewish civilians along the eastern front and the encounter of Jewish soldiers with antisemitism. The Jewish experience of the Second World War is overwhelmingly associated with the Holocaust and the desperate efforts of some Jews to resist the Nazi behemoth. There are important exceptions to all these generalizations, but for the most part when Jewish historians hear the word "war," they think of the violence it unleashes rather than the power that authorizes and directs it.

Israeli scholars, living in a society in which the army is a dominant institution and armed conflict nearly constant, have been more attuned than their diaspora counterparts to the history of Jewish military involvement. This was but one of many bonds that tied Zionist historical writing to nineteenth-century Europe's great nationalist historians. Zionism's recasting of the Jew as a fighting subject has often been attributed to a yearning, particularly among Jewish men, for physical strength and courage, an association between warrior spirit, self-respect, and the respect of the Gentiles.[10] But above and beyond salving the wounded egos of Jewish males, a fundamental premise of Zionism—one shared by most of its major streams—was a Jewish "return to history," a collective Jewish subjectivity, most commonly embodied in the state. Statecraft and warcraft are closely linked, in theory even more than in practice. The ideal type of the Jewish fighter, a metonym of collective responsibility and dynamism, was common in Zionist literature almost from the movement's beginning.

Classic Zionist historical writing placed at least as much emphasis on the historic martial valor (*gevurah*) of the Jewish people as on its oppression in Exile. Historical writing produced in the Yishuv (Palestine's pre-1948 Jewish community), and then in the state of Israel, presented the Jew in Exile as courageous and willing to sacrifice himself on behalf of his faith and community. Activists like the Labour Zionist leader Berl Katznelson praised Jewish rebels in ancient Palestine and medieval Jewish martyrs, who, by preferring death to the defilement of conversion, became symbols of national sacrifice. Zionist and Israeli authors have been less charitable about modern Jewish military service or participation in armed uprisings (except for the ghetto rebellions during the Holocaust). These actions have at times been celebrated as a manifestation of Maccabean spirit but more often dismissed as a vain sacrifice on behalf of an inimical, alien land.[11]

Zionist ideology usually conceived of diaspora Jewish heroism in terms of martyrdom and passive victimhood in times of persecution. It portrayed the Zionist militias that developed in Palestine in the early twentieth century more in terms of rebirth of the ancient Hebrew warrior spirit than as a continuation of a diaspora heritage. There were some important exceptions to this generalization. Two of the most important works of early Zionist historiography paid considerable attention to Jewish self-defense during the revolutionary tumult of 1848 in central Europe and the early twentieth century in Russia. In 1967 Israel's Ministry of Defense published a slim but useful edited volume on the history of Jews in modern armies.[12] By and large, however, Israeli scholarship has framed discussion about Jews and the military in terms of halakhic norms, not lived experience, and of marginalization rather than integration.[13]

The distance, both physical and cultural, that divides Israeli scholars from Europe and North America encourages the repetition of tried yet not necessarily true assumptions about diaspora Jewish attitudes toward war. Anita Shapira's *Land and Power* (1992), an outstanding study of Zionist concepts of force, offers a few pages on pre- or extra-Zionist history, casually asserting the "age-old Jewish repugnance for the spilling of innocent blood."[14] Ehud Luz's *Wrestling with an Angel* (1998), a thoughtful study of the Zionist ethics of power, claims that premodern Jewry had no warrior ethos and conceived physical sacrifice as "heroic service to humanity as a whole."[15] Both Luz and Shapira argue that early Zionism maintained many of the antimilitarist qualities of traditional Jewish culture, but they do not consider the contrary possibility that Zionism was influenced as well by modern Jewry's contact, in thought and deed, with the military realm.

Over the past generation, Jewish historians have demonstrated that in any land and at any time Jews took on the colorings of their social milieu, and that Jews were no strangers to fighting, dueling, and criminal activity, including extortion, assault, and homicide. Jews were participants in, and not merely victims of, violent acts. They also fantasized about bloody vengeance against Gentiles even when they did not have the ability or fortitude to act.[16] These findings are far removed from the *Edelkeyt*, or gentility, that Daniel Boyarin believes to have been the hallmark of rabbinic and medieval Judaism, or the fabricated tradition of Jewish nonviolence that the Palestinian writer Emile Habibi, wishing to separate Zionism from Judaism, invoked as the legacy of "the brothers of Heinrich Heine and Maimonides, Bertolt Brecht [*sic!*] and Stefan Zweig, Albert Einstein and the immortal Arab-Jewish poet Shlomo Ben Ovadia."[17]

The emphasis in the research done to date is on the individual and his immediate community, not the state; random or ritualized acts, not the organized instruments of domination; in short, violence, not war. My approach is different in its focus on war and the military as an arm of state power. It draws upon Hannah Arendt's classic essay *On Violence*, which defines war as a manifestation of power, power as collective action legitimized by authority, and authority as "unquestioning recognition by those who are asked to obey."[18] Violence, on the other hand, is the province of the individual, gang, or sect, which multiplies its natural strength through the use of lethal implements. "Violence," Arendt writes, "can destroy power; it is utterly incapable of creating it."[19] Although Jews, like all humans, are always capable of violence, in modern times Jews faced the particular challenge of how to accommodate new forms of state authority that demanded the donation of young bodies for military service.

I am indebted to Arendt for her distinction between violence and war, yet in this book I modify her analytical categories somewhat by distinguishing between two types of violence. The sectarian community that practices violence for ideological reasons, I argue, is not the same as the impassioned or delinquent individual or the criminal gang. The soldier, a servant of the state, and the fighter, who acts in the name of an underground or insurrectionary group, are both agents of what I call *politicized collective violence*. They both exercise collective power, belong to political communities wielding instruments of domination, and are guided by a political authority, be it the state or a competing body.

I would classify practitioners of modern politicized collective violence via five categories: (1) the citizen-soldier; (2) the uniformed civil servant; (3) the revolutionary; (4) the rebel in extremis; and (5) the indigenized colonial. The first type is globally the most widespread, because conscription is a hallmark of the modern state. Prior to the emancipation of women at the very end of the nineteenth century and continuing into the twentieth, emancipation of any specific social group was conceptually linked with military service, even in countries that did not regularly have a draft, such as the United States or United Kingdom. The second type is the career officer, as opposed to the reserve officer, whose title is more of an honorific and whose command is normally limited to brief periods in times of war or unrest. Traditionally, senior officers have enjoyed the status and privileges accorded to the highest state officials, and although their lives are ostensibly devoted to warcraft, in fact staff officers may well devote most of their career to administrative tasks not unlike those carried out by their plainclothes peers in the civil service. The third type, the revolutionary seeking to overthrow the current regime for a more just and equitable one, entered the stage of history as a civic guardsman in France, then in central Europe, from 1789 to the revolutions of 1848. These bourgeois rebels foreshadowed the decidedly more déclassé proletarian revolutionaries in eastern Europe who emerged in the early 1880s. The fourth type, the rebel in extremis, has been known by many names: guerrilla, partisan, freedom fighter, terrorist. These individuals have offered fierce, desperate responses to occupation and oppression, as in eastern Europe under Nazi occupation, and the consequences of their actions have often been suicidal. The fifth and final type is native or native-raised colonial youth, such as Euro-Americans or Afrikaners, who were indigenized yet hostilely counterpoised to the land's aboriginal population.

This fifth type is associated most closely with the Zionist project, with the young men and women, overwhelmingly of European origin, who served in the Yishuv's militias that David Ben-Gurion forged in

1948 into the Israel Defense Force (IDF). It is impossible to appreciate how the Israeli army took form, however, without taking into account the presence of the other types. In Jewish collective memory, there is a strong, even exaggerated, association between the fourth type, the ghetto rebels and partisans during the Holocaust, and the founding of the state of Israel. The Jewish variants of the other types—the soldier, the officer, and the revolutionary fighter—have largely disappeared from public awareness. This book tells their stories and, at the end, depicts their connection with the Zionist project and Israel's creation.

Modern Jews have been well aware of the beneficent as well as harmful capacities of state power. They have often accepted its legitimacy and seen it as a source of individual and collective benefit. War has inspired Jewish communities and institutions to mobilize resources for the state and for themselves. What's more, for Jews, as for all people, conscription meant far more than actually waging war. Militaries do fight wars, but much of the time, certainly in the nineteenth century and even in the blood-soaked twentieth, states in the western world have been at peace. The experience of being drafted, going through basic training, serving in a particular unit, and interacting with one's peers and superiors could have profound effects even on an individual who never came under hostile fire. The military is perhaps the single most powerful institution within the modern state, and the millions of modern Jews who performed military service were molded by forces far beyond the experience of battle.

■ ■ ■

The book's first chapter explores the Jews' historic self-image as a people that shuns what the Hebrew writer S. Y. Agnon called "the craft of Esau, the waging of war."[20] The notion of Jews as wards of divine and state authority—as "servants of kings, not servants of men" (Bahya ben Asher of Saragossa) or, more starkly, "prisoners of war" (Moses Sofer)—derives from both rabbinic tradition and the specific conditions of Jewish life in medieval Christian and Muslim civilizations. Committed to maintaining their faith and community, Jews had little reason to cross social boundaries or endanger their lives through military service. In modern eastern Europe, particularly the Russian Empire, the grim conditions of Jewish life and the prevalence of reactionary Orthodox Christianity

hardened long-standing feelings of passivity and timorousness in relation to the state. The historical memory of Russian and Polish Jewry
is replete with images of harsh military service and tales of fleeing the
country in order to avoid it. Like all historical memory, this narrative
blends fact with fiction. Eastern European Jews engaged in a variety of
paramilitary activities long before conscription into the tsar's army, and
once the draft was implemented in the nineteenth century, their experiences were not uniformly miserable. What's more, this narrative did not
apply to Jews in central and western Europe. The military experiences
and memories of eastern European Jewry may have been dominant, but
they were not normative.

Chapter 2 depicts the context in which western and central European
armies took form and how Jews were included in them. The issue of military service played a major role in eighteenth- and nineteenth-century
debates about the emancipation of the Jews. In the early 1700s, Protestant Hebraists and Enlightenment thinkers reconceived the position of
Jews in European society by presenting Jews as capable of martial valor
and so deserving of civil rights. In the late eighteenth century, new conceptions of the meliorability of humanity, combined with raison d'état
considerations by absolutist monarchs, led to the introduction of conscription for all men, including Jews. Proponents of the Jewish Enlightenment (Haskalah) paid considerable attention to the issue of military
service, especially after the introduction of mass conscription in France
during the revolutionary wars. In the German lands, early nineteenth-
century advocates of Jewish emancipation urged Jewish youth to volunteer to fight against Napoleonic France.

After 1815, Jews in central and eastern Europe frequently tried to
evade military service, but they did not necessarily do so more often
than Gentiles. In most places where Jews did not want to serve in the
military, few others did. From the mid-1800s onward, patriotic sentiment, and with it a willingness to fight for one's country, became more
widespread. During the wars of German and Italian unification, Jews
flocked to perform what they believed was their civic duty. Similar developments took place in the United States during the American Civil
War.

In the first half of the 1800s, opponents as well as champions of
emancipation marshaled arguments from the military realm to make

their case. Since Jewish emancipation was associated with the forces of revolution, conservatives seized on the image of the cowardly and incompetent Jewish soldier as the ultimate proof against the liberal claim of the equality of man. Ignoring the fact that many people besides Jews tried to dodge the draft, antisemites created a new, powerful icon of Jewish malevolence, one whose full significance would not become apparent until the First World War.

Chapter 3 presents the military as a vehicle and symbol of social mobility for Jews in continental Europe. This chapter explores the social background of Jewish military officers, the financial implications of a military career upon marriage and the formation of broader social networks, and the interplay between finance and social capital in a family that could boast of one or more army officers. Here I compare the high rates of Jewish military careerism in France, Italy, and Austria-Hungary with much lower rates in the post–Civil War United States and in the United Kingdom. This disparity suggests that Jewish military careerism was linked not only to levels of emancipation but also to the prestige of a military career in each national culture.

This chapter uses the life stories of Jewish soldiers to throw new light on the relationship between Jews, the military, and the broader societies in which they lived. For example, the hapless Alfred Dreyfus was but one of hundreds of French-Jewish captains and colonels, over whom some twenty Jewish generals served in the military during the period of the Third Republic. The French military's openness to Jewish army officers encourages rethinking of the Dreyfus Affair, as French-Jewish officers encountered support as well as hostility in their confrontations with antisemitism both within and outside the barracks. I also deal here with Jewish involvement in colonial armies, particularly those of French Africa and Indochina. Serving as a colonial officer represented a continuation of a tradition of Jewish service to the state, but it was also a means of gaining social acceptance by allying and identifying oneself with white Christian officers and colonists and against native peoples.

With Chapter 4 the focus of the book moves from peacetime to war, from the military as a livelihood to an instrument of mass death. As Jews began to serve in substantial numbers in the armies of Europe and North America, their patriotic inclinations clashed with their transnational attachments to Jews in the lands against which their country was fighting.

This problem first emerged during the revolutions of 1848, when Jews fought both as rebels and as soldiers in the Habsburg armies, and it was the object of considerable discussion in the European-Jewish press. The Franco-Prussian War of 1870–71 was far more traumatic as it sundered the French- and German-Jewish communities, which had long known close business and familial ties. Rabbinic sermons, fiction, and Jewish apologetic literature displayed a powerful transnationalist sensibility, a feeling of Jewish commonality even in times of war. The willingness of Jews to fight each other was heralded as the ultimate proof of worthiness for equal rights. A similar discourse developed among Jews in the United States during the American Civil War. In North America as well as Europe, Jewish activists took great pride in the military achievements of Jews in the armies of their homeland's rivals. This discourse was enabled by the generally benevolent tone of international relations in the century from Waterloo to the outbreak of World War I, but nonetheless it stands out for its powerful sense of intraethnic attachment and interchangeability, by which the Jew displays loyalty to all states by serving loyally in all armies.

The First World War destabilized this discourse of transnational patriotism, as Jews in the lands of the Entente and Triple Alliance began to depict the enemy in demonic terms, but even here extensive contact was maintained between Jews in enemy armies, and the moral dilemmas of Jews facing each other in the trenches of the western front became the subject of stories, myths, and even jokes. After the war, Jewish veterans the world over formed tight-knit bonds and expressed the utmost solidarity with their German brethren from the early 1930s onward. In other ways, however, Jewish veterans suffered the aftermath of the war as did many other former fighters; in Germany and Austria, for example, they shared in the prevailing fury over war guilt and reparations, and they retained a strong pride in their military service, a pride that they nurtured throughout the years of Nazi persecution.

Chapter 5 continues its predecessor's analysis of Jews in World War I, but from a different angle. It examines the combat experience of Jews in World War I and the toll the war inflicted on hundreds of thousands of Jews who fought as soldiers on all the war's fronts. Although there is a vast literature on Jews in World War I, its focus is on civilian suffering, in particular the persecution of Jews living along the eastern front. In this chapter, I analyze the war experience of Jews outside the Russian and Ottoman empires, Jews who believed themselves to be fully (or virtually) integrated into the state and its vernacular culture. Jewish sensibilities about the war shared much in common with those of non-Jews of a similar class and educational background. Yet points of intersection were accompanied by points of deflection. The war could be more meaningful for Jews than for most combatants, partly because of the ongoing sense of need to prove one's masculine and civic virtue in the face of antisemitic attacks, and partly because the Triple Alliance was arrayed against Russia, seen by most Ashkenazic Jews as their greatest oppressor in modern times. A specifically Jewish sub-culture that valorized the war was most prominent in Germany, where Jews, placed under enormous pressures to prove themselves in battle, did not allow themselves to grieve publicly over wounded Jewish soldiers and veterans, but rather commemorated only the Jewish dead, those who had made the ultimate sacrifice for their nation. Jewish veterans were far less likely than their Christian counterparts to lobby for health care, vocational training, and financial assistance for disabled soldiers.

The impact of World War I on Jewish political consciousness varied greatly across and within specific countries. It could heighten Jewish national patriotism and nationalist sensibility, a commitment either to preserve the state or to overthrow it through violent revolution. The book's last two chapters argue that the 1914–1948 period must be seen as one of nearly constant Jewish involvement in global conflicts in the name of causes that explicitly or implicitly served Jewish collective interests. The Jewish Legion that fought in the Middle East in World War I, international Jewish volunteerism in the Spanish Civil War, the global Jewish war effort during World War II, and the massive flow of Jewish money, matériel, and manpower from the diaspora to Palestine in 1948 shared certain common assumptions and operative principles despite the vast ideological differences between liberal patriotism, international communism, and Zionism. In all these conflicts Jews figured not only as refugees or inducted soldiers but also as volunteers, making a free choice to put themselves in harm's way (as in the International Brigades in the Spanish Civil War and the volunteer Machal forces in 1948) or, if already in uniform or facing imminent induction, choosing to fight within a Jewish unit (as in the Jewish Legion and the Jewish Brigade, in World War I and II respectively).

There is a substantial literature on Jewish involvement in the two world wars and the Spanish Civil War, and the 1948 war has become a scholarly industry of its own. Scholars have not, however, incorporated the spectrum of Jewish global military activity in the first half of the twentieth century into a comparative framework. Moreover, aside from some popular and autobiographical work, there is little in English on the social history of the Machal, nor on the relationship between these units and the global war that had ended just three years before. By analyzing the 1948 war against the background of earlier conflicts that also attracted international Jewish support, and by taking into account the overlapping sets of collective Jewish interests that motivated those who took part in them, the final chapter seeks to reconceive what is usually seen as a chasm between the Zionist struggle to establish the state of Israel and earlier forms of Jewish military activity.

▪ ▪ ▪

The great French-Jewish scholar Marc Bloch famously remarked that the purpose of comparative history is to highlight distinction, not similarity. The generation of 1948, and the social and military institutions they created, were unique in many ways. But they did not emerge from some distant land beyond the borders of modern Jewish civilization. The Zionist enterprise was the child of the diaspora, and even its most distinct features had diaspora counterparts, albeit not exact parallels. Throughout modern times, Jews willingly served in the military when it furthered their individual and collective interests to do so. In societies where the officer corps was prestigious and available to Jews, they sought it out. Jewish religious culture has veered less toward pacifism than toward a calculated and delimited passivity, and few rabbis have provided halakhic justification for shirking service. Although in World War I Jews fought primarily as nationals of their homelands, they also pursued specifically Jewish agendas, particularly in the fight against tsarist Russia and for a Jewish homeland in Palestine. Between 1936 and 1948 Jews displayed particular needs, predilections, and interests as they took part in a twelve-year world war on three fronts—Spain, Nazi-occupied Europe, and Palestine. As in all wars, the home and battlefronts were merged—in the diaspora as well as Israel, even if for the former the distances between the two were vast, and the conditions of daily life were far more secure and comfortable.

I am not a military historian by training or inclination, and I have seen no reason to enter the fray of Israeli scholars who have written abundantly, and often extremely well, on the history and politics of the Zionist militias that became the Israeli army and the IDF itself.[21] I am intrigued, though, by the work of European historians who have used the military as a lens for more fully understanding a whole variety of issues such as cultural sensibilities, social mobility, gender dynamics, and levels of political agency.[22] I have attempted here to do the same for Jews throughout the modern diaspora. I also hope to clarify how Zionists adapted popular ideas about the relationship between national revival and armed struggle and what practical use they made of those ideas.

These are academic questions, but they have contemporary relevance, even urgency. In recent years, Israeli governments have repeatedly presented the state as under existential threat yet possessed of a vast and powerful army that can obliterate its foes; as being the master of its own destiny yet bereft of responsibility for its intractable conflict with the Palestinians. At the same time, diaspora Jewry has been torn between those who decry Israeli militarism and those who have few, if any, compunctions against Israeli military action of any kind. One of the distinctive aspects of modernity is the need to justify ideology and action via appeals to history. Accordingly, both the dovish and hawkish camps invoke a Jewish tradition of valorizing and seeking peace, but they do so for different reasons: the former in order to justify concessions to and reconciliation with Israel's enemies, the latter to demonstrate that despite the Jews' love of peace Israel has been backed into a corner and that its survival demands frequent, tough, and bold military action. Both camps read the Jewish textual tradition and interpret the Jews' lived reality selectively, and to their own advantage. This book aims to deconstruct simplistic, ideologically driven notions of the relationship between Jews and military power, and in so doing to present the centrality of the military in Israeli politics and society as a logical, but neither inevitable nor immutable, outcome of modern Jewish history.

## CHAPTER ONE

# The Jewish Soldier between Memory and Reality

Jews in the contemporary world have a remarkably static and ho-mogeneous collective memory of their historic relationship with armed force. The memory's origins lie in the historical consciousness, transmitted by public institutions and popular culture, in which the Holocaust and the state of Israel have assumed iconic status. As Jay Winter has noted, memory is rarely fixed, stable, and unidirectionally transmitted; institutions such as schools can instill memory but not im-pose it.[1] In most of the Jewish world since World War II, however, there has been little resistance to a classic Zionist narrative that lionizes the military prowess of the Jews in the ancient land of Israel but associates diaspora Jewry with timidity and an inability to defend itself against its persecutors. In this view, Jews who served in modern armies did so as either unwilling conscripts or deluded patriots.

For Ashkenazic Jews, who constitute the vast majority of world Jewry, the dominant image of Jewish soldiers comes from their experience in the imperial Russian army. Jews think of it as a teeming mass of coarse, aggressive, and frequently drunk peasants, barely kept in check by re-actionary and disdainful, even sadistic, officers and fanatical Orthodox priests whose hatred for Jews was exceeded only by their zeal to convert them. According to this tragic narrative, the entire course of a young Russian-Jewish man's life was stamped by the threat of military service. Some Jews were drafted as tender children; others were spared the draft, and granted the chance to lead a normal Jewish life, by being the only son in their family; others entered yeshivas or married at an unseemly young age in order to avoid conscription. Jewish families resorted to any subterfuge—from hiding birth records to bribing officials to sending their beloved sons abroad—and once in the army, Jews had few qualms about deserting, despite the risk of arrest and imprisonment.

This narrative of the army as a site of torment for Jews reinforces a deeply rooted perception by Jews that throughout most of their history they have been a meek and pacific people. The book of Genesis describes Jacob, the progenitor of the Jews, as a simple man who kept to his tent, unlike his brother, the ruddy huntsman Esau. The historical books of the Hebrew Bible narrate the military exploits of the ancient Israelites, yet the prophet Isaiah likens Jacob and his issue to a worm, weak and defenseless, and dependent upon God's protection. Rabbinic texts are ambivalent toward and at times outright disapproving of military prowess. In late antiquity and the Middle Ages, rabbinic Judaism, the religious system of what has been called an "alienated minority,"[2] was detached from political power and the landed aristocracy that comprised the warrior elite. Rabbis had little reason to exult in the military exploits of Christians or Muslims or glorify wars in which Jews were more likely to be victims than participants. The dominant rabbinic view on the use of armed force was one of theological passivity—trusting that God, to cite the Jewish traditional prayer for the government, would give "salvation unto kings and dominion unto princes," and would also determine and implement their downfall. The passive Jew was not part of the Gentile body politic but had no wish to be included, and he had no reason to fight in its wars.[3]

Passivity is hardly the same thing as pacifism. Jews have rarely espoused the principled and universal rejection of war found in some Protestant sectarian groups such as the Amish, Mennonites, Moravian Brethren, and Quakers. It has not been difficult for rabbis in modern times to employ the Jewish textual tradition to justify military service in the diaspora or to look favorably upon Zionism's re-creation of the Hebrew warrior. We cannot appreciate the process by which a substantial component of Orthodox Judaism embraced Zionism, even unto its most militant forms, without emphasizing the distinction between passivity and pacifism, and the capacity of the former under the right conditions to mutate into activism, and even aggression.[4]

The corpus of Jewish sacred literature offers multiple and at times conflicting judgments regarding the ethics of military service or combat. We must neither read this literature selectively nor take it for granted that a textual tradition is indicative of lived reality. Over the span of Jewish history rabbinical authority has often directly impinged upon Jewish life, and a canon of legal and exegetical texts has been the common possession of the learned Jewish elite. Even in traditional Jewish societies, however, people did not simply do what their rabbis wanted of them. All the more so in modern times, where Jews have encountered multiple, competing sources of authority, emanating from their families, communities, civil society, or the centralizing state.

No historian interested in the social history of the military would turn first to, or rely primarily upon, the prescriptive writings of religious clerics. Similarly, students of Jewish society and culture are obliged to employ Judaic sources with care and always in juxtaposition with empirical data and a multivocal documentary base. This chapter will situate the different strands of Judaic thinking about war and military service within specific historical contexts before going on to document the extent to which military service impinged, and not always in a negative way, upon the lives of Jews in eastern Europe, the heartland of modern Jewish civilization. By juxtaposing text and context, on the one hand, and collective memory with lived reality, on the other, this chapter seeks to deconstruct popular and deeply entrenched ways of thinking about Jews and military service. It will prepare the ground for an alternative narrative of the encounter between modern Jews and the military in the chapters that follow.

## War in Premodern Judaism

Judaic thinking about war and the military reflects the specific conditions of Jewish life. The Hebrew Bible glorifies the wars by which the Israelites conquered Canaan and defeated their enemies, particularly the Philistines. Rabbinic Judaism, in contrast, emerged from the destruction of the Second Temple and failure of the first- and second-century CE revolts against Rome. The rabbis accordingly elevated passivity to a legal and ethical imperative as per the Babylonian Talmud's statement that "[a] man should always strive to be of the persecuted rather than of the persecutors because there is none among the birds more persecuted than the doves and pigeons, and yet Scripture made them [alone among birds] eligible for the altar" (Baba Batra 93a). The rabbis considered most wars to be optional, not obligatory, and permitted war within the land of Israel only with approval by the assembly of sages known as the Sanhedrin (a tall order, as it no longer existed during the final centuries of the formation of the Babylonian Talmud). The category of obligatory war was limited to the original conquest of Canaan, and therefore consigned to the distant and unrepeatable past.[5]

In late antiquity, talmudic study was verbally highly aggressive and employed the language of battle, of feint and charge, as a Jew faced off against his study partner cum opponent.[6] Despite its combative form, the content of rabbinic discussion about war emphasized respect for human life, be it that of the Jew who is not compelled to fight in even a just war, or that of the enemy, which is not to be subject to wanton destruction. The rabbinic tradition follows the sages of the Mishnah (Shabbat 6:4) who prohibited the carrying of arms on the Sabbath: Rabbi Eliezer called them "adornments" and permitted them to be worn, but the majority, citing Isaiah 2:4 ("And they shall beat their swords into ploughshares"), deemed the bow, spear, shield, and lance to be no less than a disgrace. The biblical warrior was transformed into a forerunner of the rabbinic warrior of the spirit.[7]

Biblical commandments that constrained behavior in battle and talmudic condemnations of militarism have been passed down across generations and are well known among Jews today. Less familiar is a more militant stream of Jewish thought that developed in medieval and early modern Europe and North Africa. Some of the most illustrious rabbis of the period, including Moses Maimonides (1135–1204), Menachem Hameiri (1249–c. 1310), and Josef Karo (1488–1575), justified wars of territorial expansion. The celebrated rabbi Judah Lowe of Prague (the Maharal, 1520–1609) justified the collective slaughter by Simon and Levi of the men of Shekhem (Genesis 33) as an appropriate action against violators of a Noahide commandment (the rape of their sister Dinah) or simply as members of an enemy nation: "As they [the men of Shekhem] belong to the nation which did them [Israel] harm, they are allowed to wage war against them" even though "there are many [among the men of Shekhem] who did not do anything."[8]

These rabbis did not advocate that the Jews take military action against their oppressors. But Maimonides as well as the twelfth-century polymath Abraham Ibn Ezra believed that the Jews' passivity would be temporary. In the words of the historian Haim Hillel Ben-Sasson, these great thinkers saw

> in the [Jews'] social degradation and suffering a blow and woe that must be borne so long as it is not possible to rise up against them in force; but if it is possible to cast off the yoke and to overturn the rule of those who humiliate the Jews, war is a good, as is the sword in hand, for this is the honor of the believers and the will of their God.[9]

This sort of thinking stimulated Jewish fantasies, and occasional acts, of vengeance against Gentiles in medieval and early modern Europe. It accounts for the enduring popularity of the *Sefer Yossipon*, a tenth-century paraphrase of Josephus' account of the ancient Jewish war against Rome, which provided medieval Jews the solace that their ancestors had been heroes and warriors.[10]

Both talmudic and medieval rabbinic speculation about war usually addressed the distant past, not the present, and the land of Israel, not the Jews' actual lands of residence. Medieval commentators did find a contemporary application in the Talmud's discussion (Avodah Zarah 18b) about whether it is permitted for a Jew to attend gladiatorial arenas or circuses in an army encampment around a besieged city. The core of the text, the Mishnah, says it is forbidden, but the lengthy exposition, the Gemarah, notes that one may do so in order to save the life of a Jew who was kidnapped and put in the arena, or to beseech the troops leading the siege to spare the lives of the Jews within the encircled city. At the same time the Gemarah cautions that it is strictly forbidden to be "considered to be one of the Gentiles." The eleventh-century commentator Rashi interpreted this phrase to mean taking part in the siege of the city, and later medieval commentators known as the Tosafists claimed it meant that Jews must not be "among the number of the army of the Gentiles."

Was this a blanket prohibition against Jews serving in Gentile armies?[11] If so, Jews have violated it repeatedly, for Jews have been soldiers as long as there have been Jews—not only in the land of Israel but also throughout the diaspora. There are few signs of this activity in prescriptive Jewish texts, those legal and ethical writings that are central to the Jewish textual canon. But a wide variety of sources, especially historical chronicles, document stories about Jews as defenders of their communities and warriors for their lords, stories that are well known to scholars but have not penetrated into public consciousness.

## Premodern Jews in War

In the ancient Near East, Jewish soldiering extended far beyond the wars of the Israelites that are chronicled in the Hebrew scriptures. As Judah fell under Babylonian, Persian, and then Hellenistic rule, Judean soldiers became increasingly common throughout the region. Jewish officers as well as simple fighters figured prominently in the armies of the Ptolemaic and Seleucid empires. The Christianization of Rome in the fourth century CE stimulated efforts to put an end to what was by then a millennium-old tradition of Jewish soldiering in imperial armies. Laws were promulgated, over and again, restricting Jewish access to military service and to the bearing of arms, but Jews in Christendom continued to serve as soldiers and commanders into the sixth century CE, and in the Islamic world throughout the Middle Ages.[12]

Jews in medieval Christendom were rarely soldiers but still engaged in armed combat. In the spring of 1096, after the calling of the First Crusade, a mob ostensibly en route to Palestine pillaged Jewish communities in the Rhine Valley, killing thousands. According to the Hebrew chronicle of Shlomo bar Shimon, the Jews of Mainz "donned their armor and girded on their weapons" and fought valiantly against the foe, although they were vastly outnumbered and weakened by fasting— whether motivated by the self-affliction of the penitent, or the practice of ancient warriors preparing for battle, is not clear. The Jews soon faced the grim prospect of forcible conversion or death, and they chose the latter via suicide.[13] This famous chronicle has attracted attention because of its account of Jewish mass suicide, but no less fascinating is this document's reminder that the Jews of medieval Ashkenaz had the legal privilege to bear arms, a privilege indicative of high social status, akin to knighthood.[14] The right and importance of bearing arms is evident in Jewish law as well. During the thirteenth century, the permissibility of bearing arms on the Sabbath, first discussed in the Mishnah, appeared in the responsa of Rabbi Meir of Rothenberg, the writings of Rabbi Isaac ben Moses of Vienna and Eliezer of Worms, and communal regulations in Spain. A responsum attributed to Rabbi Meir of Rothenberg determined that learning how to wield a sword was a necessary skill.[15]

Jews in medieval Ashkenaz internalized the chivalric values of the ambient Christian culture and compared their acts of martyrdom to the noble behavior of knights.[16] Images of warfare graced illuminated medieval haggadot, and in France Jews were wont to commission paintings, one of whose popular themes was the battle of David and Goliath.[17] The attraction to military imagery and the memory of the ancient Jews' triumphs over their enemies did not, however, mitigate an overpowering sense of Jewish victimhood. (The most common theme in paintings commissioned by medieval French Jews was the Binding of Isaac, which many Jews of the time, given the persecution and hatred they frequently faced, no doubt considered a form of self-portraiture.) In a number of early modern illuminated haggadot, from Barcelona (fourteenth century) to Prague (1526) and Amsterdam (1695), the wicked son was depicted as a soldier,[18] suggesting discomfort with contemporary Jews who wielded weapons more easily than talmudic logic.[19]

The interconnections between carrying and wielding weapons for personal use, military service, and town defense are clearest in the early modern Polish-Lithuanian commonwealth, home to what was at that time the world's largest, most secure, and most self-confident Jewish community.[20] In the eastern borderlands, where synagogues were fortified and occasionally housed cannons on their roofs, Jews routinely bore swords, as per the 1588 Zamosc charter: "It is permitted to them to possess and bear freely weaponry of the sort that other denizens use for their defense."[21] Twenty years earlier, a Lithuanian statute had prohibited Jews from wearing colorful uniforms and decorating their swords with precious jewels. Jews came into possession of firearms through purchase (occasionally of stolen merchandise) or as pledges on loans. Jews used weapons both licitly, as in the case of the armed Jewish guard who patrolled the Jewish quarter of sixteenth-century Poznan,[22] and illicitly, as we learn from a responsum by the sixteenth-century rabbi Moses Isserles, who dealt with the case of an armed Jew who killed a (presumably Jewish) carriage driver in an altercation.[23]

Until the intense and protracted cycle of wars in Poland in the mid-seventeenth century, Polish Jews were not required to go to war, which was waged mostly by serfs and mercenaries and commanded by the nobility.[24] Their contributions to the military were mainly financial, given that Polish Jews bore heavy tax burdens for the upkeep of the armed forces, and in some places they had to provide for the board, pay, and uniforms of the soldiers. Before the mid-1600s, Jews were covering some one-third of Poland's combined military outlays; thereafter the figure climbed to as high as half.[25] No less important, though, was the requirement, going back to the late thirteenth century, that Jews take part in the defense of towns against attackers. Jews, like townsmen of all nationalities, were required to maintain and fortify the town walls in times of peace and defend them in times of war, such as during the *levée en masse* that accompanied the Tatar invasion of 1589. Most of the time, Jews could pay special fees or hire guards to patrol the walls, but when the town was under attack Jews were called to the ramparts along with everyone else. In some cities, Jews formed their own guard units; in Vilnius, the Jewish unit carried out training exercises alongside Christians, with whom they sometimes fell into brawls. In the sixteenth and seventeenth centuries, Jews in the eastern borderlands were required to take part in military exercises and maintain heavy rifles, ammunition, and gunpowder in their homes.[26] Jews formed a powerful alliance with the nobility against their common enemies, who, depending on the time and place, included Ukrainians, Tatars, Cossacks, and Muscovites.

Polish Jewry was not content to remain within—or atop—its town walls and at times went forth to fight. A responsum of Moses Isserles refers to a Jew from Wojslawice, Silesia, who left synagogue on Yom Kippur to go to battle and was subsequently killed. (The rabbi was asked whether and on the basis of what kind of certification his widow might remarry.) Rabbis Meir of Lublin and Joel Sirkes wrote of a Berachah ben Aharon, who died in 1610 while fighting in a Cossack unit against Muscovy.[27] The Cossacks so revered his bravery and horsemanship that they called him "the hero." Polish documents from the 1650s confirm that, during the Polish wars with Muscovy, Jews went to the field of battle alongside the Poles. Some were captured, and their refusal to convert to Eastern Orthodox Christianity was read by the authors of the documents as a sign of the Jews' loyalty to the Polish king. At around the same time, King Jan Kazimierz threatened to expel Jews who had "openly and treasonously" served "as soldiers" in the enemy's army.[28]

An important source documenting Jewish self-images as a fighting people is a little Hebrew volume titled *Yeven metsula* (literally, Deep Mire; figuratively, Abyss of Despair). The book, written by Nathan Hanover (d. 1683) offers a powerful account of the Chmielnitski massacres of 1648–49. The book's emphasis is on Jewish suffering at the hands of Ukrainians and Tatars, and its narrative shapes events so as to link them with a long history of Jewish martyrdom.[29] At the same time, Nathan presents the Jews of the Polish borderlands as skilled, valiant fighters who are defeated because of treachery, not lack of courage or strength. The memory of martyrdom runs through the work, but so does a spirit of Jewish gentility, for Jews are presented as more noble than the Polish *schlachta* alongside whom the Jews fought before they were so bitterly betrayed. At the fortress of Tulczyn, according to Nathan, two thousand Jews, among them "men of valor, skilled in war," and six hundred Polish nobles, "each man and his brother," vowed to fight together against the Cossack invaders:

> [A]nd, armed, the children of Israel went up with all sorts of weaponry and stood upon the walls, the nobles and the Jews, and whenever the Greeks [i.e., Cossacks] approached nigh unto the fortress, those who stood on the walls fired arrows and flaming devices. And they smote a multitude of the Greeks who fled before the children of Israel, and the children of Israel girded their valor and they pursued them and smote them by the hundreds.[30]

According to Nathan, after a second Cossack attack was repulsed, the Poles and Cossacks made a secret alliance. The Poles disarmed the Jews, and although the Jews yearned to resist with force, they were persuaded by their rabbi to comply. The Cossacks demanded that the Jews convert, and when they refused they were slaughtered. The Cossacks then killed the perfidious Poles.

Despite its melodramatic style, Nathan's narrative appears consistent with the factual record of Polish-Jewish military service of the time. It was published in Venice in 1653, only a few years after the wars, and is probably a good deal more reliable than its Yiddish translation, published some twenty-five years later. The Yiddish version eliminates references to Jewish fighting and to political alliances between Jews and Poles while playing up, even more than in the Hebrew original, the martyrdom of Jewish communities.[31]

These cases from early modern Poland demonstrate that Jews were not averse to bearing arms in the defense of cities and at times even ventured into pitched battles. Jewish writers like Nathan Hanover commemorated these actions, yet the Jews' self-image as a victimized and powerless people was maintained by encasing Jewish valor in piety, suffering, and betrayal. Jews did not allow themselves to bathe in soldierly glory. Likewise, in central Europe, when early modern Jews engaged in civic defense, Jewish writers subordinated the Jews' secular loyalties to lord and locality to a sense of religious obligation. Fascinating evidence for this comes from a tract titled *Sefer milhamah beshalom* (The Book of War in Peace) by Judah Leon, secretary to the chief rabbi of Prague, on the 1648 Swedish siege of Prague. The text depicts Jews as loyal subjects of their sovereign, sympathetic with their fellow Praguers, and hostile toward the Swedes. During the siege the Jews build fortifications and put out fires, and at one point a group of Jewish men even try to defuse an explosive shell. In the chronicle, the arrival of imperial reinforcements results from the heroism of a lone Jewish scout, who leads the troops through "the woods and winding paths, for the Swedes were lying everywhere in wait."[32]

Despite these depictions of Jewish civic virtue, *Sefer milhamah beshalom* attributes the calamities that befall the population of Prague entirely to the Jews' sins, and Gentile military victories are presented as divine reward for the Jews' repentance. An even more pietistic work about the same event, the Judeo-German *Schwedesch Lid*, makes no claims to Jewish heroism and focuses entirely on the apparently miraculous salvation of the city and its Jews.[33] *Yeven metsula* shares much in common with these Bohemian texts, for although Nathan Hanover highlighted Jewish valor in battle, he, too, presented the disaster that befell Polish Jewry as a form of divine chastisement and martyrdom as the highest form of Jewish devotion to God.[34]

In early modern Europe, where Jewish military activity was infrequent, it was not difficult to cover tales of Jewish fighters and defenders with a tearful glaze. A more robust aggressiveness, considerably more difficult to conceal, flourished among some of the Sephardim who settled in the Caribbean and South America during the seventeenth century. Small numbers of Jews served as mercenaries in the Dutch force that invaded Brazil in 1630 and as volunteers fighting against Portugal fifteen years later. Jews as a whole were received into the general militia in Dutch Brazil from 1645 to 1654.[35] In Dutch Surinam, from the late 1600s through most of the 1700s Jews took up arms against foreign invaders, Amerindians, and bands of runaway black slaves. The Nassy family of Surinam supplied two captains of the militia, Samuel and his grandson David. According to nineteenth-century Dutch sources, on Yom Kippur of 1743 David Nassy launched a raid against slave rebels, whom he slaughtered, and whose huts he torched, without mercy.[36]

Jewish military activity usually took place on land but could also occur at sea. In mid-eighteenth-century Bordeaux and Bayonne some Sephardic Jews owned corsairs and operated as privateers, licensed by the French government to attack British shipping on the high seas.[37]

To be sure, in the Europe of the ancien régime—the period before the French Revolution—Jews did not want to serve in armies, and armies did not want Jews. Bereft of the twin pillars of Christian social organization, the landed aristocracy and peasantry, Jews had no warrior caste or mass of sturdy wielders of the musket. But this did not keep Jews from engaging in acts of violence, sanctioned by public authority, against external foes. Contemporary Jewish chroniclers documented these acts while fitting them into well-established frameworks of victimhood, passivity, and chosenness. Even in their reworked form, few of these stories have survived into Jewish collective memory, whereas the more recent history of Jews in the tsar's army has long been, and to this day remains, central to Jewish memory of the encounter between Jews and conscription.

## Jews in the Tsar's Army: Conscription as National Tragedy?

In modern times there were more Jews in Russia than in the rest of the continent put together, and despite the ravages of the Holocaust the vast majority of world Jewry today, especially outside the state of Israel, is of

Ashkenazic origin. Most Ashkenazic families have stories of relatives who fled the tsar's army lest they be forced into a twenty-five-year term of service, or of *khappers*, thugs hired by the Jewish community to round up Jews targeted to meet the annual conscription quotas, and of unspeakably cruel conditions for Jews once they did wind up in uniform. From the late nineteenth through mid-twentieth centuries, the Russian-Jewish soldier became a metonym for the collective suffering of the Jewish people and its ongoing struggle against assimilation. These themes are embodied in Joseph Roth's celebrated and melodramatic novel *Job* (1930), which tells the story of a typical shtetl family headed by Mendel, a meek man who avoids "uniformed men, horses and dogs." Mendel's son Jonas, who loves horses and holds his liquor, becomes a career soldier in the Russian army, while his brother Shemariah moves to the United States and reinvents himself as Sam, as assimilated an American as Jonas is a Russian. Meanwhile, the wayward daughter Miriam sleeps with Russian soldiers, succumbing to the physical and erotic power of Gentile masculine strength.[38]

Over the past thirty years, scholars have persistently chipped away at this grim and harsh depiction. Although popular memory has not caught up with historiography, we now are able to present a reliable historical account that neither denies the gravity of the crisis that conscription posed for Russian Jewry nor indulges in the lachrymose presentations that characterize so much earlier writing on the subject.[39]

In the early 1800s, Tsar Alexander I strove to make peasants on state-owned lands more useful to the state by creating military settlements, known as cantons, that would house entire peasant families, whose children would be trained in special regimental schools. Under Alexander's successor Nicholas I, the definition of a "cantonist" was expanded to include orphans, vagrants, and juvenile criminals as well as the children of social or political undesirables (e.g., gypsies, Polish nobles). By 1853 there were over three hundred thousand Christian cantonists living with their families and another thirty-six thousand in special youth regiments or military schools.[40] The cantonist system was to be combined with conscription of young adults in order to integrate marginal groups into the Russian state.

Conscription of Russian Jews began in 1827, with Congress Poland coming under similar legislation in 1843. Between 1827 and 1855, some seventy thousand Jewish males, forty thousand of them children, were drafted into the army. For Jews, as for all the tsar's subjects, conscription was outsourced to corporate bodies such as the Jewish *kehilla* or the peasant commune with instructions to fulfill a certain annual quota. It was possible for the leaders of a Jewish community to spare the children of wealthy and learned Jews and to send paupers, orphans, and other social undesirables in their place. Jewish draftees could be mere children, for although the minimum draft age for other nationalities was eighteen, for Jews it was twelve. During the Crimean War, quotas increased markedly, and during the last two years of Tsar Nicholas I's reign Jewish community leaders, determined to keep the children of the elites out of the army, hired Jewish press gangs to capture children far younger than twelve and hand them over to the army. The Jewish child-soldiers were not allowed to observe Judaism in the cantonist schools, and some 30 to 40 percent converted to Christianity over the course of their quarter century of service. Conversion rates among older Jewish soldiers were far lower, partly because of the Jews' own perseverance, but largely because the army did not have a policy of coercing conversion.[41] Of all the Jews who served in Russia's military between 1827 and the 1870s, perhaps fifteen thousand converted to Christianity.

The most enduring image of Russian-Jewish conscription from the days of Tsar Nicholas I is Alexander Herzen's poignant eyewitness account of Jewish child cantonists, some barely eight years old, being marched deep into the Russian interior. A less well-remembered theme, which appeared over and again in the western European press, was that of Jews being impressed into the tsar's navy. *Tait's Magazine* wrote in 1855 that the tsar ordered "30,000 [Jewish] children to be torn from the arms of their parents, and transported to the coast of the Black Sea during a most rigorous season. Many perished on the road; others succumbed to the cruel discipline of the Russian navy; and if we are to believe the Jewish archives, a few years afterward there remained only 10,000 young men alive of this first levy of Israelites."[42] In the same year the *Jewish Chronicle* published a stirring poem about an apocryphal encounter between the tsar and Jewish sailors on a warship on the Baltic Sea. The tsar asks to meet with the two finest crewmen on board; to his surprise, he is presented with Jews. At the festivities that follow, the tsar demands the Jews convert to Christianity. Rather than submit to baptism, the Jews jump into the sea and drown themselves.[43] The kernel of truth behind these stories about Russian Jews in the imperial navy was its reputation for being physically demanding—the Black Sea fleet especially so—and thus the ideal destination for Jews whom the state wished to toughen up into sturdy and obedient subjects.

Was the military experience as dreadful as this poem suggests, and was it different from the experience of other nationalities in the Russian Empire? Under Nicholas I, Jewish soldiers were required to attend daily prayers and Sunday services with their Christian counterparts. Yet Jews were not coerced to convert, and the army did allow exemptions from certain kinds of work on the Sabbath and holidays. From the 1870s, Jewish communities were allowed to donate Torah scrolls to military camps and help build soldiers' synagogues. At times, Jewish soldiers received permission to cook meat in separate pots, but toward the end of the century, as antisemitism in the army began to swell, this privilege was denied to them.[44]

Even after universal conscription was introduced in 1874, many categories of individuals remained exempt from the draft. Jews had a much harder time securing those exemptions than Christians. For example, in 1900 in the Warsaw governorship, between one-fourth and one-third of Christians, as opposed to only 2 to 3 percent of the Jews, were exempted from service on the basis of being the sole breadwinner in the family.[45] Jews could not enroll in military schools, and between 1874 and 1917 there was only one Jewish career officer, a military clerk named Getzel Tam who was promoted to captain after retirement. A law of 1892 banned Jews, along with Christian schismatics, from field promotion even to corporal.[46]

Throughout the 1800s, Russian Jews were routinely accused by government officials of draft evasion. The statistical reports compiled by the government, and reproduced in the Hebrew press, compared the total pool of youths available for the draft with the number of Jews who answered the call and showed up at the recruitment centers. Yohanan Petrovsky-Shtern has argued that in any given year, only about a fifth of Jews of conscription age were selected by lottery and commanded to report for the draft, so a more accurate measure of Jewish obedience to the call-up order would be to compare the number of Jews selected by lottery with the numbers who appeared as commanded. According to Petrovsky-Shtern, virtually all of these potential recruits reported as ordered.[47] What's more, many cases of suspected draft dodging were the result of bureaucratic error. Jews were frequently registered in official records under multiple names—a Hebrew name, a Yiddishized moniker, a Russian equivalent—or in multiple districts, as they were more peripatetic than most of the tsar's subjects, ceaselessly moving in pursuit of their studies or, most often, of a livelihood.

Nonetheless, there are numerous documented cases of Russian Jews employing bribery and various forms of subterfuge to get out of the draft.[48] The same was true for Jews in Habsburg Galicia and, as we shall see, members of many other nationalities in eastern Europe. During the Crimean War, Russian and Galician Jews alike fled to the Danubian principalities, which were under Habsburg and Ottoman occupation, to avoid conscription.[49] A half century later, at the time of the Russo-Japanese War many young Jewish men, dodging the draft or deserting their units, fled Russia for the New World or Palestine, earning the moniker "Yapanchikim" in the process.[50] Throughout the late 1800s, the Russian Hebrew press, which had to watch its language carefully owing to government censorship and dutifully show support for the tsarist regime, diligently recorded cases of Jews prosecuted for fleeing home at or before draft age or for willfully mutilating themselves to avoid conscription. *Ha-Melitz*, a periodical published in St. Petersburg, cautioned young Jewish men against cutting off their fingers, starving themselves, and engaging in other forms of self-harm that violated both Jewish and Russian law. People caught doing it, the newspaper warned, would be severely punished, and excised digits would not grow back.[51]

Before 1874, rabbis worked closely with community lay leaders to keep yeshiva students and the children of the well-to-do out of the army, sending orphans, paupers, and other socially marginal youth instead.[52] After the 1874 introduction of universal conscription, all but the wealthiest Jews, who were still exempt from service, now had to choose between reporting to the recruitment center, fleeing the country, or extracting a release through bribery or ill health. At least publicly, rabbis had little choice but to urge pious Jews to fulfill their legal obligations but to do the utmost to maintain observance while in uniform. To this end, the prominent rabbi Yisrael Meir Kagan, known as the Chofetz Chaim, published in 1881 a little tract titled *Sefer mahaneh yisrael*, a guide to

Jewish observance while in uniform.[53] This enormously popular booklet was reprinted many times in the following decades, in Europe, North America, and Palestine. It epitomizes the classic Russian-Jewish sensibility of the army as a crushing burden that one must bear to the best of his ability.

Most of the book consists of exhortations and guidelines for the observance of mitzvot, such as kashrut, Shabbat, and the ritual washing of hands. Although most Jews preferred to serve in the back lines rather than combat units, the Chofetz Chaim urges Jews to serve in the infantry, where Sabbath desecration would likely be less flagrant and frequent than in the provisioning, clerical, or medical corps, as these would demand considerable labor on the Sabbath. The author urges Jewish soldiers to be particularly diligent to observe the Torah in time of war. A soldier must take the greatest pains in wartime not to commit the cardinal sins of idol worship, sexual impropriety, or "spilling the blood of one of his brethren" in the "great confusion" of the battlefield.[54] The killing of Gentiles is not mentioned.

The Chofetz Chaim instructs the soldier going off to war to seek forgiveness for sins, make up a will, and discharge all outstanding responsibilities. The text purports to instill courage via references to the wars of Moses and the Israelite kings, claiming that God brings victory to the Jews if they are righteous. Soldiers going into battle are instructed to recite a lengthy and highly comprehensive confession of sin. There is no hint of heroic or bellicose spirit. This prayer is followed by the final chapter in the section, a discussion of the burial of the dead.

*Sefer mahaneh yisrael* glorified neither war nor military service. It was the product of compulsion, a plea for Russia's Jewish youth to obey the law of the realm as per ancient rabbinic dicta. In contrast to this book's doleful tone, the "enlightened" Jews (*maskilim*) who dominated the world of Russian Hebrew letters, including the press, saw the army in a glowing light, as a means of integrating Jews into Russian society and molding them into enlightened, productive subjects. In the mid-1800s, the Lithuanian maskil Isaac Meir Dick claimed that Jewish cantonists made better fathers than Jewish youth who had not enjoyed the benefits of military discipline.[55] A contributor to *Ha-Melitz* imagined that military service would strengthen puny Jewish lads and make them independent from their cosseting mothers. The writers evoked government policies granting Jewish veterans a wide range of occupational choices and the right to live outside the Pale of Settlement.[56] Maskilim rejoiced that Jews could now demonstrate their loyalty to their "country and homeland" (*artsam u-moledetam*), a phrase that cropped up in the popular Warsaw-based periodical *Ha-Tsefirah*.[57]

In fact, even among Russia's Jews there was more than a flicker of military valor and Russian patriotism. By the 1870s they were considered effective forces and were widely employed in the Balkan campaigns of 1877–78. Jews figured prominently in the storming of Plevna and the capture of Gali Osman Pasha, the head of the Turkish army.[58] The Briansk Regiment, one of the most illustrious combat units in the Russian army, always contained a few score Jews among its ranks, and most of them belonged to a confraternity that called its members *anashei hayil*, men of valor. The statutes of the Shomrei Emunah shel Briansk Polk Society urged its members to "gird our loins and not be lazy in serving our master the Tsar, may his glory be exalted, so that no misbehavior stems from us."[59] Even in Russia Jewish soldiers possessed manly pride, and at least some considered military service a badge of honor. Nor did military life necessarily clash irreconcilably with Jewish identity. Although Russian-Jewish folk songs bewailed the fate of the Jewish cantonist sent off to a twenty-five-year term, "turned into a Muscovite,"[60] Jewish soldiers in Russia were in fact less likely to become Christian than to develop a new form of hyphenated identity, both Russian and Jewish, as far removed from Christianity as it was from traditional Jewish religiosity and culture.[61]

Like Russia's Jewish policies in general, the treatment of Jews in the tsar's army was riddled with contradictions between accommodation and coercion, separation and integration, incipient emancipation and institutionalized discrimination. The situation was even worse in Rumania, and Jews in many other countries found the draft to be a source of acute anxiety and disruption.[62] Yet Russia has remained at the center of Jewish collective memory of military service, and this memory, whether based in fact or not, has colored popular understanding of Jewish encounters with the military as a whole. Zionist readings of Jewish history and of the Jewish textual canon reinforce each other, creating an image of a people whose warrior spirit could be kindled only by contact with the land of Israel, first in antiquity and again after two millennia of exile. Lost along the way are centuries of Jewish paramilitary activity in eastern Europe as well as the varied and at times highly positive experiences of Jews in armies in western and central Europe as well as North America. Even if due to sheer numbers the experience of Russian Jewry was dominant, it was not normative.

In Jewish memory, throughout most of their history Jews were militarily powerless. Yet who among "the Gentiles," that is, some 99.75 percent of humanity throughout much of its history, has in fact possessed such power? For many people on the globe, military power has been their nemesis, taking the form of forced conscription or the oppression of rebellions, rather than their ally. At times, in the modern western world the encounter with the military could be a happier one for Jews than Christians, who were often rough-hewn peasants torn from their lands or landless and desperate for a livelihood. Anywhere in the world, the encounter between Jews and the military, like that between Jews and the state in general, could be painful, even tragic. But, as we will see in the next chapter, it could also be a source of personal and collective liberation.

## CHAPTER TWO

# Fighting for Rights: Conscription and Jewish Emancipation

Two types of armed force characterized Europe's "long nineteenth century," the period from the French Revolution to World War I. Armies of conscripts fought to preserve or enhance the power of the sovereign, while revolutionaries strove to create a new political order. Conscripts fought for states; revolutionaries struggled for stateless nations or oppressed classes. Soldiers in standing armies had long outnumbered rebels, and the disparity between the two increased as armies grew in size and sophistication over the course of the 1800s. In previous centuries, battles were led by aristocratic warriors, and the fighting masses were paid professional soldiers and mercenaries (that is, hired fighters from foreign lands) or conscripted peasants, subject to a levy of unpaid labor akin to the corvée, but performed with weapons instead of tools. All these types of fighters—the warrior, homegrown professional, mercenary, and unwilling conscript—survived into the nineteenth century, but in public conversation they were overwhelmed by a new ideal type, the citizen-soldier, who fought out of love of king and country, and in return became an active, equal member of the body politic.[1]

In Britain and the United States, where traditions of individual liberty limited the power of central government, this new type was usually a volunteer. (The American Civil War was the only instance of conscription in the United States prior to 1917, one year after the United Kingdom implemented conscription for the first time. American society was saturated in violence but not militarism.) On the Continent, volunteerism was popular among the patriotic middle classes during moments of crisis, but from the French Revolution onward the vast bulk of Europe's armies consisted of conscripts. The conscripts were often disenfranchised peasants who considered the draft to be a curse rather than a blessing, but for any social group demanding political rights, the soldier risking his life for the homeland became a powerful rhetorical tool. The nineteenth-century French critic Hippolyte Taine was enthusiastic about neither mass conscription nor universal suffrage, but he understood them to be twins.[2] The performance of military duty became a display of citizenship, a sign of belonging, a claim for individual rights and freedoms grounded in service to the collective.

According to a Yiddish proverb, "Vi es kristelt zich azoy yidelt zich" (as with the Christians, so with the Jews). Overwhelmingly, Jews who took up arms in the nineteenth century, or who thought and wrote about the prospect of Jews in battle, did so within the context of regular armies. As in musical counterpoint, however, revolution was a countervailing, secondary theme, often subdued, but on occasion swelling into a crescendo that overwhelmed the military march. Whether Jews fought as regulars or rebels, volunteers or conscripts, they displayed multiple identities based on ethnicity and religion, gender and class, and local and national origin. The Jewish public sphere of newspapers, pamphlets, and rabbinic sermons clearly and consistently associated Jewish military service with emancipation, either already achieved and reciprocated through sacrifice (as in France) or hopefully to be gained through meritorious service (as in Russia). Jews' assertions of patriotism to their homeland were undoubtedly sincere, yet for the Jewish activist elite every war was a Jewish war in the sense that antisemitism at home was at least as powerful a foe as the enemy abroad. Jewish men drafted into the military did not always share this sentiment, and many did their utmost to evade service. But fewer dodged the draft than both Christian accusations and Jewish folklore would have it, and in lands where Jews enjoyed partial or full emancipation, and where the military was perceived as prestigious and open to Jews, draft evasion was negligible.[3]

The first steps toward Jewish conscription were taken within the framework of an absolutist state, the Habsburg Empire. These were quickly overshadowed by the French Revolution, which directed Jews, like all Frenchmen, to fight for a new regime within an existing state that claimed to regenerate humanity as a whole. After Napoleon Bonaparte's coup d'état, the paths of state building and regime change, the purviews of the soldier and the rebel respectively, began to part. Revolution or rebellion against the state was limited to a few powerful but ephemeral episodes, such as 1848–49, when Jews throughout Europe were entranced by a vision of true emancipation coming only in the wake of the fall of reactionary regimes. Similarly, in Poland many Jews supported the uprisings against Russian rule of 1830–31 and 1863. After midcentury, though, connections between military service and the state as source of emancipation grew ever tighter.

In western Europe, Jewish military service in the wars of Italian and German unification solidified the alliance between Jews and the state. From the 1870s onward, accommodation of Jewish soldiers' religious needs, promotion of Jewish officers through the ranks, and bestowal of reserve officers' commissions on eligible Jewish men were sensitive indicators of emancipation's extent and limits. Western Jewry's increasing patriotism promoted enthusiastic support for aggressive colonial militarism, manifested in the Anglo-Boer and Spanish-American wars as well as French and German colonial ventures in Africa. We have already seen that, in the east, Jews usually served effectively, if reluctantly, in the tsar's army. Similarly, in the Ottoman Empire some Jews volunteered for military service even before the introduction of conscription in 1909. As in the west, in both the Russian and Ottoman empires there were Jewish activists who proudly linked military service with emancipation and new forms of patriotic, national identity.

Toward the end of the nineteenth century, the countervailing theme of emancipation through revolutionary struggle reasserted itself. In eastern Europe, antisemitism, poverty, and political oppression forged a generation of Jewish radicals who supported the use of force not only against the state but also against those who attacked Jews. The radicals' passion for self-defense left its mark on the Zionist movement. Like Jews in revolutionary France a century previously and the Soviet Union in its first decades, Zionists combined the goals of emancipation, state building, and social transformation, though they were now projected inward toward the Jews themselves and outward toward Palestine, a distant land within the penumbra of Europe's colonial sphere.

## New Thinking about Jews as Soldiers in the Eighteenth Century

In the late eighteenth century, the improvement of the Jews' status was a subject of intense debate throughout Europe. At issue was whether Enlightenment ideals about universal human rights and abilities could in fact be applied to Jews, who had for centuries lived under a specific corporate status that was rife with liabilities. Decades before the Enlightenment, however, a cluster of Protestant Hebraists began the process of rethinking the Jews' social status. They were not reformers seeking to change the social order but rather scholars possessed of a philosemitic streak and a fascination with the Jews' historic involvement in and suitability for combat. Jacques Basnage, a Huguenot scholar whose 1706 *Histoire des juifs* was the first major history of Jews past the time of Jesus, documented Jewish soldiers in many times and places: in the civic guard in sixth-century Arles, the military command in twelfth-century Portugal, and the defense of various eastern European lands in the 1500s and 1600s. Basnage cites sixteenth-century Lithuanian statutes that Jews and Tatars, although not to be recruited as mercenaries, may be placed in the field as part of a general defensive mobilization. Referring to the booklet *Sefer milhamah beshalom*, Basnage offers a stirring account of the Jews' role in the defense of Prague during the Swedish invasion of 1648: "They were so zealous for the glory that they gained that Rabbi Judah Leon wrote the history of the siege in order to teach posterity about the services that the Jews had rendered it."[4]

A similar positive tone characterizes a Latin dissertation on ancient Jewish military service submitted to the University of Halle in 1723 by one Rudolph Colemann. Colemann's goal is to refute the most commonly given reasons for Jewish exclusion from the military. Colemann cites numerous sources, including Josephus' exhaustive documentation of Jewish valor against Rome and the exploits of Saul the Hebrew, who fought for the Roman general Stilicho against the Ostrogoths in the early fifth century, to prove that Jews are neither too weak, nor small, nor faint of heart to join battle. (Colemann also discounts the venerable accusations that Jews issue an offensive odor by pointing out that in antiquity Jews and Gentiles were indistinguishable.) In ancient Rome, Colemann notes, Jews sought and received exemption from service in the common military on grounds of religious observance.

Like Basnage, Colemann does not explicitly call for improvement of the Jews' legal status. In fact, he writes explicitly that at present the military is a mercenary force and there is no need for universal military service. Yet there is a strong foreshadowing of Enlightenment *raison d'état* in his assertion that when needed Jews have always taken part in the defense of the fatherland.[5]

Fourteen years after Colemann, the Danish biblical scholar Jacob Huid submitted a dissertation that, although less sympathetic than the works of Basnage and Colemann, is overtly indebted to the former and bears many similarities with the latter. As befits a Protestant Hebraist who considered his faith community to be the legatee of biblical Israel, Huid veritably bursts with pride in the martial accomplishments of the ancient Hebrews in the Holy Land. He also follows Basnage and Colemann in documenting Jews' valor as fighters in the imperial armies of pagan antiquity. Huid is far less kind to the Jews of the Middle Ages and his own era, when they have been, he alleges, eager to profit from the spoils of war but loath to take up arms. Yet even Huid dismisses the accusations of the Jews' allegedly revolting stench, and he scrupulously documents several examples of Jewish martial courage in recent centuries, down to the Jews' heroic defense of Buda against the Habsburg siege in 1684 and 1686.[6]

Like Colemann and Basnage, Huid did not limit his interests to the military prowess of the ancient Hebrews, whom Protestants often viewed with reverence. All these authors wrote about the recent as well as the distant past, Jews as well as Hebrews, and so their works had implications for rethinking the Jews' legal status. Colemann's and Huid's works assume added significance when we consider that dissertations, particularly in eighteenth-century northern Europe, were not known for their freshness and originality; they were exercises, and it is doubtful that the writers would have dared make positive statements about the Jews to which their supervisors would be unreceptive. The students' claims were anything but shocking.

Colemann's and Huid's concerns were, at least on the surface, antiquarian, but their arguments had a potential to be marshaled for contemporary policy. This was indeed the case in the first tract advocating the amelioration of the Jews' civil status in Germany, Aaron Solomon Gumperz's pamphlet of 1753, *Epistle of a Jew to a Philosopher, and Its*

*Response*. The pamphlet was inspired by that year's "Jew Bill" in the English parliament, which proposed to naturalize foreign-born Jews and aroused a storm of protest from merchants in the City of London who feared ruin at the hands of Jewish competition. In the early 1750s, Gumperz, who had been born into a wealthy and privileged Jewish family in Berlin, was unique in that city's small Jewish community for the depth and breadth of his secular education and his mastery of High German. In his pamphlet, Gumperz devotes most of his attention to the economic benefit that Jews could bring to the state if they were granted greater levels of freedom of movement, settlement, and occupation. Along the way, he notes that Jews are perfectly capable of military service, although he believes that it would be in both the Jews' and the state's best interests if Jews paid for mercenaries.[7]

The trail from Basnage to Coleman, Huid, and Gumperz establishes a long pedigree to the most influential Enlightenment tract on state policy toward Jews: the Prussian bureaucrat Christian Wilhelm Friedrich von Dohm's *On the Civil Improvement of the Jews* (1781–83). In this hefty, two-volume work, Dohm argues that Jews have throughout history been fully capable of military service and so have every potential to be fully integrated into the modern state. (Dohm read Colemann and cites him on one occasion, but Dohm does not acknowledge the extent to which he relied on Colemann for sources. Moreover, Dohm cites the same passage from Basnage about the Lithuanian statutes that appears in Colemann's dissertation.)[8] The second volume devotes an entire chapter to conscription, arguing that the state should restrict the size of the Jewish population or expel it altogether should Jews prove unwilling to provide military service.[9] In addition to the examples he most likely took from Colemann, Dohm also cites the presence of Jews in the militia in seventeenth-century Suriname and a rabbinical decree of 1781 that allowed the Jews of Amsterdam to fight on the Sabbath in battles between the Dutch and English. Dohm believed that changing Jews into beings capable of warfare would take two generations, but until then Jews could buy their way out of service. This did not trouble Dohm, for, like Colemann and Gumperz, he believed that modern warfare would be based on mercenary forces, not universal participation.[10]

During the period of the Enlightenment, in western and central Europe the question of military service was bound to come up in any discussion about whether or not Jews were capable of civil improvement. In his critique of Dohm, the German orientalist Johann Michaelis observed that Jewish ritual observances (e.g., the dietary laws, the Sabbath) would make it impossible for Jews to be loyal and effective soldiers.[11] On the other hand, perhaps the most famous work on the Jewish question in late eighteenth-century France, Henri Grégoire's *Essay on the Physical, Moral and Political Regeneration of the Jews* (1789) describes Jews as a formerly "bellicose nation" still possessed of a "germ of valor."[12]

Grégoire's celebrated essay points the way to the ideal of egalitarianism that would spur national conscription, the *levée en masse*, during the French Revolution. Yet during the time of the Enlightenment the bulk of the conversation about Jews' suitability for military service came from German-speaking Europe, and its motivating spirit was not revolutionary egalitarianism but rather enlightened absolutism. The ultimate goal was not to get rid of venerable legal inequalities between peasants, townsmen, the clerisy, and aristocracy but to maintain and strengthen these estates through a program of carefully supervised "civil improvement" of marginal social groups. For the Habsburg emperor Joseph II (reigned 1780–90), military reforms were key to his overall program of educating the poor, making them more productive, and improving the legal status of non-Catholics. To that end, in 1788 the emperor, supported by his Chancellery, claimed that as a matter of principle Jews should provide military service along with all subjects of the state. In Jewish historical writing, this proclamation has long been overshadowed by the Edicts of Toleration, which granted the Jews a host of new opportunities, but the introduction of Jewish conscription marked a critical point in Jewish history and provided definitive proof that modernity had come to the Jews whether they liked it or not.

## Absolute Conscription: Jews and the Draft in the Habsburg Empire

The planning of Jewish conscription in the Habsburg Empire began smoothly. Despite the imperial War Council's doubts about the Jews' capacity to serve, the army quickly agreed to provide uniforms that did not contain a mixture of wool and linen, which in Jewish law is known as *shatnez* and may not be used. The Chancellery opened itself to the prospect of Jews rising through the ranks and becoming commanders over Christians.[13] Jewish soldiers were drafted in small numbers, and those who did pass muster were consigned to the transport corps. During the revolutionary wars, conscription of Jews became more widespread, and some 15,000 Jews fought under the Habsburg flag by 1803. Over the course of the Napoleonic wars, that number climbed to 35,000.[14]

Habsburg conscription policy elicited positive reactions from followers of the Jewish Enlightenment in Trieste and Prague. The most thoughtful response to Joseph II's policy came from a twenty-one-year-old Berlin Jew named Saul Ascher, who in later years would become a pioneer of Jewish religious reform. In 1788, young Ascher published a slim volume titled *Observations on the Civil Improvement of the Jews, Occasioned by the Question: Should the Jew Become a Soldier?* Ascher acknowledges the Habsburg armed forces' need for increased manpower and in principle has no objection to Jewish military service and taking part in combat. He is harshly critical of Galician Jews who attempt to evade military service yet, in what appears to be a contradiction against his own argument, assails Jews in Trieste who have endorsed the emperor's conscription decree. The problem, Ascher notes, is that all men must receive proper treatment in return for their sacrifice. At present, Ascher complains, Jews are treated worse than "colonists," that is, other minorities with special rights and privileges, such as Huguenots in Prussia, who have been exempt from taxes and military service.[15] Ascher's goal is the creation of cultivated, upright citizens, who in exchange for fair treatment will unhesitatingly carry out all their civil duties, including service in the army. A Jewish soldier without rights is little better than a slave, not a thoughtful, autonomous subject whose obedience would stem from higher reasoning and nobility of spirit.[16] (Ascher's thinking foreshadows the early musings of Carl von Clausewitz, who in 1812 claimed that the best soldiers are self-motivated, responding to an internalized moral code.)[17]

In the late eighteenth and early nineteenth centuries, among Jews in the Habsburg Empire, the most ardent supporters of Jewish conscription were radical reformers such as Herz Homberg, who also favored drastic changes in Jewish religious observance and economic practice.[18] Staunchly traditional rabbis, on the other hand, faced a legal and ethical crisis: Jews were obliged to observe the law of the land, but what if the law tore them from their families and communities, and made the observance of the Jewish commandments all but impossible? These questions perturbed Rabbi Yehezkel Landau of Prague, who on 12 April 1789 made a memorable speech to twenty-five young Jewish recruits and their commanding officers in Prague as the Jews headed off to begin their term of service. The speech was reported a month later in the Hebrew newspaper *Ha-Me'asef*, which claimed to report the rabbi's remarks "in their original form, without change or additions as they came into our hands from a trustworthy source."[19] There are in fact different versions of the speech, but the variations between them are minor. What matters is the impact of the speech on the Jewish world, both at the time it was delivered and throughout the nineteenth and early twentieth centuries as testimony to the compatibility of Jewish piety and patriotism. It is worth reproducing in full.

According to *Ha-Me'asef*, the rabbi handed each recruit a prayer book, a packet of *tzitzit*, and a pair of *tefillin*. He then gave this speech in High German, most likely because of the presence of the imperial authorities:

> Verily you have been my brothers, are so now and always will be, so long as you act with piety and rectitude! God and our all-merciful Emperor wish that you should be taken for military service. Go forth to your fate, follow it without protest, obey your superiors, be loyal out of duty and patient out of obedience. Yet forget ye not your religion, do not be ashamed to be *yehudim* among so many Christians. Pray to God daily as soon as you awake. For prayer to God comes before all. The Emperor himself and all his servants, those who are present and those who are not, pray daily to their creator. Do not be ashamed of this sign of the Jewish faith. When you have time, perform all the prayers that each Jew, as you already know, is obligated to pray. If you however do not have sufficient time, so pray at least the *Sh'ma*.
>
> You may keep the Sabbath, because you, so I hear, will mostly [be able to] rest on this day. Grease the carriages on Fridays always before evening, do everything that you may do ahead of time. Live in harmony with your Christian comrades; see to it that you become friends with them, then they will carry out your Sabbath labor and you will work for

them on Sunday, for they, too, as pious men and Christians are obligated to observe Sunday [Sabbath] as much as possible.

Keep away from all prohibited foods as long as possible. The emperor was gracious to say that you will never be compelled to eat meat. You may thereby sustain yourselves on eggs, butter, cheese and other permitted foods until you come to be with [civilian] Jews. . . .

Should one of you fall ill, so let him strive as long as possible to sustain himself through tea, until need requires that you must consume meat broth.

Moreover, always be true to God in your heart, do not waver from the faith of your fathers and serve our all-merciful ruler with good will and unceasing activity. Earn for yourselves and our entire nation gratitude and honor so that one may see that our nation as well loves its ruler and state authority, and in case of need is prepared to offer up its life. What is more, I hope that through you, if you act with honesty and loyalty, as is incumbent upon any subordinate, also those prejudices that still somewhat oppress us will be set aside. And what glory and what love will you not then thereby gain amongst all virtuous men, as well as by your brethren.

And herewith I wish to share with you my own blessing, welling up from the depths of my heart; I will apply to you those *pesukim* [verses] in *Tehilim* [the book of Psalms], which are relevant to your current situation: [Psalms 91:10ff] "No evil shall befall thee, nor shall any plague come near thy dwelling. May the Lord turn his face to thee and give you peace."[20]

At the end of the speech, according to *Ha-Me'asef,* the recruits and Landau himself began to sob. The recruits' family members and friends gave them money and provisions and tearfully took their farewells.

The speech embodies the dilemmas facing traditional Jewish communities in the face of demands for conscription. No requirement of the modern state—surrendering legal autonomy, accepting state supervision of religious affairs, exclusion from venerable occupations such as peddling, and pressure to take up crafts and agriculture—was as invasive as the obligation to send one's sons into the army for what might be a lifetime or at least an excruciatingly long period, which in the Habsburg Empire was gradually reduced from twenty-five to fourteen to twelve years. Publicly, Landau and other prominent rabbis had little choice but to accept this "evil decree" (the traditional term for catastrophes befalling the Jews). Landau did suggest a positive aspect of military service: the attenuation of prejudice and an improvement in the Jews' legal standing. But a year after making this speech, Landau was party to a petition to the new emperor, Leopold II, that pleaded for the maintenance of the Jews' historic privileges, one of which had been exemption from military service. The petition contradicted the views so elaborately enunciated in Landau's speech.[21] (The draft for Jews was in fact rescinded in 1790, only to be reintroduced seven years later with the intensification of the revolutionary wars.) Yehezkel's son, Samuel Landau, maintained his father's ambivalent stand by urging young men to do their utmost to avoid military service until they were specifically identified by name, in which case they must serve without trying to get another to go in their place.[22]

This tension between formally accepting the sovereign's right to draft Jews and striving to keep the Jews out of uniform also characterized the writings of the rabbi commonly claimed to be the father of ultra-Orthodox Judaism, Moses Schreiber of Bratislava (aka Moses Sofer or the "Hatam Sofer," 1762–1839). The Hatam Sofer explicitly invoked the ancient rabbinic principle of *dina de-malkhuta dina* ("the law of the land is law") to classify military service as a form of taxation, which rabbis had for many centuries justified as within a Gentile ruler's purview. (The logic was that taxation by a Gentile ruler brought benefits that would otherwise accrue to Jews had they levied the tax upon themselves.) At the same time, the Hatam Sofer urged Jews to attempt to buy their way out of service if possible. In practice, this is what happened; into the 1830s, entire Jewish communities in the Habsburg Empire were allowed to exempt their males from military service through payment, and they often did so.[23] Also, various categories of well-off individuals were routinely exempted from the draft, the result being that the Jews who went off into the army were disproportionally poor.[24]

Most traditionalist Jewish authorities did not see a halakhic problem in Jews wielding lethal force. In that sense they were different from the Anabaptist Protestant sects, such as Mennonites and Moravian Brethren, which adhered to a strict, theologically justified pacifism, and which mounted fierce, if not always successful, campaigns to maintain exemption from military service as a matter of conscience.[25] (Members of these sects were usually exempt from military service, perhaps out of deference to their Christian beliefs, but also because they were usually farmers and were thought to be highly productive, useful contributors to the national economy.) Among Jews, the overwhelmingly prevalent objection to conscription was that young males would be taken, perhaps forever, from their homes, that they would be unable to observe the commandments, particularly those involving diet and prayer, and that in time they would be lost to the Jewish community altogether.[26]

As I have already argued, the thoughts and feelings of masses of Jews should not be associated neatly with those of the great sages. Grassroots Jewish reactions to conscription were less nuanced than those of Yehezkel Landau and the Hatam Sofer. On the heels of Joseph II's 1788 decree ordering Galician Jews to serve as wagoners in the service corps and artillery, Jews fled into remote areas of the province or into the remnants of independent Poland. In Brody, Jews armed with clubs chased away a press gang; armed troops were brought in from L'viv to put down the demonstration.[27] Tellingly, Polish Jews were not afraid to employ violence in order to avoid conscription into the army. Although their culture was profoundly antimilitaristic and politically passive, and though they were too widely scattered to revolt en masse even if they wanted to, they were not averse to the use of force to maintain their traditional privileges, one of the most important of which was exemption from military service.

The Habsburg Empire, the first state to conscript its Jews, has presented us with the key components of our story: a modernizing state determined to mobilize all its resources, human and material, to enhance its power, dubious of the Jews' willingness and suitability to do military service, yet determined not to exempt them; an elite of Jewish reformers convinced that the interests of the state and of the Jews corresponded harmoniously; a diffident rabbinate treading between obedience to authority and the preservation of Jewish solidarity and observance; and a fearful Jewish population, most of which was intent on avoiding service at all costs. These elements appeared in other lands, though with different balances. Throughout the Continent, the issue of Jews and conscription was part of a much larger story about the relationship between state, populace, and the army, and whether the military was seen as a progressive institution in which commoners felt a personal stake—that is, if people outside the political elites felt their interests were best served by fighting for the state, against it, or by not serving at all and keeping as low a profile as possible.

## Willing Bodies: Jewish Soldiers in Western Europe

In nineteenth-century Europe, the ideal of military service as a schoolhouse for the nation and a sacrifice gladly borne by patriotic citizens clashed with a reality in which few men actually served and fewer still relished the experience of being in uniform. France's revolutionary wars and Napoleon's bid to become the master of Europe catalyzed the largest concentration of military forces in the Continent's history. In peacetime, however, armies shrank and conscription became piecemeal. Universal male conscription developed gradually, and in most countries only a small minority of young men did any more than token service. Until World War I, the United Kingdom made do with a small and undistinguished volunteer army. France did have conscription through the 1800s, but throughout most of the century only a small percentage of the population was called up, and until 1872 a man who had been drafted could pay for a substitute to serve in his place. Truly universal conscription was introduced only in 1889. The situation was similar in Prussia. Prussia introduced peacetime universal conscription in 1858, but members of the middle class were usually exempt from active duty. For graduates of secondary school—a minuscule yet influential fraction of the population—a year of service qualified one to apply for a reserve officer's commission, which was a source of great status but by no means an indicator of military experience or prowess. In impoverished Italy, the requirements for a reduction in the term of service to one year were far lower than in Prussia—all one needed was a basic education and the money to buy one's uniform.[28]

Few young men in nineteenth-century Europe were keen on going off to the army. Karl Marx famously observed that peasants were incapable of armed revolution because their minds were fixed on their farms, but what Marx tartly called the simple idiocy of rural life could be perceived by a more charitable observer as concern for one's loved ones and a good sense of household management. In Germany, most peasants did not want to send their children into the military not only because it took them away from the farm but also lest army life coarsen their manners. During the Napoleonic wars southern Germans overwhelmingly preferred religious and regional identities to a German national patriotism, and when they were called upon to fight the French in 1813, draft dodging and desertion were rife. Until the second half of the 1800s, throughout Germany middle-class culture was decidedly unmilitaristic, and in Prussia the sons of middling landowners resorted to all sorts of chicanery, and even self-mutilation, to get out of being conscripted.[29]

In France, Italy, and Austria-Hungary draft dodging was rife and well nigh unstoppable. In France, names of male infants were kept off village records so as to hoodwink the War Ministry, and in late nineteenth-century Italy, hordes of young men avoided the draft by fleeing the country.[30] Beginning in 1872, Austria-Hungary's War Ministry kept meticulous records of no-shows at recruitment centers, and the data show a marked, and steadily increasing, rate of no-shows after around 1900 in the Dual Monarchy's eastern and southern territories. In 1888, the no-show rate for all of Austria-Hungary was 4.5 percent; in 1901, 10 percent, and by 1910 a full 23 percent. Draft dodging remained uncommon in lower Austria and Bohemia but became rampant in Galicia, Hungary, western Ukraine, Dalmatia, Croatia and Slovenia, and Fiume.[31]

It should come as no surprise that Galician Jews often dreaded conscription decrees. Community functionaries handed over the very poor and young to meet conscription quotas, Jewish conscripts were mourned as if dead, and volunteering was taboo.[32] In Galicia in 1871, the rates of Jewish no-shows for military induction averaged 30 percent. In some districts in Galicia and Bukovina, no-show rates varied widely, from 11 to over 60 percent.[33] Military reports from the previous year describe a rampant culture of corruption in which Jews and Ruthenians bribed local officials, military officers, and army doctors (both Jewish and Polish) to grant exemptions. Desperate young men hired barber-surgeons to augment existing deformities or create new ones. As one regimental commander explained, a potential recruit needed to engage in these subterfuges for only three years, the period of time when he would be liable to be called up for service.[34]

Even for those who followed the law and reported at recruitment centers, the chances of being accepted for military service could be low.

In Austria-Hungary in 1875, 63 percent of called-up young men were rejected on medical grounds, and only 15.6 percent were actually taken into the army. In Russia in 1885, 27 percent of the total pool were accepted.[35] Prospective soldiers in both countries suffered from a vast variety of ailments and disabilities, some of which were self-inflicted (e.g., tachycardia induced by intentional fasting and excessive caffeine consumption, a missing trigger finger). But lung and skin diseases were common, and real enough, as were bona fide physical disabilities (the loss of use of an ear, eye, or limb due to a work accident) and imbecility. Many were stunted owing to malnourishment. In Austria-Hungary in 1886, 21 percent of Poles did not reach the minimum height of 1.554 meters (5' 1"), as opposed to 8 percent of Austrians. In Germany, even middle-class males were often rejected for medical reasons, and only about a third of those eligible for the reduced, one-year term of service were actually enlisted.[36] In the early twentieth century, the only countries that implemented a genuinely universal conscription policy were small and constantly embattled European states such as Montenegro, whose army could field every man between eighteen and sixty-two, or Bulgaria, claimed proudly by one of its generals to be "the most militaristic state in the world."[37]

Throughout most of modern Europe's history the "people's army" was a myth, but an immensely powerful one, that forged national identities and both exemplified and stimulated new ways of thinking about the relationship between the individual and the state. The Enlightenment restored and augmented classical Greco-Roman ideals of civic virtue, according to which, as per the words of Jean-Jacques Rousseau, "Every citizen should be a soldier by duty; no citizen should be a soldier by trade."[38] The principle that every male adult could be called upon to sacrifice his life for his homeland strengthened the social contract between citizen and state, increasing the obligations of each toward the other. Celebration of the common soldier was a key component of modern patriotism, a new form of political language that extolled love of country above other affinities. Although associated strongly with the French Revolution, modern patriotic language first appeared during the Seven Years' War (1756–63), when writers in France and England, which were at war against each other, described a clash not between states or monarchs but between cultures.[39]

Jewish leaders picked up this theme with alacrity. During the Seven Years' War, English and German rabbinic sermons began to display a sense of national attachment. Over the course of the revolutionary and Napoleonic wars, incipient patriotism swelled among rabbis and communal leaders, especially those in the economic elite, who had the greatest attachments to state institutions.[40] To be sure, older forms of political identity hung on. Early Jewish expressions of patriotism bore no hint that Jews should sally forth against the enemy. In 1763, a "peace sermon" written by the famed Berlin philosopher Moses Mendelssohn was a traditional panegyric to the Prussian king and a poignant meditation on the horrors of war. ("At a time of war," Mendelssohn wrote, "Man has no recompense, the cities are burned, the palaces destroyed.")[41] Sometimes what appeared to be heartfelt exhortations by rabbis for Jews to enlist were in fact coerced. For example, in Holland under Napoleonic rule, rabbis were forced to sign letters and deliver sermons in support of the formation of special Jewish battalions. (The rabbis actually worked to undermine the conscription decrees, and there was little public support for the Israelite Corps outside the pro-French and assimilationist elites who manned the Batavian Republic's High Consistory.)[42]

In France, obligatory Jewish military service was instituted only in 1808, twenty years after the Habsburg emperor's pioneering act. Yet from the first days of the French Revolution, as Jewish emancipation was debated in the Chamber of Deputies, the Jews' fitness for military service was at the center of the discussion. In the Chamber on 23 December 1789, the abbé Jean-Sifrein Maury remarked, "I do not know of any general in the world who would wish to command an army of Jews on the Sabbath day." The Jewish response came the very next day in the form of a written address to the Chamber: the Jews have "always been ready to spill their blood for the glory of the nation and the preservation of liberty."[43] This fiery promise was realized through mass attempts by Jews to volunteer for the civic and national guards that were formed with the revolution's outbreak. Paris counted barely five hundred Jews, and at least one hundred served as volunteers in the National Guard, among them Zalkind Hourwitz, a Polish Jew who campaigned vigorously for the improvement of French Jewry's status.[44] The Jews of Bordeaux also rushed to volunteer for the guard. Two years after the revolution's outbreak, guard units were incorporated into the line army, and hundreds of Jews were thrown into combat. By the end of the 1700s, about 40 percent of Nice's combat-age Jewish males were in the military.[45]

Most of France's Jews were concentrated in the northeast, in highly traditional communities that viewed emancipation warily, fearing that it would lead to the breakdown of rabbinic authority and pressures to abandon ritual observance. Not surprisingly, they were less likely to sign up than the more assimilated Jews of Paris and the south, but there were numerous cases of Jewish volunteering in Alsace and Lorraine. In Strasbourg and Nancy, Jews who wished to serve in guard units encountered opposition not from their rabbis but from Christians, who would not let the Jews in. The celebrated rabbi Aaron Worms of Metz shaved his beard in order to keep a place in his unit. Max-Théodore Cerfbeer, a career officer whom we will encounter in the next chapter, was the son of a merchant in Metz who in 1810 lobbied to get his son admitted to the recently founded École Polytechnique, the seedbed for the empire's future engineers and military officers in the technical corps.

Jews volunteered for the National Guard or the line army not out of a desire to fight but out of gratitude for emancipation and a desire to be included with the body politic. A particularly intense outburst of patriotic enthusiasm occurred in the German states, particularly Prussia, in the wake of the emancipation edict of 1812. The removal of Jewish legal disabilities certainly had its desired effect of stimulating Jews to fight for the German states in their War of Liberation against Napoleon. About seven hundred Prussian Jews fought as volunteers, half of these in the *Freikorps*, whose members had to have the means to fit themselves out with uniform and firearms. Jews did not have to convert to Christianity to receive battlefield promotions, and over seventy received the Iron Cross.[46]

Patriotic German Jews exhorted their youth to volunteer. David Friedländer, a radical reformer and pillar of the Berlin Jewish economic elite, declaimed, "Hand in hand with your fellow soldiers you will complete the great task; they will not deny you the title of brother for you will have earned it." A pamphlet composed in 1813 by Karl Siegfried Günsburg and Eduard Kley employed the language of nation as family, and of one's own family as metaphor for the nation, that was becoming increasingly popular in times of war: "You are assembling under the colors not only for the king, but you also must fight on behalf of your fathers, mothers, sisters and little brothers, of women, brides, greybeards and children. It is their lives that you defend, their tranquility that you assure, their well-being, that you must now establish through your participation."[47] The diary entry of 25 March 1813 by one volunteer, Loeser Cohen, reads: "My heart pounded with joy; I was so thankful to be able to prove myself to ruler and fatherland. I approached my beloved parents with the words 'The time has come when we Jews have the opportunity to faithfully serve the fatherland. I am committed to sacrifice myself for the beloved fatherland.' "[48] Nor was patriotism limited to maskilim and reformers. The chief rabbi of Silesia, Aaron Karfunkel, sent sixteen young men from his yeshiva into battle, and in his farewell blessing he released them from mandatory observance of the commandments: "From the moment that you enter military service, you have to think only about king and country. Your religious duties cease!"[49]

Perhaps the most intriguing sign of any society's internalizing patriotic feeling is the integration of women into the field of battle. Women disguising their gender and fighting in men's clothing cropped up on occasion in mid-eighteenth-century French, Dutch, and British armies. They became more numerous, and more likely to fight openly as women, in volunteer brigades in the French forces during the revolutionary and Napoleonic wars. (There were perhaps eighty women out of more than seven hundred thousand soldiers.) The participation of women in battle connoted the dissemination of patriotism and also, at least after 1789, a revolutionary upheaval in human relations, ranging from high politics to the intimate sphere.[50] German Jewry got a wartime heroine of its own in the form of one Esther Grafemus, née Manuel, from Hesse. According to her own account, Esther's German patriotism was so great that when the Prussian queen Louise died in 1810, she assumed the late queen's name. Louise's husband deserted her and her children, and rumor had it that he joined the Russian army. Louise petitioned the son and daughter-in-law of the Prussian king, Prince William and Princess Marianne, to fit her out for battle so that she might search for her errant husband. The prince granted her request, Louise went with the Prussian army to Russia, and legend has it that in the midst of battle she found her husband and revealed herself to him, only to watch him die of his wounds the next day.[51]

Esther was a real person—she remarried, moved to Riga, and died in 1852—but it is hard to say how much of the story of her colorful battlefield exploits is true, especially as she was something of a publicity hound and was prone to exaggeration. Even if taken at face value, the story is striking for its overtones of passivity and conservatism, for Esther went into battle not to slaughter the wicked and degenerate foe but rather in order to be reunited with her husband. Below we will discuss the reluctance of nineteenth-century Jewish patriotic rhetoric to demonize the enemy, especially if Jews might be fighting in its camp. For now, the important point is that the tale of Esther Grafemus, like other tales of women who joined the troops, was widely circulated, and that she was admired among German Jews as a heroine. The story testifies to the development among Jews, as among western European societies as a whole, of a conception of women as part of the nation and obliged to sacrifice on its behalf. The fighting woman was a symbol, an exemplar of feminine patriotism that was practiced primarily on the home front. In many lands, women's charitable societies contributed clothing and blankets to men at the front, raised funds for hospitals and nurse-training programs, and directly supported war widows, orphans, and refugees.[52]

During the decades between Napoleon's defeat and the revolutions of 1848, the glories of Jewish volunteerism in the immediate past and promises of future sacrifice on behalf of the nation figured prominently in discussion of Jewish emancipation. In the German lands myriad sermons, pamphlets, and the Jewish press were saturated with apologetic depictions of Jews as soldiers. Moritz Oppenheim's painting of 1833–34, *The Return of the Volunteer from the Wars of Liberation to His Family Still Living in According to the Old Customs*, was enormously popular and enjoyed wide dissemination as a lithograph. In the painting (figure 2.1), the smartly uniformed son has no head covering and wears the Iron Cross, which appears to cause his elderly, traditionally garbed father some consternation. (The soldier's much younger brother, on the other hand, reaches for the soldier's saber.) This painting won high praise from Gabriel Riesser, a tireless advocate of German-Jewish emancipation, who hailed the work for its depiction of both the son's courage and patriotism, on the one hand, and his attachment to the Jewish home to which he has returned.[53] The painting perfectly suited his belief that the exclusion of Jews from military service was the most serious threat to the Jews' attainment of juridical equality.

Governments were aware that issues of Jewish military service and emancipation were inextricably bound, and this connection caused them unease. In 1806, Napoleon Bonaparte ordered the convening of a body of rabbis and Jewish lay leaders from throughout the empire. This body, known as the Assembly of Notables, was asked to respond to a number of questions, including whether France's Jews felt bound to defend their country. The assembly's vociferously positive answers to this and other questions about Jewish patriotism, and similar affirmations the following year by another assembly known as the Great Sanhedrin, did not satisfy the emperor, who in 1808 imposed a variety of punitive measures upon France's Jews, primarily those in Alsace. He also decreed that all Jewish males must serve in the army without the possibility to pay someone to take their place, as was the norm at the time. Ordinary Jews no doubt saw this as a curse, but for Jewish leaders and activists seeking to ingratiate and integrate themselves with the state, it was a godsend.

In Prussia, on the other hand, Jewish leaders had to campaign for the right to have their sons drafted. Between 1841 and 1845, the Prussian government struggled with the issue, as King Frederick William IV was suspicious of the Jews' ability to fight in his army and opposed their emancipation. In this spirit, in June of 1842 the Breslau municipality turned to the prominent Liberal rabbi Abraham Geiger and asked, as had Napoleon's government, if the principles of the Jewish faith and Jewish practices allowed for general military service. Geiger affirmed that "military service . . . is a religious duty, indeed the highest, to which all others must be subordinated, so that the pious Jew may not release himself from it." Freeing Jews from service, Geiger wrote, does them no favor; it is a blow to their spirit, as "it deprives them of the means to defend themselves and their fatherland." What's more, "the contemporary state is our fatherland and lays before us the same duties as the former Jewish one."[54] If anything, Geiger wrote, there are fewer restrictions on Jewish military activity than there were in the ancient Jewish kingdoms, as their leadership was subject to certain biblical restrictions regarding the waging of war. Since modern warfare is a skilled craft that requires extensive preparation, military service as a whole must be considered

Figure 2.1. Moritz Oppenheim, *The Return of the Volunteer from the Wars of Liberation to His Family Living According to the Old Customs* (1833–34).

a form of battle, during which, according to rabbinic Judaism, the Sabbath and dietary laws may, and at times must, be violated. Finally, wrote Geiger, since the good Prussian king only leads defensive wars, Jews are freed of all ritual obligations as they would have been in the case of a rabbinically sanctioned obligatory war in the ancient land of Israel.[55]

These positions won considerable support from German Christian liberals, and finally, after four years of bureaucratic investigation, wrangling, and procrastination, in 1845 the Prussian cabinet ordered universal, compulsory military service for the Jews, who would be eligible for field promotions but not commissions.[56] This slight would be a source of embarrassment and frustration for Prussian-Jewish men for many decades to come. More important, the freeze-and-thaw cycle of liberalization and reaction wore down the patience of idealistic

Jews, in Germany as in other European lands, who refused to sacrifice their bodies for an oppressive or ungrateful state and instead took up arms against it.

## The Jew as Rebel

Jewish volunteering during the period 1789–1815 left two overlapping and conflicting legacies. On the one hand, by the 1840s Jews in France, the German states, and the Habsburg Empire had established a practice of loyal military service in gratitude for, or in expectation of, emancipation and social acceptance. On the other hand, Jews became prominent in struggles for national liberation by the stateless peoples of the Continent's polyglot empires. The Jew as rebel became a common figure in western and central Europe in 1848, but there were earlier instances, as in Italy, where Jews were heavily overrepresented in Giuseppe Mazzini's Young Italy movement, and several died in the Naples uprisings of 1828.[57] Poland, however, was the center of Jewish fighting for nationalist causes prior to the Continent-wide revolutions of 1848.

Between 1772 and 1795, Poland was picked apart and shared between Russia, Prussia, and the Habsburg Empire. Russia, which acquired the heart of the old Polish kingdom, was a frequent target of Polish rebellion—in 1794, 1831, 1846, 1848, and 1863. Jews played a prominent role in all these uprisings.[58] One Jewish fighter in particular has become one of the great heroic figures of modern Jewish history.

According to legend, Berek Joselewicz (1764–1809), a merchant and agent of the Polish court, raised a regiment of Jewish volunteer cavalry during the 1794 Kosciuszko rebellion against Russia. (His unit may, in fact, not have been an independent regiment so much as part of the urban militia that defended Warsaw against Russian invasion.)[59] During the revolutionary and Napoleonic wars, Berek fought in Polish cavalry units in Galicia and Italy and served a stint in the Hannoverian army. After returning to Poland, Berek served in the army of the principality of Warsaw, where he rose to the rank of lieutenant colonel by the time of his death at the battle of Kock (figure 2.2).[60]

Berek was not so much a Polish patriot as an adventurer and activist who sought to enhance his own personal honor as well as that of

Figure 2.2. Berek Joselewicz at the Battle of Kock, as rendered by the nineteenth-century Polish painter Juliusz Kossak. This image was reproduced on Polish and Israeli postage stamps in 2009, the bicentennial of Joselewicz's death. *Courtesy of Eric Contesse.*

the Jews under his command. Although Berek is most famous for his service for Poland, in 1796 he proposed to the Habsburg emperor the raising of a corps of six thousand to eight thousand Jews who would be divided into cavalry and infantry units to fight against the French. At first, the proposal seems to have the interests of the soldiers at heart in its demands that they be eligible for promotion through the ranks, that ritual observance be unfettered, and that rabbis be incorporated into all units. But Berek's own ambition shines through in his demand to be appointed to the august rank of colonel, and he coolly recommends that Jews be drafted if sufficient numbers of volunteers are not forthcoming. Berek also displays an aesthetic flair in his detailed description of the soldiers' uniforms:

> The infantry will wear long Hungarian lined trousers, short boots, a Polish jacket and a Polish cap. Along the side of the trousers will be a narrow, dark green cloth stripe; the jacket will have a narrow, dark green lapel, and the cap will have, instead of a brim, a dark green cloth band. The fabric of the trousers, jacket and cap should be earthen colored, and for that reason something in salt and pepper would be best. . . . The cavalry will be accoutered like the infantry except that the lapels and edges [of the jacket] will be made of red cloth in order to better distinguish between them. . . . the overcoats for both will be made of conventional military twill.[61]

The soldiers will be armed with pikes, sabers, pistols, and ammunition; their horses will be equipped with "a Polish saddle."

Whatever Berek's actual political sentiments may have been, over the course of the nineteenth century, Berek became a hero for acculturating Polish Jews who commemorated him as an exemplar of Polish-Jewish patriotism. More traditionally oriented Polish Jews were less likely to venerate Berek, but they were not necessarily hostile to displays of male military prowess. During Napoleon's invasion of Russia in the autumn of 1806, as the emperor approached the town of Swarzedz, about eleven kilometers east of Poznan, he was met by some 120 Jews on horseback and clothed in mock Turkish cavalry costume. This act of martial pantomime was intended to demonstrate Jewish support for Napoleon as a liberator—not of Polish Jews themselves but of Poland from Russian rule, and of Palestine, which France had invaded in 1798, from the Turks.[62] In other words, this was a theatrical gesture of messianic expectation rather than a serious offer of military assistance. Still, the fact that Jews chose to display their messianic sentiments via a mock show of military force attests to their respect for the armed fighter as an admirable figure.

By the 1830s, a critical mass of Polish Jews had developed a sense of Polish national patriotism that compelled them to volunteer for guard units. During the 1831 uprising against Russia, Josef Berkowicz, Berek's son, formed a Jewish unit and spurred Jews to join guard and army units throughout the kingdom. In that year, some one thousand Jews fought against Russia. They were an odd mix of radicals and Orthodox Jews, including Dow Ber Meisels, the chief rabbi of Cracow and a prosperous banker. Meisels also supported the abortive uprising of 1846, although he was a reactionary antinationalist whose support for the Polish cause stemmed from his long-standing close associations with the Polish aristocracy.[63]

When revolution convulsed Europe in 1848, Jews were forced to choose between rebellion and order, between faith in the emancipatory state and belief in a better, freer world built upon new foundations. Many Jews remained stolidly loyal to their governments. Vienna's minuscule and wealthy Jewish community, grateful to the Habsburg emperor for promulgating a constitution in March that promised religious equality, initiated a campaign to raise money for a warship to be given as a gift to the state and christened *Emancipation*.[64] The ship was never built, but young Jewish men gave the Austrian crown more tangible support as soldiers charged with putting down uprisings by the empire's subject nationalities. At the same time, Jews figured prominently among the fighters in Hungary and the northern Italian states. Their cause was the same as that of their Gentile brethren: national independence as the indispensable precondition for universal freedom and brotherhood. According to Vienna's most prominent rabbi, Isaac Noah Mannheimer, his coreligionists were fighting as men, not Jews, for human not Jewish rights, and for universal freedom, not Jewish emancipation. Similarly, a Jewish observer in Hungary remarked, "they are not rebels because they are Jews or Jews because they are rebels."[65] Two Jews were among the first rebels killed at the onset of the March uprising in Vienna. In a street battle in Berlin on 28 March, five men died, including a Herr Weiss, who fell clutching a German tricolor in one hand and a sword in the other.[66] In June, Jewish youth in Livorno prepared and distributed among the townsfolk colorful banners praising Pope Pius IX and Leopold, the grand duke of Tuscany, who were seen as liberals at the time.[67]

The prominence of Jews among the revolutionaries is striking. Some 180 Jews from Piedmont alone figured among the 5,000 revolutionary fighters in Italy; in relation with their percentage in the Italian population, they were overrepresented by a factor of fifty-five.[68] In Germany, 750 Jews were involved in revolutionary organizations, and many died on the barricades or were executed by government troops. Here and in Austria, the cream of the Jewish intelligentsia enthusiastically supported the revolution, as shown in the pages of the German-language Jewish press, which reported excitedly about the revolutions' progress. "The messiah is freedom," thundered *Der Orient*, and "our history is concluded. It has merged with the universal." In Vienna, Adolph Fischhof and Hermann Jellinek led the uprising while Hermann's brother Adolph, who would become one of the most prominent rabbis in the Habsburg Empire, called upon the Jews: "Arm yourselves all and the communities will bring forth great sacrifice. Scholars, who only knew how to argue for or against Maimonides, stride forward with rifle and bayonet."[69] As if responding to the call, in Berlin, Leopold Zunz, the mild-mannered pioneer of Judaic scholarship, mounted the barricades. Calling upon the crowd to storm the armory, Zunz shouted that the revolution needed "weapons and a national guard, twenty thousand strong." "Plutocrats and bureaucrats, the black-robed papist police, the diplomats of Metternich—all are in the throes of fever, for the day of the Lord draws nigh. Perhaps by Purim, Amalek will be beaten."[70] Alas for the rebels, Amalek was not defeated, and after the rebellions were crushed he took his vengeance. Entire Jewish communities in Hungary were forced to pay punitive fines, while the Jewish rebels among them were summarily shot.

As in France in 1789, so in 1848 were the local and national guards the bulwarks of revolutionary zeal. In the small town of Bütztow, in Mecklenburg, almost all the men of the Jewish community, including the elderly, signed up for the guard.[71] Jews in the cities that were the center points of the revolutions—Paris, Rome, Frankfurt, Berlin, Vienna, Buda and Pest—were well situated to join the guards, which consisted mainly of middle-class family men, well-off enough to buy their own uniform and equipment.[72] At times, the guard units became sites for the performance of martial ecumenical brotherhood, as in L'viv, where each new volunteer was required to sign a declaration "that he saw Germans and Israelites as equally deserving citizens."[73] Jewish aspirations to join local militias were often frustrated, however, by antisemitism and rivalries fueled by economic competition. In Bratislava and many towns in Moravia Jews were kept out of the guard, so they formed their own units, which defended their communities from antisemitic attacks while at the same time fighting off the kaiser's armies. In July of 1848, a unit of two hundred Jews in the Moravian town of Prossnitz fought off a mob of Christians, only for violence to break out again two months later.[74] A Jewish guardsman in Pest, on duty at the town hall, was attacked by Christians, and when he defended himself with his sword, wounding one of his assailants, a mob assembled, demanding that the Jews be disarmed and expelled.[75] Throughout central Europe, riots against Jews were commonplace during the revolutionary tumult, but so was Jewish self-defense, and many of the defenders were guardsmen or veterans.[76]

Although the revolutions of 1848 had been directed against state authority, they had the unintended consequence of awakening militaristic spirit in the hearts of middle-class men and channeling that spirit into postrevolutionary patriotism. During the revolution, men who had previously shunned military service rushed into the guard units as an assertion of their right to bear arms and maintain local rights in the face of central authority. The rebellious spirit of 1848 thus inculcated militaristic values into liberal civil society.[77] The grassroots militia provided the impetus for a popular militarism that would flourish in western and central Europe the decades following the rebellions' crushing defeats. State governments successfully channeled that ethos into enthusiasm for military service.[78] Jewish society followed this general trend, manifested in both words and action. The cluster of European wars between 1854 and 1871 rendered Jews more receptive to military service, eager to promote and celebrate the integration of Jews into European armies, and supportive of sending their sons into battle. This trend extended beyond Europe, as the American Civil War of 1861–65 presented American Jews with opportunities and dilemmas similar to those found in the Old World. In eastern and southern Europe, Jews remained fearful of the army, but even here the 1860s and 1870s introduced more positive, and at times downright patriotic, feelings about the Jews' land of residence and a willingness to fight on its behalf.

As universal conscription crystallized from an ideal or short-term measure into a rigorously implemented policy, Jews identified ever more strongly with the military. In turn, armies became more receptive of Jews, taking into account their religious requirements. The accommodation and integration of Jews into the military did not put an end to antisemitism in the barracks, nor did it keep Jews in the eastern portions of Austria-Hungary or Russia from attempting to dodge the draft. But these integrative processes were universal, and they took place even in the tsar's empire, though the countervailing forces there were particularly strong.

## Integration and Accommodation of Jewish Soldiers

"Soldiers with peyos," read a headline in the 11 April 1909 issue of *Haynt*, a Yiddish newspaper published in Warsaw. The story was about Jewish soldiers in the Austro-Hungarian army, marching through Budapest en route to the Serbian border. Some of the Jews, including officers, wore *pe'ot*, the sidelocks indicative of fervently Orthodox, in this case most likely Hasidic, Jewish men. Their commander's permission of the practice attests to a far-reaching tolerance of ethnic and religious difference within the Habsburg army, which also provided halal meat for Muslim soldiers in the Balkans and, as one might expect, ensured that Christian soldiers could observe the Sunday Sabbath. Whether due to logistical difficulties or residual prejudice, the Habsburg military was not as forthcoming about giving Jewish soldiers easy access to kosher meat.[79] The army was, however, highly respectful of Jews who died on active duty. As early as 1862, the supreme commander of the Habsburg forces ordered that Jews who died in field hospitals be given a traditional Jewish burial by the nearest Jewish community and be buried with the military funerary rites due to a deceased Christian soldier. The same order authorized local rabbis to visit sick and wounded Jewish soldiers in military hospitals.[80]

Shortly before, France's army had taken steps to correct its previously negligent treatment of killed and injured Jewish soldiers. At the battle of Sevastopol during the Crimean War, a French unit lost a Catholic senior officer and a Jewish lieutenant. The Catholic was buried with full religious rites and a priest in attendance, while the Jew's burial had no religious aspect whatsoever, and the unit commander referred only to the young man's sacrifices for his fatherland. Grieving and aggrieved, the Jew's coreligionists retired after the burial to the deceased soldier's tent, where they recited the prayers for the first night of the holiday of Sukkot, keeping the tent flap wide open to view the sunset and to display their patriotic piety to the entire camp. The incident was publicized throughout Europe by a Jewish army physician on the scene, and the War and Religious Affairs ministries of the French government agreed to send rabbis to both Constantinople and the army's forward command headquarters.[81]

Jewish clerics and politicians in France also pushed the government to institute regular furloughs for Jewish soldiers to travel home for the High Holidays. In the mid-1870s, of all the Jews in uniform only those in the Paris district were given leave for Passover and for Yom Kippur. Gallingly for French Jews, their brethren across the Rhine were somewhat better treated; Jews in the German army reserve were routinely given furloughs for Passover, though soldiers in the line army rarely received this perk. Adolphe Crémieux, the most celebrated Jewish politician in France, lobbied for a standard Passover furlough of six days for all Jewish soldiers garrisoned in areas without synagogues. Over time, the leave period increased to seven and then eight days, while the leave for Algerian-Jewish soldiers serving in the Hexagon was at first fifteen and by 1882 a full thirty days, plus time to travel back to their homes in the Maghreb.[82] Impediments to holiday worship still remained, however. In 1883, the superintendent of the artillery academy at Fontainebleau refused Jewish cadets permission to pray at a local synagogue on Yom Kippur.[83]

As important as it was to Jewish soldiers to be with their families for the holidays, there was even greater symbolic meaning in celebrating the holidays in uniform, in camp, distinct from yet of a kind with one's fellow soldiers. Prayer in uniform was a simultaneous performance of assimilation and difference: the antiquity of the service, the formality of its language, and its call for a discipline of the self to God asserted a particular Jewish identity, a religious tradition no less respectable and generative of manly virtue than Christianity. A century before the praying Israeli soldier at Jerusalem's Western Wall, service rifle slung over his shoulder, became a beacon of psychic energy for diaspora Jews, the uniformed Jew at holiday services testified to the symbiotic relationship between religious and martial sentiment in modern Jewish culture.

A yearning for public recognition led German Jews in 1870 to fabricate a story of a mass prayer service by Jewish soldiers on Yom Kippur, on the outskirts of besieged Metz. Shortly before the High Holidays of 1870, Isaak Blumenstein, a rabbi from Mannheim, came to the army encampment with plans to organize a large, open-air prayer service. A plan was approved for the service to take place with leave granted to 1,147 Jewish worshippers, to be guarded by their fellow Christian soldiers. This didn't happen, however. A division was called into battle shortly before the ceremony, and only about sixty Jewish soldiers went off to hold impromptu services, without a rabbi or Torah scroll, in a couple of abandoned buildings. Rabbi Blumenstein was pleased that the commanding officer, Edwin von Manteuffel, had received him with respect and allowed the Jews a few hours to recite the prayers. (He had refused a similar request for Rosh Hashanah.) The artist Hermann Junker found this story sufficiently compelling to illustrate it in two paintings that were reproduced as popular postcards. One, which shows a throng of uniformed Jews praying in a dingy farmhouse, was inspired by not only the events at Metz but also a work from 1868 by Moritz Oppenheim, *The Prayers in Memory of the Dead*. (The painting depicted a handful of

Jewish soldiers reciting the kaddish prayer in a ruined building while two curious Christian women look on through a destroyed window.) Following upon Junker's paintings came an even more popular memorial cloth depicting the planned yet abortive mass prayer service as if it had actually taken place. The tapestry (figure 2.3) portrays Jews gathered en masse in a valley outside Metz, in full uniform and prayer shawls, facing an impressive ark, their heads covered by spiked helmets. As they pray, Christian soldiers guard them from distant hilltops. In the corners of the cloth the story of the service is told in verse, with the number of Jews claimed to be 1,200—a number that was not only impressive but also symbolic of Jewish particularity, as it subtly invoked the twelve tribes of Israel.[84]

For anyone viewing this cloth after the Holocaust, the image of Jews huddled together in prayer shawls in a valley surrounded by armed Germans evokes terrifying associations. At the time, however, this image connoted Jewish religious solidarity, patriotism, virility, and gratitude toward the German emperor for the opportunity to serve the fatherland. As the cloth wended its way into German-Jewish homes, the press was filled with reports by soldiers in the field as well as by Rabbi Blumenstein about what had really happened, but the legend proved more powerful and durable than reality.

At the center of the cloth is an ark and a uniformed prayer leader, a projection of German Jews' desires for military chaplains like those who ministered to Catholic and Protestant soldiers. In any country, Jewish military chaplains were a bellwether of Jewish acceptance within the army as a whole. Also, although Jewish soldiers did not need a rabbi to officiate at their prayers, the comforting presence of a rabbi could boost the morale and religious consciousness of a Jewish soldier on the major holidays, or recovering in a field hospital, or perplexed by a legal or moral issue that arose in the course of carrying out his duties.[85]

In central Europe, volunteer Jewish chaplains known as *Feldrabbiner* first appeared in Hungary in the late 1830s, and one such volunteer accompanied Hungarian nationalist revolutionaries in 1848. During the Austro-Italian and Austro-Prussian wars, rabbis voluntarily performed pastoral duties, and in 1874 the Bohemian rabbi Alexander Kisch was appointed as a reserve chaplain, a position without military rank or salary but still possessed of a certain amount of status. A number of other

Figure 2.3. Memorial Cloth: Yom Kippur at Metz, 1870. *Courtesy of the Leo Baeck Institute, New York.*

Jewish reserve chaplains in Austria-Hungary were appointed during the 1870s, and Wilhelm Baher, a graduate of the Breslau rabbinical seminary, had the title of chief chaplain when Austrian forces occupied Bosnia in 1878. From the 1880s, Kisch regularly carried out pastoral work among Jewish soldiers in peacetime, and he enjoyed a positive working relationship with commanding officers, including a philosemitic general who appreciated Jewish soldiers for their sobriety, honesty, and multilingualism.[86]

Prussia was far slower to recognize Jewish chaplains than its Austrian rival. The Prussian military did not authorize any Jewish chaplains at all during the Austro-Prussian War. Four years later, when Prussia went to war with France, the army allowed four rabbis to work in the field on an ad hoc, volunteer basis. (There were, in comparison, three hundred salaried Christian military chaplains.) During World War I, there were only thirty *Feldrabbiner* in the entire German army, and although they were paid a stipend, they had no rank. Austria-Hungary, on the other hand, integrated some seventy-five rabbis into its general wartime chaplaincy, where they enjoyed an official seal and the coveted rank of *Hauptmann* (captain).[87]

At the height of the Franco-Prussian War, German-Jewish newspapers remarked sourly that France had installed three salaried chaplains while Prussian Jews were left "with no demand for any kind of provisions or pay—that is the Jews' Iron Cross!"[88] French Jewry's victory in the chaplaincy wars was, however, brief. In 1874 the National Assembly approved the appointment of one Protestant or Jewish chaplain for any unit with over two hundred members of that denomination. Since no unit was likely to have that many Jews, in fact there would be no Jewish chaplains at all. Also, fervently Catholic members of the assembly made a concerted effort to require Jewish soldiers to attend Roman Catholic services.[89]

The United Kingdom and the United States, in contrast, were historically more sympathetic to the spiritual needs of Jewish soldiers despite the small numbers of them in service. The United Kingdom's first Jewish army chaplain, the Reverend Francis Cohen, was appointed shortly after the equalization of Jewry's status within the military in 1886.[90] In the United States, four chaplains were appointed on term-limited commissions during the Civil War, and several volunteered during the Spanish-American War, although the war was so brief that only one actually made it to Cuba: Joseph Krauskopf from Chicago's Knesset Israel Synagogue, a member of the first graduating class from Cincinnati's Hebrew Union College.[91] The first Jewish official wartime chaplains were appointed in World War I, when the mass influx of soldiers into the army made it impossible to maintain the old position of the chaplain as a regimental officer, whose denomination was that of the majority of the men of the unit.

Even in the most benign of environments, the integration and accommodation of Jewish soldiers was neither smooth nor complete. But it was a process that had forward momentum, and in the last quarter of the nineteenth century it appeared to be modular, replicating itself in different parts of the world—not only in the west, but in the Islamic world as well. In the late nineteenth and early twentieth centuries, the Ottoman Empire reproduced many of the military reforms that had been initiated decades earlier in northern Europe, making the army more open and palatable to Jews. Throughout the second half of the nineteenth century, the empire had undertaken systematic reforms, improving the legal status of non-Muslim minorities, promulgating a constitution, and developing a concept of imperial citizenship nourished by Ottoman patriotism. In 1856, the notorious head tax for non-Muslims was abolished, but the minority communities continued to pay a military exemption tax. During the Crimean War, Polish Jews, many of them veterans from 1848, volunteered to fight for the Ottomans against their common enemy Russia, but few Ottoman Jews signed up. In the following decades, the leaders of Ottoman Jewry became more patriotic and encouraged their youth to volunteer for service in the Russo-Turkish War of 1877–78 and the Greek War of 1897. The latter was especially satisfying for Ottoman Jews because they were allowed to volunteer in the fight against the Orthodox Christian foe, whereas Ottoman Christians were not.[92]

In some ways, events followed very much in the mold of nineteenth-century western and central Europe. In 1877–78, Jews joined the civil guard in Salonika, and in Smyrna Jews formed a special regiment complete with its own double-sided flag, with the Ottoman star and crescent on one side and the *Sh'ma Yisrael* on the other. Rabbis urged Jewish volunteers to observe kashrut but allowed the transport of arms on the Sabbath—an important ruling since almost all the longshoremen of Salonika were Jewish. Wealthy Jews donated generously to the cause. During the Greek war, the Ladino press diligently published the name, biography, and photograph of every Jewish volunteer. The Young Turk revolution of 1908 intensified the urban Jewish elites' perception of the empire as a beneficent regime promising liberty and equality. The Ladino press waxed enthusiastic about the introduction of universal military conscription in 1909, almost exactly a century after its introduction in France.

As in eastern Europe, the patriotic official voice of Ottoman Jewry did not speak for the masses, who were not at all enthusiastic about sending their sons into the army. The Ottoman army's soldiers were mostly illiterate peasants; the commanders were often cruel martinets. Unlike the Russian army, however, which happily threw Jews into the front lines, in the Ottoman army neither officers nor men welcomed religious minorities in the fighting units. (During the Balkan wars, most Jews served in labor battalions, living in unspeakable conditions, and desertion rates were high.) Unlike any European state, the Ottoman Empire allowed minorities to pay a military exemption tax up to, and even during, World War I. The tax was hefty, even exorbitant, ranging from thirty to fifty gold Turkish pounds, yet during World War I in Baghdad alone three thousand Jews paid it.[93] Some Jews were, however, eager to become Ottoman military officers, and as their numbers exceeded the paltry number of slots allocated to Jews in the Ottoman military academy, they appealed to the empire's chief rabbi to use his influence to get them accepted.[94]

At the fin de siècle, Ottoman Jewry was recapitulating the encounter with the military experienced by its northern European counterparts in the previous century. The empire's numerous wars gave Jews from the empire's urban and secularizing elites the same sorts of opportunities to wax patriotic and volunteer for service that had appealed to certain German Jews during the wars of liberation against Napoleon and the wars of unification. Throughout the Jewish world, the prospects of emancipation and integration stimulated hope and pride, feelings manifest in a vast body of apologetic literature that trumpeted the Jews' contribution to their homelands' armies in all times and places.

## Celebrating the Jewish Fighter

One of the oldest genres of Jewish literature is the apologetic, a defense of Jewish religious practices and/or an avowal of good conduct and worthiness of the respect of Gentiles. Military performance was cemented into Jewish apologetics from their very beginning in late antiquity, when Jews were numerous and highly visible in Mediterranean and Middle Eastern civilizations. Flavius Josephus built upon old Ptolemaic texts in praising the Jews' military valor in Alexander the Great's service, in return for which they allegedly received civil privileges equal to those granted to Greeks. Jews in Hellenistic Egypt, drawing on the Pentateuch's stories of the Israelites' wars in the trans-Jordanian wilderness, presented their native son Moses as a great military tactician. Jews in Parthian Mesopotamia claimed the same of Abraham, alluding perhaps to Abraham's participation in the war against the king of Elam in Genesis 14.[95]

Medieval and early modern Jews celebrated the heroism of their biblical forefathers, but they did so in order to shore up their own spirit, not to justify their existence or plead for rights of residence. Modern Jewish apologetics, intent on promoting the improvement of the Jews' social and political status, reintroduced historical narratives of Jewish military service as a means of demonstrating Jewish contributions to their host societies. During the Napoleonic wars, German-Jewish rabbinic sermons and pamphlets by Jewish activists frequently invoked the heroes of the Bible, particularly David (with France portrayed as Goliath). In April of 1813, a metal shop owner named David Hirschfeld, who outfitted a troupe of seven Jewish volunteer fighters from small towns in Brandenberg, called them the first Jewish warriors since Roman times.[96]

Such references to the postbiblical past were rare until midcentury, when Jews began, for the first time in modern history, to glorify the military exploits of the Maccabees and to compare themselves explicitly to their fighting forefathers. This self-identification broke away from rabbinic Judaism's historical deflection of attention away from the Maccabees' military exploits in favor of their rededication of the Temple. (The miraculous cruse of oil that lasted for eight days is an invention of rabbinic literature and does not appear in the ancient books of the Maccabees.) The pioneer Jewish historian Heinrich Graetz displayed this new militancy in his first major published work, a long essay of 1846 titled "The Structure of Jewish History." Graetz, a protonationalist who identified the Jews' origins more with the conquest of Canaan than with Egyptian slavery or revelation at Sinai, praised the Maccabees, who "transformed victims who feared the use of weapons into military heroes."[97]

At the end of the nineteenth century, Zionists played up the association between "old and new Maccabees," as the litterateur Max Nordau put it, but earlier in the century the Maccabean image could be linked with any number of Jewish political orientations, from radicalism to patriotic nationalism. During Hanukkah of 1848, Emil Lehmann, an attorney and Jewish activist in Dresden, penned a poem exalting the

Maccabees as fighters for human freedom and urged their descendants to "follow their colors / They fought with burning courage / For their cherished fatherland / O fight as well for yours / For Germany, the beautiful and dear!"[98] Shortly after the end of the Franco-Prussian War, anthropologist and Jewish community leader Morritz Lazarus called German-Jewish soldiers "the grandchildren of the Maccabees."[99] During the Crimean War, a mix of Polish and Jewish national pride was evident in volunteer units called the Israelite Hussars or Maccabean Hussars that were formed in London and Paris.[100]

Although the major Jewish historians of the nineteenth century rarely wrote specifically about military affairs, popular Jewish historiography, in the form of rabbinic sermons, speeches, and pamphlets by lay leaders, and above all the Jewish press, paid increasing attention to Jewish soldiers as agents of emancipation. Jewish writers in France, Germany, and the Habsburg Empire stitched together a narrative of Jewish valor that extended from Hellenistic times through the revolt against Rome and thence into the Middle Ages. One early occurrence was in the 1842 memorandum by Abraham Geiger on the suitability of Jews for military service in Prussia. Drawing on his own vast erudition as well as the work of Jacques Basnage, Geiger found Jews fighting for Alexander the Great, in the armies of Ptolemaic Egypt and its conqueror Julius Caesar, and in the Parthian Empire. From there he moved on to the Jews who fought in the service of the Thracian general Belisarius, who wrested Naples from the Goths in 536; thence to medieval Portugal and France (where "thirty thousand Jews are said to have served in 1293"[101]) and early modern Poland. As written by Geiger and others after him, these stories moved seamlessly into the modern era of *levées en masse*, conscription, and volunteering, with the Jewish press finding unlikely heroes such as a barber-surgeon who was cited for distinguished service to the wounded of Prague during its bombardment by Prussian forces in 1757.[102]

One common feature of this narrative was its emphasis on Jews' historical military service in European and Middle Eastern states and empires, not their biblical homeland, in order to drive home the message that Jews are good, even model, citizens of the states in which they live. Longitudinal surveys of Jews in armies across time and space were accompanied by detailed reports on the numbers and exploits of Jewish soldiers, and especially officers, throughout the contemporary world.

German Jews, whose full emancipation and social acceptance were often just beyond their grasp, were particularly adept at this type of literature. During the Franco-Prussian War, Ludwig Phillipson, editor of German Jewry's most influential newspaper, *Die Allgemeine Zeitung des Judentums*, issued a call to communities to provide information on their sons serving in the forces of the North German Confederation. Hundreds of communities responded to the call, resulting in a detailed list of 4,700 names. This, in turn, formed but a part of a substantial memorial volume documenting the Jews' military, administrative, and philanthropic contributions to the war effort.[103]

The Jewish press in other countries was also wont to praise Jewish valor, not only in the homeland's army but also anywhere where Jewish soldiers, particularly decorated ones and officers, were to be found. The *Jewish Chronicle* of London kept close tabs on the careers of Jewish army officers throughout Europe and the Ottoman Empire. Even in Russia, where most Jews loathed their own army, the Hebrew press boasted of the heroism of Jewish soldiers fighting in Europe and the colonial world. During the Franco-Austrian War of 1859, the pioneer Hebrew newspaper *Ha-Maggid* claimed there were some 350 French-Jewish officers (or, as they were called in the newspaper's biblical Hebraic terminology, *pekidei hayil*) and alleged that the first Austrian flag captured by the French forces was taken by a Jew, who brought it personally to the emperor and was promoted to a position on the General Staff. On top of that, according to the newspaper, the first Austrian volunteer "to go forth into the fire of the enemy of his homeland was a Jewish man."[104] In later years, the Hebrew press in Russia and Poland followed the exploits of Jewish soldiers and officers in, among other places, Italy, French Indochina, and the United States, and shared in the pain of Prussian Jews whose men were deprived the honor of officers' commissions.[105]

In Europe, Jews were quick to boast of Jewish courage under fire but more cautious about celebrating the venerable and widespread connection between Jews and war finance and supply. In western Europe, there was much admiration for the derring-do during the Napoleonic wars of the English and French Rothschilds, who smuggled funds into Spain to pay for Wellington's peninsular campaign. Usually, however, fear of antisemitic associations between Jews and money limited the apologetic benefit to be gained from documenting the deeds of Jewish bankers and provisioners in times of war. In Germany, Court Jews, who provided money, horses, food, and uniforms for German armies in the seventeenth and eighteenth centuries, were not beloved figures in nineteenth-century Jewish historiography. The situation was entirely different in the United States, where apologetic literature not only acknowledged, but even centered on, Jewish financiers.

The best example of this genre is Simon Wolf's tome of 1895, *The American Jew as Patriot, Soldier and Citizen*. Wolf wrote the book in order to refute charges that Jews had shirked military service during the Civil War. The hero of the first chapter, however, is not a soldier, but rather the financier Haym Solomon, who during the Revolutionary War lent money to the Continental Army and Virginian political leaders, served as paymaster for French troops on American soil, handsomely bribed the Spanish minister to the United States, and sold U.S. foreign debt abroad. Solomon's bravest action appears to have been to escape imprisonment by the English in exchange for a substantial payment in gold.[106]

On one level, Wolf's presentation of Solomon embodies the traditional view of military service as a form of taxation, and of Jewish financial contributions as no less supportive a gesture to the state than putting one's life on the line. Yet there is something quite remarkable about Wolf's presentation of Jewish fighters and financiers as equivalent. In lists of over eight thousand Jews who fought and died on both sides in the U.S. Civil War, Wolf includes quartermasters and paymasters, and at the end of the list he jumps into a chapter on the Seligman brothers, Joseph and Jesse, who sold two hundred million dollars of Union bonds in Germany, thus "maintaining the financial credit of the [Union] Government during the war."[107] Wolf goes so far as to claim, without a shred of evidence, that an unnamed Jewish financier saved the Union from destruction and prevented a war between the Union and England by fronting the costs for the confiscation by the British government of two armored warships that were on the verge of leaving drydock in the United Kingdom and joining the Confederate navy.[108]

Wolf was hardly alone among American Jews of the fin de siècle in displaying pride in Jewish soldiers and documenting their exploits. The masterwork of that era's English-language Judaic scholarship, the

1901–6 *Jewish Encyclopedia*, devoted considerable attention to Jewish participation in armies throughout time and space. The "Army" article is one of the longest in the encyclopedia and was penned by six distinguished scholars, including three of the encyclopedia's coeditors, Richard Gottheil, Morris Jastrow, Jr., and Kaufmann Kohler. The article is considerably longer than the "War" entry, which is mostly a dry account of biblical and rabbinic dicta on the limits of licit military action. The "Army" entry, however, identifies Jewish civilization squarely with military valor. At the outset, the article proclaims that "[a]s the terms for virtue among the Greeks and Romans . . . are derived from military prowess, so the nobleman among the Hebrews is called *ish hayil*, the man of (military) strength, warrior."[109] This sentiment is reflected throughout the encyclopedia in dozens of biographical entries about colorful and heroic Jewish officers.[110]

The literature we have been examining was apologetic in that it was designed to demonstrate the Jews' worthiness for emancipation. Even if reproduced within a Jewish space (a Jewish newspaper, a synagogue), the ultimate target of these texts was the Gentile world, upon which Jews wished to make a positive impression. Nonetheless, even assimilatory, apologetic writings on Jews as patriotic soldiers contained a strong element of self-affirmation. The literature assured Jews that they were strong and courageous, at least as much as their Gentile neighbors and perhaps even more, as Jews in the present were presented as descendants of the biblical and Maccabean warriors of old. The uniformed, armed Jew, hurled into battle and willing to make the ultimate sacrifice, was as much a source of pride for nineteenth- and early twentieth-century western Jews as the Holocaust hero or Israeli soldier is for diaspora Jews of our own day.

That said, the sunny optimism that radiates from the *Jewish Encyclopedia*'s pages and its implicit equation between patriotism and liberalism, between military service and emancipation, was challenged by a series of transformative events at the dawn of the twentieth century. Russian Jews were becoming increasingly militant in their opposition to the state, and revolutionaries and Zionists alike began to think about armed force as a Jewish, not imperial, domain. Meanwhile, although western Europe enjoyed a few decades of internal peace before 1914, its rapid expansion overseas led to a series of colonial conflicts in which the Jews' traditional instrumental patriotism gave way to an unconditional chauvinism.

## Jewish Fighters at the Fin de Siècle: Proletarian Rebels and Shock Troops of Empire

Russian military reforms of 1874, which introduced universal conscription and a reduced term of service (six years, the same as in Austria-Hungary), aroused great hopes among maskilim that Jews would be increasingly integrated into, and respected in, the army. In this hopeful atmosphere the writer S. Y. Abramovich, better known by his nom de plume Mendele Mocher Sforim, translated the new conscription regulations into Yiddish, excoriated draft evaders, and urged all Jews to do their patriotic duty.[111] But the maskilim's hopes were dashed just four years later when Russian Jews fought bravely, and in substantial numbers, in the Russo-Turkish War, only to be accused of draft dodging. The treaty of San Stefano, which ended the war, marked a victory for Russia but a defeat for maskilim, who saw their homeland become an aggressive, imperialist state, protective of benighted Orthodox Christians in the Balkans and hungry for territory. In this atmosphere Mendele wrote his most savage work, the novella *The Adventures of Benjamin III*, in which Jewish men are feckless, effeminate, and spineless, and the state that drafts them has no goals to educate or improve Jews, only to ship them to the front as cannon fodder.[112]

The pogroms of 1881 were a further blow to Russian-Jewish confidence in the emancipatory potential of the tsarist empire. Some maskilim and Russified Jews continued to see the army in a positive light. Russia's Jewish writers of the fin de siècle, however, were bitterly disappointed in their homeland and channeled their energies into two contradictory yet overlapping political projects—national revival and universal revolution, the goals of which could be achieved only through sacrifice and bloodshed, although it was not at all clear what kind of armed force would be required, for how long, or against whom it was to be directed.

Zionism, a cultural and political movement that sought Jewish collective rebirth in the ancient land of Israel, envisioned a reborn Jew who would be physically strong, psychologically unfettered, courageous, and assertive. Leon Pinsker, the first theoretician of political Zionism, adored the military prowess of the ancient Israelites, and Russian-Hebrew poetry of the 1880s and 1890s was steeped in the language of battle, valor, and honor, with constant references to Jewish heroes from biblical and Greco-Roman times. Yet enraptured though they were by myths of heroism, the first generation of Russian-Zionist poets and writers were not themselves militants. They neither advocated nor employed violence; their dream was of personal honor, not territorial conquest.[113] Eastern European Zionists looked askance at their youthful central European counterparts, who were fond of dueling as an assertion of masculine and national honor. In 1885 the great Hebrew writer Yehuda Leib Gordon penned a nightmarish satire in which the author is denied entry to the land of Israel by armed Jewish guards, with *tefillin* binding their arms and billy clubs strapped around their waists. "Their faces were Jewish," Gordon writes, "but their dress was Cossack." Like pagan necromancers, these Jewish thugs tear out the author's entrails and examine them for signs of bona fide nationalist sentiment.[114]

Gordon's anxieties were not shared by the hundreds of Jews who became involved in violent radical organizations in late nineteenth-century Russia. The shadowy anarchist group the People's Will, which assassinated Tsar Alexander II, had several Jewish members, as did the Social Revolutionaries, among them future leaders of the Zionist community in Palestine such as Moshe Novomesky, Pinchas Rutenberg, and Manya Shochat. All of them were directly responsible for murders. A mole whom Novomesky fingered was assassinated in front of his parents in Warsaw. Shochat murdered a door-to-door salesman whom she mistook for a member of the notorious Third Section of the Russian secret police. (She cut up his body into four pieces, which she dispatched to separate and distant locations in the empire.) Rutenberg personally supervised the execution of Father Gapon, a leader of the 1905 revolution who had become a collaborator with the tsarist state.[115]

Less gruesome than the terror perpetrated by some Jewish Social Revolutionaries were the self-defense squads that flourished throughout the Pale in the early 1900s. Led at times by Zionists, at times by members of the Jewish Labor Bund, or both, these groups carried out organized, armed self-defense in at least a third of the localities struck by pogroms between 1903 and 1906. By 1906, over five hundred men were involved in self-defense activity. The Bund had an arsenal of five hundred revolvers plus caches of knives, clubs, and homemade bombs. In Zhitomir in 1905, two groups of twenty-five trained fighters backed by four hundred reservists fought off a rampaging mob. Most other cases were less successful: in Odessa, self-defense at best lessened the loss of Jewish life, while armed resistance in Bialystok in 1906 did not prevent the deaths of over eighty Jews. At Kishinev, site of the notorious pogrom that inspired H. N. Bialik's immortal poem "In the City of the Slaughter," Jews attempted to defend themselves, but to little avail.[116] By and large Jewish communities did not support the self-defense activities, which often exacerbated pogroms by infuriating the police and ratcheting up the scope and duration of attacks against Jews.[117]

The Bund's fighters, who moved from one street battle to the next while striving to avoid arrest, were a far cry from a revolutionary army with permanently mobilized and trained cadres. But like other revolutionary groups in fin-de-siècle Russia, the Bund considered armed resistance a fundamental component of its program of action. In this sense, the strike forces of 1905 can be compared with the civic guards of 1848. The former were far more violent and confrontational, and they did not draw a clear line between revolutionary and criminal activity. Yet just as bourgeois Jews in central Europe had simultaneously taken up arms against the reactionary state and antisemitic assaults against their own communities, so did the Jewish proletariat in fin-de-siècle Russia consider armed struggle against pogroms to be an essential component of the general struggle to radically reconstitute the tsarist regime.

The rebellious dynamic in Russian-Jewish society emerged from a time of crisis, an unbearable pressure that was relieved by the March 1917 revolution. With the change of regime Jews once again flocked back to the state, which finally granted them full political and social emancipation. Overnight the army changed from a curse to a blessing, from a desert to a promised land. By the fall of 1917 at least half of the students in the military schools in Kiev and Odessa were Jews, foreshadowing the preponderance of Jews in the Soviet Union's Red Army.[118] These signs of integration coexisted with nationalist feelings expressed by the embryonic Red Army's separate brigades of Jewish soldiers, whose uniforms' epaulets bore Stars of David. The Petrograd Union of Zionist Soldiers, led by a hero of the Russo-Japanese War, Joseph Trumpeldor, dreamed of forging a vast army that would crash through central Asia and conquer the land of Israel.[119]

By the early twentieth century swaths of Russian Jewry were giving up on the emancipatory state and embracing revolutionary political approaches that demanded the use of armed force, if only as a means of self-defense. Meanwhile, a different kind of mass mobilization was taking place in the west. Imperial expansion catalyzed a militarization of society, which swept up Jews along with everyone else.

The Spanish-American War of 1898 gave American Jews a golden opportunity to leave behind their peculiar association with war finance and indulge in the rampant jingoism of the time. The Civil War had raised the painful issue of Jews facing other Jews across battle lines. But there were no moral qualms in hating Spain, which had expelled its Jews in 1492 and persecuted crypto-Jews for centuries thereafter, and was now both a Jewish and an American enemy.[120] Jews in Chicago, Richmond, Virginia, and Newport, Rhode Island, tried to establish separate Jewish companies, and a group of Jews in Cincinnati undertook the purchase of a battleship for the government. Four thousand Jewish volunteers served in the war; eight of them charged up San Juan Hill with Teddy Roosevelt's Rough Riders.[121] Although small in scale and short in duration, this was American Jewry's first "good war" and an indicator of the patriotic spirit that they would muster in the world wars of the twentieth century.

British Jews, formerly indifferent to military affairs, were caught up in the frenzy of chauvinism unleashed by the Anglo-Boer War of 1899–1902. Not only did queen and country call upon able-bodied British youth to volunteer; Jews had a special reason to join the fight—to combat accusations that a shadowy conspiracy of Jewish financiers and mine owners had dragged the United Kingdom into conflict with the Boer republics.[122] At a time when barely two hundred Jews served in the United Kingdom's Territorial Army, a thousand or more volunteered to fight in South Africa.[123]

The militarization of Anglo-Jewish society was visible in many forums. During the war, rabbinical sermons not only expressed unreserved support for the war but justified it within the framework of Jewish religious tradition. One of the war's ostensible aims was the protection of foreigners (in Afrikaans, *Uitlander*), many of whom were

British subjects, in the Afrikaner republics. This led the distinguished rabbi Moses Gaster as well as the chief rabbi of the United Kingdom, Hermann Adler, to justify the war as fulfilling the biblical commandment that the Israelites protect the strangers among them.[124] In 1893, the Central Synagogue in Great Portland Street hosted a modest Hanukkah celebration for about fifty Jewish men in uniform. The celebration became an annual event, and with the outbreak of the war its size and scope increased dramatically. By 1903 it attracted several hundred servicemen and guests, including the minister of war and many Christian female gentry, who looked on from the women's balcony.[125]

The Anglo-Jewish press exhaustively covered the war, listing and providing biographical sketches of Jewish volunteers, especially the nearly 130 who died in battle or from disease. (Jews fighting for the Afrikaners were also acknowledged.) The newspaper lavished attention on the Jewish officers, especially David Harris, an Englishman who immigrated to the Cape Colony as a youth and was deployed to the Transvaal as commander of the crack regiment of Kimberley Rifles.[126] The paper detailed Harris' heroic role in the defense of Kimberley and Mafeking during their prolonged sieges by Afrikaner forces. The commander of the British forces in Mafeking, the celebrated colonel (and future founder of the Scouting movement) Robert Baden Powell, singled Harris out for praise.[127] The Anglo-Jewish press also found a heroine in Rose Lina Shappere, the only Jewish woman in the nursing reserve. The *Jewish Chronicle* printed Arthur Friedlander's stirring song "The Jewish Soldier" as a pamphlet and distributed it without cost. Jingoism appeared even in the newspaper's advertisements. A kosher butcher who advertised regularly in the *Jewish Chronicle* not only assured potential patrons of his support for Britain's infantry but added "Our friend the enemy will admit that in 'kosherdom' we are the 'great guns.'"[128]

The Anglo-Boer War piqued the interest of the Anglo-Jewish press in Jewish military prowess throughout the world. The Boxer Rebellion gave the *Jewish Chronicle* a chance to demonstrate its love of country by comparing "the spirit of Boxerism" to antisemitism and observing that over a thousand Jews served in the international forces that had been sent to China to crush the rebellion.[129] The accomplishments and decorations of Jewish officers in any state—France, Russia, the Ottoman Empire, even Portugal—were an obvious source of militaristic pride in

Figure 2.4. Corps Commander General and Minister of War Giuseppe Ottolenghi (1838–1904). *Reproduced from Rubin, E. (1952).*

Jewish patriotism and manliness, and the newspaper was particularly gratified by Giuseppe Ottolenghi's appointment as Italy's minister of war (figure 2.4).[130]

The Anglo-Boer War also heightened the militaristic slant of the Jewish Lads' Brigade, a uniformed youth movement that had been founded in 1895. It was typical of youth movements of the time in its striving to inculcate discipline, cleanliness, continence, sobriety, and thrift among adolescents. It had a particular Jewish inflection, however, in its goal to, in the organization's own words, "iron out the ghetto bend"—that is, to transform allegedly narrow-chested ghetto boys into strapping, ramrod-straight-backed Englishmen.[131] Colonel Albert Goldsmid, a veteran of the South African campaign and one of the Lads' Brigade's founders, enunciated the Brigade's goal as "manufacturing Jewish soldiers."[132] Sure enough, when Goldsmid became the Brigade's commandant in 1906, the organization changed from being quasi-military to paramilitary, with rifle practice now added to the preexisting uniforms, drills, and physical education.

Compared with most of their brethren on the European continent, Anglo-Jewry had little history of struggle to attain legal emancipation or unrestricted economic opportunity. Yet Anglo-Jews continued to fret about their image (or, more accurately, the image of recent Jewish immigrants from eastern Europe) in Gentile eyes, and they embraced colonial militarism as a means of demonstrating Jewish courage and manly virtue to an at times hostile public. German Jews were similarly enthusiastic about empire and the wars that had to be fought to attain it, although Germany's overseas holdings were far smaller than England's, and Jewish colonial heroes were much harder to find. The closest equivalent to David Harris whom German Jews could claim was a Lieutenant Bendix, an engineer who had been sent to repair the railway in German Southwest Africa and was "killed by a Herero bullet" after being in Africa for only a couple of months.[133] France, on the other hand, had a vast colonial empire and, as we will see in the next chapter, incorporated thousands of Jews into its forces serving abroad. Jews at the fin de siècle proved receptive to both the increased militarism of imperialist states and the militance of radical political movements. The century-old connection between emancipation and armed struggle, as either a regular soldier or a rebel, had not been severed, but it had taken on a new and more aggressive form.

▪ ▪ ▪

H. N. Bialik's poem "In the City of the Slaughter" was historically inaccurate in its bitter accusation that Jewish men behaved with craven passivity in the face of the Kishinev pogrom of 1903. The poem, however, reflected and accelerated a sea change in European-Jewish sensibility around 1900: according to the new dispensation, Jews must actively and militantly defend themselves against physical assault. There would have been little drama in an assertion that Jews should defend themselves and were in fact doing so. Asserting that they should not and were not would have merely maintained the traditional passivity of rabbinic Judaism, and that they should not yet were would have fit the anti-Zionist position of certain strands of Orthodox Judaism but otherwise have had little appeal. Bialik's assertion that Jews should yet were not defending themselves opened the floodgates to self-excoriation as a precondition for the call to purposeful action. Unlike the continuous pattern of Jewish heroism drawn by nineteenth-century apologists, in the new, nationalist way of thinking ancient heroism was followed by a precipitous decline and then a consciously willed and painstakingly effected collective revival. Bialik's poem, when reread in the wake of the 1918–20 mass killings in eastern Europe and, above all, the Holocaust, has been treasured for its depiction of not only Gentile savagery but also Jewish cowardice, which constitutes a primal act of treachery that twentieth-century Jewish politics set out to overcome.

Underlying this classic Zionist view of the Jewish past is a thorough distrust of the state as a meliorating force, especially for the position of the Jews and their acceptance by their Gentile neighbors. Yet for more than a century Jews in many countries saw the state as a beneficent force. Jews who considered themselves or wanted to be part of the body politic longed to exercise the coercive power that inhered in the state. Military power would flow through them as neural impulses flow through human limbs, endowing them with purpose and direction. Emancipation, the release from juridical and social disabilities, was a form of liberation that could be attained and experienced only through the subordination of the self to the demands of the state. In the era of universal conscription, the highly disciplined soldier was not only the truest patriot; he was the freest of men.

For many years after the Second World War, this sensibility survived in the state of Israel, where the army assumed the dual roles of protector and schoolhouse of the nation. Military service and constant sacrifice guaranteed the collective freedom of Israel's Jewish population. Soldiering was a requirement of good citizenship and a rejection of an alleged heritage of persecution, intimidation, and lack of agency. Many a Jew in the nineteenth century felt the same way about the meaning of military service in his own homeland. For some, the military was so natural and available an object of devotion that they became career officers. It is to their story that we now turn.

## CHAPTER THREE

# The Military as a Jewish Occupation

In her classic book *The Origins of Totalitarianism*, Hannah Arendt claimed that in premodern times European Jews enjoyed a special and beneficial relationship with the state. This relationship centered on the waging of war. Jewish financiers, known in central Europe as Court Jews, provided rulers with the means to fight against their rivals by lending them money, paying them up front for the right to collect taxes and fees, and supplying armies with horses, food, and uniforms. In the nineteenth century, however, these Jews were replaced by state bureaucracies that began to collect taxes directly from the people and set up supply corps within their armies. The bureaucracy was usually closed to Jews, and its most prestigious component, the officer corps, remained a bastion of aristocratic privilege. Arendt cites the most famous example of the Jews' failure to cement themselves into the machinery of the state: Alfred Dreyfus, a captain in the artillery corps of the French army, who was crushed by a military elite that loathed "new men" promoted for their talent rather than their pedigree, and who was cursed by a nation that, a century after Jewish emancipation in the first flush of the French Revolution, remained deeply troubled by Jewish difference.[1]

Arendt's argument persists more than sixty years after her book's appearance. Dreyfus remains the first, often the only, name that comes to mind when one mentions the subject of Jews as officers in modern European armies. But Arendt was wrong about modern Jews' relationship with the state, and the salience of the tragic tale of Alfred Dreyfus extends far beyond a ruined career and antisemitic frenzy. In the nineteenth and twentieth centuries, Jews penetrated every western country's bureaucracy, including its military. There were thousands of

Jewish career military officers and administrators in western and central Europe. These officials were uniformed civil servants, a subspecies of what sociologist Pierre Birnbaum, in his magisterial study of Jews and the French state, has called *le juif d'état*.[2] Not only in France, but throughout the modern world, the relationship between Jews and the state can best be measured by the number, position, and activity of Jews who became professional vehicles of state power in its most direct and lethal form.

## Jewish Military Officers as Social Barometers

Modern militaries in the western world have been home to several types of officer, only one of which can be considered a career employee. In many states, a reserve officer's commission has been a sign of social honor, granted upon the completion of some minimal level of education and military training, although the reserve officer could be called into a command capacity in wartime. In battle, the majority of officers have been conscripts or volunteers who were promoted through the ranks while in the field and usually could not progress beyond a certain point, typically sergeant or sergeant-major (although in World War I German Jews received field commissions up to the rank of captain). Only the elite among officers have held commissions, awarded upon completion of a tertiary-level military academy and often followed by advanced, specialized training as well, after which one's military career begins with the rank of lieutenant or its equivalent. Many officers have chosen to spend their entire career in the military, retiring on a pension whose value in some states was enhanced by not only the longevity of service but also the number of campaigns fought and wounds endured. It was not uncommon, however, for an officer to serve for some number of years and then resign his commission and go into private life, bearing his title as a source of considerable social capital.

Jewish publicists and amateur historians have produced reams of apologetic literature on Jewish army officers, particularly generals and admirals. Whole books are devoted to biographical sketches of Jewish general officers, with the implicit assumption that their ascent to the summit of the military, the most aristocratic and hierarchical of state institutions, testifies to their superior qualities of mind and character, patriotism, and overall suitability for full acceptance by the countries to which they devoted their lives.[3] In their zeal to document Jewish success these books fail to take into account some important facts about the general officer contingent in modern militaries. First, there is far more to a successful military career than advancement to the rank of general. As Joseph Roth remarked memorably in his novel *The Radetzky March*, "Death lay far away for a young cavalry lieutenant, as far as the highest grade of regulated advancement. You became a colonel some day and then you died."[4] There is more than a hint of insecurity, manifest in relentless striving for the top, in the notion that only if a Jew becomes a general has he truly made it in military service. The most impressive and exciting military exploits by military officers, which richly illustrate their place and reception within the army, often occur in the midlevel ranks. Besides, although the presence of Jewish generals within a country's military is certainly an indication of a meritocratic approach to promotion and a low tolerance for antisemitism among the top brass, we need to look at what sorts of positions these generals held, in what branch of service, in order to understand how and why Jews were able to attain these high-status positions. Finally, the number of general officers in a country's military can be enormous, and the presence of a handful of generals of Jewish origin does not, in and of itself, testify to unrestrained Jewish access to positions of influence and power. (For example, in World War II, the U. S. armed forces had about 1,100 general officers, of whom 37, or just over 3 percent, were Jews, at a time when Jews were 4 percent of the general population.)

Jewish career officers have tended to crop up most frequently in countries where the military was open to Jews and highly prestigious. Whether few or many in any given country, Jews gravitated toward the technical corps, artillery and engineering, perhaps because they were less prestigious and less bound by tradition than aristocratic enclaves such as the cavalry. The connection between Jews and military technology, particularly munitions and weaponry, is striking, and many Jewish officers were instructors in science, engineering, and mathematics at military academies. In early twentieth-century Britain, Sir Frederic Nathan supervised the gunpowder factory at Waltham before moving on to direct the development of munitions for the Ordnance Department and advise the Admiralty on cordite during World War I.[5] Raimondo

Foa, an artillery commander in the Italian army in World War I, became in 1927 director of the Terni Ordnance Arms Factory.[6] In France under the Third Republic, Jews were heavily concentrated in the artillery and engineering corps; the most famous of the lot, Alfred Dreyfus, was a captain of the artillery whose first position was teaching math and design at the French army's school for the study of munitions manufacture and use. Once Jews in the United States began to penetrate the senior officer corps in substantial numbers during World War II, many of them came from backgrounds in engineering and logistics. This specialization may have reflected the Jews' own educational background, aptitude, and interests as much as the openness of the army's newer and more technical branches to accepting Jews as commanders.

With a handful of exceptions, the officer corps in the Ottoman and Russian empires were closed to Jews before the revolutions of 1908 and 1917 respectively. (The most celebrated Jewish officer in Russia was Joseph Trumpeldor, a hero of the Russo-Japanese War, whose decorations for valor in battle won him a field commission in 1906.) As we saw in the previous chapter, immediately upon full emancipation Jews flocked to the Ottoman and Soviet military academies, a reflection of an ongoing high regard in both lands for governmental service and for martial valor. In the United Kingdom, in contrast, although technically Jews in Britain could obtain commissions after 1829, and Judaism was formally recognized as a denomination by the military in 1886, the officer corps remained overwhelmingly Anglican and socially restrictive. The military drew its commanders from the sons of its own personnel, the landed gentry, and the civil and colonial service. (In 1899, four-fifths of all army colonels came from the peerage, gentry, military, clergy, or "professions," most often law.) Like the judiciary, the clerisy, and the diplomatic service, the officer corps was the province of gentlemen, as the pay was a mere pittance, leaving the officer to provide for the costs of dining and entertaining in regiment, as well as maintaining his uniform, servants, and horses (if a cavalry officer) from private income.[7]

A military career was utterly foreign to the recent immigrants from eastern Europe who made up the bulk of British Jewry by 1914. Those few Jews who became career officers were sons of the Anglo-Jewish elite, young men with surnames such as Sassoon, Montefiore, and Rothschild, for whom the Indian army was particularly popular as a site for performing an aristocratic, British imperial identity. A lifelong commitment to the military was rare and usually made by families that had converted to Christianity. Celebrated examples include Alexander Schomberg, who served in Canada in the Seven Years' War and sired a dynasty of future admiral, and Solomon d'Aguilar, a militia officer in the mid-eighteenth century, who had a son who became a lieutenant general, who in turn fathered a general who fought in the Crimean War. The most celebrated Jewish career officer of the fin de siècle, Colonel Albert Goldsmid, was raised as a Christian and became aware of his Jewish background only as an adult. A hero of the Anglo-Boer War, Goldsmid became an ardent Zionist and was much admired by Theodor Herzl. (Goldsmid, who considered himself a real-life embodiment of George Eliot's Daniel Deronda, cut a striking figure, especially when clad in his dress uniform and armed with dual decorative swords.)[8] The number of Jews in the army increased sixfold during the Anglo-Boer War, but the growth in the number of commissioned Jewish officers was far more modest, from twenty to at most fifty, and most of these were temporary, wartime appointments.[9]

In the United States, many Jewish immigrants from Europe had extensive military experience, mainly as rebels in the series of insurrections that struck the Continent from 1848 to 1863. The story of Adolph Moses (1840–1902) illustrates this point nicely. A *yeshivah bokher* from Prussian Poland, Moses interrupted his studies at the Breslau rabbinical seminary to fight as a Red Shirt for Garibaldi in Italy in 1859, and then served as an officer in the Polish insurrection against Russia in 1863. He eventually finished his rabbinic studies in Germany and then settled down as a Reform rabbi in Alabama and Kentucky.[10] Jewish immigrants who came to America's western frontier took part in the Mexican-American War and for decades afterward served in and even commanded vigilante units that "pacified" the Native Americans.[11] Hundreds of Jews served as officers on both sides in the Civil War, but the vast majority were conscripts or volunteers who were promoted through the ranks and returned to civilian life after their military stint was completed. There were some spectacular exceptions, such as Commodore Uriah Phillips Levy (1792–1862), who had several naval commands and is remembered mainly for his successful campaign to end corporal punishment in the navy. (He also fought several duels and once killed his opponent.)[12] But in a country as vast as the United States, replete with opportunities for social and economic mobility, there was little incentive for Jews to pursue a career in the military. With the exception of the *levée en masse* of the Civil War, most Jews did not assume a patriotic, republican identity before America's entry into World War I, and until then the military was far removed from the lives and career expectations of most American Jews, as it also was from those of most Americans. The army was mainly deployed in the western frontier, and the navy was minuscule.

Only during World War II did the U.S. armed forces move significantly toward religious neutrality and begin to take on substantial numbers of Jewish officers, yet even then, antisemitism ran broadly and profoundly through the officer corps.[13] Here, as in most European armies, Jewish officers clustered in the more technically oriented corps, such as engineering and artillery, and in tasks such as supply and logistics. Commodore Harry Asher Badt (1884–1967) began his career as an instructor in electrical engineering and physics at Annapolis before commanding warships during World War II. Admiral Ben Morreel (1892–1978), a civil engineer, founded and commanded the Seabees, a unit of almost a quarter million men that built bases, airfields, barracks, roads, and floating dry docks for the navy. The most famous example of an American-Jewish military technocrat was Admiral Hyman Rickover (1900–1986), who studied electrical engineering at Annapolis and Columbia, worked on the Manhattan Project in Oak Ridge, Tennessee, and then developed the navy's first nuclear-powered submarine.[14]

In central Europe, until the mid-nineteenth century the military was the scourge of peasant conscripts and of little interest to the urban bourgeoisie. During the last quarter of the century, that image began to change, and the military came to be widely perceived as both the bedrock and apex of the social order. In Germany and Austria-Hungary, a reserve officer's commission became a powerful source of cultural capital for middle-class men. In many countries, career options within the military also became more attractive and available, although the aristocracy continued to dominate the officer corps' most prestigious units, such as the cavalry.

In Germany, Jewish officers were virtually nonexistent until World War I. During the Napoleonic wars, Jews had received lower-level field promotions, but this practice stopped in 1815. It started again during the Franco-Prussian War, with about one hundred Jews getting field promotions before the cessation of hostilities. In imperial Germany (1871–1918), a handful of Jews from wealthy and influential families received commissions as career officers. It took the personal intervention of Kaiser Wilhelm I to get Walther Mossner, son of a Berlin banker, a commission in the King's Hussars, and shortly after he was reluctantly accepted into the regiment, Mossner converted to Christianity. (He went on to be ennobled, an officer on the German General Staff, a brigade commander, and major general.)[15]

The issue of reserve commissions was far more galling and humiliating for German Jews than the lack of access to military command. In Prussia, home to two-thirds of German Jewry, only a handful of the twenty to thirty thousand Jewish men who fulfilled the requirements to be considered for a reserve commission—completion of *Gymnasium* and a year of military service—received the coveted title. None received commissions after 1885. To obtain a commission, a young man had to be unanimously approved by the regiment in which he had performed his year of service, and a single negative vote from that regiment's officers was sufficient to blackball a candidate. Prussia's stubborn, continued discrimination against Jewish candidates for reserve commissions was deeply humiliating to men such as Willy Ritter Liebermann von Wahlendorf, a wealthy and assimilated youth who was so aggrieved by rejection from his regiment that he challenged his commanding officer to a duel.[16] Neither such melodramatic gestures nor tireless efforts by German-Jewish activists to win public sympathy for their cause had any effect. When the Prussian military did decide during World War I to allow Jews to be officers, it did so simply because its junior officer corps was being decimated by enemy fire. About two thousand Jews received field commissions, but none beyond the rank of captain, and after the war the Lilliputian Reichswehr was closed to Jewish senior officers.

In Bavaria, the situation was a bit more flexible, and in 1907 there were about fifty Jewish lieutenants in the kingdom's army reserve. Here too discrimination was intense. In 1906, 9 percent of the 1,401 "one-year volunteers" in Bavaria were Jews; 19 percent of these Jews were approved for candidacy for a commission versus 45 percent of their Christian counterparts. Only four Jews, or 0.3 percent of the total number of potential candidates, actually received reserve commissions. What's more, throughout the entire nineteenth century only six Jews were commissioned as career officers in the Bavarian army, and four of them were commissioned during wartime, when demand for personnel was high and restrictions were temporarily relaxed.[17]

A German-Jewish community hungry for military heroes lavished attention on a slight, stolid, and unprepossessing man named Menno Burg (1789–1853), the only unconverted Jewish career officer in pre-Bismarckian Prussia. A geometry instructor at the Prussian army's school of artillery and engineering in Berlin, Burg was the object of adulation from the Jewish community during his lifetime and long after his death. During World War I a new edition of his memoirs was published with an introduction by the prominent Liberal rabbi Ludwig Geiger. Geiger described Burg as "no hero in open battle, but a hero of self-denial, of the fulfillment of duty, a true servant of his religion."[18] Although he is largely forgotten today, in the nineteenth and early twentieth centuries Burg was for German Jewry a hero, a uniformed Moses Mendelssohn, the exception who proved that Jews could perform any service for the fatherland if allowed to do so.

Burg was born in Berlin into a family of modest means and unusually practical occupations. Although there was nothing out of the ordinary about his father's livelihood as a bookkeeper, one of his uncles was a gardener, as was one of his cousins; another cousin was a mechanic, and a third a royal building inspector. (The building inspector wrote pioneering works on urban planning and a brochure titled *Germany's Armed Youth, or Foundations for the Establishment of an Imperial Army*.) Burg was educated to be a land surveyor but volunteered to fight against Napoleon in 1813. Burg immediately encountered obstacles because of his faith, which kept him out of a guard unit and slowed his assignment as a field officer in a frontline unit. Early on, he found a protector in Prince Augustus, general of the Prussian artillery and a nephew of Frederick the Great. The prince recognized Burg's mathematical talents, and Burg quickly moved from being his company's math and writing instructor to more prestigious posts, culminating in his appointment to the new United Artillery and Engineering School in Berlin. As elsewhere, the best hopes for a Jew to advance in the officer corps lay in the army's technical branches, which lacked the aristocratic patina of the cavalry and infantry. Even so, promotions came slowly to Burg, but his tenacity was as stubborn as the army's antisemitism, and he retired with the rank of major.[19]

Burg was assimilated in dress and manner yet adhered to Jewish observance, and later in life became involved in Jewish community affairs. Burg's unflagging commitment to patriotic duty and refusal to convert in order to advance his career delighted German-Jewish activists for whom Burg was a tool in the struggle for emancipation. In 1833, Gabriel Riesser invoked Burg in his campaign for Jews to be admitted to the civil service and the professions. Burg cropped up again in debates over the 1850 Prussian constitution, which guaranteed equality of rights except for public office. Burg's funeral in 1853 brought Berlin to a standstill. (The police estimated the crowd at 60,000 out of a total population of 400,000.) Masses of Jews were present, as was the entire artillery corps in and near Berlin. An eyewitness, Kraft Karl August zu Hohenlohe-Ingelfingen, offered the following description that, although bilious and unashamedly antisemitic, also testified to the solemnity and significance of the funeral for Berlin's Jews:

> With effort space was made free for the funereal procession. With greatest difficulty the procession of riders from the Mounted Artillery pressed forth and loaded their rifles. Thousands of dark pairs of eyes over prominently hooked semitic noses squinted inquisitively at the horsemen's gestures. The formalities lasted for hours, the hundred horsemen held their place for hours, the curious, unbaptized throng tarried for hours.

According to Kraft, after a eulogy delivered in the presence of Jewish community officials and military officers, the body was handed over for burial away from Gentile scrutiny, "for the fulfillment of [the Jews'] secret practices."[20] Kraft was clearly indulging in antisemitic fantasies, although the graveside ceremony was, in fact, limited to a small number of Jews. Taken as a whole, the funeral testified to the respect that Burg enjoyed among his comrades in arms as well as the Jews of Berlin, and it, like Burg's life, became an oft-told and beloved story among Jews who looked enviously at the ease with which their coreligionists in neighboring lands obtained commissions and pursued military careers.

The Dual Monarchy offered Jews immensely more opportunity within the military than Germany. Austria-Hungary was a multinational empire, united by dynastic loyalty rather than a single nationalist identity, yet committed to a gradual process of economic and political liberalization. The multiethnic, multilingual armies (the Austrian Landswehr, the Hungarian Honvéd, and the imperial joint army) needed educated, polyglot officers and officials, and Jews fit the bill nicely. The manifold differences between central Europe's twin empires were epitomized by the status of Jews in the reserve officer corps. In Austria-Hungary they comprised 18 percent of the corps in 1900 although they were less than 5 percent of the empire's population. Jewish reserve officers concentrated in the transport corps, fortress artillery, and engineering, but they were overrepresented even in the aristocratic cavalry. The Jewish reserve officers were called into battle in World War I, where they, along with Jews promoted in the field, added up to some twenty-five thousand Jewish officers in uniform.

Relatively few Jews in the Dual Monarchy, however, were officers by profession; they were somewhere between 0.6 and 1.2 percent of the entire career officer pool.[21] Antisemitism no doubt placed an obstacle in an ambitious Jewish officer's career path; up to 1911, over half of the Jewish colonels and generals in combat branches converted to Christianity. Yet the high command did strive to rein in overt Jew hatred, and Christian officers were explicitly commanded to give Jews "satisfaction" in matters of honor; that is, the Christians were obliged to accept a Jew's challenge to a duel and not scornfully dismiss it, as was often the case in Germany.[22] The highest-ranking Jew in the common army, Lieutenant Field Marshal Eduard Ritter von Schweitzer, kept kosher and attended synagogue regularly in Budapest. Alexander Ritter von Eiss, who was promoted to the rank of general in retirement, was an ardent Zionist and used to attend Zionist meetings in his imposing dress uniform. These colorful cases aside, most Jews avoided the career officer path, mainly because aspirants were required to attend a military boarding school from late childhood and to make a lifelong commitment to military service. Jews were far more attracted to careers as military officials such as medical officers, judge advocates, accountants, and teachers. These positions granted their holders prestige, flexible-term appointments, sedentary employment, and a decent income, giving them the opportunity to marry and raise a family. In 1897, almost 13 percent of Austro-Hungarian military officials were Jews. Their numbers fell markedly during the first decade of the 1900s, perhaps because of competing economic opportunities, or perhaps because the antisemitism that permeated Austrian political life percolated into the army as well.

The experience of serving as a military official played a sufficiently important role in the lives of Austro-Hungarian Jews to have wended its way into the novelist Joseph Roth's masterpiece, *The Radetzky March* (1932). The novel offers a rich and empathetic portrait of Lieutenant Demant, a melancholy regimental surgeon. Ill-favored by an "eternally bowing head on his thin neck" and "narrow, sloping shoulders," as awkward on a horse as he is conversing in polite company, Demant is the grandson of a tavern keeper and the son of a minor postal official. Demant sees himself as both a failure and a success in his ancestor's eyes: "Had [Demant's grandfather] known that his grandson would some day stroll through the world murderously armed an in an officer's uniform, the old man would have cursed his old age and the fruit of his loins." Demant's father, however, was fiercely proud of his years of service to the civic guard and of his assistant paymaster's uniform, which he cleaned once per week along with his saber and wore in public on the kaiser's birthday. In his own kitchen, Demant's father used to get drunk, draw his saber, and pretend to command a regiment: "The pots are platoons, the teacups troops, and the plates companies." Demant appears to be realizing his father's dream of assuming a command, but in fact he was driven into the military by poverty, and he has no leadership or fighting ability. Demant challenges an officer to a duel over an antisemitic slur but does not know how to fence, and so he must choose the far more lethal option of dueling with pistols. Musing during the night before the duel, Demant says, "Tomorrow I'm going to die a hero, a so-called hero, completely against my grain, and against the grain of my forebears and my tribe and against my grandfather's will." Unwilling to raise a pistol against another man, Demant shoots with his glasses off, without seeing or aiming at his foe.[23]

Demant's integration into the Habsburg officer corps is partial at best. The same dynamic was present in most countries in Europe, with a shifting balance between triumphant integration into the state bureaucracy, including its highest military command, and betrayal by society manifested by virulent antisemitism. The balance between the positive and negative forces was most favorable to Jews in two countries that demand separate attention, Italy and France. These cases demonstrate that under the right circumstances, the military could be a normal and highly respected career option for Jews.

## The Armed *Juif d'État*

Both the kingdom of Italy and French Third Republic had highly bureaucratized states in which civil service of any sort was highly valued; both were based upon the principles of confessional neutrality. The fact that one was a kingdom and the other a republic was less important than both countries' transcendence of religious difference and support for Jewish emancipation. Italy's Jews were loyal servants of the state bureaucracy; in 1920, an astounding 3,250 Italians of Jewish origin served in state administration, this in a country whose total Jewish population did not surpass 50,000.[24] In a country fissured by regional and cultural differences, and saddled with endemic poverty, the relatively prosperous and well-educated Jews were a boon to all forms of government service, including the army. Between 1859 and 1938 Italy produced 58 Jewish generals and admirals, including Giuseppe Ottolenghi, appointed minister of war in 1902. There were some 700 Jewish officers of all ranks in service in 1895. Relative to their share of the general population, Jews were overrepresented seventeenfold in the officer corps.[25]

The bulk of Italy's generals and admirals came from the small communities in Piedmont, Lombardy, and the Veneto as opposed to the larger communities in Italy's main cities, and Rome did not produce a single Jewish general officer. A lack of opportunities for social mobility in the smaller communities may partly account for this lopsided distribution, but high levels of assimilation, intermarriage, and conversion were also important factors. Jews who intermarried tended to find mates among members of the large cities' liberal and secular Catholic bourgeoisie, who were deeply attached to the Italian state and even more likely than Jews to send their children into military careers. Intermarriage between Jews and Christians reduced the number of self-identified Jews in Italy by almost 30 percent between unification and World War I.[26] The military historian Alberto Rovighi, born and baptized as a Catholic in 1921, did not even know that his father was a Jew until 1938, when the father was classified as Jewish according to the Fascist racial laws.[27] At that time, there were some 3,400 families in Italy like Rovighi's, with one parent classified as Jewish and the other as a Catholic "Aryan." Not only did these families produce a number of career officers; they tended to do so, at least for the most illustrious cases, in the form of military dynasties. Umberto Segre, a brilliant artillery commander during World War I and future general, was the son of Colonel Giaccomo Segre, who entered his son into the Military College of Milan at the age of thirteen. Emanuele Pugliese (figure 3.1), Italy's most highly decorated general in World War I, was the son of a colonel who had fought for unification.

Italy had many Dreyfuses, but no Dreyfus Affair. In 1888, Italian Jewry's leading periodical, *Il Vessillo Israelitico*, took great pride in Ottolenghi's promotion to the rank of general, recalling his service back to the Austro-Italian War of 1859 and presenting him as a model for other Italian-Jewish officers to emulate.[28] A decade later, the newspaper noted with pride that Italy's Jews had virtually unrestricted access to high military and political offices, yet their presence occasioned no scandal like the one that was tearing France apart.[29] In June of 1914, the newspaper organized a ceremony in Turin on behalf of then-captain Pugliese, who two years previously in Libya had been wounded by shrapnel in the midst of battle yet stubbornly remained at his post. The captain was presented with a sword of chiseled silver while a variety of Gentile and Jewish dignitaries, including two Zionist activists, heaped praise upon him and their beloved homeland.[30] Italy's Jews were well aware of the reactionary and Judeophobic forces lurking inside parish churches and behind the walls of the Vatican. But the Italian kingdom's embrace of the *juif d'état* ensured that Italy's Jews would not go the way of their central and eastern European brethren, who during the interwar period embraced radicalism, antiauthoritarianism, and antimilitarism. Even under the Fascists, who took power in 1922, the Italian army remained an attractive and welcoming institution for Jewish officers for sixteen years, and precisely because there were so many Jews in positions of high command the racial laws of 1938 proved difficult to implement.

Although mostly forgotten today, Italian-Jewish military officers were a source of pride for Jews throughout Europe. The distinguished German-Jewish scholar Abraham Berliner concluded the preface to the

Figure 3.1. Corps Commander General Emanuele Pugliese (1874–1967). *Reproduced from Rubin, E. (1952).*

second volume of his magisterial *Geschichte der Juden in Rom* (1893) with this brief yet stirring eyewitness account of a visit by the German kaiser to the pope, with a Jewish commander at the head of the Italian honor guard escorting the kaiser:

> I am still feeling the great emotion of those days. My memory delights in dwelling on that grand moment—at 15:10 yesterday—when the German Emperor was on his way to visit the Vatican, accompanied by Italian troops under the command of General Ottolenghi, a Jew. The sight made my heart shout in praises: Praise be to God, He who changes the seasons. With these lines . . . I conclude my book.[31]

The same display of military splendor was visible in France, home to hundreds of Jewish career officers, including twenty generals, under the Second Empire and Third Republic (1852–1940).[32] German Jews looked on enviously at their French coreligionists, who attained positions of power that the former could only dream of. In the early 1890s, Jews, barely 0.25 percent of France's population, were 3 to 4 percent of the entering classes into the École Polytechnique, France's premier institution for the training of civilian engineers and officers in the artillery and engineering corps. Graduates of the EP were automatically given officer status, and many Jewish EP graduates, like their Christian counterparts, chose military careers. Jews also made up about 1 percent of the entering classes of France's illustrious and strongly Catholic École Spéciale Militaire at Saint-Cyr, which trained junior officers for the cavalry and infantry.[33] Jewish graduates of the École Polytechnique regularly attended the prestigious École Supérieure de Guerre, which groomed staff officers. Because of the relatively small size of the engineering and artillery corps as opposed to the infantry—in 1894, there were 900 active officers in engineering and 3,700 in the artillery versus 12,000 in the infantry[34]—Jews may have comprised 3 to 4 percent of all artillery officers and as much as 10 percent of those in the engineering corps.

The French sociologist Pierre Birnbaum coined the term *juif d'état* to describe the thousands of Jews who, over the course of the Third Republic (1870–1940), served in France's governing elite as prefects, parliamentarians, cabinet ministers, judges, and military officers. The term is not merely descriptive; it is also normative, evoking French Jews' intense loyalty to the ideals and institutions of the state. The French title of Birnbaum's book, *Les fous de la République* (Fools of the Republic) suggests that Jews were not merely supportive and patriotic citizens but besotted with gratitude for their emancipation, pride in their social and economic mobility, and scorn for the republic's enemies, particularly reactionary, "ultramontane" Catholics. As in most cases of infatuation, so it seems, French Jewry's love affair with the Third Republic ended badly, and during their many decades of romantic association, the Jews were often treated cruelly by their beloved.

In 1892, a series of articles in *La Libre Parole*, the mouthpiece of the notorious (and wildly popular) antisemite Edouard Drumont, impugned the honor of Jewish soldiers and claimed that Jewish officers got promotions and choice assignments through bribery and pulling strings. (During the height of the Dreyfus Affair, another antisemitic newspaper, *L'Anti-juif*, obsessively listed the names of Jewish officers, especially at the most senior ranks, as if to suggest that the very presence of so many Jews in the army could be attributed only to trickery and malevolence.)[35] The scurrilous articles in *La Libre Parole* led to a series of duels. The first was between the headstrong Jewish cavalry lieutenant André Crémieu-Foa and Drumont's colleague Paul de Lamase, a shooting contest that ended without a clear victor. There swiftly followed a sword fight between Lamase's chief second, the Marquis de Morès, and a young Jewish artillery captain, Armand Mayer, who despite being the fencing master at the École Polytechnique was mortally wounded.[36] (One of Mayer's seconds was none other than the villainous Ferdinand Esterhazy, the German spy whose treachery would be falsely attributed to Dreyfus. Esterhazy apparently had a knack for seeking out Jewish officers as sources of money and aristocratic ones as sources of prestige.)

Antisemitism lay behind this whole sorry chain of events, but so did an obsessive yearning for male honor, a yearning that Jewish officers in France were allowed to fulfill. Crémieu-Foa was, we should keep in mind, an officer of the cavalry, the most aristocratic of the army's corps. What's more, although Mayer's death was a terrible blow to the French-Jewish community—he was the nephew of a prominent Parisian rabbi—it was also seen as an assault against the republic's supreme value of secular patriotism, and his funeral was a public affair, attracting somewhere between 20,000 and 100,000 spectators. The French-Jewish press predicted confidently that Captain Mayer's brave death had dealt antisemitism a mortal blow.[37]

Seldom has a prediction proved more inaccurate. Less than a year after Mayer's death, the young lieutenant Alfred Dreyfus endured antisemitic abuse at the École Supérieure de Guerre, where one of his final examiners awarded him a zero in the field of moral conduct because he could not abide the notion of a Jew serving on the army's General Staff, the prize awaiting the twelve top scorers on the exam. (Perhaps unfortunately for Dreyfus, he did so well on the other tests as to finish ninth and thus win one of the coveted spots.)[38] Dreyfus' arrest and trial, and even more so the public accusation in 1898 by Émile Zola that the army was suppressing evidence of Dreyfus' innocence, catalyzed an explosion of political antisemitism such as France had never seen before.[39] Within the army, hazing of Jews by Christians became increasingly vicious, in one case causing the death of a Jewish cavalry officer. An anonymous group of officers wrote to *La Libre Parole* that they eagerly awaited the "order to try out the new canons and new explosives for the 100,000 Jews who poison the country."[40] Some battalions refused to accept an aspiring officer without a baptismal certificate. Frustrated and aggrieved Jewish officers became increasingly wont to challenge their bigoted comrades to duels, at times fatal. Many Jews resigned their commissions out of fear that their career advancement would be stifled. Between 1895 and 1906 one-third of officers with characteristically Jewish names such as Bloch, Cahan, and Mayer, and half of those named Levy, left the army, as opposed to only a quarter with the robustly Gentile surname Dupont. In 1899, Colonel Émile Mayer was forced to resign his commission after publishing articles in *Le Figaro* defending Dreyfus and criticizing French military strategy. Not surprisingly, at the end of the century the numbers of Jews entering the École Polytechnique and Saint-Cyr plummeted. In 1907, the percentage of Jews at the École Polytechnique was half what it had been a decade previously.[41]

Nonetheless, even at the height of the affair Jews continued to graduate from the École Supérieure de Guerre and receive promotions from lieutenant to captain, battalion chief, lieutenant colonel, colonel, and general. Jewish officers who died in uniform continued to receive elaborate and respectful military funerals. At the turn of the century, as the forces of republicanism in the government reasserted themselves, Catholic and monarchist officers, not Jews, were the targets of investigation by the War Ministry. After the official separation of church and state in France in 1905 and the exoneration of Dreyfus the following year, France's liberal political parties affirmed their support for the army.[42] Jews continued to flow into the École Polytechnique, albeit at reduced numbers, leading to the training of a whole new generation of Jewish officers who would take command during and after World War I.[43]

If we evaluate the integration of Jews into the French officer corps solely through the lens of the Dreyfus Affair, if we equate antisemitic incidents in the French military with the attitudes of the army toward Jews *tout court*, we miss fundamental truths about the military in almost any society, and certainly in that of France at the fin de siècle. First, the army is a vast machine possessed of enormous bureaucratic inertia.

Administrative procedures change slowly and are constrained by the dicta of instrumental rationality. The French army was formally, rigorously meritocratic. In the 1870s, fully one-third of its officers, versus only 5 percent for the British army, had risen from the rank and file.[44] A commitment to meritocracy could coexist with snobbish or bigoted sentiment within a single corps, regiment, or even individual commander's mind. Second, unit and regimental commanders might have an entirely different perspective from that of the general staffs of their corps or the army as a whole. Jewish officers encountered supportive as well as hostile comrades and superiors throughout their careers. Third, the history of any particular religious or ethnic collective's encounter with the military cannot be separated from broader developments within the military as a whole. Before asking whether the military was a desirable place for Jews and whether they were desired by it, we must ask about the status of the military within French society as such. Add to all these factors the tenacity with which French Jews pursued military careers well into the interwar period, and the tangible benefits—social, economic, and psychological—that they derived from this occupational choice, and it becomes clear that we need to go beyond existing frameworks for analyzing the subject.

We can begin with the general decline of the prestige of the military in France in the late 1800s. Between 1897 and 1911 the total number of applicants to Saint-Cyr dropped by 60 percent, and there was a 40 percent drop in the number of noncommissioned officers reenlisting for additional terms of service. The army was in increasingly bad political odor, but also salaries were unattractively low. A newly commissioned junior lieutenant earned 175 francs per month, of which at least 125 were needed for room and board. Owing to a glut of junior officers from previous cohorts, career advancement became ever slower. A lieutenant might wait a dozen or more years for promotion; a captain might sit in place for fifteen to twenty years. Most officers made it to major in their mid- to late forties, and they dreamed of reaching the august rank of colonel on the cusp of retirement. This was the lot of the very best graduates of Saint-Cyr and the École Polytechnique; those who came up through the ranks as noncommissioned officers rarely rose higher than major.[45] Not surprisingly, in a society that increasingly valued the pursuit of wealth, the *haute bourgeoisie* of bankers, merchants, and entrepreneurs began to question sending their sons into the military or marrying their daughters to officers.[46] The increased percentage of Jesuit seminarians and aristocrats entering Saint-Cyr was a sign that the number of applications from bourgeois families was declining. Antisemitism may well have deterred some Jews from pursuing a military career or spurred them to resign their commissions prematurely, but perhaps Jews preferred alternate career paths, which for Jews were likely to be more numerous and attractive than for most Christian officers given the Jews' heavily urban and educated backgrounds.

In popular accounts of the Dreyfus Affair, little is explained about the General Staff except that Dreyfus was the first or only Jew to serve on it. The emphasis on Dreyfus' exceptionality smacks of foreboding that any Jew who rose too high or too fast in Gentile society was doomed to be struck down, and hard.[47] But a closer look at how the French army's administration developed in the late nineteenth century, and what role Jews played in it, challenges such simplistic views. Over the second half of the nineteenth century, the terms *état-major* and *état-major général* referred to multiple and constantly developing institutions. The army had a central administrative corps, and each branch of the army— cavalry, infantry, and so forth—had an administrative staff of its own. Before the late 1880s, the General Staff (*état-major général*) was a cumbersome and ineffective body that crafted neither policy nor strategy. It was directly subordinate to the minister of war, so its leadership changed every time the government fell and a new minister was installed. Its permanent membership included all of the army's generals plus hundreds of staff officers.[48] Since there were Jewish generals going back to the early years of the republic, there were by definition Jews on the General Staff. What's more, as early as 1881 a Colonel Abraham Samuel was a member of the General Staff's highest administrative cadres.[49]

The French General Staff underwent a major restructuring between 1888 and 1890 under War Minister Charles de Freycinet, whose fear and antipathy toward Germany was matched by admiration for its military's General Staff, a politically independent body that engaged in military planning in peacetime. Officers for the old General Staff had come largely from Saint-Cyr and the École d'Application d'État-Major, a sort of finishing school, admission to which was based on pedigree and comportment. The new General Staff would draw on the best and brightest from the École Supérieure de Guerre, which had been founded in 1876, also in response to the French military defeat of 1870–71 and a desire to create a cadre of officers as savvy as they were brave and honorable. These new institutions represented an unprecedented opportunity for ambitious young men like Alfred Dreyfus, who indeed was the only Jew in the new, far more powerful General Staff. Yet in 1893–94, when he served as a *stagaire* in the General Staff, there were several Jewish officers on the staffs of the army's various corps.[50] Dreyfus was hardly the only high-placed Jew in the army's administration. Besides, three of the four units of the General Staff with which he served thought extremely well of the young artillery captain, and officers from two of those units defended him when he fell afoul of colleagues in his fourth and final posting in the statistical (i.e., counterintelligence) branch and was accused of treason.[51] Sadly for Dreyfus, the General Staff's statistics bureau was controlled by officers who loathed not only Jews but also any bright young men of talent who had gotten through the École Supérieure de Guerre and onto the General Staff by achievement alone, rather than family background or connections.[52]

Dreyfus' exceptionality can be demonstrated by studying the careers of his fellow Jewish officers. Fortunately for historians, the French military kept excellent records, and thousands of dossiers of career officers are preserved in the Service Historique de l'Armée Territoriale, nestled in the regal seventeenth-century outbuildings of the medieval Vincennes castle on the eastern edge of Paris. The personnel dossiers include the officers' career ladder, educational records, correspondence from family members related to their military education, annual evaluations (by regimental and corps commanders as well as the inspector general), and, for those who married, exhaustive evaluations of the intended's family background, dowry, and what was referred to as "moral virtue." Since Jewish officers were frequently referred to by name in the Jewish press and apologetic literature, it is possible to locate most of their dossiers. (Some have been lost along the way.) An exploration of the dossiers of officers with common Jewish names yields more information, and although a number of French names are ambiguous regarding religious origin, the contents of the dossier as a whole always establish the officer's background.

## Lives Reconstructed: French-Jewish Officers at Home and Abroad

The connection between Jewish officers and the French republic could not be more intimate or immediate. No sooner had the École Polytechnique been transformed into a military academy in 1805 than the Alsatian merchant Théodore Cerfbeer enrolled one of his five sons in the school, from which the young man emerged as an artillery officer. Another son, Max-Théodore, was born in 1792, "the first year of the republic," according to his birth certificate, and like his brother (and several of his cousins) he pursued a military career, though without the benefit of a higher education. Unable to afford to send Max-Théodore past high school, in 1810 Theódore successfully petitioned the War Ministry to send him directly into a commission in the army of the line.[53] Max-Théodore rose through the ranks to become a successful staff officer, serving as aide-de-camp to several generals and, in 1834, as director of the War Ministry's cabinet. He retired in 1846 at the rank of full colonel. (He also served in the Chamber of Deputies between 1842 and 1848 and as president of the Jewish Central Consistory between 1846 and 1871.)

From midcentury until the 1890s, Jewish officers often came from humble backgrounds, and although most attended the École Polytechnique, a substantial minority were simple volunteer soldiers who rose through the ranks. Adolphe Hinsten (1831–1905), who reached the rank of general of the artillery, and his brother Charles, a naval officer, were the sons of a tailor.[54] The father of Eugene-Abraham Levy (1825–99), who would become a general in the engineering corps, was a "professeur de belles-lettres." The future artillery colonel Edouard Anatole Lippman, who graduated the École Polytechnique in 1855, was the son of a postmaster in Verdun.[55] The previous year, an Alsatian peddler named Ephraim Weil celebrated the birth of his son Samuel, who signed up as an infantryman in 1875 and retired at the rank of captain.[56] Another *engagé volontaire* in the infantry who wended his way up the ranks, Hippolyte Solomon Weil, was the son of a kosher butcher from Strasbourg.[57]

Under the Second Empire and Third Republic, aspiring officers from middling to poor families depended on the generosity of the French state to pay for tuition, room, and board at the École Polytechnique, and soldiers who had signed up without clear career prospects benefited from stints of free officer-training courses as they worked up the ladder into administrative and command positions. A father seeking a *trousseau*, or bursary, for his son was required to submit detailed information about his own finances and testimonies to his probity as well as to the child's own promise. We see from the dossiers how Jews benefited from the state's largesse. Alphonse Albert Valabregue, who died tragically in 1892 while serving with the artillery in Dahomey, was the son of a merchant with six children and an income of less than a thousand francs per year. He received a full bursary, as did Lucien Levy, an engineering general during World War I who was the son of a rabbi and schoolteacher from Alsace. When Levy's father requested a full bursary in 1878, the École Polytechnique's examining committee determined that his income amounted to barely two thousand francs per year and took note of his "forty-three years of service" to the community as well as glowing recommendations from his municipal council.[58] The military was also sympathetic to formerly well-to-do parents who had fallen on hard times. In 1881, a banker in Paris named Lazare Levy requested a scholarship to the naval academy for his son Pierre Joseph. Levy was a respectable man: a member of the Paris consistory and a former inspector of Jewish schools in Nancy, involved in Jewish philanthropic societies in Paris, and the author of several works on linguistics. But he had gone bankrupt, and his lawyer allotted him an income of six thousand francs per year. Lazare's oldest son had been an army officer but resigned his commission when his father's bankruptcy became public news. Given that Lazare had four other children to support, the Paris municipality recommended that young Pierre be granted a bursary.[59] After graduation the officer went on to spend many years in Africa and Indochina, after which he commanded torpedo boats in the North Atlantic.

France's Jewish officers were born into unmistakably Jewish homes, where the paterfamilias could as easily be a religious functionary or teacher as a merchant or professional. The officers almost invariably married Jewish women as well, and often the brides were considerably higher on the social ladder, suggesting that at least until the end of the century a captain's epaulets were source of considerable social capital. Dowries were an essential component of any French officer's income: in 1890 a captain's salary including perks was a bit over four thousand francs per year, which barely covered a bachelor's room and board plus the costs of maintaining an officer's lifestyle (uniforms, equipment, socializing, gambling.)[60] As early as 1817, the French military decreed that all officers who wished to marry must be assured a certain minimal dowry, which was fixed at 1,200 francs per year (i.e., 24,000 francs, assuming a 5 percent annual return) and remained in place until 1900. This income did not adequately cover the cost of maintaining a household, but almost a third of officers' marriages between 1855 and 1890 involved dowries below this minimal amount, so exceptions to the rule were made on a routine basis. Most dowries were under 50,000 francs, and only 8 percent were above 120,000 francs.[61]

The brides of Jewish officers usually brought into marriage dowries that were far higher than average. Elisa Ratisbonne of Strasbourg, who in 1829 married Max-Théodore Cerfbeer, brought 100,000 francs. In 1864, Captain Abraham Auguste Samuel married one Leanne Levylier, a widow from Luneville, whose dowry was 150,000 francs, with another 300,000 in expected inheritances.[62] In 1868, Léopold See, who would become the first Jewish general under the Second Empire, married at the age of forty-seven while serving as a colonel in the infantry. His wife, Frederique Ellison, was the daughter of a prosperous banker who lived on Boulevard Hausmann in Paris, owned three horses and two carriages, employed six servants, and dowered his daughter with 150,000 francs in cash plus an additional five thousand per year in income.[63] In 1871, Joseph Simon, a landowner from Mulhouse who moved to Paris, most likely after the German annexation of Alsace-Lorraine, dowered his daughter Adele with 150,000 francs worth of stock, government bonds, and cash when she married the then battalion commander and future general Adolphe Hinsten. The following year, Captain of the Artillery Georges-Henri Halphen, who came from a poor family and graduated second to last in his class from the École de l'Artillerie et du Génie, married Marguerite Rose Aron, the daughter of a banker, with a dowry of 240,000 francs.[64] When Captain (Second Class) Samuel-Paul Naquet-Laroque married in 1875, his wife brought 100,000 francs in cash plus an income of two thousand a year.[65] Emilie Lang, who in 1879 married Captain (and future general) Justin Dennery, came from one of the most distinguished families in Verdun, with a home worth 450,000 francs, though her dowry was a mere 100,000.[66] Anna Katz of Paris was, according to the military investigators of officers' brides, a "brilliant marriage" for Captain Mardochée George Valabrégue, a future general and infantry commander in World War I. The dowry was indeed a fortune: 225,000 francs with expectations of 250,000 to 300,000 more.[67] Lucien Levy's wife, Jane Wolff Lamont, brought 140,000 francs into the marriage—quite an upward economic leap for the son of a poor rabbi. (Jane's sister had also married a Jewish officer, a Captain Bloch.)

These marriages often, but not always, involved grooms who were headed for the highest positions in the French army, so one might argue that these young men were unusually well connected, brilliant, or wealthy themselves and so attracted rich brides from distinguished families. Indeed, there are some cases of Jewish officers, usually volunteers who rose through the ranks and retired as captains or majors, who married women with modest dowries. Out of scores of dossiers, however, I found only three cases of dowries below the average figure for officers as a whole of 50,000 francs, and only one of those was below the 1,200 francs/year minimum.[68] More common than Jews marrying poor women were those who never married at all—some died in service, others simply stayed single, perhaps because of personal preference, but more likely because they could not afford a household. (In the late 1800s, about a quarter of all career officers had not married by the age of fifty.)

From the 1850s until 1871, French officers frequently took part in campaigns on the Continent—in the Crimean, Italian, and Franco-Prussian wars. After that, the only fighting they saw was in the colonies, in North Africa, and Indochina. Much of an officer's time was taken up by a routine of disciplined idleness (drill, inspections, equipment maintenance) punctuated by training exercises. The army's vast bureaucracy afforded ample opportunities for young men who lacked the constitution or desire to be warriors to make successful careers as staff officers. Abraham Auguste Samuel was in delicate health but managed to graduate near the top of his class at Saint-Cyr and devoted his career to administrative work. Georges-Henri Halphen was lazy, undisciplined, and disobedient but also a mathematical genius who became an examiner and instructor at the École Polytechnique, a position so august that it elevated him to the category of "celebrity" in the French military archives' filing system. Being Jewish did not necessarily stand in the way of being assigned to a particularly sensitive or prestigious position. In 1867, then colonel Léopold See (figure 3.2) was assigned to the French forces preserving papal control over Rome, and he fought against Garibaldi's republicans. (See's Jewishness kept him from being put in command over the garrison, as the War Ministry was concerned about the locals' reaction to a Jew so visibly protecting the Pope.)[69] In 1881, Eugene-Abraham Levy was appointed director of fortifications for Paris and France's northern forests, and three years later he became supreme commander for engineering operations in Algeria.

Levy's dossier contains a number of tart comments from his annual inspections: he is "small and skinny" with a "nervous constitution" (1881); "small, nervous" (1887); "very small of stature" (1888). Was antisemitism lurking underneath such evaluations? Or was he, in fact, small, skinny, and prone to anxiety? (I cannot verify his mental state, but his medical records reveal his adult height to be four foot eleven, short even by the standards of the time.)[70] The evaluations in this and other Jewish officers' dossiers throw light on the contradictory nature of the French military, where antisemitism was certainly present but, with the exception of the worst years of the Dreyfus Affair, does not seem to have penetrated deeply into the military's bureaucratic culture.

Every officer received at least three written evaluations per year, by the commanding officer, regimental officer, and inspector general. Of the thousands of evaluations I have looked at, many are glowing: "very honorable . . . very capable in directing his battalion" (Captain Bernard Avraham, 1878); "has all the qualities of an engineer and of an eminent warrior: intelligent, courageous, vigorous, extraordinary. He should quickly reach the higher ranks where he would exert the most useful influence" (Captain Adolphe Hinsten, 1872); "Well-intentioned and has no weaknesses [in dealings] with his inferiors and demonstrates experience in the way he directs officers placed under his command. His value is real" (Abraham Auguste Samuel, 1881). Virtually all the evaluations are free of overt or even implied antisemitism. Just a year before his tragic death at the hand of the Marquis de Morès, Captain Joseph Armand Mayer's commander wrote that he was smart, erudite, tactful, an excellent horseman, "certainly called to a brilliant career" and "a remarkable officer from all points of view." An evaluation from earlier in his career suggests some antisemitic sensibility as it alludes to his Jewish origin only to dismiss it through praise for his physical and moral

Figure 3.2. General Léopold See (1822–1904). *Reproduced from Rubin, E. (1952).*

virtues: "Israelite of tall stature and very blond, correct and military bearing . . . should make a good officer."[71] Such direct references were, however, rare. Some evaluations refer to a Jewish officer's "zeal" in what might be a coded way, but negative evaluations tended to be specific and varied, which lends credence to their accuracy. André Crémieu-Foa, who initiated the sorry chain of duels that led to Mayer's death, was said to be a good horseman but to have poor judgment—a fair assessment, given later events.[72] Captain Émile-Emmanuel Oppenheim, who was killed in Tonkin in 1892, was called a stolid, capable officer, good with details but perhaps a bit hard on his subordinates.[73] Another colonial officer who died overseas, Alphonse Albert Valabrègue, was said to have trouble expressing himself.[74] A squadron commander named Lucien Levy (not the same as the future general) was consistently described as indecisive and timid.[75]

We noted earlier that most officers considered themselves fortunate to retire with the rank of colonel, and many did not reach that lofty goal. Jews who experienced slow or fitful promotion may have been subject to the same vagaries of military mobility that affected all officers, or they may have suffered specifically from antisemitic prejudice. It is hard to determine why in the early 1800s Max-Théodore Cerfbeer spent almost twenty years at the rank of captain, as he lobbied consistently for promotion from the line army to a staff officer's position. A report of 1821 claimed that Cerfbeer lacked an adequate knowledge of math and military science and that other candidates for promotion had greater seniority.[76] This does not, however, explain why Cerfbeer was not promoted until 1837, especially since one of his commanding officers emphatically recommended him for promotion in 1832. A similar dynamic developed decades later in the case of Lucien Levy, who sat at the rank of captain for sixteen years despite regular comments in his annual inspection reports that he was more than ripe for promotion. An officer could be well thought of by his unit and regimental commander yet run afoul of decision making by anonymous individuals who knew nothing of the man but only his dossier—and, so it seems in these cases, his religion.

At times, though, Jews were promoted with astonishing speed. In 1870, Léopold See was promoted to brigadier general at forty-eight, an unusually young age for so high a position. Advancement of Jews into the most senior positions continued even during the nadir of the Dreyfus Affair. In 1898, Squadron Leader Mardochée-George Valabregue was appointed director of a corps-level artillery school, and in 1902 was promoted to colonel and placed in command of the prestigious École Militaire d'Artillerie et du Génie. (He was promoted to brigadier, then division general in 1905 and 1908 respectively.) In 1900, Colonel Samuel-Paul Naquet-Laroque was attached to the General Staff; in that same year he was promoted to brigadier general, and became a division general in 1903.[77] Dreyfus may have been the first Jew on the newly revamped General Staff, but he was not the last.

An intriguing alternative to Dreyfus' fate was that of Edmond Isidore, a squadron commander in Tunisia and Tonkin who in 1892 requested permission to marry a young woman whose father was of German-

Jewish origin. Smarting from defeat by Prussia and obsessed with fears of German espionage, the military denied the request out of fear that the father had been a spy for Germany during the Franco-Prussian War. But in this case suspicion was amenable to reason. The would-be father-in-law wrote a lengthy testimony vowing that he was no spy, but merely a successful manufacturer of hats who had spent the war holed up in Switzerland. Further investigation bore out the man's claim, and the marriage took place.[78] The loyalty of the officer himself was, apparently, never called into question.

Despite this minor kerfuffle surrounding his marriage, Isidore's career was ordinary in every way, including his stints in North Africa and Indochina. We have already encountered Eugene-Abraham Levy, commander for engineering operations in Algeria between 1884 and 1886, the infantry general Jules Heymann, who spent most of his career in the Maghreb as an assistant to the army's section of native affairs, the naval lieutenant Pierre Leo Levy-Bing, Émile-Emmanuel Oppenheim of the colonial infantry, and Alphonse Albert Valabregue, who served in Dahomey. The impetuous André Crémieu-Foa was dispatched from France to North Africa after the duel with Lamase, and he died of disease shortly after arriving in Dahomey. In that same year, both Valabregue and Oppenheim died, the former of disease, the latter from a gangrenous gunshot wound inflicted by what his commanding officer called a "pirate band."[79] (The French frequently referred to Tonkinese insurgents as "pirates." In this case the "pirate" was Doc Ngu, who was also killed that year.)

Proud as the French-Jewish community was of all its soldiers, it was particularly devoted to its native sons serving in foreign lands, and in December of 1892 a grand memorial service was held in the Rue de la Victoire synagogue for the officers mentioned above and other Jewish soldiers who had died overseas. According to *Les Archives Israélites*, "The Temple was illuminated as bright as day," and black sheets covered the choir area. Representatives of the War Ministry, the Ministry of the Navy, and the president of the republic were in attendance, as were Generals See and Levy, and a smattering of other military dignitaries sat with the heads of the Central and Paris consistories, Alphonse and James de Rothschild. The afternoon prayer service was followed by solemn organ music, a choir singing the traditional funerary Psalm 91, and remarks by the chief rabbi of France. The rabbi's remarks about Oppenheim "salute[d] the valiant expeditionary unit that, under the command of a leader as brave as he was experienced, in a savage and hateful confrontation, defended the honor of France, bringing luster, through their victories, to the national flag." The rabbi "offers warm praise for the army, this school of duty and sacrifice, which is the microcosm of the homeland, where all Frenchmen, regardless of origin and religion, blend together in the same love for the flag and a similar will to assure it its respect."[80]

Surely, such patriotic pomp was motivated in part by the desire to counter antisemitism. But it was also a genuine, sincere assertion of devotion to the homeland, *la patrie*, and of the inseparability of *patrie* and empire. French Christians were no less likely than Jews to equate colonial service with laudable self-sacrifice. It is no surprise that, in public, Jewish support for empire was declaimed repeatedly, elaborately, and unequivocally. In private, however, the association between patriotism and imperialism, between the army and antisemitism, in short, between French Jews and the French state, was subject to intense interrogation. A remarkably thoughtful expression of all these issues emerges from the writings of a young Jewish officer in the colonial artillery named Fernand Bernard (1866–1961). Bernard was a younger brother of the writer Bernard Lazare (born Lazare Bernard, but he reversed the names, perhaps a sign of rebellion against his bourgeois upbringing). Bernard Lazare was a man of fierce and volatile intellectual convictions: an anarchist, a vociferous Dreyfusard, and a Zionist, although of a heterodox sort that caused his friendship with Theodor Herzl to be as brief as it was passionate.[81] Fernand shared his brother's idiosyncratic and independent spirit but turned it in a quite different direction: toward military service, which he both loathed and loved, and to the French Empire, of which he was deeply critical but which would in later life be the source of his fortune. Correspondence from the late 1880s through early 1900s between Fernand, Bernard, another brother, Armand, and their parents has survived intact and is preserved in the National Archives in Paris.[82]

Bernard was the son of a wine merchant who was hit hard by the phylloxera epidemic that in the 1880s ravaged the vineyards of southern France. Given a full bursary to the École Polytechnique, Bernard graduated in the top third of his class, though he failed the admissions examinations for the École Supérieure de Guerre. Bernard's early evaluations uniformly described him as gifted, curious, and particularly well-spoken. One report referred to him, accurately enough, as "brash." As Bernard wrote to his parents, and as his service dossier confirms, in February of 1897, while on board a ship anchored off the coast near Hué, Bernard struck a shipmate, a drunken lieutenant who made antisemitic remarks to Bernard's face. Bernard was let off with a token punishment of three months leave in Hué at his current rank and lodgings. The "disciple of Drumont," as Bernard called the lieutenant, was relieved for a full year. Bernard's career continued to flourish. Between 1897 and 1899 he worked on planning the Annamese railway, but life in the tropics took its toll on him and he went on medical leave until 1901, when he was reassigned to various staff positions in France. The apple of his commanding officer's eye, Bernard was brought back to Indochina in 1904 to direct the expedition that delimited the Indochina-Siam border. Bernard retired from the army in 1908 as a lieutenant colonel, only to be called out of retirement in 1914 to command artillery installations in northern Paris.

Bernard loved the Far East. He spent most of his career stationed in East Asia, where he developed a profound appreciation for Chinese culture and a prescient understanding of the power of Vietnamese nationalism. Bernard's letters contain lengthy travelogues peppered with homages to the splendor of native architecture and Buddhist ritual as well as barbed critiques of the incompetence of French colonial rule. Bernard protested that he was no "annamitophile": "this unfortunate people has for so long been steeped in rule at the hands of so many masters that it has contracted the basest faults caused by servitude: it is cowardly and deceitful."[83] Yet Bernard was even more enraged by the arrogance of Catholic missionaries, the brutality of the French administration, and the parochialism of French bureaucrats who were fluent in ancient Greek and Latin but knew not a word of Chinese, the language of a civilization no less great than those of the west.[84] In 1901, while still in uniform, Bernard penned a journal article, followed by a full-length book, that predicted the rise of Annamese nationalism and the overthrow of French colonial rule.[85] After his retirement from the army in 1908, Bernard combined business with pleasure as he made practical use of the knowledge he had so painstakingly acquired. During the 1920s and '30s, he got involved in rubber plantations in Indochina and by 1933 was acting director of the Cochin Chinese Company for Rivertime Freight. Although highly critical of the practices of the Bank of Indochina, he became a member of its directorial board, president of Indochina's Chamber of Commerce, and France's official representative to an international body that regulated the production and price of rubber.[86] During World War II, Bernard put the money he had made overseas to good use: the elderly colonel, now retired in France, was a key organizer and funder of the resistance group Combat.[87]

In the winter of 1898, Ferdinand Esterhazy was tried and acquitted in a closed military court, and Émile Zola, who had dared attack the army for covering up evidence of Dreyfus' innocence, was convicted of criminal libel. These events shook the usually confident Bernard to the core. He put on a good face to his parents, dismissing their concerns for his career advancement and expressing every confidence that he would in no way suffer "although no one does not know that I am the brother of Bernard Lazare and that moreover I take from this a most legitimate pride."[88] Bernard saved his authentic feelings for his brothers. He adored his "cher gros" Lazare and urged him to expose the antisemitic forces that prevented the airing of evidence casting doubt on the accusations against Dreyfus. In turn, Lazare sent Bernard parcels of newspapers as well as his pamphlet *Antisemitism: Its History and Causes*, about which Bernard commented, "There is no one, no one who is loyal and intelligent (I do not speak of the mental defectives who are content to read *La Libre Parole*) who will not be convinced in reading it. It is certain that Dreyfus is innocent."[89] Early in 1898, Bernard confessed to Lazare that he had lost all respect for the army; an institution that he had previously seen as the embodiment of integrity, honor, and discipline had degenerated into a mass of petty servants who blindly did the bidding of their masters.[90] By September he was rueful and bitter about the "illusions I had held for this career that eight years ago, on my exit from the academy, I had believed to be the most noble and glorious." On the very same day that Bernard wrote a breezy, upbeat letter to his parents assuring them that Dreyfus would be acquitted at his upcoming retrial, Bernard wrote to Lazare that he was disgusted to wear the same uniform as that of Dreyfus' tormentors and was considering resigning his commission: "Where is my former pride, my former faith? I ask today only to leave the army and be me, Fernand Bernard, and not Captain Bernard."[91]

Bernard did not resign his commission in 1898. He stayed in the army for another decade, racking up accomplishments and gaining experience that served him well in his second career as a man of affairs. For all its vicissitudes, Bernard's life was one of success—as an officer, businessman, writer, and, when he was well into his seventies, a steely resistance fighter against the Nazis. There were among Jewish officers failures as well, tragedies that were self-inflicted or caused by family trauma rather than malevolent external forces.

The celebrated Jewish actress Rachel Felix (1821–58) had numerous lovers, including a son and nephew of Napoleon Bonaparte, the future emperor Louis-Napoleon, and one Arthur Bertrand, who fathered an illegitimate son, Victor-Gabriel (1848–88), who never knew his father and took his mother's last name.[92] After a spell in the army, Victor-Gabriel Felix signed up for the navy and was promoted to lieutenant in 1878 despite what his commanding officer admitted was a highly checkered past:

> He was covered in debts that will never be paid. His morality was, however, not compromised. His youth was an excuse, his bohemian birth was a mitigating circumstance. He is not undeserving of interest: he is disfigured by a wound received in the army of the Loire; moreover, he has outbursts of disorderly generosity, from a weak heart.[93]

Unfortunately, everywhere Felix went in Africa, gambling and other debts mounted up, and his commanding officer lost patience, writing "M. Felix is *decidedly* a *lost* officer. The dregs, madness or suicide are his only and imminent fate." Felix responded that he must stay in Africa and begged to be allowed to join an expedition to Gabon, part of what he called France's "honorable struggle" in Africa, which would enrich the homeland with ebony, ivory, and rubber. Felix promised to make himself useful making astronomical observations and learning local idioms.

Indeed, Felix turned himself around. In 1884, he wrote a memorandum titled "Considerations on the Method of Lunar Distances," which was published in the *Revue Maritime et Coloniale*, and he was appointed to be head of post in Lambaréné and N'Gove in Gabon. At the time, an official on site wrote optimistically, "I am sure that in Gabon, this officer, well known amongst the blacks who love him and fear him even more, can render us more useful services than anywhere else." But Felix, the bastard son of a *tragédienne*, could not escape a tragic fate. Although it is not clear if he was drunk, Felix almost foundered a boat under his command, causing his crew to mutiny. By 1888, he was utterly mad, sobbing and shouting uncontrollably. The cause of his death is not certain, but it may well have been self-inflicted.

Victor-Gabriel Felix did not suffer for being of Jewish origin; his demons came from within. For that matter, although antisemitic slights hurt Fernand Bernard's pride, his career was as fortunate as Felix's was disastrous. Comparisons between Bernard and Dreyfus are limited because Bernard spent most of the years when French antisemitism reached its peak far from the maelstrom of the metropole, and although his criticisms of French colonial rule were unorthodox and carried some risk, they did not touch upon the truly taboo subjects that could get an officer disciplined or even cashiered. If we want to locate a French-Jewish officer who can truly serve as a counter to Dreyfus, it should be someone who, like Dreyfus, suffered for being Jewish, who was in France during the thick of the crisis and beyond, and who doggedly remained in the army despite all he had to endure. Émile Mayer (1851–1938) was such a man: a state Jew who was intimately tied to the mechanisms of power yet an outsider to them; a republican patriot who was excoriated by the nationalist right (figure 3.3).

Mayer's family story was one of classic Jewish social mobility *à la française*: one of his grandfathers was a horse trader in Lorraine who made a small fortune and sent one son into academia and another, Mayer's father, to the École Polytechnique. When Mayer was five his father was appointed director of a gunpowder factory in southwest France. As a child, Mayer hardly fit the bill of a future officer—he was nearsighted, deaf in one ear, and plagued by a frail constitution that his mother (the eldest niece of the prominent banker Michel Goudchaux) strove to combat through regular ministrations of goat milk and cod liver oil. He loathed sport, swimming, and dance and seemed happiest when reading alone. Neither fit nor keen to become an officer, Mayer nonetheless followed in his father's footsteps and attended the École Polytechnique,

Figure 3.3. Colonel Émile Mayer (1851–1938). *Reproduced from Duclert (2007). Courtesy of Armand Colin.*

entering and leaving at almost the very bottom of his class, and after that the École d'Application de Guerre at Fontainebleau. Mayer's health, and with it his outlook on a military career, slowly improved, and he took a position with a construction garrison for the artillery, rising in the 1890s to the command of an artillery battery, though he longed for a teaching position at Saint-Cyr. Despite strong backing from the school's commandant, the appointment was blocked by the War Ministry; as one general said, with Mayer at Saint-Cyr, "*La Libre Parole* would have raised a ruckus."[94]

Kept away from a teaching career, Mayer began to write on military theory and policy. In 1890 he wrote that war was bound to become increasingly static and dependent upon technology rather than courage, strength, or esprit de corps. These ideas did not please his superiors, but Mayer got into much more serious trouble during the Dreyfus Affair, when he penned articles decrying the officer corps' isolation from the nation, the travesties of the military judicial system, and the primitive, baleful culture of honor and *omertà* within the General Staff. As late as 1898, Mayer was not sure of Dreyfus' innocence but condemned the savagery of the proceedings against the young captain and the flimsiness of the evidence upon which he was convicted. The following year, the General Staff's counterintelligence section, the source of Dreyfus' torment, accused Mayer of publishing sensitive information without permission. For this infraction he was placed on a temporary leave of absence, then forced into retirement.

This was not the end of Mayer's career, however. He became a public intellectual, launching a journal, *L'Armée et la nation*, and serving the socialist leader Jean Jaurès as a military adviser. During the Anglo-Boer and Russo-Japanese wars, Mayer developed further his youthful musings about the future of war as a multifront affair that would see vast reservoirs of soldiers hunkered down in trenches, fighting over the space between them but forced into protracted stalemates. Not only did Mayer become increasingly respected; he also had a chance to return to the army after Dreyfus' pardon in 1906, now as a lieutenant colonel in the reserves. In 1914, at the age of sixty-three, the doughty military theorist was put in charge of artillery emplacements for western Paris. (At that time, we will recall, Bernard was in command in the north of Paris.) Yet once again Mayer's pen got him into trouble. On 3 February 1916,

Mayer wrote a letter to a fellow French officer in which he displayed admiration for German military theory and sympathy for German suffering: "Perhaps," he wrote, "this sympathy has something to do with my origin? I need go back only three generations to find only Germans among my ancestors. My father's family's origins were in Frankfurt, I think. My maternal grandmother was from Stuttgart. . . . The current war thus to my eyes has the character of a civil war. I find it only more atrocious and I suffer cruelly from it."[95]

After the war, now fully (and, no doubt for the military command, thankfully) retired from the army, Mayer went back to his calling as a public intellectual, calling for the League of Nations to maintain an international peacekeeping force—a novel idea at the time. Even more novel, albeit bizarre, was a proposal that the League also develop a mobile gendarmerie consisting of civilian aircraft equipped with chemical weapons that could be rapidly deployed in order to nip incipient conflicts in the bud. Mayer had the chance to espouse his futurist theories at a weekly salon run by his daughter Cecile, a close friend of the future prime minister Léon Blum, and her husband, Paul Grunebaum-Ballin, who had a similar connection with Aristide Briand, who served as prime minister on and off throughout the 1920s. In 1932, the young lieutenant colonel Charles de Gaulle, who had first met Mayer in 1925, began to attend the salon. De Gaulle did not take Mayer's military theories seriously—at this time De Gaulle was developing his own theory of the centrality of a mobile armored corps as the key to future wars—yet the elderly colonel did serve as an intellectual mentor to the aspiring commander and statesman.

Until his death, Mayer remained obsessed with the deconstruction of conventional land armies and their replacement by a small permanent army of experts and a technologically advanced air force. This technophilic vision has a pedigree among French Jews, dating back to the embrace by prominent Jewish businessmen of the Saint-Simonian movement of the mid-nineteenth century. Perhaps the rebellion against aristocratic, entrenched elites and their replacement by a pure meritocracy, with technology constantly pushing forward the boundaries of the possible, was especially appealing to Jews seeking not merely to be accepted within current society but to mold it in their own image.[96]

Mayer's Jewishness, however, manifested itself in more obvious ways. Like most French-Jewish officers, Mayer married a Jew, and his daughters married Jews, albeit secular ones, and in civil ceremonies. Mayer, who was raised in a mildly observant home, never denied his identity, yet he was clearly uncomfortable with public identification with Judaism while in uniform. In 1892, as a young artillery commander, Émile refused a young conscript a furlough for Passover. (The disappointed soldier was Orly André-Hesse, a cabinet minister during the 1920s.) André-Hesse appealed to Mayer's superior and for good measure asked his cousin, an officer named Dreyfus (not Alfred) to use his influence as well. According to Mayer's memoirs, Mayer wrote to Dreyfus that André-Hesse, "being Jewish, had to refrain from fueling anti-Semitic passions, at that time carried to the point of apoplexy."[97] Mayer also stressed the difficulties for a Jewish commander to maintain discipline when challenged by a coreligionist. The Dreyfus in question agreed that "too many of our coreligionists justify by their acts or their words the movement that, every day, became stronger against them."[98] This attitude underlay the behavior of those Jewish officers who remained in the military throughout the Dreyfus Affair. They kept their heads down and, in public at least, never questioned the authority or infallibility of the army to which they had devoted their working lives.

▪ ▪ ▪

There is a profound difference between suffering and martyrdom. Captain Alfred Dreyfus became a martyr for the republic, although he was a particularly lucky one in that he survived his torments and died in his bed at the age of seventy-six. Other Jewish officers suffered for their origins, yet despite the rage directed against them by journalistic hacks, demagogues, and at times their comrades in arms, the military remained a desirable and, within France's Jewish community, socially prestigious livelihood well into the interwar period. This pattern repeated itself in any country where Jews were accepted as officers. As in other lands, French-Jewish officers flowed disproportionately into the military's technical branches, which were more meritocratic than aristocratic, and which demanded an advanced education that Jews acquired out of all proportion to their numbers. In a modern state, officers are a form of uniformed civil servant, and there has been a direct correlation between the openness of the bureaucracy as a whole to Jews and the presence of Jews in the career officer corps.

Even for assimilated French Jews, loyalty to the state was not the same as unreserved identification with the nation. Mayer's letter of 1916, in which he alludes to his German origins, asserts a form of transnational identity. His decrial of the Great War as a "civil war" is reminiscent of a substantial body of writings of the time by European Jews whose support for the war, however passionate at its outbreak, quickly turned to uneasiness, even strident opposition. That opposition had little to do with pacifism, which was espoused by a small (albeit vocal) minority of Jewish intellectuals and activists. Jewish leftists who opposed the war as a battle between imperialist powers quickly changed their tune after the March 1917 Russian Revolution. Russia, formerly seen as a tyrannous, hulking anachronism, now became an infant socialist state in need of military protection. As we will see in the next chapter, Jews frequently expressed misgivings about going to war, but their sentiments were less likely to be opposition to war as such, but rather fear of facing their coreligionists on the other side of the line of battle.

## CHAPTER FOUR

# When May We Kill Our Brethren?
# Jews at War

During World War I, Emile Zaidan, editor of the Cairo-based news-paper *Al-Hilal*, offered a fascinating observation about the military behavior of European Jews:

> The Israelites are distinguished from among the rest of the peoples by their preservation of their nationality and their customs and practices, despite the passage of time and their subordination to different states. Israelitism is simultaneously a religion [*d'in*] and a nationality [*jinsiyya*], unlike Christianity and Islam. So if we are surprised by fighting between Christian and Christian in this war, we are all the more shocked by fighting between Jew and Jew.[1]

Like other Arab writers of the time, Zaidan professes a neutral, even re-spectful, attitude toward Jewish particularity and describes Jews as com-prising a nation as well as a faith.[2] Amidst the chaos and mass bloodshed of the war, Zaidan sees a particular tragedy in Jews, members of a single nation, facing each other across the lines of battle. If the spectacle of Jew killing Jew could affect Zaidan, a Christian Arab writing from Egypt, how much more so did it traumatize Europe's Jews themselves.

Modern Jewish identities have frequently blended national attach-ments to a homeland with a transnationalist, pan-Jewish sensibility. Military service was a core issue in debates about Jewish emancipation and the most powerful manifestation of Jewish allegiance to the state. Yet coincident with Jewish patriotism was a transnationalist sense of

Jewish commonality even in times of war, when Jewish soldiers in one country faced Jews in a rival army. This sentiment reflected the reality of Jewish transnationality, that is, the global social and economic bonds that linked Jews across borders, continents, and oceans.[3]

Jews have been but one of many collectives divided between hostile polities in modern Europe. During the First World War, over one million Poles fought in the Russian army while half that number served Germany, and the army of Germany's ally Austria-Hungary included more than forty thousand Polish officers. Polish regiments were formed in all three armies, and at times they directly clashed along the vast expanse of the eastern front.[4] Little research has been done on how Poles made sense of this fraught situation, nor on Ukrainians who fought for both the Russian and the Habsburg empires during the war.[5] This chapter's analysis of Jewish wartime sensibilities can not only throw light on Jewish history but also suggest how international conflict can be used to study the extent and limits of transnationalist sentiment among stateless peoples in modern Europe.

## Civil Wars within Civil Wars

By the early nineteenth century, when Jews began to face the moral dilemma of fighting against one another in combat, the religious civilizations in which they dwelled, those of Islam and Christianity, had for many centuries condoned warfare between believers. War was justified as a crusade against sectarianism or heresy, even when it was a simple case of a struggle for political power. No sooner had Islam entered world history than it was plunged into bloody struggles over authority that resulted in the division between Sunni and Shiite Muslims. Muslim clerics prohibited Muslims from fighting one another and limited licit warfare to battle against the lands of the unbelievers. There developed in the ninth century a caste of non-Muslim, Turkic warrior-slaves, but over time this caste adopted Islam and became a ruling elite, which waged war against Muslims and infidels alike.[6] The Ottoman Empire's major wars were against Christian Europe, but in the 1830s the empire was embroiled in conflict with Egypt's rebel governor, Muhammad Ali, who had previously waged war against the Wahabi Muslims of Arabia and massacred Egypt's long-ruling Mamluk elite.

In Christendom, the great Protestant-Catholic schism of the sixteenth and seventeenth centuries occurred at the time of the introduction of gunpowder technology. The result was lethal on a massive scale. Christian unity, always more fictitious than real, was obscured by cannon smoke until the exhausted European powers agreed to a policy of toleration, a policy motivated more by pragmatic than religious sensibilities. In Europe's wars of the eighteenth through twentieth centuries, the Protestant and Catholic churches alike almost invariably supported state authority. *Ad bellum*, the Vatican offered appeals to Christian love and Catholic unity, but *in bello* it retreated to the margins, especially after 1870, when it lost the Papal States and with them its temporal power. Even Pope Leo XIII's policy of worldly reengagement in the 1890s focused on social reform, avoiding high politics, diplomatic affairs, and the making of war.

While Christians and Muslims made war, against their coreligionists or each other, Jews usually stood on the sidelines (when they weren't caught up as victims). As shown in chapter 2, in the medieval Islamic world Jews did occasionally serve as soldiers, even commanders, and in early modern eastern Europe, Jews took part in municipal defense and, on occasion, in battle.[7] But until the turn of the nineteenth century, nowhere in the Christian or Muslim worlds did Jews serve in the military in substantial numbers, and so the issue of Jews facing each other in battle did not arise. They did face a legal and ethical problem, though, that foreshadowed the physical clashes between Jew and Jew that would follow.

Traditionally, Jews were obliged to pray for their sovereign's wellbeing, and by the 1600s the Jews' political loyalties were expressed in a prayer known as *Hanoten Teshua*. Some versions of the prayer contained the phrase "May he [the sovereign] subdue nations under his feet and make his enemies fall before him. . . ."[8] As the eighteenth-century Bohemian Rabbi Samuel ben Nathan Ha-Levi Loew wrote in his supercommentary on the *Shulkhan Arukh*, Jews praying for the well-being of their king may not pray for his foreign enemies' downfall lest Jews elsewhere do the same, the result being an ineffectual and inappropriate prayer. (In Mishnah Berakhat 9:3, this is called a *tefilat shav*.) Thus prayers that God cast down the king's enemies must be limited to his foes within the kingdom.[9] This idea permeated a powerful sermon delivered on 19 October 1803 by Rabbi Isaac Luria at London's Bevis Marks Synagogue, as England faced the threat of a French invasion. Acknowledging that French Jews, being loyal to their sovereign, were praying for his well-being and the success of his troops, Luria asks, "Is it probable then, nay possible, for brethren in one common state of affliction to court a measure that would pierce their own bowels at every stroke their weapons plunged into the entrails of their same brotherhood?"[10] Jews in enemy lands, Luria claims, are praying for their armies, not for our defeat. Surely continental Jewry would not pray for Britain's downfall, which would damage the global commercial economy in which Jews are intertwined and upon which they are dependent: "on the tranquillity and security of these favoured kingdoms depends not only our preservation, but likewise that of the greater part of our brethren elsewhere."[11] Luria was struggling with conflicting supplications for the application of divine power, but his dilemma became vastly more complex once Jews began to fight in rival armies.

Jews in France were subject to the revolutionary government's *levée en masse* of 1793, five years after they were first conscripted into the army of the Habsburg Empire, which was soon at war with France. In 1806, Jews in Prussia began to volunteer in the fight against Napoleon. For the first time in history, Jewish leaders had to acknowledge and think through the consequences of Jews fighting in rival armies. The first response was that this situation was painful yet indicative of the Jews' overwhelming love of their homelands and worthiness for emancipation. The yearning for integration into the *patrie*, and acceptance by it, led to the famous declaration by the 1806 Assembly of Notables about the military spirit of the Jews of France:

> The love of country is in the heart of the Jews a sentiment so natural, so powerful, and so consonant to their religious opinions, that a French Jew considers himself in England, as among strangers, although he may be among Jews; and the case is the same with English Jews in France. To such a pitch is this sentiment carried among them, that during the last war, French Jews have been seen fighting desperately against other Jews, the subjects of countries then at war with France. Many of them are

covered with honorable wounds, and others have obtained, in the field of honor, the noble rewards of bravery.[12]

The Assembly of Notables' declaration aside, during the revolutionary era the problem of Jews fighting each other did not receive explicit attention in rabbinical sermons and other Jewish texts. But perhaps we can detect an indirect sign of the Jews' situation in the differences between Jewish and Gentile patriotic discourse in Napoleonic Germany. Even Jews who did serve as volunteers appear not to have been attracted to the cult of German military masculinity that originated in the teachings of Father Jahn and was disseminated by Prussian officials, eager to harness the fighting power of the peasantry by equating the nation with the family, and the soldier's fight for German liberation with the paterfamilias protecting his wife and children. One looks in vain for Jewish statements at the time equating physical fitness with the emergence, survival, and triumph of the German nation. Whereas German patriots waxed lyrical about the German fatherland and excoriated the degenerate and brutal mores of the regicidal French, Jewish discourse on military mobilization was tied to the rational value of service to the state.[13]

This muted or neutral tone was present in rabbinical sermons from the period, not only in Germany but also in Great Britain. British sermons of the early 1800s rarely vilified the enemy. They did not refrain from detailing the horrors of war, and they acknowledged that all combatants were praying, and beholden, to the same God.[14] I have not found a rabbinic equivalent during the Napoleonic wars of the language of Spanish clergy who, when justifying the killing of French Catholics by guerrilla insurgents against Napoleon, called the French "former Christians and modern heretics" and "wild animals."[15]

Notions of masculinity are not static, and militarism made few inroads into middle-class society in Europe until well after 1850. Some scholars have argued that German-Jewish bourgeois men were particularly likely to retain the gentle form of masculinity that was popular in the early nineteenth century well into later decades. Liberal rabbis embraced the feminine as the ultimate source of virtue and devotion, and the Viennese rabbi Adolph Jellinek not only asserted Jewish ethical superiority over Christians but attributed that superiority to the Jews' feminine nature.[16] He turned the common Christian negative stereotype of Jewish men as feminine on its head and transformed it into a source of pride.

On top of this gentle masculinity, Jews often displayed a particular sensitivity to the common divinity worshipped by all nations and the suffering endured by all sides in a conflict. These sensitivities derived directly from the ties linking Jews across national boundaries and first became manifest during the 1848 revolutions. Let us consider two pieces published by Ludwig Philippson, the renowned rabbi and editor of the *Allgemeine Zeitung des Judentums*, during the height of the 1848–49 revolutions. In a sermon delivered during Passover of 1848, Philippson vociferously denied that Jews comprise a corporate body among the nations; Jews in France are French, and their coreligionists in Germany are Germans. "Should two nations enter into a struggle today, we do not ask, 'Are there Jews in the enemy army?' No, we fight against them."[17] Ten months later Philippson turned again to this theme, asserting that throughout the vast bulk of their history the Jews have lived in diaspora. The Jews' enemies accuse of them of forming a mighty cabal, but "What are we? A scattered, powerless mass without force or energy." And the proof that Jews do not form a united mass is the diversity of Jewish political affiliations within countries and the presence of Jews on all sides of military conflicts between countries: "In the battle camps of fighting nations there are now frequently Jews standing as enemies against each other, and not hesitating, as brave soldiers, to engage in armed conflict against themselves."[18]

Philippson's remarks bespeak an ongoing sense of Jewish commonality, if not solidarity, a sense expressed far more pointedly by his newspaper's correspondent in Pest. Writing in the spring of 1849, the correspondent observed that Jews combine aspects of nation, religion, and ethnic community (*Stamm*): "The solidarity of the Jews, which has played such a great, albeit in former times natural role, still exists, and now where Jews find themselves in two opposed, fighting camps, it will be always felt in the one when Jews play a role in the other camp."[19] There is a pathetic note in the correspondent's plea for Gentiles to accept Jews based on the sacrifices they are willing to make for their homelands:

There stands the army of the Croatian viceroy, in which there are Jews enough present as fighters; there lies Croatia, in which stand Croatian Jews in the National Guard, ready to defend against the invading foe. And here there stream thousands of Jews into the Hungarian camp, brought together under the *levée en masse*, who observe neither sabbath nor holiday nor dietary laws. They have forgotten that they were scornfully driven out of the National Guards; they do not think that only a few weeks ago they were fallen upon, plundered, persecuted; they do not remember, that only a little while ago rights were given to them and then taken away. The fatherland is in danger, freedom is threatened—and they struggle forward to fight, to battle, to defend, to die. Then will the scales fall from your eyes, o people? Then will prejudice be wiped from your hearts? Do you still say that we are a separate nation, when, in the two hostile camps Jews take up weapons against other Jews? Do you still say that Jews have and pursue special interests, when they have forgotten all but not the interests of the fatherland and of freedom?[20]

In this remarkable tirade, the Jews' suitability for inclusion is based on their willingness to fight on all sides of the revolutionary conflict—for Croatia, allied with the Habsburgs, against Hungary's struggle for independence; for the Hungarians as they sought to crush the independence movements of all peoples except themselves. The Jews' willingness to fight on any side, at any time, for any land that will accept them produces a disturbing image of a sort of mercenary who is paid in rights rather than money.

The revolutions of 1848 brought to the fore a number of motifs in Jewish consciousness that would be repeated and strengthened over time. First was Philippson's argument that the willingness of Jews to fight one another was the ultimate proof of Jewish assimilation. The more readily they fought, the more truly passive they were, passive in the sense that they submitted themselves fully to the bidding of their sovereign and no longer constituted a separate corporate body. This theme cropped up again during the Austro-Prussian War of 1866, which the *Allgemeine Zeitung des Judentums* described as a "double sorrow," a civil war, or *Brüderkrieg*, in which Germans were forced to kill other Germans and Jews faced off against their own coreligionists. Such was the price of emancipation, claimed the article's author, for although before the era of mass conscription Jews had formed a separate juridical entity in Europe, this corporate structure was now undone and Jews were fully integrated into their lands of residence.[21] Similar arguments appeared around every subsequent war of the nineteenth and early twentieth centuries, especially the Franco-Prussian War, where the sacrifices made by Jews on both sides were celebrated by Jews in not only bystander nations such as Britain but also the combatant nations themselves.[22]

In the Anglo-Boer War of 1899–1902 Jews fought on both sides (though far more for the British), each willing to pay the ultimate price for the British Empire or Boer republics. American-, German-, and French-Jewish sources all followed the war carefully, remarking on the heroism displayed by Jews on both sides. Even the *Jewish Chronicle*, which emphasized Anglo-Jewish contributions to the war effort, paid homage to Jews who fought for the Afrikaners.[23] *Les Archives Israélites* invoked the heroism of hundreds of Jewish volunteers in the Boer republics, shopkeepers taking up weapons against not only the British but also marauding "kaffirs" ("il y a le grand danger des nègres," the newspaper warned). The paper praised the Natal fusiliers Landsberg, Stichel, Abrahams, and Goldmens as well as the key role in the defense of Kimberley played by Colonel David Harris. (Harris, whom we encountered in chapter 2, was a professional soldier who two years before the war's outbreak had commanded an expedition in Paquana and been wounded in action. Harris was also a mining director at De Beers and president of the Kimberley Jewish community.) The main lesson of the war, according to the French-Jewish newspaper, was that Jews are "far from forming a bloc in politics or business but rather are divided into diverse camps according to their affinities and interests."[24]

The integration of traditional notions of Jewish passive suffering with modern patriotic sacrifice was especially notable in Russia, where prospects for emancipation were far less bright than in the west but where Jews had had a long and painful encounter with the military. Much more than the western Jewish press, the Hebrew newspapers produced in eastern Europe offered highly emotional and detailed descriptions of the wounds and disabilities suffered by Jews in battle. The imagery of death and disfigurement is invoked in order to demonstrate Jewish obedience to their sovereign, but it attests as well to a great wellspring of sorrow, anger, and even a repressed hostility toward the tsar and state that had deprived many a Jewish family of its loved ones. An article in *Ha-Tsefirah* in 1878, in the wake of the Russo-Turkish War, depicted the pain of:

> ... the myriad parents mourning their sons who fell in the field of battle on the shores of the Danube, and in the Balkan mountain passes and beyond the Caucasus Mountains, or were stricken with malignant disease resulting from air fouled by rotting bodies in terrible battles. There are thousands of groaning fathers amongst our Hebrew brethren, whose children of delight went forth hale and whole, filled with the verve of youth, to fulfill their duty to the sovereign, and did not return, or returned wounded with mortal blows, disfigured and shorn of limbs, to the heartbreak of their parents to see them suffer without remedy, and instead of their hope for a time when their children shall care for them in old age, the children become a burden to their parents and themselves, like men who cannot find a livelihood by labor with their own hands, and who envy those who already died by the arrow.[25]

Similarly, a long article of *Ha-Melitz* in 1901 offered the following stirring threnody, which invokes the sorry spectacle of Jews killing their brethren in battle as a sign of both love of country and a fundamentally passive acceptance of the political conditions of life in *galut*:

> Let not the readers think that we have come to recall the wars of our ancestors when they dwelled upon their land: [these wars] may be found in the sacred writings and in later writings and in the books of the generations until the exile of Israel from the Land of the Hart. For from then onward Israel did not stand in connection to war—commanded war or discretionary war for its holy land, the inheritance of its ancestors, but only obligatory wars for the new homeland [*moledetah ha-hadashah*] to which [Israel] had been exiled, to save [the homeland's] honor and to extend its border and on its behalf and on behalf of its government [Israel] spilled its blood like water on the high fields together with the other children of its land of birth [*mekhorato*]. And this is the sign— that more than once the Jew stood in the array [of battle] for his king and country, and he fired lethal bullets toward the heart of his brother, son of his people or even the son of his mother, who went forth girded

for the country where he dwelled, as a citizen and resident of it, as the leaders of the armies were aware in the days of the wars between Russia and Turkey, France and Crete (1854–56) in the Crimean Peninsula, between Germany and France (1870–1), and in the Balkan mountains (1877). And except for these obligatory wars, it did not occur to the Jews who preserved the laws of their faith to try to return to their land with an outstretched hand, but rather they would wait for salvation from the Lord as his prophets promised. And this became second nature to the Jews not to incite the Gentiles but rather to bear and tolerate all distress and restrictions and persecutions and comprehensive expulsion and not to come up with the strange thought in their heart to extend their own power to throw off the yoke that bore down upon their neck and to attempt with all their strength to come to terms with their enemies.[26]

The article's tone is not so much patriotic as it is nationalist, reflecting the newspaper's association with the early Zionist movement in Russia, and universalist, as it invokes the 1899 Hague Peace Conference and convention in order to associate the Jewish ethos with a yearning for global peace:

> There is no doubt that if God had had the hand of the Hebrews to turn the scales on its spiritual and intellectual power, it would first be lent to the league that was founded some years ago in Western Europe whose orientation is to negotiate piece between peoples and to influence their leaders not to declare wars of man against brother and to spill the blood of man without reason.

Such associations between Judaism and the pursuit of peace became increasingly common from the fin de siècle on through World War II, but throughout most of the 1800s public conversation among western Jews shunned outright pacifism in favor of a patriotism that was both active and passive: active in its embrace of military service and passive in its acceptance of the necessity of fratricide as the price of emancipation and citizenship.

The passive patriotism of Jews in central and western Europe was also nourished by cosmopolitan conceptions of Jewish political identity. This idea was nicely expressed by the scholar Samuel Spitzer in his booklet of 1869, *Das Heer- und Wehrgesetz der alten Israeliten im Vergleiche zu den in Ungarn-Österreich bestehenden diesfälligen Bestimmmungen.* He begins as follows: "The cosmpolitanism of the Jewish tribe is well recognized in scholarship."[27] Over the ages, Jews have lived throughout the globe and adapted with alacrity to every land, both physically and psychically. Spitzer approvingly quotes Vienna's celebrated rabbi Adolph Jellinek on the Jews' lack of a nationality and possession only of ethnic or, literally, "tribal" particularities (*Stammeseigenthümlichkeiten*). The crucial point in Spitzer's argument is that the Jews' exemplary cosmopolitanism is enabled by the universality of Jewish law and ethics. For example, he claims, the Hebrew Bible's laws of war adumbrate and are in perfect resonance with those of the Dual Monarchy.

Indeed, during the Austro-Prussian War, in which between ten and twenty thousand Jews fought for Austria, Habsburg rabbis delivered stirring sermons that were revealingly vague in the designation of the Jews' historic object of loyalty. For example, a sermon by the Bohemian rabbi Adolph Ehrentheil traces the long and glorious history of Jewish military service for empire, going back to the days of Justinian, when Jews combated the Goths and took part in the conquest of Naples under the command of the Thracian general Belisar. The Jew always fights for his homeland, whatever it might be:

> The Jewish soldier knows like any other how to bear arms; he knows how to use them bravely, when the fatherland calls, and he will not stray in cowardly fashion from the path toward death for the Fatherland, for when the voice of the patriarch Jacob says, "Judah, your brothers will praise you" (Gen. 49:8), it does not wish to encourage virtuous deeds only in peacetime, no![28]

Only toward the very end of the sermon is there a specific reference to the Austrian homeland, but Ehrentheil quickly moves on to a political message: that the Jews' death in battle should prove Jewish worthiness for equality, as opposed to mere toleration, in the fatherland. Similarly, a sermon by Adolph Jellinek in 1867 glorifies not the ancient Hebrew fighters of Eretz Israel but rather the Jews who fought for Alexander the Great, and who allegedly decided Julius Caesar's battle against the Egyptians. There is nary a mention of the Prussian enemy or the cause over which the war was fought. The sermon is replete with terrifying images of the horrors of war, whose saving grace is bringing the nations and creeds of the empire together in brotherhood.[29]

From 1870 onward, the counting and glorification of Jewish soldiers was part of a great apologetic project to demonstrate Jewish worthiness of emancipation and equality. This project produced sermons like the ones mentioned above, historical studies of Jewish volunteerism, and, above all else, attempts to count Jewish soldiers in armies and in wars. Ludwig Philippson's listing of every one of the 4,700 Jews who served the North German Confederation in the Franco-Prussian War was outdone by a massive, folio-size tome, published in Berlin in 1896, titled *The Jew as Soldier*. German Jewry's military prowess received the greatest amount of attention, as one might assume from a book published in Germany by a committee for defense against antisemitism. Yet country by country, the book lists the numbers of Jews in uniform in every nation in Europe as well as the United States. Jewish officers are listed individually. (The substantial numbers of Jewish officers in the United States, France, and Italy are striking, as is the involvement of Jews in colonial armies in Africa and Southeast Asia.) The reader is struck by the placement of lists, side by side, of Jews who fought against each other, or at least whose countries were frequently enemies. Herein, the Jew who dies for England lies alongside the Jew who dies for Russia, or for Prussia or France.[30]

Nor were German Jews unique in producing Herculean apologetic projects of this type. The long entry titled "Army" in the 1901–6 *Jewish Encyclopedia*, which we discussed in chapter 1, glorifies Jews who fought on behalf of medieval Christian and Muslim kings and commanders without noting that the Jews' lords were each other's sworn enemies. For the early modern period, the Jewish defense of Prague, ruled by the Habsburgs, against the Swedes in 1648 is seamlessly followed by the Jews' defense of Ofen, ruled by the Ottomans, against the Habsburgs in 1686. For the nineteenth and early twentieth centuries, the article proudly places Jews in the armies of both Napoleon and Wellington, the Union and the Confederacy in the American Civil War, and Afrikaners and British in the South African conflict that had barely ended when the encyclopedia was published. And as with the German folio volume discussed above, the article exulted in the military achievements of French

Jewry, which, as we saw in the previous chapter, was the most militarily oriented Jewish community in the world.

The military universalism to which I have been alluding reached its pinnacle in a lecture titled "L'esprit militaire des juifs," delivered, appropriately enough, during Hanukkah of 1903, by the chief rabbi of Belgium, Armand Bloch. Jumping across time and borders, Bloch claims that the Jewish soldier, regardless of where he lives, "gives testimony to the lofty and grand spirit of tolerance of Jews, who consider the first of their duties, even before that of religion, the obligation toward the homeland."[31] Here, as throughout the apologetic literature we have examined, the "homeland" is nonspecific. In 1914, the Florentine attorney Alfonso Pacifici noted this contradiction between patriotism and ethnoreligious solidarity. Writing of the ceremony, referred to in the previous chapter, where Captain Emanuele Pugliese was honored by *Il Vessillo Israelitico*, Pacifici entreats his readers:

> Let us think a little! This soldier of Italy has fought, has comported himself with valor . . . what then is this supplement of honor that these other soldiers of Italy did not have and that the Jew Pugliese is about to receive? Is it the *Italian* Pugliese or rather the *Jew* Pugliese who is being honored? Is it Italian patriotism or, yes, Jewish patriotism that he is about to perform at Turin on 7 June? . . . Here is the turning-over of the coin, the other side of the sword, which makes this act thoroughly *anti*-Jewish. . . . [This honor] stands for the homage rendered by the Jews to Jewish military valor. Yes, but military valor for whom? For Italy! Against whom? Turkey! And then tomorrow there could be, if there isn't already, in Turkey another Vessillo that will wish to offer another sword of honor to another captain of Mosaic faith, but this one Ottoman. And what will the other sword of honor mean? That one too is an homage to Jewish military honor. But for whom? For Turkey! And against whom? Against Italy![32]

Unlike Bloch, Pacifici saw this moment as an occasion for mourning, not celebration. The Jews formed a transnational community that was obligated to engage in fratricide in order to attain rights and acceptance.

Did this cosmopolitan patriotism stem from Jewish transnationality, that is, the presence of Jews in many lands, in constant communication, linked by blood, marriage, commercial partnerships, philanthropic and political organization, or, failing all those, the imagined community of *am yisrael*? And did cosmopolitan patriotism in turn militate against demonization of the enemy, as one's own coreligionists might be among its ranks?

In general, throughout the nineteenth century and until World War I, the answer to both questions was yes. During the Franco-Prussian War, Jews were acutely aware of the presence of their brethren on both sides of the conflict, an awareness implicitly reflected in a plaintive query in *L'Univers Israélite* in 1870, "Do the tears that flow in the German homeland sting less than ours, and are they not of the same weight in the balance of humanity?"[33] To be sure, during the war there were expressions of genuine animosity between French and German Jews, both in the field and on the home front and as far away as Los Angeles, where a brawl between French and German Jews broke out at a meeting of the local chapter of the Alliance Israélite Universelle (an organization founded in Paris in 1860 to promote and protect the rights and well-being of Jews worldwide).[34] In public conversation, though, rabbinic sermons, addresses, and newspaper articles by both French and German Jews trod a thin line between patriotic support for their homeland and denigration of the enemy country's leadership, on the one hand, and compassion for enemy civilians and combatants alike. Like other French citizens in Alsace-Lorraine, Jews who lived in the region often had familial and business connections across the border. German Jews were in a particular quandary because France was both Prussia's enemy and the Jews' historic emancipator. German-Jewish journalists engaged in analytical gymnastics to present the French as having betrayed the values of 1789 and Prussia as having internalized the spirit of human liberation.[35] No wonder rabbinic sermons in both countries frequently presented Judaism as committed to peace and yearned for a quick end to the fighting.

Later in the century, eastern European Jewish newspapers were even more likely to distance Jews from the warrior ideal. According to *Ha-Tsefirah* in 1884, "Love of peace and hatred of war are stamped into the soul of Israel," whereas throughout the world "the Christians display greater lust and drive and persistence for military service than Jews . . . in the Christian soul the quality of heroism and a warlike tendency are dominant."[36] The article noted with approval the calls for an end to war issued by Jews in high positions in the west, men such as the German politician Eduard Lasker and Adolphe Frank, a leader of the Alliance Israélite Universelle. Fifteen years later, in 1899, a lead article in *Ha-Maggid*, written by its coeditor, Shimon Menachem Lazar, compared the Hague Peace Conference in May of that year with the Third Zionist Congress, which was held in August. Lazar described them both as components of the prophet Isaiah's vision of a universal peace accompanying the restoration of the Jews to Zion.[37]

Jewish pacifism had definite limits. Jewish antimilitarism melted away in the case of wars in which one of the sides was clearly associated with long-standing persecution of the Jews. During the Crimean War, European Jews solidly supported the alliance of the Ottoman Empire and western European countries against Russia. Russian Jews who had fled military service in their land of birth and taken refuge in the west volunteered for the Polish Cossack forces that fought on behalf of the Ottoman Empire.[38] A messianic nationalist named Armand Levy, a Catholic of partial Jewish origin who as an adult claimed his Jewish identity, strove to organize a Jewish legion within the Ottoman forces in the belief that it would promote Jewish emancipation:

> When the Jews will prove today that they are not only as intelligent as the others but also no less brave, our religious and civil emancipation will be sealed throughout the entire world. The only means of showing our racial bravery is through combat as a group, in Jewish regiments. It is very good that the Jews have acquitted themselves bravely at Sebastopol. But it would have been much better, had they done so in a separate unit. Our bravery would have resounded throughout the world. Much is being done in our century to emancipate individual Jews, but today we must work above all for our racial emancipation, if we do not want our race to disappear.[39]

Levy's scheme had the support of the Polish nationalist leader and bard Adam Mickiewicz and the prominent Jewish bankers Alphonse de Rothschild and Abraham Camondo. Levy went so far as to submit a formal proposal for a thousand-man Jewish legion to the Ottoman Ministry of War. Ottoman officials received the proposal coldly, as they feared that masses of armed Jews might congregate in Palestine and wrest it from Ottoman control.

This blatant attempt to form an international Jewish fighting force was unique for its time. But there were other conflicts where Jews had no qualms identifying a single enemy and expressed little sympathy for those who fought and died for the opposing side. In 1859, *L'Univers Is-raélite* solidly endorsed French support for Italy in its war of unification against Austria, for this conflict could strike a fatal blow against the papacy, the Jews' historic nemesis.[40] A similar clarity characterized global Jewish support for the American war against Spain in 1898, and the clear conscience with which central European Jews went to war against Russia in 1914, even though hundreds of thousands of Jews served in the Russian ranks. (In chapter 6, we shall observe even more morally unambiguous situations in the Spanish Civil War and World War II.)

Another situation where Jews were unlikely to preach pacifism was a war in which there could not possibly be Jews on the enemy side. In Europe, these wars were by definition limited to colonial conflicts. As we saw in the previous chapter, in France rabbis and activists unreservedly lauded the heroism of Jewish officers in skirmishes in Indochina and Africa, and they painted the natives in the darkest hues, both physically and psychologically. At the turn of the century, both the French and the Jewish press waxed enthusiastic about the thousand or more Jewish troops within the Russian brigades sent to China to suppress the Boxer Rebellion. The *Jewish Chronicle* claimed that Boxerism was a political evil akin to antisemitism.[41] The newspaper was more circumspect and respectful in its treatment of the rivals' claims in the Anglo-Boer War, in which Jews fought on both sides. In 1901, an article in the *Jewish Chronicle* claimed that Jews lacked the bloodlust that Gentiles brought into war, and some readers' letters endorsed this position, although one did claim that the Boers lacked humanity.[42]

Underlying the language of Jewish cosmopolitan patriotism was the reality of Jewish transnationality, a reality that translated into solidarity with Jews across enemy lines. Although Jewish apologetic literature about military service had an assimilatory intent, its affect was dissimilatory. During the Crimean War, when Britain and its western allies faced off against Russia, the Board of Deputies of British Jews urged an inquiry into the state of Russian and Polish Jewry, "for although we are at war with Russia, yet means may be devised for assisting them."[43] The U.S. Civil War, in which Jews within the same families wound up fighting for both the blue and the gray, attracted the attention of the German-Jewish press, while in Philadelphia in 1864 Rabbi David Einhorn spoke on the tragedy of Jews facing off against each other in the Prussian-Danish War.[44] The tone of Einhorn's and similar sermons is somber, yet underneath the pathos evoked by the spectacle of Jews in battle, never sure if they will smite one of their own, is an assertion of Jewish strength and particularity.

Here I return to Adolph Ehrentheil's sermon. In his citation of Jacob's deathbed blessing of Judah, Ehrentheil reproduces only the first phrase, leaving out the verse's conclusion: "Your hand shall be on your enemies' neck; Your father's sons shall bow down low to you." Many a listener would have known this celebrated verse by heart, along with its successor: "Judah is a lion's whelp; On prey, my son, have you grown. He crouches, lies down like a lion, like the king of beasts—who dare rouse him?" Was this elision intentional? Did Ehrentheil wish to avoid any hint of malice and bloodlust? Or was he, rather, afraid of slipping over that very fine line dividing Jewish valor in the service of the fatherland and the might of the Jewish people, to whom its many "brothers" shall bow? Indeed, in the European wars that followed, rabbis and activists routinely referred to fighting Jews as "new Maccabeans," imbued with vigor, righteousness, and zeal, simultaneously subordinate and equal to their Christian counterparts.

Another form of Jewish wartime transnationalism appears in a speech delivered in 1857 by Esdra Pontremoli (1818–88), a rabbi and educator who coedited Italian Jewry's flagship periodical, *L'Educatore Israelita*. The speech, titled "The Importance of the Sacred Tongue for Israelite Religious Nationality," is a panegyric to the Hebrew language, which Pontremoli sees as the glue that bonds the people of Israel together across space and time.[45] Hebrew preserves Jewish distinctiveness, fortifies Jews during their all too many times of sorrow, and engenders trust among Israelites scattered across the globe. The most striking example of this trust may be found in a time of war:

> Follow me, gentlemen, with your imaginations. Here, our pilgrim is a warrior fighting between his homeland's defense lines. The enemy who

stands face to face with him sees him as nothing but an enemy uniform, and he seizes him, and he strips him, and, abusing the barbarous laws of war, drags him away as his slave.

But why does the victor suddenly extend a hand to the vanquished and lead him amicably to his canteen? Who must these men then be? On the battlefield they are enemies, implacable enemies: after the victory, one should emerge as hangman and the other as his victim, but the sweet words of paternal recognition have sounded between them; the ruthless law of victory is mitigated; it is superseded by the dignity of man, piety, sympathy: these men have recognized each other as brothers in faith.[46]

The rabbi's language moves suddenly from the abstract to the concrete as he tells a story that would become a fixture in modern Jewish consciousness, a story whose peregrinations we shall soon follow, but which we now reproduce from its 1857 iteration:

These miracles are more than just a figment of our own imaginations; they occur in every country, almost every day. Who does not remember the moving case of the French-Jewish soldier brought down to us from the stories of the Napoleonic wars? This man is lying on the ground soaked in his own blood; the shadow of death already covers his eyes; he cries out in vain. The bloodthirsty victor stands over him, lays on him a foot ready to deliver the fatal blow. Steel flashes, the vanquished man falls to his knees, a cry rings out: *Shema Yisroel!* And what do we see now? We see the steel fall from the hand of the victor: we see that same victor reach down to the fallen soldier, dress his wound, and help him to his feet. The final cry of the dying believer rose from the throat of the wounded man. These men recognized each other in that moment: they were brothers in faith.[47]

The tale of a Jew about to kill, or who does kill, an enemy soldier, who turns out to be a Jew, is ubiquitous in Jewish conversation about war from the time of Pontremoli onward. Although the story is projected back to the Napoleonic wars, it did not appear at that time, nor during the revolutions of 1848, although the general phenomenon of Jews facing other Jews in battle was routinely invoked in patriotic sermons and newspaper articles. I believe that this story gained currency precisely as

Jewish emancipation took hold in western and central Europe, allowing Jews to assert more comfortably a transnational identity as well as new national attachments. During the Franco-Prussian War, French Jews fought heart and soul for *la patrie* and were devastated by the loss of the French-Jewish heartland of Alsace-Lorraine to the Prussians, while German Jews identified the war against France with the last battle for emancipation and exulted in Prussia's victory.[48] In this circumstance the story of the Jew who almost slays his brother in enemy uniform took on a new, complex form, reflecting the tension between cosmopolitan patriotism, international Jewish solidarity, and the demands of the Gentile state.

Consider a long, serialized story published in *L'Univers Israélite*, the official journal of the French-Jewish central consistory, in 1871, in the aftermath of the Franco-Prussian War. The setting is an old synagogue, at the beginning of a weekday *maariv*, in a countryside occupied by enemy forces, who have pillaged and plundered the terrain. An enemy soldier and a sickly young lad both enter; both are mourners and need to recite kaddish. The boy, we soon learn, is an orphan, his father killed in the recent conflict. The enemy Jewish soldier is deeply disturbed by this. After the prayers are over, the soldier lingers behind and approaches the rabbi, who greets him with a phrase from the biblical book of Joshua: "Are you one of us, although you are of the enemy?" (5:13). The Jewish soldier is conscience-stricken that his actions may have caused the death of other Jews:

> Your hand rips asunder those who are triply bound as brothers to you: by faith, by race, and by common misfortune. Alas! Those for whom I pray daily, though they dwell apart in all countries of the globe, and to whom I am inextricably bound by ancient struggles from the past and the promised future that we invoke in all our prayers; those among whom I would share joy and sorrow, fortune and misfortune, it is against them that I must act with fury, dip my sword in their blood, pitilessly increase their misery![49]

The rabbi responds with a parable about a king with two sons, both of them hateful, spiteful, and arrogant. The king banishes them; they eventually settle in separate lands and, in time, overcome their evil ways. But their countries go to war, and it is decided that each side will provide one champion; the two will fight to the death, with the fate of the war to be determined by the outcome of this contest. The brothers are chosen as champions, and they are overcome with love at seeing each other again yet also horror at what they have been compelled to do. They do fight, and one strikes a blow that causes the other to drop his weapon, but the first does not kill the second, but rather takes him in his arms. The war's fate is decided, and the two are reunited with their father.

We have here an imagined act of medieval single combat, in which warriors from opposing sides do battle while their men look on. In this case, the Jews as a collective take on the quality of the solitary champion. Liberal universalism is represented by an aristocratic cultural practice.[50] We learn from this story that when Jews are forced to fight each other, the fate of humanity rests on the struggle. Jews must fight with courage, scorn death, and strive to win glory for their "race," but they must also honor the enemy and prepare for the days when warfare shall cease. The rabbi says, "If in combat you prove yourself to be an intrepid warrior, you show yourself to be a true Israelite; if after battle you behave like an upstanding Israelite, you prove as well that you are a true soldier." The rabbi bids the soldier farewell, calling him "noble enemy."

In some ways, the internationalist message of this story is peculiarly French. There has been a long intellectual tradition in France, encompassing Saint-Simon, Comte, and Durkheim, of perceiving international engagement as serving national interests and internationalism as the highest form of patriotism.[51] Moreover, mid-nineteenth-century notions of "solidarity" held by French Jews envisioned international linkages among Jews not as an end in themselves so much as a means to the unification of all humanity. To borrow language from Benedict Anderson, whereas in previous centuries solidarity had connoted the corporate autonomy and liability of a bounded seriality (i.e., the Jews in a particular community), now the seriality becomes unbounded, borderless yet finite ("world Jewry," eventually blending into "humanity" as such).[52]

There were limits, however, to French internationalism, including its Jewish variant. In the wake of the Franco-Prussian War, French calls for *révanche*, no less than the exultant chauvinism of the triumphant Germans, eroded liberal faith in progress toward a reign of perpetual peace.

While legal theorists pondered the import of the combatants' failure to honor the terms of the recently established Geneva convention, Frenchmen called for German blood and the restoration of Alsace-Lorraine to *la patrie*. Major public figures in French-Jewish life such as the politician Adolphe Crémieux, the writer Alexandre Weill, and the politician Joseph Reinach looked forward eagerly to what Weill called "the blood of fire" in which France would "find her revenge."[53] Isidore Cahen, editor of *Les Archives Israélites*, was less bellicose but expressed deep concern for the future of Jews in Alsace-Lorraine, torn between increasingly implacable foes.[54]

There is a further problem with attributing a particularly French quality to the story of the rabbi and the enemy soldier. The story was a translation and expansion of a prose poem published in the *Israelitische Wochenschrift* in Magdeburg early in 1871. The poem itself had been mailed anonymously, possibly from Brno.[55] The fact that the national origin of a poem about war is murky and indeterminate nicely illustrates my point that Jewish patriotism could be as cosmopolitan as it was heartfelt. There was also an indubitably German-Jewish version of the story, in which two friends, one Christian and one Jewish, fight side by side for Prussia, and both are taken captive. The Christian is executed, but the Jew's' life is spared because as he is reciting the *Sh'ma Yisrael*, in what he believes are his final moments of life, a French-Jewish major passes by and orders that the soldier's life be spared. This story's origin may be unambiguous, but its political valence is not, as it could easily justify antisemitic accusations of Jewish tribal loyalty trumping duty to one's country.[56]

German-Jewish apologetic literature had no qualms boasting about the military prowess of French Jews, including those who went to war against their German coreligionists. In the midst of the war, *L'Univers Israélite* published an article, translated from a Jewish newspaper in Mainz, that enviously compared the laurels of French-Jewish officers with the "odious ingratitude" of Prussia, which conscripts the Jews but will not allow them to receive commissions.[57] Moreover, the author admits that when Napoleon invaded Germany, Jews saw the French as "liberators from a hard and unbearable yoke." Yet "none of these matters diminishes our patriotism. The love of our homeland is not only for us a civil duty, but also a religious obligation, completely independent of the level of rights that we are granted." It is the tragic fate of German Jewry to fight and die for the country, only to be ghettoized and oppressed after the war. The author concludes: "We are filled with sadness when foreign periodicals tell us, 'France is the bastion of civil and religious equality. In France there are Jewish colonels, chief justices, [government] ministers. Once France is conquered, the Prussian idea of the 'Christian state' will decree the banning of the Jews [la proscription des Juifs].'"

Throughout the war, German Jews simultaneously asserted not only German patriotism but also transnational Jewish solidarity and a particularistic religious identity. For the former, we have numerous examples from the German-Jewish press, which noted with satisfaction that Jewish soldiers served as guards for French-Jewish prisoners of war and that they attended religious services together.[58] The press took pride in the achievements of Adolphe Crémieux, France's minister of war and the first Jew to hold such a post in a modern state. Crémieux's long history of involvement on behalf of Jewish causes, dating back to the Damascus Affair of 1840, made him particularly worthy of admiration.[59] For the latter, we have a memoir, composed shortly after the war by a German-Jewish veteran, who at one point tells of marching with his unit in Champagne on a Shabbat morning. While the Christian soldiers sing German patriotic songs, the author and his Jewish mates (who conveniently amount to ten, the minimum required for a prayer quorum, or minyan), talk nostalgically among themselves about how if they were at home they would be praying in synagogue. A church clock strikes ten; the Jews remark that it is the time for reciting the *Ein Ke-eloheinu*, and, taking advantage of a lull in the singing by the Christian soldiers, one of the Jews begins to chant, and the others join in. "It is thus that this oriental melody, chanted by ten powerful voices, resounded across the plains of Champagne and the members of the semitic race affirmed loudly that we have no other savior but God!"[60] A German field officer, utterly unaware that what was being sung was a Hebrew hymn, scolds the Jews not to sing French songs. Esdra Pontremoli could not have been more pleased by this display of Jewish particularism in the form of recitation of the Hebrew liturgy.

Toward the end of the 1800s, the rise of Jewish nationalism brought new varieties of, and meaning to, the story of the Jewish soldier who almost kills, or does kill, his coreligionist on the field of battle. In the journalistic writings we have looked at so far, ostensibly patriotic tales reveal an undercurrent of Jewish transnational solidarity, but in Zionist writings the latter is unreservedly dominant. In 1897, the year of the First Zionist Congress, the Ottoman Empire and Greece fought a thirty-day war over rival claims to the island of Crete. In Odessa, home of the great Hebrew poet Shaul Tchernichovsky, a rumor that a Jew had slain his own brother in the Cretan war circulated among the city's bustling Jewish community and may have inspired Tchernichovsky to write his heart-wrenching poem *Bein ha-Metsarim*. The title, drawn from Lamentations 1:3, can be translated in many ways: "Between the Straits," "In Dire Straits," or, most literally, "Between the Narrow Places." The first is the most common, and it is the sense applied in Jewish tradition to the three weeks of mourning between the seventeenth day of the Hebrew month of Tammuz (the day when, according to tradition, the walls of Jerusalem were breached by the Romans in 70 CE) and the ninth day of Av (when the Jewish temple was destroyed). This phrase, redolent of inevitable national tragedy, is applied by the poet to the story of one Rabbi Shmuel of Salonika who has two sons: the firstborn, Joseph, lives with his parents and at the war's outbreak volunteers for the Ottoman army. The younger brother, Moshe, who is living and studying in France, volunteers for the Greek army.

The impending tragedy is all the greater for the fact that neither brother had to serve. Ottoman Jews were not conscripted until 1909, and Joseph's volunteering to fight was precisely the sort of patriotic gesture that Prussian Jews made during the Napoleonic wars. In both cases, Jews fought in gratitude for emancipation gained and hopes for further steps toward equality in the future. For the former, the holy writ of emancipation was the decree of 1812; for the latter, the *Tanzimat*, the era of reforms in the mid- nineteenth century. Yet also in both cases only a few hundred Jewish volunteers came forward, most Jews maintaining a traditional distance from the state and fear of military service.[61] For Tchernichovsky, Joseph is thus more a symbol of the destructive consequences of Jews in exile, divided among many lands and unable to call any of them truly home, than a critique of Ottoman Jewry per se. As to Moshe, the poet makes his motives for volunteering explicit, as he writes to his parents: "I am volunteering / With a band of my fellows from France we set forth, / For Greece, the eternal, our lives we shall lay down."[62] Like so many Europeans of the time, Moshe mistakenly identifies the rather shabby Greek kingdom with the glories of ancient Athens and the progenitors of western civilization.

In the poem's final section, the opposing armies meet in a valley in the shadow of Mount Othrys in the central Greek mainland. (Perhaps Tchernichovsky chose to set the battle here because Mount Othrys was, in Greek mythology, the base of the Titans during their war with the Olympian gods.) The valley is dark, rocky, almost barren of life. The predawn stillness is broken by an Ottoman cavalry charge on the encamped Greek forces. The Greeks battle valiantly but are crushed by the onslaught of horses, guns, and swords. The Turks push their way forward to the Greek flag, and one soldier leads the charge:

> Back under their flag they [the Greeks] were pressed, driven back;
> Enemy horsemen had them all surrounded
> To that bluest of flags—they pushed forth and aspired.
> Among them the one: upon sounding his thunder
> And tune of triumph his opponents were aghast;
> On his right, on his left as his fiery sword flew
> More than one had fallen wallowing in his blood,
> And near to the flag upon his horse he arrived,
> And with the flames of rage his pupils did shine.

But at that very moment "destroyed he then sank from his horse to the ground." The poem's final, deliberately incomplete line reads: "To the light of the shot the brothers recognized—." Moshe has killed his brother Joseph. The line refers to another case of estranged brothers, in Genesis 42:8, "For though Joseph recognized his brothers, they did not recognize him." In this poem, unlike the story in Genesis, each brother fully recognizes the other, but there is to be no familial reconciliation. In the biblical story, Joseph's brothers debate killing him, but instead throw him into a pit and then sell him into slavery. The Bible's Joseph lives, and rises to greatness in Pharaoh's court, but the poem's Joseph will never return.

Tchernichovsky's voice was uncommon, even among Zionists, most of whom dutifully joined their nation's armies in the First World War. The fear of slaying one's fellow Jew paled in comparison with the longing by German and Habsburg Jews to display loyalty and gratitude toward their homelands and to defeat the much-hated tsar. Yet Russian Zionists, and their counterparts in France and Britain, with whom Russia was allied, invoked loyalty and duty to the homeland and vilified Germany as militaristic and expansionist. If transnational solidarity among Zionists was threatened by the war, all the more so was this the case for assimilationist Jews possessed of a heartfelt patriotism that they were eager to demonstrate. The Jewish financial elite constituted yet another category: a group of individuals bound not by transnational Jewish solidarity, nor by national pride alone, but rather by a complex blend of collective attachments inflected by the global flow of capital, labor, and markets.

## Jews and War Finance: Between Patriotism and Internationalism

One of the most common tropes in modern antisemitism is the Jew as war profiteer—the banker who rakes in vast sums by financing all parties to a conflict after goading them to fight each other in the first place; the supplier of matériel to the army at inflated prices; the merchant who gouges the common man for scarce consumer goods in a war economy. These images are but extensions of common economic antisemitic stereotypes, which are in turn thinly veiled abstractions of the venerable phantasm of the Jew feasting on the blood of Christian youth. Revulsion against hateful stereotypes should not blind us to the sizable presence of Jews in finance and business who made money from war. By the nineteenth century, the Court Jew as he was known in early modern times no longer existed, but the long-standing connection between Jews and war finance continued, and even grew. Although perhaps less colorful than uniformed Jewish officers, Jews in sober business attire provided invaluable service to the state as they shuttled between their banks and the marmoreal edifices of government offices. The motivations behind their business activities were a blend of national patriotism, transnational Jewish solidarity, and, most important, international economic interests that knew no borders.

Financing wars and supplying armies are two historically linked yet distinct activities. In early modern central Europe, Court Jews provided both kinds of services for the region's constantly squabbling rulers. In the nineteenth century, the historic functions of the Court Jew were gradually divided as the provisioning of troops fell under the aegis of the state.[63] In much of continental Europe, new quartermaster corps took charge of the clothing and victualing of troops, though in Britain Jews continued to dominate the manufacture and sale of uniforms and boots.[64] In Russia, attempts at midcentury to incorporate provisioning services within its Military Commissariat failed miserably. After its humiliating performance in the Crimean War, the Russian government reluctantly went back to subcontracting military services, often to Jews. Stories about these services dot the memoirs of Pauline Wengeroff, a Lithuanian Jew whose father and grandfather built canals, roads, and military fortifications and provisioned the army on government contracts.[65]

In comparison with military purveying, the relationship between modern Jews and war finance was more durable, secure, and lucrative. Jews were prominently involved in an international banking system that derived considerable profit from lending funds directly to governments or packaging and selling government debt. Much of this activity took place during or in the wake of wars. During the American Civil War, the Union government's debt skyrocketed from $65 million to $3 billion, some 30 percent of the Union's gross domestic product. (Today such a percentage would be considered a sign of rock-solid financial stability.) Much of that debt was marketed in the form of government bonds in small denominations and bought by ordinary citizens. The Rothschilds had pioneered this practice in France during the 1830s, and the banker Joseph Seligman picked it up in the United States during the Civil War. After the war, the Seligmans, along with the bankers Mayer Lehman and Jacob Schiff, energetically marketed U.S. bonds as well as those of cash-strapped southern-state governments.[66]

Jewish bankers may have had patriotic feelings about the beneficiaries of their loans, but for the most part these were business transactions without a specific political agenda. During the Russo-Japanese War, although Russia was the most feared and hated country among Jews the world over, the English, French, German, and Austrian Rothschilds sold Russian bonds, as did the Mendelsohn and Bleichroeder banks in Germany. The Rothschilds did not lend directly to Russia during the war, but other Jewish bankers in Europe had no qualms about doing so, including Theodor Ritter von Taussig, president of an Austrian bank and member of the directorial board of Vienna's Jewish community.

There was no European equivalent to Jacob Schiff, the New York banker who prevailed upon his own firm of Kuhn, Loeb as well as upon Isaac Seligman not to lend funds to the tsarist regime. Instead, Schiff worked with a consortium of bankers to provide some $200 million in loans to Japan, whose expansionist designs upon the Far East did not trouble him, as they did not entail the persecution of Jews. During World War I, Schiff continued to support Japan even though its notorious twenty-one demands upon China would have reduced the Middle Kingdom to a Japanese protectorate. Similarly, the Seligmans encouraged the United States' intervention in Colombia in 1903 to carve out a quasi-independent Panama, where the Seligmans had invested in land along the prospective route of the canal.[67]

There were limits to Schiff's influence over his fellow bankers. During the Russo-Japanese War, Schiff was not able to persuade the Morgan bank not to lend to Russia, and at the outbreak of World War I his own bank did not heed his attempts to forestall loans to the Allies of which Russia would be a beneficiary. Schiff's German origins and strong pro-German sympathies played a part behind his reluctance to lend to the Allies, but in general his support for military conflict of any kind was highly selective, as peace, especially peace within Europe and between Europe and North America, was good for business. Schiff had been an antijingoist during the Spanish-American War and in the early twentieth century had been involved in a number of groups that advocated mediation between conflicting states as well as an international league of nations. When war broke out in 1914, Schiff was as reluctant to deal in German war bonds as he was supportive of American neutrality. Only in the wake of unrestricted submarine warfare by the Germans and the United States' entry into the war in 1917 did he fully support the Allied cause.[68]

Schiff's position was typical of Jewish financiers and industrialists leading up to and during the First World War. Gerson Bleichröder, one of the wealthiest bankers in imperial Germany and a confidant of Otto von Bismarck, exulted in Prussia's victory in 1871 over France, but in general he opposed war as harmful to his business interests. Over the years 1906–11, Max Warburg in Hamburg and Nathan Mayer Rothschild in London shared concerns over Germany's rising government debt caused by massive spending on its fleet of battleships. One of the most prescient, dire, insightful, and accurate predictions of the course of twentieth-century warfare was the work of a Polish-Jewish banker, Jan Bloch, whose conversion to Calvinism in no way diminished his identification with, and concern for, the Jewish communities of eastern Europe. In 1899, Bloch published a four-volume tome, *The Future of War in Its Technical, Economic and Political Relations*, which claimed that technological advances would doom future wars to be fought from entrenched positions, dragged out over years without a clear victor, ruinously expensive, and horrifically, massively lethal. By diminishing the security of collateral and the likelihood of repayment, war would drive up borrowing costs, forcing governments to finance the fighting through compulsory loans and printing money, both of which would lead to a devastating inflation.[69] Bloch may have inspired, and certainly took an active part in, the 1899 Hague disarmament conference that was convened by Nicholas II of Russia. (The tsar had not embraced pacifism; Russia was militarily less advanced than the other great powers, and so slowing down the drive toward conflagration was in the military's own interests.)

Bloch's views were hardly unique to Jews. In the early twentieth century, the English writer Norman Angell and the French socialist leader Jean Jaurès thought that international capital was a guarantor of world peace because investors from all over the globe held the bonds of one another's governments. In 1905, Alfred von Schlieffen, chief of the German military's General Staff, authored a notorious war scenario that called for a rapid German victory on two fronts (first the west, then the east) precisely because of the assumption that a prolonged war would wreak havoc on the German and international economy. Schlieffen's colleagues in Germany's political and military elite did not share his confidence that Germany could defeat France quickly or easily, and their private musings about the next war were almost as dark as those of Jan Bloch, but they could not bring themselves to adopt Bloch's conclusions that future wars must be avoided at all costs.[70]

Jews, who were heavily represented among the European and American financial elite, were particularly sensitive to the threat that a prolonged European war posed for the world economic order. During the crisis of July and August of 1914, the English and French Rothschilds fretted about the prospect of a war that could divide the great banking dynasty, and Max Warburg began to dump his shares in companies trading on the Vienna exchange. The Rothschilds feared that if governments printed up bonds to pay for war, existing bonds would plummet in value. (They were right: prices of consols, British government bonds, fell by more than 40 percent in England and France between 1914 and 1920, and the English Rothschilds lost half of their capital.) Baron Rothschild predicted that war would be a "calamity . . . greater than anything ever seen or known before."[71] He urged the *Times* to tone down the bellicosity of its editorials, only to be met with a sneer over this "dirty German-Jewish financial attempt to bully us into advocating neutrality."[72] Shortly after the outbreak of the war, the German-Jewish shipping magnate Albert Ballin watched despondently and helplessly while his merchant fleet sank to the bottom of the Atlantic.

War can be as profitable as it is destructive, and the German army's early conquests along the western and eastern fronts awakened the interest of German financiers and industrialists, Jews among them, in taking hold of the natural resources and labor markets of the conquered territories. Walther Rathenau, who inherited the directorship of the German conglomerate AEG from his father Emil, embodied all the contradictions of a patriot and strident nationalist who was also a farsighted businessman. Today, Rathenau is best known for an essay titled "Hear O Israel!" that he wrote in 1897. The essay is a scathing critique of German-Jewish behavior as well as a painful display of self-hatred and of a troubled soul. Yet this essay is but a drop in Rathenau's vast oeuvre of writings on technology, entrepreneurship, and politics, writings reflective less of any specifically Jewish cultural orientation than of the worldview of a director responsible for a vast, export-oriented business concern.[73]

As a youth carrying out his mandatory military service, Rathenau reveled in the splendor of his corporal's dress uniform (figure 4.1). Young Rathenau claimed to despise the army yet desperately wanted to be an officer. As he matured into an elegant, prepossessing adult, a master of essayistic prose as well as industrial management, Rathenau continued to oppose war in principle yet exult in Prussia's militaristic ethos. When war broke out in 1914, Rathenau wrote, "We must win, WE MUST! And yet we have no clear, absolute right to do so."[74] The following year, when he took the helm of AEG, Rathenau predicted that future wars would be won or lost based on the combatants' economic strength, which led him to the gloomy conclusion that Germany was bound to lose in a conflict with England. Spending a fortune on battleships and armaments, Rathenau warned, could not compensate for the limitations imposed on the German Empire by a rigid class rule that throttled economic growth. In 1913 Rathenau had called for a western European customs union that was far more predictive of the European Union of the post-1945 era than the rapacious German empires of the First and Second World Wars. His envisioned commercial and industrial union would "equal and perhaps surpass that of America, and within the league there would be no longer any backward or unproductive regions. At the same time the most potent cause of international hostility would be removed."[75]

Indeed, the First World War was hard on AEG: it lost its export market, which had accounted for a fifth of its sales, and half of its employees were in uniform by 1916. Yet Germany's conquests also offered promises of vast riches. Rathenau traded in his pacific dream of a pan-European customs union for an aggressive agenda involving Germany's forced acquisition of Belgian and French industry, an enforced common market within the zone of occupation, and a vast pool of forced laborers from Belgium and Poland. Throughout the war Rathenau remained torn between visions of AEG as the center of an imperial war economy based on conquest versus an international economic order promoting social and economic justice. He attempted gamely to reconcile the two in his directorship of the German government's War Matériel Department (Kriegsrohstoffabteilung, or KRA). Rathenau hoped that the KRA, which allocated raw materials to industries based on their commitments to use them for military purposes, would be a first step toward state socialism. Things didn't turn out that way, as the industrialists who invested in the KRA expected and received preferential treatment in the allocation of resources.[76]

Antisemites were wont to attribute Rathenau's schemes to allegedly "Jewish" motives and designs such as internationalism, socialism, rapacious capitalism, or, more simply, world domination. It is a fact, not an antisemitic fantasy, that Jews played vital roles in coordinating the allocation of raw materials during the First World War, not only in Germany but also in the United States. (The Wall Street speculator Bernard Baruch became chair of the United States' War Industries Board, which

Figure 4.1. Young Walther Rathenau in military dress uniform. *Courtesy of the Leo Baeck Institute, New York.*

set production quotas, allocated raw materials, and encouraged standardization of production methods.)[77] Jewish industrialists and financiers were, however, much less likely to condition their business dealings and economic worldview on Jewish transnational solidarity than on hard-nosed considerations of profit and loss, considerations that often militated in favor of global peace although they could just as easily endorse imperial conquest so long as its benefits outweighed its costs.

Patriotism and capitalist internationalism could coexist in the heart of an industrialist just as easily as patriotism and socialist internationalism flourished in the multinational, polyglot empires of central and eastern Europe before the First World War. Once war began, most of Europe's citizens fell behind their countries' respective flags, and internationalism evaporated in the heat of battle. For the Jewish masses, however, whether on the front line or on the home front, transnational Jewish solidarity retained a visceral power, often competing with patriotic sentiments that were no less sincere.

## World War I: The End or Pinnacle of Jewish Transnationalism?

Earlier we saw that the traditional Jewish prayer for the government refers only in the vaguest terms to the ruler's enemies, lest Jews in different lands place themselves in the compromising position of praying for the downfall of each other's sovereign. During World War I, the United Kingdom's official prayer book for Jewish soldiers and sailors maintained the traditional Hebrew wording, and the English rendition called upon God to "make His enemies fall before him."[78] A German wartime version, however, went much further; the Hebrew text calls for God, "in wrath and fury," to "destroy them when they go toward us; each time, cause our foes to surrender to us. And with trembling and shaking they shall fall. . . . Weaken their army and swallow up their designs, and bring them and their ships down to the depths of the sea."[79] (The reference is possibly twofold: Moses' "Song of the Sea" in Exodus 15 and Germany's ruthless practice of submarine warfare.)

Vigorous, even chauvinistic, support for the war came from a wide swath of the German-Jewish intelligentsia. As for urban and bourgeois Germans as a whole, the greatest enthusiasm was expressed at the beginning, and by 1916 it had largely evaporated. But during the war's first months Victor Klemperer, whose World War II diary decried the gratuitous hatred inherent in Nazism, prayed that for every German soldier who fell in battle, an English civilian would be killed by a zeppelin.[80] Writer Arnold Zweig, who would claim in the 1920s that he was a pacifist from the outbreak of the war, actually favored it at first.[81] At the tender age of nineteen, the future Zionist leader Nahum Goldmann penned a propaganda brochure on the splendors of German militarism. Even more egregiously nationalistic was the poet Ernst Lissauer, author of the notorious 1914 "Hate Song against England." (Rather than endearing himself to German patriots, Lissauer was accused of possessing a pathological and uniquely Jewish strain of misanthropy.)[82] Franz Rosenzweig, while serving on the Macedonian front, penned essays celebrating Germany's geopolitical mission to create a vast *Mitteleuropäisches* empire "from Antwerp over Strasburg towards Trieste, Salonika, Cyprus, Suez."[83] The philosopher Martin Buber accused Belgian women of defiling German corpses and claimed that the war would unite Germans and Jews in their great mission to civilize the Middle East. "Incipit vita nuova," wrote Buber upon the outbreak of the war, jarringly citing Dante's words upon first sighting Beatrice.[84]

Meanwhile, in France, rabbinic sermons painted the German foe in the blackest of hues, associating it with Amalek, even with Satan. In 1916, *L'Univers Israélite* produced a powerful parody of the biblical creation story, with a "good old German god, an officer of the hussars of death, with handlebar moustache and a sabre, [who] called out one day, Let the depths be, and there were depths. He created in turn poison gas to kill men, firebombs to destroy houses, zeppelins and the 420 cannon to bombard open cities. And seeing that his work was evil, he was pleased." This evil god then sets out an inverted Decalogue, commanding men to steal, rape, murder, and covet.[85]

Jewish attitudes toward the war and willingness to serve were, however, complicated, contingent, and subject to change over time. For the most part, businessmen and scientists of Jewish origin thought of the war less as a redemptive, world-historical moment than as a vast challenge that they, as loyal German citizens, were obliged to meet. The chemist Fritz Haber, a convert to Christianity, devoted himself heart and soul to the war effort; he directed the army's chemical warfare program, and after the war he labored futilely to extract gold from the sea so that Germany could make reparation payments.[86] Walther Rathenau, who marshaled raw materials from the Reich and the conquered territories, was from the war's beginning highly ambivalent about Germany's war aims and chances for victory.[87] The Jewish upper stratum tended less to chauvinism than to pragmatism. Their enthusiasm for the war stemmed from a desire not so much to slay the enemy as to demonstrate Jewish worthiness for acceptance by German society.[88]

Eastern European Jewish immigrants in both the United Kingdom and France were willing to fight for the latter but not the former. In Great Britain there were some thirty thousand young Jewish men who had been born in Russia and were collectively exempt from conscription. They vigorously resisted calls for conscription by Anglo-Jewish leaders, refusing to fight on behalf of the oppressive tsar and to kill fellow Jews from the Triple Alliance.[89] In France, on the other hand, eastern European immigrant Jews, although banned as noncitizens from serving in the French army, streamed to volunteer for the French Foreign Legion. The Jewish immigrants in France were, like their brethren in England, largely socialist and antimilitarist, yet in France the immigrants supported the war as a struggle against "autocratic and feudal" Germany and Austria, which were accused of being "the main forces of imperialism in the world."[90] The embarrassing truth that France and its ally England were the world's greatest imperial powers, and that both were allied with the much-hated Russia, was obscured. In France, Jewish immigrants were captivated by the national myth of France as the birthplace of revolution. While in England it was the established Anglo-Jews who invoked the ancient Maccabean spirit, in France this rhetoric came from Yiddish-speaking volunteers. Jewish patriotism ebbed and flowed depending on the specific circumstances and interests of particular Jewish communities.

Many Jews did not wish to fight, but few were principled pacifists. There were a few extraordinary figures like Aharon Shmuel Tamares (1869–1931), a rabbi from Brest-Litovsk who at the turn of the century flirted with Zionism but withdrew in revulsion against the thought of Jews becoming like other nations and lifting up a sword against their fellow men. "How terrible is that corruption," he wrote, "which would result from any evil example set by 'Jacob, selected by God, Israel, His special treasure,' were he also to adopt the faith of Esau."[91] Tamares remained a pacifist throughout the rest of his life, but most Jews, leaders and rank and file alike, were more flexible.

In the United States, many Jews were uneasy about the war or opposed it outright. Among middle-class Jews, women took the lead in promoting pacifism. The president of the National Council of Jewish Women, Janet Harris, shunned any charitable activity that smacked of military preparedness, yet after the United States' entry into the war in April of

1917, many NCJW activists plunged into philanthropic work on behalf of the war effort.[92] Jewish radicals of both genders staunchly opposed the war until Russia's March revolution, which overthrew the despised tsar and installed a social democratic government. American-Jewish socialist organizations did not, however, immediately endorse America's declaration of war in the following month, as they clung to hopes for an immediate peace without losses or annexations by any party. For many American-Jewish radicals, the November 1917 Bolshevik Revolution was a betrayal of their democratic ideals, but in the wake of the punitive Treaty of Brest-Litovsk that Germany imposed upon Russia the following March, all but the most hardened Jewish radicals endorsed the war effort in the hopes that it would bring down not only the German invaders of Russia but also the Bolsheviks themselves.[93] Although there was a good deal of antisemitic grumbling about Jewish draft dodging, and many Jewish recent immigrants claimed to have fled Russia for the New World to avoid the draft, district draft boards in heavily Jewish neighborhoods in major East Coast cities had little trouble filling their quotas. (The social work activist Lillian Wald, who founded the Henry Street Settlement in New York, allowed recruiting stations to operate on the premises even though she personally opposed the war.)[94]

During the interwar period, peace activism would become popular throughout the western world, and it found staunch advocates among liberal rabbis and Jewish women active in organizations such as the Women's International League for Peace and Freedom.[95] Peace activists often spoke of themselves as pacifists, but this was a capacious term that could mean everything from a principled rejection of force under any circumstance to a cautious acceptance of the legitimacy of purely defensive wars. By the end of the 1930s all but a handful of Jewish public figures believed that the line between unjust and just war had been crossed, and, as we will see in chapter 6, in World War II Jews were far less likely than Christians to be conscientious objectors.

In World War I, for Jews living in Germany and Austria-Hungary "revenge for Kishinev" provided the justification for a war that pitted Jew against Jew. Still, a painful cognitive and emotional dissonance remained. As the German Zionist Andras Moritz Goldstein wrote in 1916, "in order to fight we must forget that Israel is a people—if not . . . it would be impossible for us to let off a single shot."[96] The year before, the liberal German-Jewish newspaper *Israelitisches Familienblatt* claimed straightforwardly that the Jews' transnational connections impeded chauvinism. The Jew who fights on the side of the enemy is our enemy, yet conversely, the article argued, respect for one's fellow Jews compels respect for the enemy.[97]

Jews stood out for their international linkages, be they professional or personal. These ties crossed enemy lines and were preserved by philanthropic activity on behalf of Jewish civilians in eastern Europe and prisoners of war in the various belligerent countries. It was the responsibility of the belligerent state governments to negotiate proper care for their soldiers who had been taken prisoner by the enemy. The numbers were staggering; over the course of the war more than eight million soldiers were taken prisoner, half of them Russian POWs in Germany and Austria-Hungary. (At least thirty thousand Russian-Jewish POWs were held in Germany.) Governments of the belligerent states worked with neutral governments, the Red Cross, and the YMCA to provide goods and health care for their citizens in captivity, but Jews took, and were allowed to take, the initiative in caring for their own. Jewish POWs "consistently received assistance from co-religionists in Galicia and Russia"; Russian-Jewish families regularly invited Jewish POWs to their homes for the Sabbath and holidays.[98]

Three Russian-Jewish interned aliens in Berlin initiated a scheme to provide reading materials in Yiddish and Hebrew to Germany's Russian-Jewish prisoners. (The Jewish POWs were usually placed in specific camps, given the German practice of separating POWs by ethnicity. There were special camps with kosher kitchens for Orthodox Jews, and two camps for Muslims—one for Tatars and one for North Africans.) An international Committee for the Provision of Jewish and Hebrew Literature for Russian-Jewish Prisoners of War was established in July of 1917 under the protection of the Spanish embassy in Berlin.[99] Technically, only the eighty thousand Jews with Russian nationality living in Germany were solicited for donations, but the committee's chair, Rabbi Meir Hildesheimer, was a German subject, and it is doubtful that he refused any assistance from other German Jews. Whereas German Christians were asked to help German POWs languishing in Russia, Jews in Germany assisted Russian Jews in Germany itself. Ironically, the

Jews' lack of a sovereign state limited their ability to truly nationalize within their own homelands, as there was no government they could turn to to spearhead the welfare work done by Jewish transnational organizations. Unlike the Red Cross, which was an explicitly international organization that stood above all states, Jewish wartime philanthropy was anchored within specific states and forged bonds between them.

Jewish writers and activists were bedeviled by the impossibility of reconciling patriotism with collective solidarity. The conflation and confusion of the two led to some revealing statements. The *Jewish Chronicle* praised the bravery of Jewish soldiers in all the combatant nations and, in 1916, proffered a single Jewish casualty count of sixty thousand for the Entente and Triple Alliance combined. The official organ of the stridently patriotic Central Association of German Citizens of the Jewish Faith proclaimed that "Jewry had deputized an army of over 800,000 soldiers"—an underestimation of the total number of Jews in uniform but, more important, a presentation of Jewish soldiers throughout the world as a single bloc.[100]

Never before in history had so many Jews been mobilized for battle—over one million in the Allied forces and some 450,000 among the armies of the Central Powers. Jews made up about 5 percent of Russia's armed forces (650,000 out of 12 million) and 4 percent of Austria-Hungary's (320,000 out of 7.8 million.) (Only a fraction of the men in any army were actually in combat units, and once in combat men fought for only a few weeks at a time, but the numbers do demonstrate that Jews were a significant component of the two states' armies.) Russia and the Dual Monarchy, along with its German ally, clashed along the eastern front, which ran through the Pale of Settlement and Habsburg Galicia, home to millions of Jews. As the lines of battle seesawed back and forth, Jewish civilians were subject to expulsion, persecution, and atrocities, particularly at the hands of Russian forces. Antisemitic fantasies of Jewish treachery prompted Jews to create rumors of their own, rumors filled with hope as well as fear and desperation. While Russians accused Jews of having secret telephones with which they communicated with the enemy, Jewish versions of the rumor identified the true perpetrators as Poles disguised as Jews.

A more popular and enduring rumor, given the substantial number of Jews fighting on the eastern front as well as the turbulent, fearful atmosphere in the zones of occupation, revived the old myth of the Jew who almost slays, or does slay, his coreligionist in battle. Its most famous versions were documented by the Yiddish writer S. Ansky, who spent the war years gathering and distributing relief throughout the Russian Pale of Settlement and Russian-occupied Galicia. In St. Petersburg, Ansky heard of a Jew who had bayoneted a soldier, who, just before expiring, gasped the *Sh'ma*. His killer, so the story went, went mad. In Kiev, he was told that a Jew had killed another, who had produced a pouch of money and entrusted it to his killer to give to his widow and orphaned children. At a military hospital in Moscow, a soldier avowed that he had almost killed another Jew but had withdrawn his bayonet at the last second and had taken the Jew prisoner. A few weeks later, Ansky ran into the same soldier, who changed his story completely, now saying he had killed the other man, riffled through his belongings, and found a pouch containing *tefillin*. Ansky assumed that the man was telling unconscious lies, acting out his emotional anguish about fighting in general and the prospect of killing a fellow Jew in particular.[101]

Such stories were less common along the western front, perhaps because far fewer of those who fought there were Jews. (The French and British armies fielded over 15 million soldiers, of whom some 100,000 were Jews.) In 2003, the daughter of a German-Jewish veteran claimed that her father had been deeply scarred by having killed a fellow Jew in battle and often spoke of it.[102] It is of course possible that this happened, although it is far more likely that the same psychological mechanisms that Ansky saw at work on the eastern front were present in the west as well. Intriguingly, I have not found a single documented case of a Jew killing another Jew in battle and then feeling remorse, or going mad, or vowing to return the fallen Jew's belongings to his bereaved family. I did, however, come across a credible story of something quite different—a Jew who blithely killed an enemy coreligionist. On 2 July 1915, the *Jewish Chronicle* published a letter from a Sergeant Major V. Rathbone of the King Edward's Horses, to his brother, a Mr. M. Rathbone:

> I was up and down the trenches for twenty-four hours, with one hour's rest. We captured a German officer, Lieut. Max Seller, of a Bavarian Cavalry Regiment. He and about fifty men were attacking us with hand

bombs and the officer was bayonetted on the parapet. I helped to bury him with our own casualties. He was a Jew so I had the services altered by the Chaplain. Possibly his people might be glad to know, and if you asked the *Jewish Chronicle* and the *Jewish World* to mention it they might learn of it. He was a plucky chap and our fellows could not help expressing admiration at his effort to bomb us.[103]

Here, we have real names, a concrete situation, and an at-best curt nod to Jewish solidarity, a far cry from the high melodrama of the literary works and rumors we have discussed thus far. Yet this is an isolated incident, whereas the rumors and stories of the Jew who slays his brother doggedly accompanied Jews in uniform from the mid-nineteenth century through the Great War.

These stories communicate a sentiment embodied in the fortunate tale of Chaim Berezin, a Ukrainian-Jewish immigrant to the United States who enrolled in the Thirty-ninth Fusiliers and served as a musician in General Allenby's army, which conquered Palestine in 1917 and 1918. In his memoirs, composed immediately after the war, Berezin writes of an encounter with German and Turkish prisoners of war, one of whom turned out to be his next-door neighbor from childhood:

> As soon as I heard his voice, I screamed out at the top of my lungs, "Meylikhzon! Oh my friend Meylikhzon! A Turkish officer! Just a day ago, my enemy, I shot at him and perhaps he at me. And now we are friends again. Oh great God! The Jewish people, [what] a cursed people."

Meylikhzon claims that in service to the sultan he had himself taken three Jewish prisoners of war from the Thirty-eighth Battalion of Royal Fusiliers, the North American and British component of the Jewish Legions.[104]

Both Chaim Berezin and his boyhood friend Meylikhzon went to war out of a sense of obligation, not staunch Russian or Ottoman patriotism. The situation was very different for European Jews, particularly in the west, as the bonds between German and French Jews remained a source of pain, envy, and confused identity. In the published diary of the German Jew Julius Marx, an entry from September 1916 tells of his conversation with a French farmer, whose home Marx and some companions briefly requisitioned for High Holiday prayers. Marx asks the farmer what he thinks they are praying for:

> "I think, for the German fatherland, as the French Jews [pray] for France."
> "Do you know many French Jews?"
> "Not many. But my company commander back then, he was a Jew. No officer in the regiment was as beloved as he. Now he is a general and fighting somewhere for poor France."[105]

Eight months later, Marx visits an old Jewish acquaintance in Valenciennes. The French Jew asks Marx why he is not yet an officer. Marx replies rather defensively that he does not wish to be one but that there are plenty of German-Jewish officers. His French interlocutor is skeptical. He tells Marx about having quartered German soldiers in his home, not letting on that he was Jewish, and goading them to speak their mind about the Jews. The French Jew tells Marx that he was happy to hear how intolerant, thick-headed, and mean-spirited the German soldiers were, because such people, more concerned with rank and class than with faith and patriotism, must lose the war. Seeking the last word, Marx invokes the Dreyfus Affair, which, he claims, could not have happened in Germany. "'If you lose the war,' responds the Frenchman—'and you will lose it—then Germany will be ripe for such affairs.'"[106]

By jotting these conversations down in his diary, Marx was reproducing a long-standing French-Jewish discourse of pity and condescension toward German Jews for being excluded from the German officer corps and the status it conferred. These feelings were reproduced on a global scale during the interwar period, when Jewish veterans the world over joined forces to condemn the persecution of German-Jewish veterans under the Nazi regime.

## Jewish Veterans as a Transnational Community

Jewish veterans' organizations, founded in various lands from the early 1920s through the mid-1930s, formed an interlocking framework. On one level, they were an extension of the general international veterans' movement that organized fighters from formerly combatant nations to advance both their own economic interests and a broader pacifist agenda. The Paris-based Association Républicaine des Anciens Combattants, founded in 1919, had a broad pacifist agenda and communist orientation. (It was also idealistically internationalist; at the association's founding congress in 1920, the British delegation proposed that all future meetings be held in Esperanto.) This association did not last long, but the politically more moderate Fraternité Interaliée des Anciens Combattants, founded in 1920, represented all the major French, British, Italian, and American veterans' organizations, with a combined membership of over eight million. (Despite the FIAC's internationalist flavor, old national rivalries died hard; the French veterans steadfastly prevented their German counterparts from joining.)[107]

Similarly, the Jewish veterans' organizations maintained extensive personal and institutional contacts. In 1925, a memorial service in Paris for the French-Jewish war dead, especially those in the Foreign Legion who had died at the battle of Carency, received favorable attention in *Der Schild*, the newspaper of the German Reichsbund jüdischer Frontsoldaten (RjF).[108] As a rule, the sundry Jewish veterans' organizations' journals reported on the others' activities. When the Austrian Bund jüdischer Frontsoldaten (BjF) was founded in 1935, it received warm greetings from Jewish veterans' organizations in Bulgaria, Hungary, Latvia, Lithuania, Poland, and the United States.[109] At the first international conference of Jewish veterans' organizations, held in Paris in 1935 and representing some 400,000 individuals, the assembled delegates vowed, as their counterparts did in general veterans' groups such as the British Legion, to strive for understanding among nations and world peace while also lobbying for their members' economic interests.

There was a distinctive quality, however, to the Jewish veterans' organizations. In addition to appealing to the common war experience to promote international reconciliation, the Jewish veterans asserted their military honor. In 1925, *Der Schild* printed a major article, based on a recently published piece in the *American Jewish Year Book*, on Jews in the armies of the Entente. Paying particular attention to Jews in Britain and its empire, the German article expressed pride in Anglo-Jewish valor, which demonstrated that British Jews richly deserved the civil equality that had been bestowed upon them in the previous centuries. British Jewry, the newspaper claimed, did honor "to the entire Jewish collective

[*Gemeinschaft*]," employing a term with undeniably transnational, albeit ethnically specific, connotations. (The article also implicitly linked Anglo-Saxon Jewry to a German point of origin by pointing out that Sir John Monash, commander in chief of the Australian Expeditionary Force in the war, was the nephew of the pioneering historian Heinrich Graetz.)[110]

The peculiar features of the Jewish international veterans' movement became even more evident after the Nazi seizure of power in Germany. The absence of the RjF from the 1935 world conference of Jewish veterans had nothing to do with old resentments held against Germans by other national organizations of Jewish veterans, but rather the RjF's forced dissolution under the Nazi regime. The persecution of German Jewry, and in particular the fallen honor of Germany's Jewish veterans, was a central topic at the conference. The Austrian BjF, supported by other Jewish veterans' organizations, expressed solidarity with its German counterparts over Nazi propaganda minister Josef Goebbels' decree that Jewish names were to be expunged from Germany's war memorials. The BjF went so far as to propose that the international Jewish veteran community establish in Palestine a village for the orphans of the twelve thousand German-Jewish soldiers who had died in military service during the war. Although this gesture was partly philanthropic, it was overwhelmingly commemorative and apologetic:

> This village, a monument to the fallen, a refuge for their persecuted children, will become, in its name and in the fact of its establishment by Jewish soldiers of the entire world, a monument to the eternal disgrace of this Germany, which rewards life sacrifice with perfidy.[111]

The twelve thousand German-Jewish war dead were sanctified in the eyes of Jewish veterans the world over. Jews who died for one fatherland died for them all, and if the deaths of Jewish soldiers in one land were to be held of little account, then the Jewish fallen everywhere would have made the ultimate sacrifice for naught. In this spirit, the second international congress of Jewish veterans, held in Vienna from 27 June to 4 July 1936, declared it would begin to gather statistics on world Jewry's participation in the war and establish at the memorial village a monument in honor of the Jewish dead on all sides.[112]

At the 1935 Paris conference the assembled veterans proclaimed their love of each soldier's native land; yet they did so as Jews, bound together in what German Jews had since the nineteenth century called a community of fate—a *Schicksalsgemeinschaft*. The veterans blended statements of love of home with a growing nationalist consciousness. On the eve of the convention, the French association of Jewish veterans proclaimed that Jewish veterans have a right and obligation to solve the Jewish Problem through any of three avenues: "Jewish honor, Jewish security and the Jewish National Home."[113] According to the manifesto, not all veterans would agree about the priority order for each of these three, but all would surely agree that "not a single Jew should be insulted, massacred, or deprived of the right to participate freely in the development of the Jewish National Home." This rapprochement with, even embrace of, Zionism was far removed from the assimilationist patriotism of the elderly retired officer who was the most honored attendee at the convention, one Colonel Alfred Dreyfus, who rose from his sickbed to make a brief appearance, and who passed away a month later.[114]

The moment of assertion of the deepest patriotic sentiment coincided with a performance of transnationality: the transnationality that had underlain Jewish discourse on military service and combat since the beginnings of Jewish conscription. To be sure, during Europe's "long nineteenth century" there were increasing numbers of individuals of Jewish origin who attenuated or severed ties with their communities and possessed little Jewish ethnic consciousness. But as I have argued here, the active claim of patriotic attachment, even when accompanied by the willingness to die in battle for one's native land, did not, in and of itself, demonstrate a loss of Jewish identity. Until World War I, and even at times during that horrific conflict, Jewish patriotism was expressed within a framework of liberal universalism and even, at times, of prenationalist concepts of military service as an obligation toward the monarch—any monarch, in any land.

Also in 1935, the motif of Jew killing Jew in battle made what may have been its final appearance, in the *English Ex-Servicemen's Journal*.[115] "The Symbol" is a short story about a Jewish Tommy named Stern who, during the war, kills a "Hun" at close range and, viewing the body, notices a Star of David round the man's neck. The English soldier, wracked by guilt, declares "My brother, we were enemies, our countries are at war—all unknowingly I killed you." Many years later, the ex-serviceman is a solicitor in London and is active in philanthropic activity on behalf of German Jews persecuted under Nazism. He is approached by a friend who has just returned from Germany and who asks if Stern can take on as a clerk a young German-Jewish law student who was orphaned during the war. Not surprisingly, the youth turns out to be the son of the man Stern killed.

This particular story's resonance derives not so much from its recollection of events almost twenty years past as in its placement of a venerable motif into the service of a moral lesson about the obligations of Anglo-Jewry toward its persecuted brethren. During the 1800s, when Jews were striving for emancipation and often attaining it, assertions of Jewish transnationality in wartime were often implicit or indirect. In the politically charged atmosphere of the 1930s, when the fate of German Jewry was precarious, eastern European Jews were experiencing increasing oppression, and Jewish nationalism had become commonplace, there was no reason not to proclaim the commonality of Jews even when their nations were at war. During the Second World War the motif of Jew killing Jew in battle disappeared, not because of a decline in transnational Jewish solidarity—far from it—but because, so far as Jews in the Allied nations were aware, there were no Jews in the Axis armies.

■ ■ ■

Before World War I, a variety of connections linked men and women across national lines on the European continent. Aristocrats shared bonds of class identity, kinship, and marriage. Liberal humanitarians and social democrats preached the brotherhood of mankind and the proletariat respectively. These forms of extranational solidarity were ravaged by the First World War. Jewish solidarity fared somewhat differently. Jewish concepts of collective identity, along with a dense network of business and familial connections, generated a vast cohesive force. For many Jews, military service was a blood sacrifice on the altar of emancipation, a tragedy without precedent in Jewish history in that never before had so many Jews been arrayed against their brethren on opposing sides.

There was another aspect to the war for Jews, one that rendered it empowering, even exhilarating. It offered a chance to fight side by side with Christians and thus to meld into a national community as powerful as, or more so than, the transnational community of Jews. The act of war could be as thrilling as it was terrifying. As we will see in the next chapter, Jewish soldiers constructed the war as a meaningful, affirming experience. As veterans they attempted to perpetuate the memory of active participation in battle into the 1930s and 1940s, when they were deprived of their rights and, retroactively, of their masculinity through the denigration, and then erasure, of their wartime valor and suffering.

## CHAPTER FIVE

# The Jewish Soldier of World War I: From Participant to Victim

In 1924, the German-Jewish physician Felix Theilhaber published a book celebrating Jewish flying aces of World War I. The book's cover features a photograph of a Fokker fighter aircraft with a swastika painted onto its fuselage (figure 5.1). The plane had been flown during the war by one Fritz Beckhardt, a highly decorated flyer who, Theilhaber assures the reader, had no idea that the swastika, an ancient and ubiquitous symbol, would be appropriated after the war by the National Socialists for their nefarious purposes.[1] By putting the swastika-adorned airplane on the cover of a book about Jewish valor, Theilhaber was claiming the Jews' right to use this symbol and their status as an inseparable and essential component of the German nation.

If the previous chapter was about anxiety, this chapter is about empowerment. Aside from sheer compulsion, Jewish men had many reasons to serve their countries in World War I. They fought for social acceptance and masculine pride. They believed they were liberating Jews in enemy lands or occupied territory that had been a cradle of venerable Jewish communities. Like millions of their fellow soldiers, they were doomed to suffer disease, injury, and death. If suffer they must, they longed to do so as nationals and subjects of their homelands, as Germans, Frenchmen, and so on, and not as Jews. Jewish suffering was historically associated with the persecution of Jewish civilians, with assaults, expulsions, and pogroms—in short, with victimhood. (The ancient, original meaning of the Latin *victimus* is a sacrificial offering of an innocent animal, its fate entirely in the hands of the slaughterer,

Figure 5.1. Fritz Beckhardt's swastika-bedecked Fokker on the cover of Felix Theilhaber, *Jüdische Flieger im Weltkrieg* (1924).

the *victimarius*.) The mass slaughter of the First World War called into question neat separations between the deaths of soldiers and civilians; in Germany battlefield casualties and their bereft families alike were known as *Kriegsopfer*, victims of war. But many soldiers, and especially veterans who became politically active during the 1920s, insisted on distinguishing the battlefield experience from the fate of civilians, even if the lines of battle ran straight through Belgium, northern France, and a vast belt of territory running from the Baltic to the Black Sea, devastated by years of fighting and military occupation. Jewish veterans as well insisted on the singularity of the experience of battle.

Historian Antoine Prost has written a poignant description of the experience of French, and by extension all, soldiers in World War I. The unspeakable terror of omnipresent death, the hideous assault against the senses (the stench of the dead, the deafening noise of artillery and the gentle hissing of gas escaping a bloated corpse, the squish of mud and body parts) could not be depicted to those who were not part of it. During and in the immediate aftermath of the traumatic event, "the experience of death was too close to be recalled." The experience of war, Prost continues, engenders numbness, callousness, and selfishness. Soldiers could behave toward each other with great cruelty and look upon mass death with hardened indifference. They could also form intense emotional connections. After the war these connections were hard to maintain; the camaraderie of the trenches was, paradoxically, both "ephemeral yet indestructible." Comradeship kept the soldiers alive; they fought for each other long after their initial patriotism had worn away. The survivors of the war found meaning in their awful experiences: pride in their integrity and conscientiousness in extreme situations, and solidarity with their fellows.[2]

Studying Jewish soldiers and veterans of the Great War shows how, under circumstances of inclusion (even if incomplete) rather than vicious persecution, Jewish suffering in wartime, and with it the forms of collective memory and strategies for commemoration of the dead, could closely parallel, and even intersect with, the suffering of soldiers from sundry faiths and ethnicities. Medieval Jews had perceived themselves as obedient sacrifices, called upon in times of persecution to sanctify the name of God by being killed or even killing their own family members lest they fall into Christian hands and endure forcible conversion.

Jews had read themselves as an extension of the biblical Isaac, who was prepared to die (and, in some medieval versions of the story, did in fact die) to fulfill a divine commandment.[3] In World War I, however, Jews in western and central Europe barely referred to the Isaac story. They preferred to conceive of sacrifice in a more active and universalist spirit, reflecting their status as citizens as well as Jews.[4]

To be sure, the points of intersection were accompanied by points of deflection. Even when Jews served, fought, suffered, and died as soldiers of their homelands, their interpretations of the war experience, and their communities' postwar memory and commemorative practices, had distinctive characteristics. Most fascinating is the case of German Jewry, the main focus of this chapter. German Jews' overwhelming burden to prove their worthiness of equal rights and fair treatment caused them to mourn publicly only the Jewish dead, those who had made the ultimate sacrifice and so were the most unequivocal victims. The Jewish war wounded were far less visible as objects of communal concern in Germany than in the United Kingdom or France. Nor did they play the political or cultural role in postwar Jewish life that their Christian German counterparts carried out in founding veterans' organizations that lobbied for disabled soldiers. In other ways, however, German-Jewish veterans suffered the aftermath of the war as did other Germans; they shared in the prevailing fury over war guilt and reparations, and they retained a strong pride in their military service, a pride through which they interpreted the events of 1933–45. Fighting in the Great War solidified the Jews' faith that Germany would not betray them, and when it clearly did, the memory of agency, of participation in a war as soldiers and not as victims, salved their pride. German-Jewish suffering between 1933 and 1945 was that of the victim, but of an unwilling one, who had been a dutiful, at times enthusiastic combatant when allowed to be so.

▪ ▪ ▪

Like most men in World War I, Jews fought because they were drafted. In general, war enthusiasm was limited to the urban middle classes, which were more likely than laborers and peasants to take nationalist ideology seriously. Even among the bourgeoisie, by 1916 most of that support had worn away. In some countries Jews had specific reasons to fight that did not hold for much of the rest of the population. Jewish men going off to war could anticipate a tangible benefit, that is, social acceptance, whereas for most young men, especially peasants and urban workers, the war promised only ruin.[5] French Jews fought to regain Alsace-Lorraine, which for them was not merely a historic part of France that had been torn from the country by the Prussians but also the cradle of French-Jewish civilization. France's status as the birthplace of Jewish emancipation and of modern democratic revolution endeared it to thousands of Jewish foreign nationals who were domiciled in France and volunteered for the Foreign Legion.[6] The combination of French patriotism and *révanchisme* overpowered solidarity toward the Jews of Russia, whose wartime persecution by the tsarist government was covered up by the French-Jewish press. The French-Jewish press was also silent in the face of antisemitic outbursts against Jews in Algeria, preferring instead to focus on Algerian Jews' mass enlistment into the French army and their sacrifices on the country's behalf.[7]

The Anglo-Jewish elite also kept silent regarding the persecution of Russian Jewry, while its sons were among the first to enlist to fight against the Hun. England's alliance with Russia and its lack of a specific grievance against Germany's treatment of its Jews made it difficult for Anglo-Jews to justify the war in specifically Jewish terms, as seen in the mass refusal of the recent immigrants from Russia to follow their established coreligionists' model and volunteer for service.[8] Yet a quarter of Russian Jews in the United Kingdom returned to Russia after the revolution of November 1917, many of them before Russia's withdrawal from the war the following March. Those who came home right after the Bolsheviks took power were returning to a war zone and to near-certain mobilization for battle.[9]

The specifically Jewish aspects of the war were most apparent in Germany and Austria-Hungary. Taking part in a campaign to crush the Jews' historic oppressor was worth the risk of fratricide that we explored in the previous chapter. In Austria-Hungary Jews had a second motive for fighting, a fierce dynastic loyalty that was akin to French-Jewish republicanism in its stalwart identification of the governing regime with the protection of Jewish rights.[10] The German states and imperial government did not have nearly so strong a record of meritocratic treatment of Jews, as we saw earlier when comparing Austro-Hungarian and German policies toward admitting Jews to the officer corps.

For German Jews, the fight was for both the preservation of opportunities gained and for the attainment of greater access and acceptance. For the liberal German-Jewish elite, the war offered Jews the chance to fight side by side with Christians, to meld with them into a common nation, in a newfound unity born of common crisis. The kaiser's own call for a truce among the country's warring political factions elicited these heartfelt, if clumsy, verses that adorned the front page of the newspaper of the Central Association of German Citizens of the Jewish Faith upon the war's outbreak:

> That Germany's inner strife
> Finally had abated
> And that in trust and unity
> All had joined together
> That Germany as a tight-knit realm
> Should range amongst the rest
> This made the envious soul pale
> This they could never bear![11]

Similar views were expressed by Germany's Jewish military chaplains, a group of about thirty rabbis who provided pastoral care for Jewish soldiers in the field.[12] In an address given three weeks after the outbreak of the war, the *Feldrabbiner* Bruno Italiener proclaimed that the outbreak of war had undoubtedly made Germans a "better, more mature people":

> Yes, a war can be beautiful. A war that is so accepted, as it began and has been shouldered in Germany, is beautiful despite all the horrors that it brings and will yet bring to all of us, despite all the wounds that it has already struck and will strike, [such a war] brings blessing. . . . A people that with such simplicity throws aside its scythes, its pens, its books, and thereby takes the sword into its fist, a people among whom each man pulls himself away with fervor and as a matter of course from wife and child, from father and mother, from sister and bride and goes forth, perhaps never to be seen again; a people that marches through the streets with such a firm step, such clear eyes, such clear, joyful blood, as if it were going to a festival, such a people carries within it a guarantee for the future.[13]

Here, the family of the nation has priority over the nuclear family, although German militarism could be praised from an entirely different direction. In 1915, the prominent Orthodox rabbi Joseph Carlebach wrote that the German military should be a model for the raising of Orthodox children.[14]

According to the *Feldrabbiner* Reinhold Lewin, Germany's Jewish and Christian soldiers unstintingly assisted each other in the trenches, yet in general the trench experience was alienating and isolating for Jews, for endemic antisemitism throttled the development of intimate social relations.[15] Lewin claimed that Jews fulfilled their duty with the utmost devotion but also grimly, soberly, without the bloodlust against which the Jewish tradition has long expressed revulsion. Jewish soldiers, he claimed, had deeper attachments to home and family, to rituals and holidays, than those of Christians. Lewin's remarks were most certainly sincere, but they were also self-serving and represented a projection of his own sensibilities onto the Jewish soldiers. What do we know of the actual war experience of German-Jewish soldiers? Was Jewishness an aggravating, mitigating, or inconsequential factor affecting levels of militarism or pacifism? Did Jews experience the war any differently for being Jews, and if so, how?

In seeking to answer these questions we run into some methodological problems. The existing scholarship on German Jewry and the First World War has neglected the experience of war as combat and the suffering that inevitably followed. There is a vast literature on wartime antisemitism and Jewish reactions to it, and on the effect of the war on Jewish political disputes between liberals and Zionists, but most of this writing is about civilians, not soldiers.[16] Even when soldiers are the specific subject of attention, as in the encounter between German-Jewish soldiers and eastern European Jews in the zone of German occupation, the questions that historians ask and the analytical framework in which they operate center on individuals grappling with issues of personal and collective identity, not armies of men in mortal combat.[17]

Jewish historians have all too often mapped the sensibilities of the articulate elites, and particularly of a few representative intellectuals and activists, onto the community as a whole. Over the past twenty years, however, European historians have emphasized continuity more than rupture in characterizing the psyches of ordinary soldiers before and after their war experience. The war profoundly affected many writers and poets, radicalizing them toward the extremes of pacifism and celebration of brutal violence. For ordinary soldiers, however, the war experience was unlikely to lead to a Nietzschean reevaluation of values, though it often produced horrific injuries and lasting psychological trauma.[18] German-Jewish soldiers at times felt powerful solidarity with their Gentile fellow fighters, glorified the community of fighting men, and believed in heroic, redemptive death. They were longing for belonging, which is a necessary but hardly sufficient precondition for fascism. They were indifferent to assertions of the will to dominate or to merge one's self into a fighting collective.[19]

The error of conflating the views of elite and ordinary Jews has been particularly egregious in the case of the notorious "Jew count" of 1916, when the German military, suspicious that Jews were not pulling their weight in combat, ordered a census of Jews serving on the front lines. The census infuriated and deeply worried many rabbis and Jewish activists. It received a great deal of attention in the Jewish press, and it deeply disillusioned some prominent Jewish intellectuals, most notably the Zionist thinker Ernst Simon, about the possibilities of Jewish integration into German society.[20] But one wonders how much the census mattered to Jewish soldiers in the field and how likely it was to turn them, like Simon, into Zionists. The census is not mentioned in any of the more than seven hundred wartime letters that were written by former residents of the Berlin Jewish community orphanage and sent from the field to the institution's director.[21] Perhaps self-censorship provides an explanation, but the letter writers did not hold back from bitterly criticizing the German government or calling for socialist revolution. Furthermore, memoirs written by German-Jewish veterans during the 1920s devote little attention to the census; the collapse of the empire was a far graver concern. The census gained significance retroactively, after the Nazi accession to power in 1933, as shown in memoirs written at and after that time.

Throughout Europe, relations between Jewish and Christian soldiers varied greatly. Jews in the Dual Monarchy's military forces documented brutal, unremitting, and oppressive antisemitism.[22] Yet there were also displays of tolerance, friendship, and respect. Among the Austro-Hungarian forces on the eastern front, *tefillin* gained a reputation as a talisman, protecting its wearer from harm or even stopping bullets fired into the small box affixed by leather straps to the forehead.[23] Jews in the British and French forces were more likely than their central European counterparts to document warm relations with Gentile soldiers and officers. Here as well, however, there was no shortage of antisemitic incidents, involving Yiddish-speaking immigrants in particular. British soldiers were suspicious of the Yiddish language, which closely resembled that of the Hun, and suspected immigrants of Bolshevik sympathies.[24] Even Jewish servicemen from established British families encountered rude remarks, prompting J. Kemper, the only Jew in the Flying Corps, to urge his coreligionists to "learn to take a joke like the Scotsman. To see red whenever the word Jew is mentioned [is] rather unfair to your comrades and make[s] life beastly unpleasant for yourself."[25]

German Jews' relations with their fellow soldiers ran the gamut from comradely to hellish, and their experiences of the war depended heavily on where and in what capacity they served. German Jews fought on all fronts: the west, east, Italy, and Middle East. Galician Jews working or studying in Germany volunteered for the Dual Monarchy's army, serving overwhelmingly on the eastern front. Many German Jews fought in both the west and the east, sometimes being injured on both fronts.[26] Not every Jewish soldier, however, was put in harm's way or stolidly accepted his duty to die for the fatherland. One in five Jewish soldiers served behind the lines, a ratio typical of the distribution of the German army as a whole yet a source of antisemitic rumormongering. The clear intent to avoid death or injury characterizes the fascinating, bizarre memoir of Louis Liebmann, the son of a cattle trader and kosher butcher from Ellar, a town in Hesse-Nassau. Quite unselfconsciously, Liebmann describes himself as a timid, hypochondriac lad with an overprotective mother and who developed an unhealthy dependence on his parents. Liebmann's memoir protests patriotism and a love of adventure, but the narrative is primarily about Liebmann's constant efforts to avoid serving at the front. Thanks to constant complaining and a genuine, if mild, heart problem, on several occasions he was temporarily invalided out, only to be sent back into service, finally winding up well behind the front line in a unit engaged in livestock transport and slaughter.[27]

Soldiers' and veterans' writings have a limited capacity to express affective states. In general, soldiers' letters home and diaries tend to be dry and factual, whether due to censorship, self-censorship, or the writers' inability to make sense out of what they were experiencing.[28] Letters and diaries written by German-Jewish soldiers rarely narrate battlefield conditions in gruesome detail.[29] Letters could be expansive and reflective, but even so they recycle discursive patterns that originated before the war (e.g., love of the fatherland, the value of faith). Memoirs written after the war are more introspective but are colored by apologetic, self-exculpatory, or political agendas as well as the imprecision of recollection. For German-Jewish veterans, one must make a further distinction between those memoirs composed shortly after the war's end and those written after 1933, in the face of Nazi persecution. The former tend to display greater levels of militaristic sentiment and sympathy with Germany's war aims than the latter, which are more personal, concerned with the bravery and suffering of the individual German Jew, whose plight foreshadows the tragic events of the Nazi era.

Let us consider the case of Samuel Jacobs, an Orthodox Jew from a small town near Hannover. Shortly after the war's end, Jacobs stitched together a memoir out of letters sent home to his parents, along with new introductory and connecting passages. The memoir begins with a rather vague reference to being shell-shocked and depressed after the armistice. Nursed back to health by his mother, Jacobs claims that reading the letters he had sent home from the front filled him with resolve to write a memoir:

> I have striven to depict everything truthfully and as it appeared, so far as it was possible for me, as an ordinary man. I have avoided reporting upon the scenes of misery and cruelty that the battlefield often offered. May the youth who read this report recognize what a man can accomplish, may the youth take a stand and hold fast to that which sustained me during the entire war—to faithfully adhere to the faith of our fathers, to loyally sacrifice all one's being if it is required in order to preserve and nurture the interests of the German fatherland.[30]

Jacobs avoids detailing the horror of the battlefield but leaps forward to its aftermath: his and his comrades' shattered bodies and nerves, and Germany's defeat. Jacobs identifies his suffering entirely with that of Germany, and Germany's suffering as that of an innocent victim. A letter of May 1916 speaks of the war as entirely caused by the envy and greed of Germany's neighbors. In a later passage narrating his being wounded and transported back to Germany near the war's end, he writes of his yearning, along with that of all the "old soldiers at the front," that Germany would "wrest the laurel of victory and thereby be redressed for all our superhuman efforts." Claiming that Germany was defeated only because of American intervention, Jacobs heaps praise upon General Ludendorf and the heroes of the German air force, "who despite [the enemy's] superior force accomplished daily wondrous deeds of heroic courage and scorn for death." He describes himself as a "true German fighter," filled with "sorrow, which I carry with me daily as a result of my nerves shattered by the bloodbath, so filled am I with woe for the defeated German fatherland."

Jacobs writes extensively about his faith, and the letters are filled with references to Hebrew liturgical and biblical texts. But religion is, for Jacobs, a means to the end of doing his patriotic duty, which is inseparable from his German and Jewish identity. As he writes in a letter of May 1918:

> For more than three years I have been in the vortex of the great global conflagration. I have done my duty, as is fitting for a loyal German Jew. I have been hardened in body and soul. I have helped to alleviate suffering, have been and am always laboring to win for us Jews the recognition that we deserve. The faith that you, my parents, implanted in my soul as a child is a precious jewel. I cherish and defend it unto my last breath. We Jews have a right to respect and we are always worthy of it, for we have defended the fatherland in loyal fulfillment of duty alongside our comrades of other confessions; we have suffered and endured for father and mother, for wife and child, for brother and sister.

Jacobs fights as a Jew, but he suffers for being a German. In memoirs composed after 1933, the writer is more likely to present himself as fighting in the mistaken belief that he was a German, and to suffer for being a Jew.

German-Jewish activists had no qualms about exploiting Jewish suffering—that of civilians as well as soldiers—as a means of serving the interests of the Reich. During the war, regular contact took place between the umbrella organization for the provision of philanthropic services to Jews, the German-Israelite Communal Federation (*Deutsch-Israelitischer Gemeindebund*, or DIGB), and the Central Office for Foreign Service, a propaganda agency of the Foreign Ministry that was active in neutral countries. DIGB officials received reports of atrocities committed against Jews in Russian territory, translated them into German, and passed them on to the propaganda office for dissemination abroad. For example, in November of 1914 the DIGB heard from an eyewitness to a pogrom in Biezun, a small town in central Poland: "The Russian military commander who had just recently been in Biezun called for the rabbi on 16 October and asked him why the Jews do not pray that the tsar be favored in his war with Germany. The rabbi answered that Jews as Russian subjects pray for his welfare, as is commanded to them: 'Pray for the welfare of the kingdom [Avot 3:2]'" This answer apparently did not satisfy the commander, and a pogrom ensued, though it was squelched thanks to intervention by the Prussian army. The propaganda office rendered the report into German for publication, whereas neither it nor the DIGB considered information about another pogrom that took place several months later in Gorlitz to be suitable for dissemination abroad, most likely because it took place in German Silesia and there was no heroic rescue by the German military.[31]

No less instrumental were proposals offered by the celebrated Jewish feminist and philanthropic activist Bertha Pappenheim for aid to the children of eastern European Jewish refugees who had been driven from their homes as a consequence of pogroms or expulsion decrees by the Russian government. Comparing the Jewish refugees with children of German and Austrian nationality who fled Belgium and were welcomed in Germany, Pappenheim argues that the eastern European Jewish youth must be taken in, as they would be of great benefit to Germany as a whole and to its Jewish communities in particular. This would not, she wrote in October of 1914, be a humanitarian gesture alone, but also a "quiet, clever form of social policy." It would increase Germany's overall youth population and, if the refugees were directed away from the big cities, stabilize Germany's small, rural Jewish communities that had long been in decline owing to low birthrates and emigration. "Fresh blood would be infused into the Jewish communities through healthy elements, also in the biological sense, that are religiously conservative yet capable of assimilation." This policy must be implemented quickly, writes Pappenheim, lest the refugees crowd into the major cities and become a public burden.[32]

By far, however, the Jewish activist elite's most common form of instrumentalizing Jewish suffering was by presenting fallen Jewish soldiers as sacrifices for the fatherland. The apologetic literature took two different forms: as massive lists, with little more information than dates of birth and death, place of origin, and rank; and memorial volumes with details about the dead soldiers' lives and, no less important, deaths in battle. This latter type of literature began to appear within a month after the war's outbreak, with the appearance in Vienna of a bimonthly *Kriegsgedenkblatt* narrating the life stories of Jewish officers who had fallen in battle. Similarly, throughout the war the German-Jewish press published obituaries of distinguished Jewish fighters. The former type of literature, which demanded exhaustive statistical research, appeared in a flood of publications after the war, culminating in the RjF's massive volume of 1932 that listed every one of the twelve thousand Jews killed in battle.[33] Volumes of this type were hardly unique to German-speaking Jews; French and British Jews produced similar tomes.[34] These books all shared something in common with the many memorial volumes produced by non-Jews for the fallen youth of a particular town or school. As Daniel Sherman has observed in his study of commemorative practices in interwar France, communities strove to memorialize their dead as sons of a particular place, and not merely as sacrifices for the nation.[35] In the case of the Jews, however, an entire ethnoreligious community was displaying its dead, not only for the purpose of mourning and commemorating but also to impress others with the extent of Jewish sacrifices in order to combat, or ward off, antisemitic accusations of Jewish "shirking" (*Drückebergerei*). Within this genre of Jewish apologetics, the German-Jewish case was unique in the range and depth of efforts to count and display the Jewish dead.

Scholars usually date the onset of the statistical project to the "Jew count" of 1916. This was a time of increasingly hysterical antisemitism in the German press, accusing Jews of not only shirking military service but also growing rich from profiteering on war contracts, price gouging, and black marketeering. In fact, however, the statistical project began at most a month after the outbreak of the war. The DIGB archives contain protocols of meetings, dating back to January 1915 but referring to meetings as early as October 1914, of a Committee on War Statistics, which consisted of highly experienced leaders of German-Jewish philanthropic institutions and social scientists who had published widely on Jewish topics before the war. At the January 1915 meeting, it was decided to produce a statistical survey of the number of Jews in service, but the next month a disagreement arose between Heinrich Silbergleit (who, in addition to serving on this committee, directed the city of Berlin's statistical office) and Jacob Segall, the committee's primary researcher and analyst, over the desired end product of their inquiries. Segall preferred a quantitative approach that would yield statistics documenting overall Jewish participation in the war effort, whereas Silbergleit thought it more important to demonstrate Jewish soldiers' "taking part in the suffering of the soldiers, [by documenting] death and wounds."[36] As time went on, antisemitic accusations of Jewish war profiteering began to vie with the question of military service for the attention of the committee members, but the committee continued to focus on gathering statistics of dead and decorated Jewish soldiers. Thus the German-Jewish statistical project needs to be seen as less an anguished reaction to the "Jew count" than a continuation of long-standing forms of statistical inquiry, often with an apologetic orientation, dating back to the early 1900s.[37]

In 1915, the committee was gathering statistics on the Jewish wounded as well as the dead and decorated. This information was provided by the Berlin War Aid Commission and could at least indicate numbers of Jews in Berlin military hospitals. Committee member Louis Maretzki, chair of the German B'nai B'rith, recommended expanding on this information and actively soliciting hospitals for statistics about incoming wounded Jewish soldiers. There is no sign that this specific suggestion was acted upon, but even if it was, virtually no work published by this committee or any of its successors so much as mentioned the Jewish wounded.[38] In the committee's own private papers, wounded soldiers were set aside in a separate category, and if they died, they were moved into the ranks of the honored dead and featured in the published lists of fallen Jewish soldiers.[39] Otherwise they remained nameless and unknown. This neglect of the Jewish war wounded continued into the Weimar period and constitutes a fascinating area of distinction between German-Jewish commemoration of wartime suffering and that of German society at large.

Modern societies have frequently been slow to publicly acknowledge the suffering of wounded soldiers and to care adequately for those who are permanently disabled.[40] (The most recent example of this phenomenon is the 2003–11 Iraq War, in which at least thirty thousand American soldiers were physically wounded and many more than that number suffered severe battle-related mental illnesses, yet whose plight is all but ignored.) World War I veterans throughout Europe complained bitterly of their neglected state. As a British veteran turned MP, a double amputee, said on the occasion of the July 1919 Peace Procession in London, "The Dead are brought to memory by the noble Cenotaph, the lucky living are in the procession, but where are the wounded?" Three months earlier in Germany, a group of disabled veterans enraged by the lack of state assistance threw the Saxon war minister into the Elbe, where he drowned.[41] In 1921, disabled veterans in Hamburg protested plans to erect an enormous Heroes' Hall of Memory for the city's war cemetery. State funds, they claimed, should not be expended on an edifice commemorating the dead "until the misery of the living . . . has been expunged."[42] This anger was an incentive to public action and national, then international organization.

In the United Kingdom, France, and Germany, the original motivation behind the founding of veterans' associations was to advocate for the wounded. During the 1920s, the fate of the wounded veteran received considerable public attention. In the United Kingdom, care for wounded veterans came mostly through local and private philanthropies, and this grassroots approach maintained public awareness of the veterans' plight. In France and Germany, a massive state bureaucracy took charge of veterans' affairs, although France was far more generous than Germany, accounting for German veterans' greater tendencies to political radicalism.[43] By the end of the war there were in Germany more than 700,000 disabled out of 5 million men who had been mobilized and 3 million surviving veterans. By 1920 there were seven war survivors' organizations, the largest of which, the socialist-oriented Imperial League of War Wounded and Former Fighters (Reichsbund der Kriegsbeschädigten und ehemaligen Kriegsteilnehmer), had over 500,000 members.[44]

Jews were welcome in the Reichsbund, less so or not at all in the others, which were rightist or Catholic in orientation. Some 68,000 Jews served on the front lines and survived the war, and most of them eventually joined the RjF. (Its membership reached 55,000.) There must have been a substantial number of disabled Jewish soldiers (anywhere between 14,000 and 17,000, if disabled in proportion with the general mobilized or fighting population), yet the Jewish wounded scarcely appear in RjF publications, other Jewish newspapers, publications by Jewish activists, rabbinic sermons, or other voices from the Jewish public sphere.

During the war, German Jewry's major philanthropic institutions—the DIGB, the B'nai B'rith, and the individual communities' welfare agencies—devoted considerable money and effort to the care of war widows and orphans as well as the families of Jewish teachers and communal officials who had gone into battle. The Berlin community's War Aid Commission featured separate men's and women's sections and twelve district offices, which provided food and clothing for refugees, employment referrals, and day care for working mothers whose husbands were at the front. Much of this work was spearheaded by a group of female activists such as Ernestine Eschelbacher, director of the B'nai B'rith's Confederation of Women's Associations, which had twenty-three offices in Berlin alone.[45] This activity was very much in keeping with Jewish philanthropic services for the deserving poor, services that had expanded greatly during the Wilhelmine period.[46]

Far less was done for the soldiers themselves, even though at this time the German state had not yet taken charge of soldiers' welfare and was entrusting it to church and local agencies. The DIGB instructed Jewish communities along the western front to take charge of burying fallen Jewish soldiers,[47] but both the DIGB and Berlin community leadership consistently resisted pressure from other communities to create special facilities for wounded Jewish soldiers. At times local activists prevailed, as in the case of a Jewish women's organization in Hamburg that dedicated a kosher convalescent home for summer use by Jewish soldiers.[48] There were also efforts in Berlin to set up an employment exchange for the war wounded, with a particular eye to sending them to the colonies or the Orient.[49] In general, however, it was far better in the eyes of German Jewry's national leadership to mix them with the general population in military hospitals and sanatoriums.[50] This policy represented a rupture with long-established practices of funneling poor and needy Jews into separate welfare programs and institutions so as not to be a drain on the public purse and a potential source of antisemitic wrath.

These practices intensified under the Weimar Republic, with the creation of a vast national network of Jewish welfare agencies that imagined a coherent, distinct German Jewry as a "social body" (*Volkskörper*).[51] The Jewish soldier, however, was not part of that body. He was German Jewry's unconditional offering to the nation, and in return for risking life and limb he was worthy of the same services received by his Christian comrades.

At the time of its founding in 1919, the RjF discussed obtaining agricultural tracts to settle Jewish veterans on the land. The RjF's director, Leo Lowenstein, raised the matter again in 1922, but it languished, and in the following years discussions about agricultural training for veterans dropped the disabled component altogether.[52] The RjF newspaper *Der Schild* only began to seriously cover the issue of veterans' welfare in 1926, when it launched a series of discussions about the desirability of establishing a long-term care facility for disabled Jewish veterans. The newspaper mentioned a variety of soldiers' welfare initiatives that had been undertaken in previous years by local RjF chapters but bemoaned the lack of a coordinated, public strategy for such activity. In fact, the article continued, the RjF had made a conscious decision at the time of its founding not to deal with welfare issues but to concentrate on the campaign against antisemitism through public demonstrations and the production of apologetic literature.[53] This decision is all the more puzzling given that no other Jewish political or communal organization during the Weimar period took up the cause of Jewish veterans in general and the disabled in particular. Only in 1932 did *Der Schild* make a clear statement that the needs of the surviving scores of thousands of Jewish veterans deserved at least as much public attention as the twelve thousand Jewish war dead.[54] The following year, in the wake of the Nazi seizure of power, the RjF officially took care for war victims under its purview, and in 1939 the organization was effectively disbanded, its activity limited to care for war victims.[55] The RjF's final duties were those furthest from its heart.

A comparison with the Jewish communities in other lands highlights the oddity of this situation. In England, there was extensive conversation in the Jewish press throughout the war about the Jewish wounded. True, much of this conversation took the form of complaints by disabled soldiers about inadequate care, but these complaints were published in the

*Jewish Chronicle*, the official voice of Anglo-Jewry. In August 1918 the *Jewish Chronicle* devoted a series of articles to disabled Jewish soldiers, and issues of employment and vocational training for Jewish veterans, able-bodied and disabled alike, continued to be discussed throughout the early postwar years.[56] The Board of Guardians, Anglo-Jewry's coordinating body for philanthropic activity, ran a convalescent home for Jewish veterans and provided small loans for them as well.[57] In postwar publications, Anglo-Jewish organizations included the numbers of wounded in statistics of Jewish casualties; the same was true for Jewish organizations in France, the United States, Rumania, and Belgium. The *Archives Israélites* commemorated Jewish soldiers who had died of illness as well as wounds, and the newspaper's accounts of the death of decorated Jews dwelled on the wounds that accentuated the bravery and merit of the act for which the decoration had been bestowed.[58]

Why did the RjF neglect what must have been a major source of concern for their constituents? The most obvious reason is that Jewish veterans' organizations were primarily defense organizations, dedicated to combating antisemitism, rather than interest groups like their general counterparts. The first Jewish veterans' association in the United States, founded in New York City in 1897, combated the growing antisemitism and anti-immigrant sentiment of the time. When the various Jewish veterans' groups amalgamated in 1923 into the Jewish War Veterans of the United States of America, the organization claimed its duty was to "act as an advance guard, protecting the Jew against unjustifiable assault . . . it is our mission to bear the brunt of the attack, to protect from assault, to safeguard against treachery and deceit, and to act as their body guard and defenders." The Jewish War Veterans' statutes did, however, include "aid and comfort" to their "sick and distressed comrades and their dependents."[59]

A similar balance of functions was at work among Jewish veterans in the United Kingdom. An Anglo-Jewish veterans' organization was first founded in 1921, but it maintained a low profile until the Palestinian riots of 1929. The Association of Jewish Ex-Servicemen, or AJEX, as the organization is known, championed the rights of Jews to immigrate to Palestine, live there in peace, and defend themselves against Arab attack. During the 1930s, they took up the campaign against fascism, usually peacefully, via apologetic publications and public demonstrations, although the Jewish veterans also engaged in more direct action, such as tossing marbles under the hooves of horses bearing police escorting the fascist leader Oswald Mosley when he and his Blackshirts attempted to march through London's East End.[60] Philanthropy wasn't AJEX's main brief, but it did provide services for disabled Jewish veterans, and one of its cofounders, Jon Grinnel Cohen, was a double amputee whose disability was always apparent to the eye.

So we must look elsewhere for an explanation to our query. It is hard to draw definitive conclusions from absences and silences, rather than that which was said and done, but I can suggest a provocative explanation. Among the RjF and the organized German-Jewish community as a whole, the muted public discussion during the war about the Jewish wounded and the near silence for many years thereafter stemmed from a common source. In any society people do not deal comfortably with the war wounded, or with disabled people of any type. Viewing the disabled evokes fear lest their fate befall the viewer. It also evokes guilt over being hale, not doing enough to assist the unfortunate, or both. In the case of the war wounded, there is a distinct type of guilt, that engendered by the knowledge that the war is not really over, that even the victorious paid a heavy price, that life will never, in fact, be the same. For the wounded in defeated countries, that guilt is aggravated by shame, for the broken body of the veteran symbolizes the humiliation of the nation. Thus German society, despite its elaborate welfare bureaucracy, treated its veterans more harshly than France or the United Kingdom. Veterans were forced to undergo frequent and rigorous examinations to determine whether they were worthy of a pension, and many who suffered from debilitating shell shock were dismissed as "hysterical," a word that carried powerful connotations of effeminacy and irrationality.[61] It appears that Jewish activists, smarting under long-standing accusations that Jews lacked masculine virtue, were particularly ashamed of their wounds, physical and mental. They were ashamed of antisemitism, which they believed to be a blot on German as well as Jewish honor, but wounded veterans shamed them as well. To display the Jewish wounded was tantamount to an admission of the frailty of the Jewish corporate body.

Consider the case of Julius Fuhrman, a severely wounded Jewish soldier who lived in Kreuznach. One day, upon lurching into a café on crutches, he was accosted by a drunken furniture dealer named Jean

Ehrenhardt, who called him both a cripple and a shirker. (The matter was prosecuted, and although the lay assessor's court in Kreuznach let Ehrenhardt off, the criminal court in Koblenz fined him five hundred marks, and would have given him jail time had he not claimed inebriation as an extenuating circumstance.)[62]

Given antisemitism's astonishing capacity to fit conflicting data into a uniform worldview, for Jewish activists the most effective apologetic technique was to obscure the wounded Jewish body, and all the more so the shell-shocked Jewish mind, altogether. This is seen in a remarkable series of articles in *Der Schild* titled "Frontartzt und Frontsoldat," penned by Eugen Neter, a physician and member of the RjF's Mannheim chapter. Neter claims that the battlefield experience was, overall, a positive one that strengthened body and soul. Despite dreadful conditions in the field, he avers, men rarely fell ill. Shell shock, according to Neter, was a fiction; people claiming to suffer from nervous disorders either fabricated them or suffered from them before the war.[63] Neter's claims are breathtakingly audacious and wildly inaccurate. But the RjF must have approved of them, as the newspaper devoted considerable space to them over three weeks.[64]

Rather than look nervously upon the living reminders of the war, Jewish activists in Weimar Germany took comfort in the dead, whose names were engraved on monuments in every community, the dead who amounted to 12,000, a number evoked constantly in German-Jewish public discourse of the interwar period (figure 5.2).[65] In a country that had lost 1.5 million, 12,000 was minuscule, yet among Jews that number had a quasi-mystical quality. The number evoked the twelve tribes of Israel, the twelve apostles (German Jews were not shy about appropriating Christian symbols), and the duodecimal system of much of the ancient Middle East. The number maintained its aura in the face of the Nazi abrogation of Jewish emancipation. In 1935, the Austrian equivalent of the RjF, the Bund jüdischer Frontsoldaten, proposed the establishment of a village in Palestine, "Das Dorf der Zwölftausend," to house the widows and orphans of the German-Jewish war dead.[66]

As Benedict Anderson has wryly observed, nationalist ideology legitimates itself far more comfortably via appeals to the unborn and the dead than to the living. Writing of a war memorial in New Haven, Connecticut, Anderson notes that in death, immigrants of motley ancestry become "'pure American,' and it is in this purity that Goodness lies

Figure 5.2. German Jewry laments its dead: The cult of the 12,000 fallen soldiers in World War I. *Courtesy of the Deutsches Historisches Museum, Berlin.*

secured."[67] On one level, the Herculean labor of the RjF to produce a book listing the name of each one of the twelve thousand Jewish dead exemplified the practice of individualizing the victims of mass death, a practice introduced during the war throughout the western world.[68] But the total was greater than the sum of its parts. Jews who had suffered and died as Germans were seen as having bequeathed to their survivors the right to live as Germans. The RjF's Munich chapter prefaced its memorial book with the assertion that "what the fallen had of human weakness disappears before the great horizon of their fate, to which they freely surrendered themselves."[69] The dead are completely absent, freeing remembrance to take myriad forms. One cannot remember the wounded, because they are present; they cannot be re-membered because part of them is forever absent.[70]

During the Weimar era, German-Jewish veterans sought to expunge their dual shame—as defeated Germans and as despised Jews—by constructing an aggressive, masculine self-image. Before the war, German-Jewish activists, particularly Zionists, had written a good deal about the military prowess of ancient Israel, producing articles with titles such as

"On the Military Fitness of the Jews" and "War as Master Instructor." This martial spirit was to be restored in the present via fencing and gymnastics. During the 1920s, the RjF favored less genteel forms of athletics, such as boxing, jiujitsu, and wrestling. In 1925, a Jew became the German national jiujitsu champion, an event celebrated in *Der Schild*.[71] (That same year, a correspondent for the newspaper, reporting on a boxing evening during which Jewish youths won the first three bouts, wrote that one Jewish boxer's "broad shoulders sloping sharply to slender hips, developed muscles—filled me with particular joy. I only regret that Buchman was wearing a shirt.")[72] Between 1926 and 1932, the Berlin RjF chapter was a nursery for German jiujitsu champions—eleven in all— and the RjF won the Reichsverband für Jiu Jitsu's Challenge Trophy in 1929, 1930, and 1931.[73] As in interwar Europe as a whole, team sport was seen by the RjF as a vital source of collective, masculine pride. ("Sport is battle!" according to *Der Schild*.) Gliding, which required a team of sturdy men to portage the machine to its launching point and a fearless soul to pilot it, was popular among postwar German youth, including Jewish veterans. According to the RjF, the purpose of gliding was to "toughen our hearts and lungs, practice with our eyes and hands, raise our Jewish youth in the spirit of the Spartans, teach them courage, self-mastery, cold-bloodedness, bravery, mental presence in the spirit of our heroic forefathers [so that they] fight strongly and prove victorious!"[74]

The RjF's fascination with sport grew out of and paralleled its commitment to self-defense. Throughout central Europe, Jewish soldiers had formed self-defense squads, at times with direct authorization from state government, amid revolutionary chaos in the fall of 1918 and winter of 1919.[75] In Berlin, at the time of the Kapp putsch in March of 1920 and again when riots threatened Jewish neighborhoods in November of 1923, RjF units armed with pistols and rubber truncheons went into the streets and brawled with German toughs. (A leader of the Jewish paramilitary forces, Emanuel Simon, claims to have facilitated Albert Einstein's flight to Holland during the 1923 disturbances.)[76] The RjF was a typical paramilitary force in Weimar Germany, and its leaders were imbued with the camaraderie of the trenches. As Neter wrote in 1929, "The frontline experience connects our souls in this association, and only this creates the visible and palpable camaraderie of our association."[77] If German Jews experienced modernity within what David

Sorkin famously termed a subculture, then Jewish veterans constructed a sub-subculture, distinct from those Jews who had not tasted battle, and linked psychically with non-Jewish veterans, even when the latter did not tolerate Jews in their midst. The dilemma of the Jewish soldier who had been imbued with German patriotism and socialized by the war experience, yet was excluded by virulent antisemitism, is epitomized in the memoirs of Joseph Kurt. Kurt, raised in Berlin in an acculturated family with Conservative leanings, served during the war in the air corps and returned to Berlin during the Spartacist rebellion. Deeply opposed to socialism, Kurt hurried to the Potzdammerplatz where, he writes, he assembled a phalanx of government supporters who took on a group of advancing Spartacists, disarmed them, and took them prisoner. After the suppression of the uprising, Kurt volunteered to command a *Freikorps* unit on the German-Polish border. When troops in another unit threatened to kill him for being a Jew, he returned to Berlin, where he continued to confront antisemites but also attended Communist meetings in order to shout down the speakers.[78]

Not content to celebrate Jewish sacrifice in Europe during the Great War, the RjF constructed a narrative of Jewish military prowess throughout the history of the Reich, from the Franco-Prussian War through the Southwest African colonial wars of the early twentieth century and the Middle Eastern front in 1914–18. *Der Schild* located twenty Jews, some of them settlers in Winhoek, who took part in the "campaigns" against (i.e., extermination of) the Hereros and Witbooi.[79] The invocation of Jewish colonial valor served a dual purpose: to share in the general mourning for Germany's lost colonies and to present differences between Jews and other Germans as indistinguishable when contrasted against the Dark Continent. During the 1920s, Jewish veterans' tales of colonial adventures were assertions of racial identity with Germans in the face of an increasingly vicious and biologically framed antisemitism. But such attempts were doomed to failure as the Nazi regime took control in 1933 and began to build the infrastructure of a racial state.

Already in 1932, Jewish organizations had been excluded from taking part in services for the Day of National Remembrance. Once the Nazis were in power, Jews were driven out of most of the veterans' organizations, and in 1934 the National Association of Blinded Soldiers refused membership to Jews. Jews who had fought at the front or whose fathers or sons had been killed in combat were exempted from the April 1933 law that Aryanized the civil service. Iron Crosses for Jewish veterans continued to be issued.[80] The exemption for veterans raised the hopes of the RjF leadership that Jews could continue to serve in the German army, but in May of 1935 military service was limited to Aryans, and the Nuremberg Laws applied to all racially defined Jews, including veterans. Nonetheless, awards and allowances continued to be disbursed to veterans. In June of 1935, one Franz Münzer, now living in Palestine, received the Iron Cross, and in December of 1936, a medical doctor named Alexander Walk, from a small town in Lower Silesia, received permission to wear the armband for wounded veterans.[81] In this atmosphere of deepening gloom and fading hope, the RjF made final, desperate efforts to display the suffering of Jews as Germans. It published a collection of *Feldpostbriefe*, letters sent by Jewish soldiers from the front to their friends and families. The collection was prefaced by the tragic epigram "We died for Germany." During the last few years before it was shut down in 1935, the RjF espoused support for authoritarian government, and some of its leaders openly embraced fascism.[82]

By and large, however, the RjF's final political stance was not fascism so much as a reactive and imitative form of right-wing German nationalism. There was no cult of the leader, no internal enemy or internecine violence, and little interest in irredentism or territorial expansion. In the 1920s, the RjF leadership had been, to cite Thomas Mann's memorable phrase, *Vernunftrepublikaner* (republican by reason); during the organization's final years they became at worst, to coin a phrase, *Vernunftfaschisten*.[83] In many lands, Jewish veterans' organizations of the time were sympathetic to militant and authoritarian nationalism. Jewish support for fascism was far greater in Italy than in Germany; over seven hundred Jews took part in Mussolini's March on Rome in October of 1922 or were members of the Fascist Party at the time. Twenty Jews were injured in the fighting against the Fascists' opponents, and three, killed in battle, were posthumously declared to be "Fascist Martyrs."[84] In Poland, there were two Jewish veterans' organizations, one intensely patriotic and the other enamored of right-wing Revisionist Zionism.[85] Jewish veterans' organizations engaged in paramilitary activity, at times as auxiliaries of state governments (e.g., in Poland and Czechoslovakia). One of French Jewry's veterans' organizations, the Union patriotique des Israélites français (f. 1934) was sympathetic to the antirepublican, irredentist, and fiercely nationalist Croix de feu.[86] (Unlike Germany, however, in France there was a sufficient critical mass of leftist Jewish veterans of eastern European origin to found a rival organization that espoused Bundist and left-Zionist views.) Even the relatively pacific Anglo-Jewish veterans' association showed its militaristic colors when writing in 1934 of Palestine's Mitzpah colony, made up entirely of veterans and their families, and suffused with a "team spirit, reminiscent of the trenches in the Great War. Like that spirit of brotherhood in the face of shell-fire and other horrors, it has enabled these people to accomplish superhuman things in the face of terrific odds."[87]

If young Jewish men throughout Europe had absorbed the militaristic sensibility of the era, how much more so in Germany, where vigorous assertions of patriotism and fighting spirit were a salve to a macerated masculine identity. The RjF's jarring rhetoric stemmed from a desperate longing for acceptance and dignity, to honor and mourn the dead, to restore a gravely wounded pride. Self-esteem, not patriotism alone, impelled German-Jewish veterans to react to the 1 April 1933 Nazi boycott by standing in front of their stores in their uniforms, bedecked with medals. Many German Jews, including historian Peter Gay's father, took their war medals with them into exile. The first leader of the Austrian-Jewish veterans' association, a retired general in the Habsburg armed forces, wore his uniform when ordered by Nazi thugs to clean the streets of Vienna.[88] This display of patriotic valor was not limited to men. Alfred Meyer, a native of Bielefeld who immigrated to the United States in 1939 at the age of twenty, writes in his memoir that his mother, who had been an army nurse during the First World War, wore her nurse's boots when, during the Second, she reported for transport to the east and to her death.[89]

Between the introduction of the Nuremberg Laws and the beginning of World War II, the suffering Jewish soldier came increasingly to be seen within a particularistic framework, not necessarily Zionist but imbued with a sense of a common Jewish fate throughout time. German Zionists associated the death of Joseph Trumpeldor, a Russian-Jewish army officer who fell in defense of the Zionist settlement Tel Hai in northern Palestine in 1920, with the 12,000 Jewish dead from World War I. As German Jews fled to North America, Palestine, and China, they continued to stage Remembrance Day observances, now framed within the context of Nazi persecution. The 12,000 became a metonym for the 600,000 German Jews whose lives were shattered—at this point, few had been extinguished altogether—by the Nazis. The trope of the 12,000, previously invoked only by German Jews, now became part of the discourse of global Jewry, as Jewish veterans in the United States, the United Kingdom, and elsewhere protested the maltreatment of their fellow Jews whose dear ones had sacrificed their lives for their homeland.[90]

During the Second World War, while Jews remaining in Germany suffered as Jews, some comfort could be taken in the time when they had suffered as Germans. Victor Klemperer's memoirs of the war years provide an invaluable source on this point. "The Jews' favourite topic," he wrote in Berlin in March of 1942, "immediately after the Gestapo and the current situation: their participation in the 1914–1918 World War." Compared with his current miserable situation, he asserts, "the last war was such a decent business." Klemperer writes of two Jewish acquaintances for whom World War I had been their central and greatest experience. According to Klemperer, working as a forced laborer in a factory or asking a fellow worker about his war service was a natural icebreaker. And in June of 1944, he and other Jews, holed up in a cellar at night, chatted "naturally" about their war experience. "A grotesque conversation, really, in a Jews' cellar. But it goes without saying that each of us is attached to the German army of the First World War and to its opponents in this world war with the same degree of passion."[91]

Memoirs composed by German-Jewish émigrés after the Nazi seizure of power contrast the enthusiasm with which they served their fatherland and the cruelty with which they were treated. Writing from Argentina, Edwin Halle notes that he left Germany during the 1920s for economic reasons but that after 1933 he became a forced exile despite having received the Iron Cross. Only serendipity, he writes, prevented him from being gassed, "which was the lot of the bravest among my comrades with high decorations as 'reward' for their service!"[92] Felix Kaufmann's memoir, composed a half century after the Nuremberg Laws, consists of a three-page letter in shaky, spidery handwriting and is devoted mostly to military affairs—his father's service in the Franco-Prussian War, his own experience in World War I, and then an apparently random, yet in fact meaningful, digression on the fate of General Wilhelm Ritter von Leeb, a third-generation baptized Jew who was turfed out when Hitler came to power. This story of the downfall of the high, mighty, and baptized softens the blow of the final portion of Kaufmann's memoir, where he tells of being sacked in 1935 and forced into exile.[93]

For most of Germany's remaining Jews, the sacrifice of their fellow Jews killed in the First World War symbolized the futility of fighting for Germany and the need for ethnic solidarity with Jews the world over, particularly with Israel. In the sizable colonies of German Jews abroad, however, surviving Jewish World War I veterans continued to pay separate homage to their dead. In New York, German-Jewish veterans of World War I held a remembrance ceremony barely six months after V-E Day.[94] It would not be correct to interpret these practices as a perverse expression of attachment to a country that had spurned and betrayed them. Rather, it was an exercise in nostalgia and a sign of ongoing need to remember the dead within the original context of their death—as Germans, not as Jews; as vibrant men, not as living corpses stripped of all humanity—and to associate with one's wartime comrades. Even when soldiers have long given up fighting for king and country or God, they fight for each other, and they remember each other, the dead and living alike.

▪ ▪ ▪

Writing from exile in Amsterdam in the 1930s, the German-Jewish journalist Fritz Heymann fantasized about Jewish power. As a teenager, he had volunteered to fight for Germany; shortly after the war he served with a *Freikorps* unit in the Rhineland. A fifth-generation soldier and strident German nationalist in his youth, Heymann became during the 1920s a staunch political Zionist, an admirer of Herzl and Trumpeldor. In the early 1930s, Heymann began research for a book on Jewish adventurers throughout history, a book that he thought would thrill Jewish youth and inspire them to greatness. "Perhaps Jewish history would have followed a different course," he writes at the beginning of *Der Chevalier von Geldern* (1937), "if it had been written differently."[95] The book is about heroes: "A hero is he who accomplishes the impossible, attains the unattainable, achieves the unreachable, takes hold of the taboo, masters the monstrous."[96] Heymann's heroes are a motley lot: not only kings, warriors, viziers, and generals but also Marranos, false messiahs, rebels, conquistadores, pirates, swindlers, highwaymen, boxers, and gangsters. It is a curious mixture of those on or beyond the fringes of the law and respectable society and those deeply embedded in, indeed pillars of, the state. They share little in common save a repugnance for book learning and a love of action, often of a violent sort. Jewish children, Heymann wrote, love the story of the biblical robber-king David and other Hebrew heroes of the Bible: "Here Jews fight! . . . The lad in the Jew-alley dreams of the clash of weapons no less than the Christian child."[97] Heymann expresses his own yearning to take vengeance against those who drove him from his own country, and to mobilize the Jewish nation into battle, through the words of the fourteen-year-old Ferdinand Lassale, the future Socialist leader who in 1840, at the time of the Damascus Affair,[98] wrote in his diary of his longing to lead masses of armed Jews in a struggle for independence: "Cowardly people, you deserve no better fate! . . . You do not know how to die, you do not know the meaning of proper vengeance, you do not know how to bury yourself with your enemy and to rip him asunder while locked in the death struggle. You are born to be slaves!"[99]

Heymann would not live to see Lassale's, or his own, dreams fulfilled. He went into hiding when the Nazis occupied Holland in 1940, was ferreted out and sent to Westerbork, and thence to Auschwitz, where he was murdered. Focused as he was on exceptional individuals, Heymann may well have gone to his death unaware of a seismic wave of political and military transformations that overtook Jews throughout the world during the 1930s and 1940s. I do not speak of the battering of World War I's Jewish participants into victims, but rather of the mobilization of Jewish men of all sorts—soldiers and civilians, young and old, from all the inhabited continents of the planet—into participants in the global fight against fascism and the struggle for a Jewish state. This transformation was both envisioned and documented by Hannah Arendt, the epitome of German-Jewish humanism and a champion of a binationalist state in Palestine, who during World War II spoke unequivocally in favor of a separate Jewish army within the Allied forces. In language reminiscent of the Revisionist Zionist leader Vladimir Jabotinsky, Arendt wrote that the Jews would not benefit from a defeat of Hitler unless they took part in that defeat. "Freedom is not a gift, as per an old and oft-cited Zionist maxim. *Freedom is also not a reward for sufferings endured.*"[100] The Jewish Brigade of the British army, formed in 1944, was for Arendt the most important possible Jewish response to Hitler.[101] The Jew, attacked by antisemites for being a Jew, having suffered repeatedly and horrifically for being a Jew, would now have to fight as a Jew, accepting the undeniability of his identity while, like the Jewish partisans, refusing to follow the "natural law of the Jews' peculiar fate."[102]

For Arendt, to fight "as a Jew" did not mean adopting a chauvinistic, aggressive nationalism, any more than fighting "as a German" necessarily imbued Jewish soldiers with German militarism, or suffering as a German demanded denying the existence of Jewish ethnic bonds. In our final chapters, we will see to what extent Arendt's delicate balance of particularism and universalism was realized in the Jewish world wars of the twentieth century.

## CHAPTER SIX

# The World Wars as Jewish Wars

The Jewish soldier in the First World War served his country and suffered as a citizen, but he also fought to demonstrate Jewish valor, and he suffered as a Jew. Throughout the world, the war intensified Jews' commitments to causes that clearly served Jewish collective interests, even though those causes could radically oppose each other. This chapter demonstrates the effect of the mobilization of ideas and manpower on the Zionist movement during the two world wars as well as a smaller international conflict that adumbrated World War II. During World War I, the Zionist movement sponsored the formation of Jewish units for the British armed forces, and although these units' military accomplishments were modest, they had a galvanizing effect on Jewish collective solidarity throughout the western world. A very different type of international mobilization sent thousands of Jews into the International Brigades in the Spanish Civil War. Jews the world over gave their utmost support for the Allied struggle against Hitler's Germany. Ideologically, these wars were perceived as serving Jewish interests, albeit often conflicting ones such as Zionism, on the one hand, and international socialism, on the other. Operationally, these were, for Jews, international conflicts, involving mass movements of Jews not only as refugees or inducted soldiers but also as volunteer fighters.

By presenting these conflicts as a unity, and by analyzing the overlapping sets of collective Jewish interests that motivated those who participated in them, I will set the stage for the book's final chapter, a study of the transnational Jewish dimensions of the 1948 war out of which Israel emerged as an independent state. Taken together, these two chapters seek to narrow what is usually perceived as a chasm between the Zionist struggle to establish the state of Israel and previous forms of Jewish military activity. These conflicts were not the "Jewish war" of the antisemitic imagination, which believed that the elders of Zion fomented wars in order to bring about global chaos from which Jewish financiers and Bolsheviks would both profit. These were wars in which, as Jews saw things, the only profit was their very existence. They were not "world wars" in the conventional sense of conflict occurring simultaneously in multiple continents, but rather wars in which Jews from all over the world took part in a common struggle for a cause, a place, or for sheer survival.

## The Jewish Legion and Palestine: The First Global Jewish War?

Throughout most of World War I, the international Zionist movement took an official stance of neutrality, not wishing to antagonize Palestine's Ottoman sovereigns and endanger the land's Jewish community. Some of the movement's most talented and energetic leaders, however, pursued a pro-British policy from the start in the hopes that in return for international Jewish assistance Britain would favor the Zionist cause and, after the war, nurture a Jewish national home in Palestine. In London, Chaim Weizmann engaged in diplomatic maneuvers with the British war cabinet, maneuvers that led to the December 1917 Balfour Declaration and the formal entry of the Zionist movement into the Entente camp. In Palestine, the Zionist agronomist Aaron Aaronsohn led a clandestine pro-British intelligence operation that functioned for more than two years before the Turks discovered it and imprisoned or executed most of the group's members.

Within a few months after the war's outbreak, the Zionist leader Vladimir Jabotinsky and the Russian war hero Josef Trumpeldor lobbied the British government to create a Jewish unit within the Entente forces.[1] Jabotinsky had his eyes set on England as the postwar lord of the Middle East, and he, like leaders of stateless peoples throughout the polyglot empires of eastern Europe, believed that taking part as a distinct force in the great struggle against the Central Powers would strengthen his people's claim to a place at the negotiating table after the war. Trumpeldor shared Jabotinsky's vision of an independent Jewish unit as the most visible and effective means of winning British support for Zionism. The first Jewish military unit in the First World War, however, was a decidedly unglamorous affair. Like the first Jewish conscript wagoners in the Habsburg Empire of the 1780s, Jews here were relegated to transport services in the form of the Zion Mule Corps, which is best known for supplying the Entente troops at the tragic battle of Gallipoli. A bona fide Jewish legion became possible only when Britain introduced conscription in 1916 and the British government began to think seriously about how best to mobilize the thirty thousand Jewish citizens of Russia residing in the United Kingdom. The entry into the war the following spring of the United States, home to an exponentially greater number of new Jewish arrivals from Russia, heightened the appeal of the Jewish legion to the British authorities as a source of highly motivated manpower.

The Jewish Legion was a rather motley group. It consisted of three distinct units, the Thirty-eighth, Thirty-ninth, and Fortieth battalions of Royal Fusiliers, about five thousand men in all, hailing from the United Kingdom, North America, and Palestine respectively. The Russian Jews living in Britain were not eager to fight on the same side as tsarist Russia or imperialist Britain, and their main reason for signing up was to avoid being shipped back to Russia and dropped into battle on the eastern front. After Russia's withdrawal from the war upon the signing of the Treaty of Brest-Litovsk, most of the men of the Thirty-eighth (known as the "*shnayderim*," or tailors) stayed in the service voluntarily, not out of patriotism so much as a desire to gain British citizenship in exchange for military service.[2] There was more Zionist fervor among the North American members of the Thirty-ninth Battalion, which was a purely volunteer force, as many as a third of which consisted of members of Zionist organizations.[3] Many of the rest were not ideological Zionists, though they had a visceral Jewish identity that had been catalyzed by a sense of marginality in the new North American environment. The experience of training together in Nova Scotia and then serving together in Palestine and Egypt further sharpened the volunteers' Jewish identity yet also filled them with a sense of American pride.[4] There were also among the Thirty-ninth many adventurers and at least a few criminals.

Jews in the Yishuv were, like their diaspora counterparts, ambivalent about fighting for Britain and against their suzerain of the moment, the Ottoman sultan. A strong antimilitarist streak ran through *Ha-Po'el Ha-Tza'ir*, one of the two major workers' parties of the time.[5] Here, as abroad, some signed up out of desperation or loneliness. But in general, the members of the Fortieth Battalion shared the sense that fighting would establish a right to the land and provide the nucleus of a future Jewish army.[6] The volunteers reflected the spectrum of the Yishuv, ranging from Orthodox to secular, including Sephardim as well as Ashkenazim, and Jews from the two major centers of Jaffa and Jerusalem. Naturally there arose tensions amid so diverse a group, especially between the Palestinian Jews and their often unenthusiastic diaspora counterparts. The lack of a sense of unity emerges from one legionnaire's characterization of the Egyptian Jews in the Fortieth, most of whom were not Zionists and had joined for economic reasons, as "Arabs by temperament," suffused with "primitive fear."[7] Even more jarring were the memoirs of the Anglo-Jewish officer Redcliffe Salaman, who divided the legionnaires into strict racial categories:

> The moment they rolled into the station I spotted a nigger amongst them, and before the train stopped I cleared that question up—his mother was a negress, his father a Sephardi (these Sephardim are a fearfully mixed lot; give me Ashkenazim for blue blood!). Then the types varied from blue-eyed handsome pseudo-Gentiles to dark purely semitic Yemenites—and scattered between were a dozen, perhaps, of semi-negroid, but often very handsome, Moroccan Jews. . . .
>
> The Yemenites are for the most part undersized and rather poor-spirited *natives*. They are *not* racially Jews. They are black, long-headed, hybrid Arabs. They have scarcely any Jewish blood; they are much closer to the Falashas. The real Jew is the European Ashkenazi, and I back him against all comers.[8]

On the other hand, a powerful loyalty to diaspora Jewry was displayed by a legionnaire from Montevideo, an acolyte of Jabotinsky, who attempted with a gang of comrades to bolt camp and trek to L'viv in the wake of that city's dreadful pogrom of November 1918.[9]

During the war, the Zionist justification for the legion had been both instrumental and demonstrative. Zionist leaders wished to be of service to the Entente, in the hope of a postwar quid pro quo, but even more so they believed that demonstrating Jewish commitment to fight and die for Palestine would win international respect and strengthen the Zionist claim to a Jewish national home. In both these senses there was a direct connection between Zionist thinking about military action and diaspora Jewish discussions, going back to the Napoleonic wars, about conscription into diaspora armies or fighting in national uprisings. Zionists faced the same disappointments encountered by their patriotic predecessors. The Jewish Legion was a source of pride to Zionists the world over, but militarily it did not accomplish very much. The British contingent of the Thirty-eighth Fusiliers took part in General Allenby's northward march through Palestine, but the North Americans of the Thirty-ninth wound up in the Egyptian desert, guarding prisoners of war at Tel El-Kabir. Nor did the legion play a major role in British calculations behind the issuing of the Balfour Declaration and the formulation of British Palestine policy thereafter. After the war the British saw the legion as more a liability than a benefit. Most of its members were expeditiously demobilized and the rest incorporated into the First Judean Battalion, which performed guard duties and other ancillary tasks.

The Jewish Legion had a few lasting effects on the Yishuv. Some of the veterans of the Fortieth Battalion were among the founders of the Yishuv's primary militia, the Haganah; others founded a settlement in Palestine, a moshav called Avihayil. Some of modern Hebrew's military terminology was coined by legionnaires.[10] All in all, however, the contribution of the legion to the postwar Yishuv was modest. The legion did have a somewhat greater influence in enhancing Zionism's postwar profile among international Jewry. During the war itself most Jews were not Zionists, and it was the Balfour Declaration, not the exploits of the legion, that shifted the tide of Jewish public opinion to endorse, and vicariously take part in, the Zionist project. Years and even decades later—in the wake the establishment of the British Mandate for Palestine, the development of the Yishuv into a going concern, and the tireless efforts of Jabotinsky and his acolytes to trumpet the legion's accomplishments—the legion became a symbol of international Jewish involvement in the struggle for Palestine.

The British army was not the only site of separate Jewish units during the First World War. In the chaotic days following the Bolshevik Revolution in November of 1917, a separate Jewish army unit was founded in St. Petersburg. Trumpeldor, who was in Russia in 1918, saw this as the first of many such units that would protect Jewish communities throughout the Pale of Settlement and could coalesce into a great Jewish army that would battle its way through central Asia and eventually into the land of Israel.[11] His dreams of an armed Jewish horde were not realized. The Jewish battalion was disbanded after a month, and although there were some separate Jewish units in the Red Army in 1919, they were deployed on the front lines and not given the opportunity to be stationed in and defend Jewish communities. Large concentrations of Jews in Red Army units unleashed fierce antisemitism among their Gentile fellow soldiers as well as civilians, who felt confirmed in their suspicions that the Bolsheviks were dominated by Jews.[12]

Some fifteen years after the end of the Russian Civil War, a new opportunity arose for Jews on the left to fight for the values of socialism. The site of this opportunity was not Palestine, or, for that matter, anywhere in the Jewish diaspora. The next battlefront in the Jewish world wars of the twentieth century was a land that had expelled its Jews four and a half centuries previously—Spain.

## Mobilized Jewish Internationalism: The Spanish Civil War

In 1931, Spain became a republic for the first time since the 1870s. In 1936, a coalition of leftist parties known as the Popular Front defeated a coalition of right-wing parties in a national election. Military officers who opposed the republic attempted a coup d'état, and when that failed they launched a full-scale rebellion. The Civil War that followed became a center of world attention as a rocky alliance of socialist, communist, and anarchist forces supported and increasingly controlled by the Soviet Union attempted to fight off a nationalist and authoritarian movement abetted by, and in some ways sympathetic with, Nazi Germany.

Throughout North America and western Europe, the Spanish Civil War successfully mobilized the eastern European Jewish immigrant masses that had for the most part looked upon World War I with indifference. Jews were present at the very beginning of the war. Several dozen had come to Barcelona in July of 1936 to take part in the international workers' Olympiad, which had been planned as a response to the Nazi-sponsored Olympics in Berlin but was canceled following the outbreak of civil war. Many of the athletes, including the Jews among them, stayed on to fight for the Republic in the first battles against the Nationalists in Catalonia and Madrid.[13] Foreign volunteers from around the world arrived by the thousands, and in the winter of 1936–37 they were formally divided by national origin and language to form the International Brigades. At their height the brigades numbered some 30,000, of whom at least one-fifth were Jews. Six commanders of the fifty-odd brigades, and three of their divisional commanders, were Jews.[14] Estimates about both the total population of the brigades and the Jews within them vary widely, and many of them are the work of former brigadistas combing through membership lists and picking out Jewish-sounding names, which is a highly unscientific enterprise. But the figure of 30,000 appeared in a report by the League of Nations, and no estimate of Jewish brigadistas is lower than 5,000, while some go as high as 7,500. Moreover, according to Martin Sugarman's statistical studies, which involve diligent cross-tabulation among multiple sources, 45 percent and 38 percent of the Polish and American contingents respectively were Jewish.[15] There is also telling qualitative evidence of Jewish prominence in the brigades, such as the story told by one Rumanian brigadista who claimed that the only way for members of the Abraham Lincoln Brigade to communicate with the Spanish commander of the Rumanian brigade was by speaking to Sharf in Yiddish, which he then translated into Spanish.[16]

Jews were not always overrepresented within the brigades, however. In Canada, as few as 38 out of 1,500 volunteers were Jewish. The low numbers might be explained by Canada's Foreign Enlistment Act, which prohibited its citizens' enlistment in the armed forces "of any foreign state at war with any friendly state," and which technically applied to Canadians fighting on either side in Spain.[17] But this act did not prevent Canadian Jews from volunteering in large numbers to fight for Palestine in 1948. True, the Ministry of External Affairs determined in 1947 and 1948 that the Enlistment Act was not applicable to Palestine,[18] but Canadian Jews in 1948 operated under the assumption that volunteering to fight for Israel was illegal and that the operation had to be carried out with the greatest secrecy. A far more likely explanation for the low volunteer figures for the Spanish International Brigades was the relative weakness among Canadian Jews of Soviet-brand communism, and the corresponding strength of Labour Zionism, which focused Jewish collective energy far more on Palestine's state in the making, the Yishuv, than on Spain.[19]

The Spanish Civil War coincided almost exactly with the Palestinian Arab revolt, which threw the Yishuv into turmoil and reinforced the Yishuv leadership's preexisting propensity to concentrate on state building and pay only lip service to international socialist solidarity. The Yishuv's reigning political party, Mapai, shared the United Kingdom's official position of nonintervention; as Yaakov Hazan, leader of the leftist party Ha-Shomer Ha-Tsair, put it, "Hanita [a kibbutz in the northern Galilee] is preferable to Madrid."[20] The official stand of the Yishuv leadership was to send money, not men. The Yishuv's newspapers rarely wrote about Palestinian volunteers in Spain and only broke their silence in late 1938, after the International Brigades had been disbanded. The fight against fascism, and the Spanish Republic's leftist tinge, appealed powerfully to certain segments of Yishuv youth, and all but 14 of the 344 volunteers from Palestine were Jews. Most of these Jews, however, were communists, and so technically anti-Zionist; only eleven came from left-Zionist parties and from the kibbutzim, and the latter expelled members who went off to fight in Spain.[21] Both the British authorities and the Mapai leadership saw the Jewish communists as troublesome undesirables who should be forced out of the country. The British authorized Jewish supernumerary police to bully and threaten jailed Jewish communists to, as one historian put it, "prefer the war of courage and glory in Spain [over] a long period of arrest."[22]

One such communist without a home was Pinchas Hafetz, a great-grandson of a disciple of the Vilna Gaon and a child of Jerusalem's old Orthodox community. As a young man, Hafetz gave up on Orthodoxy and embraced communism. Jailed by the British, he went off to fight in Spain, where he was temporarily blinded and invalided out of service. After a stint in the Soviet Union, Hafetz yearned to return to Palestine, but he was denied an entry permit and was forced to stay in the USSR until the early 1950s when he put an end to his misery by hurling himself in front of a train.[23]

Regardless of national origin, the vast majority of the brigadistas were communists, and the brigades' command was effectively handled by Moscow, which sent both military and cultural commissars to Spain. The brigades were infused with the spirit of communist internationalism, an essential component of which was the celebration of the role of particular nationalities to the workers' global struggle. The fifty brigades were named after national and/or revolutionary heroes such as Garibaldi for Italy, Masaryk for Czechoslovakia, Washington and Lincoln for the United States, Papineau and Mackenzie for Canada, and Mickiewicz and Glowacki for Poland.[24] Communism of the time not only embraced nationality as a vehicle of cultural and social unity that could boost fighting spirit and effectiveness; it also recognized the need for a common language of command and operation within each brigade. Cultivating the national languages of the sundry brigades through newspapers and radio programming became ever more important in maintaining morale as, throughout 1937, losses mounted steadily among the brigades, who were often used as frontline shock troops or, less charitably put, cannon fodder. In this spirit, a French-Jewish communist named Albert Nahumi (né Arieh Weits) proposed to the brigades' General Commissar Luigi Longo that a Jewish company be created within an existing brigade. Moscow approved, thinking the scheme would attract more Jewish volunteers. The Polish-Jewish Comintern representative suggested naming the unit Bar-Kokhba, while other Jewish brigadistas (including Pinchas Hafetz) proposed naming the company after Judah the Maccabee or Berek Joselewicz, both of whom were constructed in the left-Jewish tradition as champions of human liberation within a particular Jewish framework. In the end, though, the unit was named after Naftali Botwin, a Polish communist executed in 1925, and, at the time of its official formation in December of 1937, was incorporated as the second company of the Palafox Batallion of the Polish Dombrowski Brigade.[25] The company endured heavy and continual losses, but its numbers usually held steady at around two hundred, although estimates of the percentage of Jews within the company vary from 15 to 90 percent.[26]

One Botwin Company member's journal describes his comrades as "people not of blossoming youth, rarely younger than twenty-five years old. The majority are over thirty. Over forty is not rare."[27] Few had had previous military experience. They died in staggering numbers: for example, at least a third of the Palestine volunteers were killed. In all these respects—age, inexperience, and high casualty rates—Jewish volunteers differed little from their Gentile comrades. They were all highly imperfect soldiers, driven to fight because of the threat that fascism posed to their world. Their worldview was strongly and nearly consistently influenced by communism, but also inflected by particular ethnic concerns.

The balance between the two is difficult to measure. In their memoirs, many Jewish former brigadistas write of having volunteered purely out of internationalist motives but claim that they harbored deep-seated Jewish sensibilities that were only awakened years later—following the Holocaust, Israel's establishment, and Stalinist persecution. One scholar has described this type of narrative as a reconstruction rather than a realization of past identities, for during the 1930s the Jewish brigadistas were internationalist communists pure and simple, and subsequent events restructured their memory of their past selves.[28] The Botwin Company's anthem mentioned the word "Jew" only once, in the penultimate line of the final verse.[29] The company's manifesto of July 1938 emphasized brotherhood across nations as indispensable for the "struggle against antisemitism, race hatred and pogroms."[30]

Yet there were clear indications that at least some Jewish brigadistas felt, and wished to foster, a Jewish collective identity. In May of 1937, a group of Jewish officers and political commissars gathered to discuss founding a Yiddish-language newspaper. The paper, *Der Frayheyts-Kemfer*, first appeared in August, at a time when there were only eight other newspapers for specific nationalities in the brigades. The Botwin Company had its own newspaper, whose first issue called for a united struggle against not only fascism and dictatorship but also "Inquisition." The term meant more than generic clerical reaction, as the issue featured an article specifically about the suffering of Spanish Jews of Teruel under the Inquisition. As one American volunteer, Wilfred Mendelson, wrote to his father in June of 1938, "Today Jews are returning welcomed by the entire Spanish people to fight the modern-day Inquisition, and in so many cases the direct descendants of the ancient persecutions . . . yes, Pop, I am sure we are fighting in the Maccabean tradition."[31] In that same month, the fourth issue of the Botwin paper, in June of 1938, proclaimed a specific Jewish solidarity among the brigadistas:

> The appearance of each Botwin edition is impatiently awaited by not only Botwin soldiers but also by many hundreds of Jewish volunteers in other units. Jewish volunteers came from all corners of the world to Spain in order to combat fascism. Not all could be taken into the Jewish company; many did not want to be separated from their non-Jewish fellow countrymen. The Hungarian Jews went and stayed with the Rakoczi

Battalion; English and American with the Lincoln Brigade. These volunteers have, however, not forgotten that they are Jews and that they, in fighting against fascism, also smite barbaric antisemitism, along with the Nuremberg Laws and the accursed regime of the ghettos and pogroms.[32]

The company had a choir and theatrical troupe, and at one of its concerts, a forty-year-old volunteer, a cantor from Hungary, began by singing operatic arias, then *chazones*, traditional Jewish liturgical music. An article about battle stated that "the bullets piercing the air recall the slurping of a *Tehilim-Yid* [a Jew reciting Psalms, in this context as part of the morning prayer] when he drinks a glass of hot tea at the frosty dawn of a winter day."[33] And in the final issue, prepared after Moscow had ordered the withdrawal of the brigades, the company's newspaper left class solidarity and internationalism behind and focused only upon "the Jewish combatants [who] are fighting for the freedom, honor and well-being of the entire Jewish people."[34]

The final issue of the Botwin Company's newspaper also called for the "preparation of an extensive book, with a rich content, which would in popular form depict the various phases of the Jewish combatant's fight, from the outbreak of the war until today."[35] This project was similar to that envisioned in the Soviet Union during World War II by the writers Ilya Ehrenburg and Vasily Grossman, who hoped to compose a trilogy on Soviet Jewish suffering and heroism—a "black book" on the Jews' destruction, a "yellow book" on the partisans, and a "red book" on Jewish soldiers in the Red Army. (Only the *Black Book* was completed.)[36] The purpose of such projects was apologetic, very much as it was for the countless tracts produced by bourgeois Jews from the Napoleonic wars through World War I. Marxist internationalism and the united struggle against fascism occasionally dimmed but never extinguished antisemitic stereotypes, nor did they moderate the Jewish impulse to, in the words of one young volunteer, "show the world that we can be heroes."[37] Apologetic themes run throughout the monumental history of the Jewish volunteers by the ex-brigadista David Diamant. The fighters, he writes, "raised the esteem of the Jewish people" by giving "with deeds an answer to antisemitic propaganda that Jews were cowards and were not capable of risking their lives in battle."[38] In Diamant's exhaustive account, one of the first volunteers to fall in battle, as well as the last, was

Jewish. Over and again Diamant relates how non-Jews held the Jewish fighters in the highest regard.[39]

The Spanish Civil War was "Jewish" on two levels: as part of the global struggle against Nazism and antisemitism, and as a performance of a Jewish virility and heroism that historically had been tied to national patriotism but was now put in the service of internationalist Marxism. Both of these aspects mobilized and united, however briefly or imperfectly, large swaths of the Jewish left. In the United States and western Europe, Jewish communists, Bundists, and members of the Left Poalei Tsion, which combined commitments to Zionism and global proletarian revolution, supported the Paris-based Jewish-Spanish Solidarity Committee, which gathered money, clothing, food, and cigarettes for distribution to the Republican forces.[40] In the United States, the war was meaningful to immigrant and established Jews alike. Journalist Gina Medem filed copious dispatches from Spain for the American Yiddish press, while the yearbook of the staid American Jewish Committee offered lengthy accounts of the war and its consequences for the Jews. At the war's outbreak, American Zionist leader Stephen S. Wise vociferously supported the Republicans and condemned the "fascist rebels." According to a Gallup poll in 1938, 75 percent of American Jews supported the Republic, and rabbis in the United States took an unequivocal pro-Republican stand, as seen in proclamations of both the Conservative Rabbinical Assembly and the Central Conference of American Rabbis.[41] Although rates of volunteering for the International Brigades varied greatly from one land to another, Jewish sympathy for the Republicans was nearly universal—"nearly" in that there was a smattering of Jews among the thousands of Italians who fought for Franco.[42]

A Jewish former brigadista wrote in 1972 of a direct link between the Jewish fighting effort during the Spanish Civil War, the Warsaw Ghetto Uprising, and Israel's War of Independence.[43] Many Jewish brigadistas did, in fact, go on to play distinguished roles during the Second World War and, in fewer cases, in Israel's War of Independence. From the Botwin Company alone, two members became generals in the Polish People's Army. Emanuel Mink fought with the partisans in France, Pinkus Kartin took part in the Warsaw Ghetto Uprising, and David Smulevitch photographed the crematoriums in Auschwitz. Several Jews from the Balkans who had fought in Spain later served in partisan units during

World War II. Mirko Dojht, a footballer for Maccabi Zagreb, fought on and off from 1936 to 1948 in the brigades, the French Foreign Legion, and the Haganah before settling down as a shopkeeper in Haifa. In the United States, Leopold Berman of Baltimore fought for the Republicans, served in the U.S. Navy during World War II, and then worked in the Haganah's weapons procurement program.[44]

Proximity of action, however, does not amount to propinquity or causality. Jewish brigadistas who survived the conflict in Spain found themselves plunged almost immediately into an even more extreme situation, in which they fought for their lives in the only ways available to them. Many former brigadistas wound up after 1948 in Israel, not out of conscious choice but because of the presence of friends and family in the young country or, more often still, sheer happenstance. Just as the Spanish Civil War was, for all its horrors, a mere overture to the Second World War, so were the Jewish brigadistas, and the international Jewish support they commanded, a tributary of the international Jewish crusade against Nazism between 1939 and 1945.

## The Second World War: Fighting Amalek

Over one and a half million Jews fought in the Allied forces during the Second World War.[45] About a third served in the Red Army and another third in the United States' armed forces. The rest were mainly from Europe, the largest contingent being some 100,000 Polish Jews who took part in the futile defense of their country against the Nazi blitzkrieg. Many of them went on to serve in the various Polish armies in exile under British or Soviet command.[46] Similar patterns characterized Jewish soldiers in other eastern European successor states. Czech soldiers, for example, formed a separate unit within the Red Army that was over two-thirds Jewish, with mostly Jews in positions of command.[47] Over time, this force expanded into an entire corps with separate divisions for infantry, artillery, paratroopers, and armor. Jews also figured prominently among the French resistance forces. They constituted some 10 percent of the Free French and were prominent as leaders of the resistance groups Combat, Franc-Tireur, and Liberation. These three combined to form the Mouvement uni de la Resistance, commanded in southeastern France by the celebrated medieval historian (and Jew)

Marc Bloch. There were also within the French resistance several specifically Jewish groups, peopled mainly by recent immigrants who did not speak French well and who were divided between communist and Zionist factions.[48] Add to these various types of soldiers and rebels the thousands of Jewish partisans and ghetto rebels in eastern Europe, and the resulting total of Jewish fighters far exceeded the number of Jews killed at Auschwitz.

Of all the armies in which Jews took part, the Red Army had the greatest level of Jewish involvement and sacrifice. In keeping with the general patterns of mortality among combatants in the Soviet Union and the United States, over one-third of Soviet Jewish soldiers perished during the war as opposed to only 1.5 percent of American-Jewish soldiers. There were almost twice as many Jews in the United States as the Soviet Union, yet Jewish generals and admirals in the USSR outnumbered their American counterparts ten to one.[49] In other ways, however, certain patterns of specialization and placement united Soviet and North American Jewish soldiers. As in earlier conflicts, so in World War II Jews were concentrated disproportionately in branches of service that required education and technical expertise. In the Red Army of the 1930s, the professor and major general G. Eierson had developed new theories of mobile warfare, and other Jewish officers had been prominent as inventors and developers of tanks and other armored vehicles. Twelve of thirty Red Army armor specialists sent to Spain had been Jews. In 1939, the Spanish war hero Yakov Smushkevich was appointed commander of the Red Army's air force, only to be liquidated by Stalin in 1941. During World War II, Jewish engineers developed the Red Army's most successful tank and fighter aircraft. Three of the Red Army's twenty most highly decorated submarine commanders during World War II were Jews.[50] Similarly, Jews comprised 30 percent of the American army air corps, admission to which required higher education.[51] In Canada, in the spring of 1943 there were almost as many Jews in the air force as in the army, and over the course of the war Jews, who constituted 1.5 percent of the general population, were 2.66 percent of the Royal Canadian Air Force but only 1.44 percent of its army and 0.6 percent of its navy. The combination of higher levels of education and a slightly older demographic profile than the general population caused

Canadian Jews to be somewhat overrepresented in administrative as opposed to combat positions and underrepresented in the infantry, which tended to enlist the least educated soldiers and incur the highest casualty rates.[52]

It is not my purpose here to provide a comprehensive history of Jewish participation in the Allied forces in World War II. My focus is the conceptualization and implementation of a global Jewish world war that blended Allied and Jewish, especially Zionist, interests into a seamless whole. This idea was the work primarily of Jewish lay leaders, as the attitudes toward the war of American rabbis, especially in the liberal movements, were ambiguous. Rabbinic rhetoric featured a strong pacifist streak that persisted into the early years of the war. In 1939, the influential Reform rabbi Judah Magnes agonizingly abandoned pacifism in the face of Hitler's threat to Jewish and world civilization, but Rabbi Bernard Gross continued to favor a Jewish pacifist position so as to deflect accusations that the United States was being goaded by Jews into a war its citizens did not want. In 1940 the Reform movement's Central Conference of American Rabbis debated the legitimacy of conscientious objection and declared by a 38-30 vote that one could, within the spirit of the Jewish tradition, justify a refusal to serve. In that same year, the Conservative movement's Rabbinical Assembly also gave its sanction to conscientious objection. As late as June of 1942, the Reconstructionist Foundation recognized the right of Jews to interpret Judaism within a pacifist framework.

During the 1940s Orthodoxy never tolerated conscientious objection, whether out of a traditional obeisance to state authority or a stronger sense of attachment to persecuted European Jewry. Even within the more liberal movements, publicly vocal pacifists like rabbi Ed Feder were few. The Jewish Peace Fellowship, founded in 1941 by Rabbi Abraham Cronbach, had fewer than one hundred members in 1943. (Cronbach remarked memorably in 1937 that the worst thing about Hitler was that he had destroyed the Jews' love of peace.)[53] In fact, Jews were the least likely of any religious community in the United States to register as conscientious objectors. There was one Jewish CO for every 2,200 Jewish soldiers, while for Christians the figure was one in 653.[54] Jews, lacked the principled pacifist tradition of Protestant sectarian groups such as Quakers or the Brethren, and although in World War I many Jews had invoked radical socialist justifications for pacifism, in fact they were expressing an ideological opposition to fighting an imperialist war, and the combination of America's entry into the war and Russia's transition from a tsarist autocracy into a socialist republic caused all but the most hardened Jewish opposition to war against Germany to melt away. The pattern repeated itself in World War II; after the Nazi invasion of the Soviet Union, many a red or pink Jewish "pacifist" became a fervent supporter of, or participant in, the war.

As Deborah Dash Moore has written, military service in the Second World War was a means of both Americanization and intensification of Jewish ethnic identity.[55] Powerful, pervasive antisemitism was the experience of many a soldier, whose written memoirs and oral testimonies tell in particular of nasty altercations with redneck drill sergeants.[56] Yet Jews also felt that they were an essential component of a multiethnic yet quintessentially American war effort against Nazi and Japanese aggression. Even at its most difficult, the position of American Jews in uniform was drastically superior to that of African-Americans, who served in segregated units and faced supreme difficulty advancing into the officer corps. (The navy commissioned its first black officers only in 1944.) American Jews benefited by presenting themselves as members of a religious, as opposed to ethnic or racial, minority. They took pride that for the first time Jewish chaplains held officers' rank and that a considerable number were accepted into the service—311, a fifteenfold increase over World War I.[57] Apologetic literature of the era emphasized the commonality of spirit among American Jews, Protestants, and Catholics. *Jews Fight Too!* a popular book for youth published in 1945, consists of vignettes of Jewish heroism, and one of the stories, "A Tale of Tolerance," is about three soldiers, a Jew, a Catholic, and a Protestant, who fight and die together.

Intriguingly, *Jews Fight Too!* was in no hurry to dispense with older stereotypes of Jewish mildness of character. The book begins: "Yes, Jews fight too! Perhaps they do not fight any better, not more heroically than other people—but certainly no less bravely do they fight."[58] One vignette tells of a "shlemiel" who volunteered to join a commando squad charged with capturing Field Marshal Rommel, only to be caught and executed, dying as a shlemiel, but a heroic one.[59] Moreover, the preface to the book, penned by congressman and former Boston mayor James M. Curley, frames the Jewish contribution to the war effort within a broader "contribution" to American society that includes philanthropy (Julius Rosenwald), jurisprudence (Louis Brandeis), and "the financial well being of America in the critical period of the World War by Morgenthau and Baruch."[60] Most of the book is about more conventional forms of heroism, displayed by Jews the world over, including partisans and ghetto rebels, Moshe Dayan's daring nighttime raid in Vichy Syria, which cost him his eye, and the death of Irgun leader David Raziel while fighting against the forces of Rashid Ali during the Anglo-Iraqi War of 1941. But its display of pride in Jewish financial activity, and its affectionate evocation of the mild-mannered Jew as a hero even in defeat, is unique to American-Jewish apologetics and is a sign of both American Jewry's relative comfort in its surroundings and the valorization of commerce and capitalism in American culture.

The easy blend of commercial and military heroism represents a continuation of the prewar propaganda of the Jewish War Veterans of the United States, which published an article in 1938 praising the great leaders to whom American Revolutionary War financier Haym Salomon lent money. By lending money, usually without notes and interest-free, to warriors such as Baron von Steuben, General Arthur St. Clair, and Thaddeus Kosciuszko, Salomon essentially rose to their ranks.[61] The consonance between this spirit and that of broader currents in American society is made clear by a monument to George Washington, Haym Salomon, and fellow Revolutionary War financier Robert Morris that was unveiled in downtown Chicago in December of 1941, the product of six years of fund-raising by an ecumenical organization and led by a non-Jewish mayor and campaign chairs.[62]

On this point there are interesting distinctions between American- and Anglo-Jewish wartime propaganda. The latter indulged in a variant of the American-Jewish distaste for vulgar militarism, as seen in Cecil Roth's 1946 paean "The Jews in the Defence of Britain":

Like most extremely pacific persons, the Jew is a good fighting-man, and he has never failed to demonstrate his devotion (not merely his loyalty) to this country on the battlefield when the opportunity has offered. This is no cause for pride. It is a question of duty; and the whole of Jewish history is a demonstration that we of all people do not shirk our duty wherever it may lead us.[63]

But Roth does not breathe a word about the great Jewish banking families' historic contributions to England's victories, dating back to Nathan Mayer Rothschild during the Napoleonic wars.

Canadian-Jewish propaganda, on the other hand, shared American Jewry's eclectic and capacious definition of military heroism. In 1944 and 1945, the Canadian-Jewish Congress published a three-part series of comic books titled *Jewish War Heroes* (figures 6.1–6.3).[64] The issues employed the classic graphics of comic books to illustrate the lives and heroic deeds of decorated fighters in the Allied forces. Deftly combining narrative and fictionalized dialogue with illustrations of dogfights and battles on land and at sea, the booklets also made space to document their figures' contributions to civilian life, especially Jewish education and philanthropy. The series paid particular attention to Canadian and British flyers, but it also honored Americans (such as the celebrated boxer Barnie Ross) and Russians (twenty-nine-year-old submarine commander Israel Fisanovitch). For some, a colorful prewar past was more important, and received more attention than, wartime service, as with Bert "Yank" Levy, a Canadian adventurer who saw combat in the Middle East in World War I, Nicaragua in 1926, and Spain during its Civil War before becoming an instructor for the British Home Guard and U.S. Army. Similar were the primarily prewar exploits of the Anglo-Canadian Morris Abraham Cohen, aka "Two-Gun Cohen." According to the comic, Cohen first met the Chinese reformer and nationalist leader Sun Yat-sen in Calgary, became his aide-de-camp, and, after Sun's death in 1925, foreign secretary of the Chinese Nationalist Party, the Kuomintang. In fact, Cohen was more of a bodyguard and drill instructor than an aide-de-camp, and during the interwar period he worked for a number of Kuomintang leaders and warlords opposed to the Nationalists' nominal leader, Chiang Kai-shek.[65] Understandably, given the nature and format of a comic book aimed at youth, specific contributions to the war effort at times took a back seat to overall displays of derring-do.[66]

In the comics, interspersed between the biographical sketches, are brief narratives of the presence of Jews in the Allied forces: "Jews every-

Figure 6.1. *Jewish War Heroes* comic book cover (Canadian Jewish Congress, 1944). *Courtesy of the Canadian Jewish Congress Charities Committee National Archives.*

where have declared war on Hitler, war to the death, without reserve and without compromise." In an illustration from an issue released just after the end of the war, Palestine's contribution to the fighting receives as much space as that of the Jews of the British Empire, the United States, and Russia. ("The Jewish University fought a war of science," the caption reads, while "the Jewish Brigade fought on the Western Front.")

Figure 6.2. *Jewish War Heroes*: Soviet submarine captain Israel Fisanovitch (Canadian Jewish Congress, 1944). *Courtesy of the Canadian Jewish Congress Charities Committee National Archives.*

The number 12,000, which as we have seen showed up repeatedly in Jewish apologetic literature about World War I—it was the tally of fallen German-Jewish soldiers, wounded and killed Polish-Jewish soldiers, and foreign French volunteers in World War I—is invoked here as the number of Canadian Jews in uniform and the total number of Jewish servicemen in Australasia and Africa. Perhaps this is all coincidence, but given that all the numbers in the apologetic literature about

Figure 6.3. *Jewish War Heroes*: Sergeant Meyer Levin (Canadian Jewish Congress, 1944).
*Courtesy of the Canadian Jewish Congress Charities Committee National Archives.*

Jews in both world wars are estimates, and are at times artfully cobbled
together (sometimes combining Jewish communities in separate states,
or the killed and wounded, into a single category), one wonders about
the enduring power of this particular number in Jewish consciousness.

American Zionists made a particular effort to present the Yishuv as
the center of a global Jewish effort on behalf of the Allies. During the
early years of World War II, while the battle for North Africa raged and

the future of Palestine was in doubt, Palestinian Jewry's contributions to war industry were portrayed as part of world Jewry's commitment to fight for Britain and against Hitler by any means necessary. Abba Hillel Silver, national chair of the United Palestine Appeal (UPA), wrote in its 1941 yearbook that Hitler's war against the Jews had triggered a unanimous Jewish response to fight "to the hilt and to the finish." The hundreds of thousands of Jews in the Allied forces, Silver wrote, were "men whose hands are on machine guns, or hurling hand grenades, or driving tanks, or piloting bombers, who give blow for blow."[67] Not only are the world's fighting Jews valiant, they are also united against Hitler as is no other people, for "there is not a single Jew fighting in the Axis armies." This was not precisely true. There were Finnish and Soviet Jews who allied with Hitler against the Soviets, thousands of men of Jewish origin fought for Nazi Germany, and Iraqi Jews were conscripted into the pro-Nazi Rashid Ali's army during his brief war against England. Still, the prospect of Jews facing other Jews across the lines of battle, which, as we saw in chapter 4, was a major theme in public conversations amongst Jews from the mid 1800s up through World War I, was no longer a visible dilemma.

Palestine's Jews receive the lion's share of praise in the yearbook; according to Silver, "almost from the first day of the war, the entire Yishuv mobilized as one man." "They Work and Fight," blares the title of one article, whose text details the contributions of the Yishuv's Jews as both skilled laborers at home and soldiers in the armed services abroad. According to another article, the Yishuv's rates of volunteerism were behind only those of Australia and New Zealand among the British dominions.[68] In this article, poignant testimony of the Yishuv's commitment to the war against Hitler came from the survivors of the *Patria*, a ship loaded with refugees that in November of 1940 was denied entry into Palestine and exploded under mysterious circumstances in Haifa's harbor. Eighty-two survivors, representing about a third of the surviving able-bodied men, signed up for the British army.

In fact, before the Nazi invasion of the Soviet Union there had been considerable opposition, particularly among the pro-Soviet factions within the kibbutz movement, to fighting for imperialist Britain, author of the notorious 1939 White Paper that throttled Jewish immigration, and less ideological souls simply resisted leaving behind farms, factories, and families. Venerable Jewish fears of the standing army as an agent of assimilation and hostile to Jewish observance blended with a Zionist strategy of focusing military efforts at home both to defend the Jewish national home and prepare the way for statehood.[69] The UPA yearbook acknowledged some shirking by Palestinian Jews from volunteering to serve in the British army but claimed that "the closely-knit Jewish community of Palestine is strong enough to make life extremely uncomfortable for such individuals," yet without "injustice or discrimination."[70]

The 1941 UPA yearbook's emphasis on Jewish military service to the Allies takes on a special meaning when we realize that its text was composed in November, before the Japanese attack on Pearl Harbor and the United States' entrance into the war. American-Jewish activists were in the delicate position of fervently supporting the war against Hitler without expressly advocating American entry into the fight lest they be accused by antisemites of fomenting a "Jewish war." Similarly, until the end of 1941 the organ of the Jewish War Veterans of the United States officially supported the United States' policy of nonintervention, but it waxed enthusiastic about the Lend-Lease Act of 1941, and it painted in the most positive colors the situation in Canada, which was geared up for the war effort, and whose Jews were allegedly volunteering in large numbers and for every corps, especially the air force.[71] The truth was somewhat different. Until the spring of 1942 Canadian conscripts were not sent overseas unless they volunteered for overseas service, and Canada's Jews were less likely to do so than others. One in five Canadian Jews in uniform was a "Zombie," or a draftee who refused to be sent abroad. A community of recent immigrants from eastern Europe, Canadian Jews had little affection for the British Empire, and the radical leftists among them adhered to the provisions of the Molotov-Ribbentrop Pact (the nonaggression treaty between the USSR and Germany) until the Nazis brutally and unilaterally abrogated it.[72]

The cover illustrations of the UPA's 1941 and 1942 yearbooks, drawn by the celebrated artist Arthur Szyk, depict the profound difference in American-Jewish self-representation before and after the United States' declaration of war on Germany. The 1941 cover (figure 6.4) depicts a male British soldier in khaki shorts, armed with a rifle and knife, his right sleeve adorned with a Star of David atop his sergeant's chevrons. (In World War II, the Star of David appeared on British uniforms only with the formation of the Jewish Brigade in 1944, so this depiction is a carryover from the uniforms of the Jewish Legion.) The young man has oversized, muscular arms and legs, and while his right hand clutches his rifle, the left fist is clenched in a confident "thumbs up" gesture. Behind the soldier's profile is a larger Star of David surrounding a V for victory, along with the visual representation of the Morse code for the letter V, dot-dot-dot-DASH. (This rhythm was reminiscent of the first four notes of Beethoven's Fifth Symphony, which was the signature of the BBC World Service.)[73] The V is framed by twin lions, a deceptive reference to the lion and unicorn representing England and Scotland in the United Kingdom's coat of arms, as here the Scottish unicorn is replaced by the Lion of Judah. Between the lions is a Hebrew inscription, Rabbi Hillel's "If I am not for myself, who will be for me?" Toward the bottom of the page, at the soldier's knees, are two smaller pictures: on the left, a family of traditionally dressed Jews, sitting dejectedly on the ground, eyes closed or staring blankly forward, while on the right a young pair of Zionist pioneers, shovel and rake in hand, and carrying a basket of produce, stride purposefully into the future. The image's referents are Jewish and British, but not global.

The 1942 yearbook cover (figure 6.5) communicates a very different message. It depicts a male and female soldier, bearing the Star of David and the word "Palestine" on their lapels and clutching a large Zionist flag, which flies against a background of the flags of the Allied powers—with that of the now-combatant United States on top and, in the very center of the frame, the Free French. The "Jewish war" of the antisemitic imagination has now truly become a world war in which Jews are enthusiastic players.

Similarly, according to veteran Zionist propagandist Rufus Learsi, the Italian bombing of Palestine in June of 1940 catalyzed the homeland to gird for "total war," mobilizing the Yishuv's industry, agriculture, and scientific research along with its fighting men and women.[74] For Learsi, heroism among Jews has been evenly distributed over history between diaspora and Eretz Israel. In an unusual reference to early Islam, he singles out for praise the Jewish tribes at Yathrib (the former name of Medina), who rejected Mohammed's claim to prophethood, thus inviting Mohammed's resolve "to destroy them." The Jews, writes Learsi, would have defeated Mohammed but for their tribal disunity. No doubt he was

Figure 6.4. Arthur Szyk, cover drawing for the 1941 United Palestine Appeal year-book. *Reproduced with the cooperation of The Arthur Szyk Society, Burlingame, CA. www.szyk.org.*

making a reference to Jewish-Arab tensions of his own day, as well as to the ongoing splits between Labour and Revisionist Zionists, which many feared would mire the Yishuv in civil war just when it needed to make common cause against the Arabs.

During World War II, a cluster of Zionist activists in the United States combined propaganda, fund-raising, and political lobbying into a massive consciousness-raising campaign among the American

Figure 6.5. Arthur Szyk, cover drawing for the 1942 United Palestine Appeal yearbook. *Reproduced with the cooperation of The Arthur Szyk Society, Burlingame, CA. www.szyk.org.*

public on behalf of the future Jewish state.[75] Most of this activity was the work of Revisionists, in particular a delegation of Palestinian Jews led by Hillel Kook, a nephew of Abraham Isaac Kook, who went under the pseudonym of Peter Bergson. The "Bergson group" worked alongside, and at times clashed with, the Revisionist New Zionist Organization of America (NZOA), itself led by émigrés such as Ben-Zion Netanyahu and Meir Grossman. Support for these relative newcomers came from more established second- and third-generation American Jews who had not been lured by the siren call of socialism and who would have assimilated into a comfortable American bourgeois identity had it not been for Hitler.[76] Revisionist-inspired initiatives led by the American Friends of a Jewish Palestine, the Committee for a Jewish Army of Stateless and Palestinian Jews, and other organizations appealed to an array of colorful American Jews, including playwright Ben Hecht, journalist Max Lerner, advertising executive Alfred Streslin, and actor Eddie Cantor. Non-Jews were also prominent advocates for a separate Jewish army within the Allied forces. As we noted earlier, there were several national armies in exile during the war, and the idea of a Jewish army fighting both against Hitler and for Palestine was appealing to Irish-Americans, who were anti-British, and to liberal Protestants such as Reinhold Niebuhr and Paul Tillich. The Bergson group was particularly effective at winning endorsements from national political leaders such as congressmen, senators, and governors.[77]

The idea of a Jewish army was hardly unique to Revisionists. The Labour Zionist leaders of the Yishuv had proposed it as early as 1938, and Zionist Organization president Chaim Weizmann did the same in a letter to the British government of 3 September 1939.[78] David Ben-Gurion continued to expound upon it from 1940 to 1942, thinking less in terms of the fate of European Jewry (the extent of whose genocide was not fully understood until the summer of 1942) than of the defense of Palestine against Rommel's Afrika Korps and the postwar emergence of new states out of the British Empire.[79] It was not American Revisionist pressure, but pure manpower needs, that led the British to create the "Palestine Buffs," which was supposed to be an equally weighted force of Jews and Arabs until summer 1942, when the British gave up on parity, as the number of Arab volunteers was paltry.[80] The Palestine regiment served mainly in North Africa, but after the invasion of Italy in 1943 the British preferred to integrate the Palestinian Jews into the European theater, removed from the Palestine Question. The Zionist leadership's ongoing efforts to create an independent Jewish Brigade within the British forces finally came to fruition in the fall of 1944, mainly because the British wanted to shore up Jewish support for the Allies in the wake of the destruction of Hungarian Jewry.[81] The brigade, which was about five thousand strong and commanded by a mix of Jewish and Gentile officers, was deployed in Italy, Yugoslavia, and, at the war's end, the Netherlands.

In 1942, as Palestinian Jews increasingly entered the British forces and American Jews wholeheartedly embraced the American war effort, Bergson's scheme for a Jewish army became ever more tightly linked with the plight of European Jewry. At this point the American-Jewish home front displayed a talent for public relations, as Bergson placed advertisements in major newspapers calling attention to the growing Holocaust (the term was used in the 1 December 1942 issue of the NZOA's organ *Zionnews*).[82] Some of Hollywood's and Broadway's biggest names—Billy Rose, Kurt Weill, Dean Martin, Jerry Lewis, Frank Sinatra, and Leonard Bernstein—were enlisted to create and mount a theatrical pageant celebrating the Jewish contribution to civilization and calling for a Jewish army. The pageant, *We Will Never Die*, was seen by over 100,000 people in New York City, Washington, D.C., Boston, Chicago, and Los Angeles. In 1946, another Bergson initiative, the League for a Free Palestine, kept the cause of a Jewish army alive with another pageant, *A Flag Is Born*, written by Ben Hecht and directed by Luther Adler, starring Marlon Brando (whose acting instructor was Stella Adler, Luther's sister).[83] Brando plays David, a Holocaust survivor, in despair and on the verge of suicide, who is revived by the sounds of Hatikvah and the arrival onstage of three soldiers, representing the Haganah, Irgun, and Lechi.

Mainstream American Zionist organizations as well as the American Jewish Congress opposed the pageants as unduly provocative and even tried to prevent their performance. Much of what was at stake was a power struggle between the Zionist Organization of America and its Revisionist counterpart, as between the Revisionist movement as a whole and the leadership of the World Zionist Organization and the Jewish Agency Executive. The pageants were undoubtedly popular, but how effective were they? There is no evidence that they directly influenced American or British foreign policy, nor did they raise much money for the Zionist cause. Ben Hecht claims that *A Flag Is Born* raised over $1 million, but according to historian Judith Tydor Baumel, only $166,000 of this can be confirmed.[84] Similarly, the Jewish Army Committee, which disbanded in 1943, raised some $250,000 over its eighteen-month life.[85] These numbers pale in comparison with the fund-raising prowess of mainstream American Zionist organizations such as Hadassah and the National Labor Committee for Palestine, which between 1941 and 1945 raised $11 million and $4 million respectively, not to mention the United Palestine Appeal, whose wartime campaigns brought in some $40 million.[86]

After the war, Revisionist Zionists in the United States continued to engage in high-visibility actions such as organizing rallies, holding benefit basketball games at Catskill resorts featuring talented athletes working in the kitchens (one of them was the young Wilt Chamberlain), or, on a more militant note, occupying the British consulate in Manhattan. Revisionist-sponsored newspaper advertisements compared the Zionist fighters in Palestine with the American minutemen from 1776, and Dov Gruner, an Irgun guerrilla executed by the British, with Nathan Hale. Just as leftists during the Spanish Civil War appropriated the heritage of American liberal republicanism by creating Abraham Lincoln and George Washington brigades, so did the Irgun form a "Sons of Liberty Committee" and an Irgun volunteer brigade for Palestine called the George Washington Legion.[87] (One of its most celebrated activists, boxing champion Barnie Ross, claims to have signed up more than two thousand volunteers, though it's not clear how many of them got to Palestine, as the total number of American volunteer fighters in 1948–49 did not exceed twelve hundred, and few of them identified with Revisionism.)[88] If Jews were minutemen, then the Palestinians fighting for their own independence were deemed "Arab mercenaries" and likened unto Hessians. This rhetoric influenced the liberal American press; Henry Wallace, editor of *The New Republic*, himself made the 1776–1947 analogy, and I. F. Stone wrote in *The Nation* that the Jewish rebels in Palestine were "no more gangsters than were the men of Concord or Lexington." Walter Winchell wrote of the British, "You tried the Palestine policy in America and got your answer in 1776."[89]

There is no doubt that American public opinion favored the Zionists in 1948, and Revisionist publicity may have had something to do with that, although given the horrors of the Holocaust and the Americans' lack of connection with the Arab world it is difficult to imagine public opinion at the time would have been so different had the Bergsonites not been around. The Bergson group and American Revisionist Zionists, in fact, played a minor role in the overall American-Jewish effort on behalf of Israel's struggle for statehood in 1948. Many parties took part in this struggle, and, taken together, their contributions were essential. For many Jews in the United States and Europe, a robust, militant Zionism represented both a structural and ideological continuation of World War II, a war that would not be truly won until a sovereign Jewish state had been created in Palestine.

## CHAPTER SEVEN

# 1948 as a Jewish World War

The Israeli-Palestinian conflict emerges from and constantly returns to 1948. For over twenty-five years, ever since Israel's archives made sources from 1948 available for historical research, scholars have striven to understand why Israel emerged victorious in its war against the Palestinians and Israel's neighboring Arab states. There is a broad consensus among scholars that Israel enjoyed relative military strength compared with its Arab foes. Although far smaller in population and land mass than the array of Arab states, Israel was able to field more soldiers, its army was better trained and had higher morale, and, although at a material disadvantage during the war's first months, in time it was able to acquire superior weaponry.[1] For all that has been written on the subject, however, scholars have paid only cursory attention to the connections between international Jewish assistance and the fledgling state's strength. We know a great deal about the autonomous political institutions of Palestine's Jewish community and how they inculcated a fighting, nationalistic spirit into its youth, but little serious thought has been given to the scores of thousands of Jews who flowed from the diaspora into the ranks of Israel's new army, nor to the international sources of money that purchased the weaponry, provisioned the armed forces, and sustained the civilian economy throughout the period of the war. In Israel, victory in 1948 was made possible by not only the tenacity and innovative spirit of its fighters, but also the marshaling of credit and capital, both within Israel and throughout the Jewish world.

For all its important discoveries, recent historical writing on Israel's origins has remained steadfastly parochial, focused on the leaders of the Yishuv's institutions and militias. The war could not have been won, however, without a stream of men, money, and matériel from the diaspora, especially North America, western Europe, and South Africa.

## The Global Battle for a Jewish State

The ideal type of the Israeli soldier in 1948 is the native-born (or close to it) Palestinian Jew who manned the Yishuv's militias during the 1930s and '40s and led the IDF to victory in 1948. The embryonic IDF was not, however, cut off from previous traditions of diaspora Jewish military service. For example, there were Haganah leaders in the interwar Yishuv who had cut their fighting teeth in European armies during the First World War and Bolshevik Revolution. There were those from the Red Army, like Yitzhak Sadeh; or officers from the Habsburg military, like Raphael Lev[2] or, more important, Sigmund (Edler von) Friedmann, the second head of the Austrian World War I Jewish veterans' association, the Bund jüdischer Frontsoldaten.

Friedmann was born into a military family; his father was a colonel and staff officer in the imperial War Ministry. Highly unusual for a Jew in fin-de-siècle Vienna, young Sigmund had only military schooling; with his lieutenant's commission, he went into the heavy artillery and commanded a unit on the front before being called to the War Ministry as a staff officer. Arrested at the time of the Anschluss, he was released largely thanks to intensive lobbying by Jewish veterans' groups throughout the world. Upon his release, Friedmann went to Palestine and, on behalf of the Committee of the World Congress of Jewish War Veterans, issued a broadsheet under his signature that displayed his conversion to the Zionist cause: "The blood given by our brothers is no longer acquiring rights for the Jews who fought in the front line nor for their fellow." The greatest tragedy befalling the Jewish people, Friedmann wrote, is its lack of a homeland, and "the conviction that this is really so is now permeating the mind and soul of every Jew who was a combatant in the World War."[3] Shortly after issuing this statement, Friedmann changed his name to Eitan Avisar, and in 1939 joined the Haganah staff. Avisar ran the Haganah's Planning and Operations Department, and in 1943 became its deputy chief of staff. He created a nationally organized militia and strategy out of what had been localized units and defensive schemes. After the war Avisar, now a general, became head of the Israel

Defense Force's supreme military court, and he wrote a comprehensive history of tactical warfare, the first of its kind in Hebrew.

Avisar's talent for administration, planning, and operations was shared by other immigrants, both minor and major figures in the history of the Israeli military. For the former, we have the colorful character of Max Reihan, an officer in the German infantry in World War I who served on all its fronts. A proud bearer of the Iron Cross First and Second Class, Reihan immigrated to Palestine in 1938 and served the Haganah in a variety of capacities, including organizing training exercises for the first battalion of the Haganah's field units in Haifa. Reihan relied on German military training manuals and swore in new Haganah members by having them place one hand on a Bible and the other on his officer's sword, whose hilt bore the golden Prussian eagle.[4] For the latter, there are the cases of the American Mickey Marcus and the Canadian Benjamin Dunkelman, both of whom held senior command positions during the 1948 war.

During World War II, and during the years of Israel's struggle for statehood, the line dividing a "diaspora" from an "Israeli" fighter was porous to the point of dissolution. In June of 1940, the British began to recruit Jews and Arabs as sappers for the French front. The Jewish volunteers were a mix of idealists, adventurers, young men fleeing personal or family trouble, and most often new immigrants, lonely and rootless, newly arrived and looking to leave. Newcomers who had been in Palestine for less than a year comprised 80 percent of the sapper force. The ratio of new Jewish immigrants in the British forces declined as the war progressed, but the presence of newcomers as volunteers remained significant.[5]

This sense of diversity was captured in the opening issue of the short-lived newspaper *Ha-hayal ha-'ivri* (1943), produced for the twenty thousand Jews scattered across more than a dozen units in Britain and North Africa. (Another ten thousand served in local forces, including the supernumerary police, in Palestine.)

> Like the Yishuv, so are we a gathering of exiles and a unity of differing ages. From sundry lands and cultures, veterans and youth and new immigrants, rooted dwellers in the land, and illegal immigrants. Not a single bloc in our origin, in the customs of our culture, in its age, in its

experience in Eretz Israel, in its spiritual life and aspirations. In addition, we are few among the many and scattered among small units without a connecting framework beyond that of general military command. For we have no Hebrew army.[6]

Another article in the same issue, poignantly titled "On the Holocaust," clearly associated the genocide, the unity of the Jewish people, and the urgent need for a distinct Jewish fighting force within the Allied armies:

We cannot be satisfied that many Jews participate on various fronts. They take part in them as soldiers of various peoples. Their heroism and sacrifice are not recorded in the name of their people. Our brethren are slaughtered as Jews. *As Jews.* In Jewish units we want to meet in battle, we will not agree to purchase the right to active participation in the campaign at the price of erasing our Jewish face and Hebrew name. Our infantry battalions carry in them this right in the essence of their being. The volunteer movement is born out of the burning desire to fight, out of the evil decree, and out of the vision of a Jewish war. Do not throttle this movement. Do not destroy its will. Do not stand by the blood of our people. Do not join the deniers of our rights in your prohibiting us this basic right. We cannot accept this evil decree. We cannot stand by it. The time has come to fulfill our demands—to the front![7]

Late in the war, among the new arrivals were Jewish maquis from France and Yugoslavia who made their way to Palestine, joined the Jewish Brigade, and made the return journey to Europe, now fighting in Italy. Moreover, partisans figured among the first wave of recruits for the Gahal (*giyus hutz la-aretz*), those brought to Palestine before Israel's declaration of statehood in May of 1948.[8] That first wave also included many Jews with experience serving in various eastern European armies, and from the spring of 1948, by which time most of the Haganah representatives who had begun the recruiting drive had returned to Palestine to fight against the Palestinians, Jewish veterans offered paramilitary training in camps near Marseilles and Bari and on Cyprus. To be sure, most of the Gahal had been neither partisans nor soldiers, and the military training they received was limited to ten days of drill and exercise. But contrary to myths that have developed in Israel since 1948, the Gahal were not a mass of civilians unfit for battle. At the notorious first battle for Latrun where, legend has it, the Gahal were thrown into the field as cannon fodder, only eight of the seventy-four who died in combat were new arrivals. The total number of Gahal fighters killed in the 1948 war did not exceed their percentage of the total IDF fighting forces. Most important, despite profound cultural differences between them and veteran Israeli soldiers, Gahal fighters distinguished themselves in the middle and last phases of the war, such as the battle for the Negev.

The Gahal constitute only part of the global Jewish dimension of the struggle for Palestine leading up to and during the 1948 war. The creation of an effective Jewish fighting force during the War of Independence cannot be separated from the international mobilization of armaments, supplies, and volunteer fighters (as opposed to the immigrant Gahal). This mobilization was spearheaded by Haganah forces in Europe, South Africa, and North America working in cooperation with a collection of diaspora Jewish activists. The post-1945 network of Jewish aid for Palestine was a direct outgrowth of decades of international Zionist and Jewish philanthropic activity, the difference being that now the activity was illegal and much of the material was contraband.[9]

While Jewish businessmen were doing their utmost to smuggle matériel and recruits into Palestine, some 3,500 volunteer fighters (Machal) came to Palestine, then Israel, to take part in the 1948 war. The Machal hailed mainly from the United States, Canada, and South Africa, but volunteers came as well from North Africa.[10] Most were Jewish, though some were Christian, motivated by biblical philosemitism, a love of adventure, or the need for a job. Among the Jewish fighters, the line between volunteers and immigrants was at times fuzzy, not so much in the fighters' intentions as in the perceptions of the Yishuv bureaucracy, which assumed, for example, that any new arrival from North Africa was an immigrant, much to the consternation of those Moroccan Jews who saw themselves as helping Israel in its hour of need but planned to return home after the fighting was over.[11] The South African and North American men of the Machal forces supplied the bulk of the pilots and crew for Israel's embryonic air force, which played an essential role, not as a combat force so much as a transportation corps. The air force did not provide a significant level of tactical support for ground troops, nor did it engage in decisive aerial raids, as the Arab states' planes were quickly grounded owing to a lack of spare parts. But Machal airmen were indispensable as transporters of supplies to besieged Israeli communities in the Negev and of arms purchased abroad. (The most famous weapons airlift was Operation Balak, which brought Czech arms and fighter aircraft to Israel.)[12] Machal forces were also highly overrepresented in Israel's newborn navy. Paul Shulman, first commander of the Israeli navy, was an Annapolis graduate who received his appointment at the age of twenty-six after coming to Palestine to work in illegal immigration activity.[13]

Machal commanders served in ground units as well, as in the Eighth Armored Brigade, which had an English-speaking heavy tank company and a light tank company consisting of Russian speakers. (The brigade commander, Yitzhak Sadeh, communicated with this company's commander in Russian.) Toronto's Ben Dunkelman commanded the Seventh Brigade in the Lower Galilee, and two of his battalion commanders, Joe Weiner and Baruch Friedman-Erez, were also volunteers.[14] And the most celebrated Machal ground commander was Colonel David (Mickey) Marcus (figure 7.1), who commanded the Jerusalem front with the rank of major general before he was mistakenly killed by a Palmach sentry at Abu Ghosh on 10 June 1948, on the eve of the United Nations truce. Marcus' exploits in Palestine have been celebrated in a popular 1962 biography by Ted Berkman[15] and a Hollywood film, *Cast a Giant Shadow* (1966), with Kirk Douglas in the starring role.

Marcus was one of those rare men who were just as remarkable as hagiographical representations make them out to be. He was the epitome of American-Jewish success. Born on Washington's Birthday in 1902 on the Lower East Side's Hester Street, son of a Rumanian pushcart peddler, Marcus received a basic Talmud Torah education but became a star student and athlete in public high school. He stunned his immigrant parents by announcing his intent to attend West Point and become an army officer. This decision corresponded to Marcus' ambition and determination not merely to Americanize but to penetrate the bastion of the United States' warrior elite, a caste that historically had had few Jewish members. Agile as well as brawny, a powerful gymnast and boxer, Marcus was also intellectually gifted (he memorized great swaths of classic literature, especially Shakespeare). He excelled at West Point

Figure 7.1. Colonel David "Mickey" Marcus (1901–48) on graduation from West Point. *Courtesy of the 1924 Howitzer yearbook, United States Military Academy.*

and was offered a Rhodes Scholarship, but declined so as to remain with his bride Emma (who would outlive him, becoming the loyal custodian of his grave and his memory, by thirty-five years). Before the war, Marcus was an attorney, New York district judge, deputy commissioner of New York City corrections, and then commissioner under Fiorello Laguardia. While deputy commissioner, he led a 1934 police raid on New York's lawless Welfare Island penitentiary, run by gangsters with Tammany Hall connections. (Marcus wrestled one of them, the 210-pound Joey Rao, off a barber chair and onto the floor.) Marcus' cleanup of the New York prisons became the subject of a 1939 Hollywood film, *Blackwood's Island*, starring John Garfield as Marcus. Before World War II even began, Marcus was already a national celebrity.

During the war Marcus trained some eight thousand Rangers for service in the Pacific theater, then served as a senior staff officer in the army's Civil Affairs Division, attending the inter-Allied conferences at Cairo and Teheran and planning the postwar occupation of Europe. Bored by what he considered a desk job, Marcus got himself dropped into France without authorization just after D-Day and was present at the liberation of Dachau. (His late-war exploits were chronicled by Walter Winchell in his widely syndicated newspaper column.) After the war Marcus was appointed head of the Pentagon's War Crimes Division.

Berkman's biography of Marcus, from which this information is taken, has a strong Technicolor tinge to it.[16] There is a good deal of fictionalized dialogue and narrative in the book (in one scene, when Marcus warns Ben-Gurion that the Arabs, if united, could take Tel Aviv in ten days or less, Ben-Gurion "slammed shut the huge Bible open on his desk.)"[17] Trying to make his story accessible to an American audience, Berkman describes Israel as "a kind of miniature California,"[18] with Tel Aviv as Los Angeles, Haifa as San Francisco, and, most improbably, Jerusalem as Sacramento. More important, Berkman makes a fair number of factual errors. (He describes Dachau as "the most terrible of the Nazi prisons in that it was devoted exclusively to mass murder" and Hatikvah as "a traditional Jewish song of yearning for the homeland.")[19] Yet many of the most fascinating aspects of Marcus' life are a matter of public record; Berkman's sketch of Marcus' warmth, charm, and commanding presence is confirmed by numerous other accounts, and, most salient for our purposes, Berkman's narrative of how Marcus got involved in the Palestine War is largely corroborated by the meticulous Israeli historian Uri Milstein in his exhaustive history of the 1948 war. Both authors present Ben-Gurion as in dire need in winter 1948 of a foreign expert to help build an Israeli army out of the land's scruffy militias. Ben-Gurion entrusted Shlomo Shamir, the Haganah emissary to the United States, to find the right man—not necessarily a Zionist or even a Jew, but someone sympathetic to the cause and who could bring a staff of assistants with him. The Haganah considered more than twenty individuals, none of them Jewish, and at first called upon Marcus as a consultant to the process, not a prime choice.[20]

Marcus' decision to volunteer when no other suitable candidate would take on the job stemmed from a profound conviction that the Zionist cause was a direct continuation of both classic American republican values and the new, postwar order of collective, international resolution of ethnic conflict. Very much in keeping with the parallels drawn by postwar Revisionist propaganda between the Zionist fighters in Palestine and the American revolutionaries, Marcus saw the Zionists as brave pioneers who wrested a living from the ungenerous soil and as victims of religious tyranny, democratic and individualistic, organized into a citizens' militia. Just as the American revolutionaries had been aided by friends from abroad—Lafayette, von Steuben, and Kosciuszko—so did the international community owe assistance to the Zionists, successors to the colonials of 1776. Marcus believed that the principles of international cooperation under United States tutelage, which he had helped formulate at Dumbarton Oaks, demanded the establishment of a Jewish state. For Marcus, Palestine represented the final theater of the Second World War, and a Jewish defeat would discredit the cause for which the war had been fought.

Marcus' first major task in Palestine was to compose manuals on military organization, tactics, and logistics. The effective mobilization of the Yishuv's home industry was a top priority, as soldiers on military bases often lacked proper clothing and footwear. In May of 1948, Marcus focused his attention on the development of a motorized (jeep) corps in the Negev, and thereafter he was appointed commander of the Jerusalem front, overseeing the Harel, Etziyoni, and Seventh brigades. As the assaults against the Jordanian Arab Legion's stronghold at Latrun failed and the position of besieged Jerusalem grew ever more desperate, Marcus accomplished what had appeared impossible by engineering the construction of the legendary "Burma Road," the alternative route through the Judean hills that enabled the transport of goods to the starving city.

Marcus accomplished the impossible as well in terms of human relations. The veteran militia commanders were usually suspicious or dismissive of outsiders, but they admired Marcus, who also was able to overcome the mutual suspicions of Haganah and Palmach commanders toward IDF officers who had served in the British army's Jewish Brigade. As a rule, during the 1948 war there were considerable tensions between the North American, South African, and western European volunteers from abroad and the veteran Israelis. On occasion, the bona fides of a volunteer was cast into question, as in the case of Fred Grunich, a colonel and career officer in the U.S. Army who came to Palestine briefly in June 1948 under the pseudonym Fred Harris as an adviser to the IDF chief of operations. Grunich was suspected by the Palmach and the leftist political parties of being a confidant of Ben-Gurion and even an American spy, sent to rupture the solidarity between Israel and the Soviet Union and to enmesh Israel into an American alliance. Harris lacked Marcus' colorful, jovial personality and warmth, and, as Teddy Kollek noted, he did not have the good fortune to be killed and thus to be remembered as a hero.[21]

More typically, the Israeli and Machal fighters trusted each other's intentions but were two distinct types of soldiers with differing self-images and conceptions of each other. By and large, the Machalnikim saw themselves as highly trained soldiers with much to offer the infant Israeli army. They were volunteers, intending to return home after the war was won but nonetheless dedicated to Israel (except for the handful of pure adventurers and mercenaries, many of these not Jewish, among them). Veteran Israelis saw the Machalnikim as helpful but unfamiliar with the terrain—political and cultural as well as geographic—of the new Jewish state and so as subordinates to the natural masters of the land, who had emerged from the Haganah and Palmach.[22] The Machalnikim, in fact, did not fit into a clearly established framework of Israeli-diaspora relations. They were not conscripted soldier-citizens fighting for their homelands, nor were they the indigenized colonials of the Yishuv. They were a phenomenon unto themselves, manifested precisely at the time when the war for Israel's creation took on a global dimension, demonstrating the inseparability of the diaspora from the land of Israel in all aspects of the Zionist project, including its military.

An excellent case study is provided by Benjamin Dunkelman (figure 7.2).[23] Born and raised in Toronto, he lived in Palestine during the early 1930s, returned to Canada for several years, and served in World War II with the Canadian forces in Europe. Decorated with the Distinguished Service Order, Dunkelman returned briefly to civilian life in Toronto but in 1948 went back to Israel. At first he was assigned to the Harel Brigade, and in July was appointed commander of the Seventh Brigade, which took part in the conquest of the Galilee. As a seasoned officer in the Canadian army, Dunkelman valued military discipline as well as personal initiative, and he strove to introduce rank insignia on soldiers' clothing and recognition in the field of a chain of command. But he encountered fierce opposition from Palmach commanders such as Yitzhak Tabenkin and Haganah commanders Yisrael Galilee and Yigael Yadin. Dunkelman aroused hostility for his use of maps to plan an operation; one dour Palmachnik growled, "In the Palmach we have to see the ground—we don't do our planning from *maps*."[24]

Dunkelman's adherence to appropriate norms of military behavior led to a clash with Dunkelman's superior, Haim Laskov, who, shortly after Dunkelman's forces had taken Nazareth, ordered that the city's civilian population be "evacuated," that is, expelled. In a page of his autobiography that Dunkelman deleted from the final manuscript, he tells of his refusal to follow the order:

> I was shocked and horrified. I told [Laskov] I would do nothing of the sort. In view of our promises to safeguard the city's people, such a move would be superfluous and harmful. I reminded him that scarcely a day earlier he and I, as representatives of the Israeli army, had signed the surrender document, in which we solemnly pledged to do nothing to harm the city or its population.

Twelve hours after Dunkelman openly defied his superior officer, he was replaced as military governor of the city. He agreed to the transfer of authority only if the security of Nazareth's population would be assured; and in his autobiography, published thirty years after the fact, he expresses satisfaction that these guarantees were maintained. (David Ben-Gurion, concerned lest the expulsion of the Arabs of Nazareth provoke an outcry throughout the Christian world, approved of Dunkelman's action.)[25]

Dunkelman very much wanted to stay in Israel after the war, but his ventures were all unsuccessful, as they clashed with vested interests. The Histadrut's construction enterprise Solel Boneh was furious about his plans to have U.S. Steel come to Israel and build Quonset huts for immigrants. Israeli soft drink manufacturers were unhappy with his acquisition of the license to sell Coca-Cola in Israel. And his idea for a clothing factory to make uniforms also ran afoul of the Zionist trade union Histadrut, as he wanted it to "be run along piecework lines."[26] Although admired by Ben-Gurion, who offered him a promotion to general and command of the armored corps in the new IDF, Dunkelman remained an outsider. If he had stayed in Israel and worked in business, it would

Figure 7.2. Major Benjamin Dunkelman (1913–97). *Portrait of Benjamin Dunkel-man, Second Lieutenant of the Queen's Own Rifles of Canada, ca. 1940. Ontario Jewish Archives, fronds 2, series 4.*

have been as a subordinate, not a leader, and that was something Dunkelman could not accept.

Dunkelman, like Marcus, was not an Israeli—if Marcus had spoken Hebrew he might not have been killed by a sentry on that fateful night in June of 1948. But Israel would most likely not have won the 1948 war without them and their ilk. They were motivated not so much by a clear Zionist ideology as by a sense of Jewish solidarity, a search for meaning in life, a love of adventure, and an acceptance of war as no less inevitable than it was hellish. Few of the Jewish volunteers were mercenaries. They were paid half as much as the Gentile volunteers who were prominent among the air force pilots and technicians. (The pay rates for Gentiles were quite good—as much as $550 per month.)[27] Late in life, Jewish volunteers spoke of their service as having infused their life with meaning and purpose, as a destiny fulfilled.[28] A Jewish pilot, Art Yadven, explained his volunteering in less lofty language: "I'd never been occupationally Jewish, but why not? I hadn't been in a good war for a couple of years."[29] Wars often induce a thrill of danger, dominance, and intimacy that civilian life cannot replicate, and the Machalnikim were hardly the first or only veterans to find themselves enlisting in one conflict shortly after having emerged from another. Unlike his mercenary predecessor, the modern serial soldier acts out of internalized longing for community, be it abstract and politicized (here, the state of Israel) or concrete and experiential (the community of the trenches, beautifully described by historian Antoine Prost as "ephemeral yet indestructible.")[30]

Many American volunteers in 1948 were students at the Hebrew University, beneficiaries of a benefit within the G.I. Bill that paid for tuition and a living stipend at foreign universities, including the Hebrew University or Technion, as part of an effort to relieve the crunch of American veterans attending universities in the United States. In 1948, the American consul in Jerusalem became aware that some of these students were fighting for a foreign power and asked for clarification from the university registrar. The registrar's reply was that the American students were studying just like their Israeli peers, and this misleading answer was accepted at face value by the American consulate.[31]

Despite the presence of American GIs at the Hebrew University, and the highly sympathetic stance toward the Zionist project taken by all the major Jewish organizations in the wake of the war, American-Jewish volunteer rates for the Machal were only a fraction of those from other countries. Whereas one in 5,000 American Jews volunteered, the ratios were one in 1,000 for Canada, about one in 500 for Britain and France, and a stunning 1 percent for South Africa's Jewish community, even higher if one takes into account the streams of South African Jewish youth who volunteered but were not mobilized.[32] The United States sent slightly·more American Jews to the International Brigades during the Spanish Civil War (1,250) than to Palestine in 1948 (1,100). Why was this the case? To be sure, America's Jewish veterans were weary after their service in World War II, concerned about the possible illegality of fighting for a foreign power, and cosseted by protective Jewish parents. But the same was true for Jews elsewhere in the world. Canadian and South African Jews were far more likely to have been involved in pioneering youth movements and to have a familial connection with, or previous life experience in, the Yishuv. (Some 15 percent of the Machal, many of them South African, stayed in the country after the end of the war.)[33] American Jewry was less connected with Palestine than its diaspora counterparts, and its Zionism was far more likely to be philanthropic, manifested through donations of money, not bodies.

These remarks are not, however, intended to diminish the signal role of American Jewry in 1948. American Jewry was akin to a vast and distant home front, and the same spirit of national commitment that motivated a paltry thousand or so men to don IDF khaki also stirred beneath the suited breasts of thousands of North American Jewish businessmen and professionals who eagerly worked with Haganah representatives to raise funds and purchase both arms and arms-production machinery for the infant state of Israel.

Fighting the 1948 war was a far more expensive affair for Israel than for the Arab states that attacked it. The Arab states deployed only portions of their armies, and with the exception of brief fighting in the Sinai, the war was carried out entirely on the soil of the lands designated for the Jewish and Palestinian states. Yet unlike Jordan and Iraq, which were plummeted into financial crisis by the war, Israel mobilized its entire population and economy in what Moshe Naor has described as a situation of total war.[34] The need and ability to attain this level of mobilization were far more significant markers of Israel's exceptional situation in the war than oft-made claims about Israeli military weakness or strength vis-à-vis its foes. A sign of this remarkable mobilization is the fact that Israel extracted almost three-fourths of the $300 million direct costs of the war from its own citizens—through loans (subscribed by patriotic individuals, especially the Yishuv's small entrepreneurial class of bankers and manufacturers), taxes, and bonds (bought by patriotic and desperate banks).[35] Since Israel's very survival was far from certain, the purchase of government debt was an expression of fervent patriotism, collective solidarity, and desperate hope. Even the robust civic spirit of the Israeli population, however, could not compensate for the exclusion of the Palestine pound from the sterling bloc in February 1948,[36] rendering the Israeli currency nonconvertible on the international market and useless for the purchase of arms abroad. The final and crucial quarter of the costs of Israel's war of independence came from diaspora Jewry.

Diaspora Jews provided far more than money. They worked closely with Zionist emissaries, mainly from the Haganah, in the acquisition of arms both before and during the war. Israel's situation was quite different from that of the Arab states, which did not have an arms acquisition network abroad and were denied access to weapons after the imposition of embargos on arms sales, first by the United States (declared on 14 December 1947 and strengthened by executive order, effective 15 April) and then by the United Nations (29 May).

On 1 July 1945, United Jewish Appeal director Henry Montor convened a meeting at the New York home of industrialist Rudolf Sonneborn. The meeting was attended by seventeen prominent Jewish businessmen and Zionist activists. The guest speaker at the meeting was David Ben-Gurion, who told the gathered guests that Great Britain would leave Palestine within three years and that an Arab invasion was sure to follow. He called upon the assembled to raise money for arms purchase. All present at the meeting agreed to take part in this largely illegal activity. The meeting resulted in the creation of a steering committee that established what became known as the "Sonneborn Institute."

The 1 July 1945 meeting has become the stuff of legend. Memoir accounts differ widely as to the composition of the meeting as well as its participants' later activities. Late arrivals to what became known as the "Sonneborn Institute" depict themselves as present from its creation, and peripheral characters claim to have played central roles. There is also a confusion of the institute's illegal activities, such as raising funds to acquire arms production machinery and smuggle it out of the country, and the legal collection of tents, clothing, and other nonmilitary materials. Fortunately, despite the secrecy attached to the meeting and its outcome, an archival document with the guest list has survived.[37] This list can serve as a point of departure for exploring what kind of prominent American Jew would commit himself to breaking the law to assist in the founding of a Jewish state.

Most of those present were already deeply involved in Zionist affairs. Some were modestly successful attorneys or businessmen, such as Atlanta's Howard Travis, president of the Zionist Organization of America's southeastern region and a founder of Camp Judaea in North Carolina, and Cleveland's Ezra Shapiro, who was to became world chairman of Keren Hayesod–United Israel Appeal.[38] Eleven of the seventeen, however, were highly affluent, and several had penetrated American elite society. Sonneborn himself was "old money," being the grandson of an immigrant who became a prosperous textile manufacturer. Like his father, Rudolf Sonneborn attended the elite Johns Hopkins University, and once in business he turned the family concern successfully from textiles toward petrochemicals. He also married into the German-Jewish aristocracy, becoming the fourth husband of Dorothy Schiff, the granddaughter of financier Jacob Shiff. Charles Rosenbloom, son of an immigrant Jew from Lithuania who became a liquor distributor in Pittsburgh, attended Yale, became an attorney, and then went into business with his college friend Alex Lowenthal, who also was present at the 1 July 1945 meeting. Lowenthal was a developer and a pillar of Pittsburgh civic affairs; he amassed sufficient wealth to retire at the age of fifty. Rosenbloom was at least as successful as a financier and developer and became a trustee of Carnegie Mellon University, to which he donated masterpieces of European art from his private collection, and the Yale University library. Shoe magnate Philip Lown, perhaps best known today for his endowments to Brandeis University, was an immigrant from Lithuania but a graduate of the University of Maine who had worked in the army's chemical warfare service during World War I. William Sylk owned a chain of drugstores in Philadelphia, and Julius Fligelman was a wealthy furniture manufacturer from Los Angeles.[39] These men were, as a whole, not only well-to-do but, by the standards of a mid-twentieth-century American immigrant community, reasonably genteel. True, one of the most active leaders of the group, Shepard Broad, had been born into poverty in Pinsk and clambered his way to great success as a banker, lawyer, and real estate developer in Miami. Broad had a reputation as a tough, savvy businessman who was not unaccustomed to skirting the edge of the law, but he was also a pillar of the Miami business and philanthropic community. Although the men of the Sonneborn group were mostly of eastern European origin, and several were first-generation immigrants, they were all respected figures within a variety of communities outside the Jewish realm and were unlikely to have flouted the law in any serious way.

The Sonneborn group created a bourgeois underground, replete with decentralized cells, safe houses, and noms de guerre. Some of the group's leaders had been involved in weapons production and supply during the Second World War, and they hired a staff of technical experts to locate surplus army machinery for manufacturing guns and bullets. Zionist youth volunteered to package munitions in deceptively marked crates; respected lawyers rented warehouse space for the production of weapons and stored vast amounts of cash in their office safes. With over three-fourths of the American trucking industry in Jewish hands, and many of the truckline owners supportive of the Sonneborn project, licit goods such as tents and foodstuffs were easily transported to New York and thence to Palestine.[40]

Through word of mouth, the Sonneborn Institute's members grew to several thousand, with professional connections to key industries including textiles, naval surplus, and telecommunications (for radio transmitters and walkie-talkies; ten thousand of the latter were smuggled to Palestine). Sonneborn created a permanent administrative structure, with a Finance Department headed by stockbroker Louis Rocker. Within the first four months of 1947, the group had raised a half million dollars and had purchased, among other things, two Canadian corvettes and a freighter, the *President Warfield*, later to be rechristened *Exodus 1947*. By the end of 1947, two million dollars had come in, and total fundraising by 1948 was six to seven million dollars. The money went to the acquisition of ships for illegal immigration, airplanes, especially transport craft, and, most important, equipment for arms manufacture. Seventy percent of Israel's machinery for the production of small arms and munitions was bought in the United States through these mechanisms.[41]

The Sonneborn project was tightly linked with Haganah efforts to raise funds and acquire arms and arms-manufacturing equipment in the United States. Between 1946 and 1949 three Haganah bureau chiefs—Yaakov Dori, Shlomo Shamir, and Teddy Kollek—and a staff of experts headed by Yehuda Arazi nominally supervised the operation, but in fact they and the Americans operated as equal partners. The Haganah engaged in fund-raising on its own, pulling in some three million dollars between 1945 and 1948.[42] Nevertheless its acquisition operations were not only dependent upon, but symbiotically linked with, American-Jewish activists. Haim Slavin, who headed up arms machinery purchases until the end of 1946, knew a lot about engineering from his work for the Palestine Electric Company, but he knew nothing about North America, let alone its arms industries, and could not speak English. (He taught himself by reading Sherlock Holmes stories.) Hence Slavin's need for Harry Levine, a millionaire plastics manufacturer from Massachusetts with extensive wartime experience in arms manufacture. Levine made connections with arms merchants throughout the United States and rented a warehouse in the Bronx to house contraband. He also rented factory space in downtown Toronto where Slavin and Karl Ekdel, a Swedish arms expert, crafted a prototype machine gun. Slavin's aide, a mechanical engineer named Phil Alper, was able, as an American citizen, to purchase military surplus equipment, including machinery for the production of arms and munitions.[43]

At times, it was simply impossible to determine if an initiative originated from a "Palestinian" or an American Jew or as a result of interaction between them. This is particularly true if we look beyond the philanthropic elite within the Sonneborn group to the scores of American experts who assisted the Haganah's acquisitions operations. For example, although Haganah commanders in Palestine were from the start enthusiastic about importing machinery for manufacturing light arms, until late 1947 they were reluctant to think in terms of a multistate Arab invasion and the need for air power for ground troop support or transport. The idea of buying airplanes came from the United States, most likely from Al Schwimmer, a former TWA navigator who founded Service Airlines, a front corporation that purchased aircraft and then flew them to Palestine. Schwimmer also directed the recruiting of American airmen, rendering his contribution to the war all the more essential.[44]

With the American arms embargo in place and firm restrictions on foreign involvement in arms purchase and transfer, American Jews assumed most of the legal responsibility for the acquisition project, reasoning that if they were caught the consequences for them would be far less grave than for any Palestinian Jews who might be caught. In fact, on several occasions, some of the Americans were caught red-handed: crates filled with dynamite spilled open on a New York dock; Royal Canadian Mounted Police at Niagara Falls apprehended the prototype submachine gun being smuggled from Toronto; volunteer pilots were apprehended while trying to fly planes from the United States to Europe and thence to Israel. Yet out of all these incidents, only one participant in this vast enterprise went to jail. Schwimmer was convicted of conspiracy, fined heavily, and stripped of his civil rights, but was not imprisoned. (He was pardoned by President Clinton in 2001.) Many others received suspended sentences or fines, at times nominal. The courts were sympathetic to the Zionist cause, the defendants had astute legal representation, and the FBI was never able to pierce beyond one local cell and expose the national operation in its entirety. Apparently it did not try very hard once FBI director J. Edgar Hoover had ascertained that the weapons would not be used within the United States.[45]

The American Jews involved in the Sonneborn project were not mere writers of checks. They understood the import and consequences of their actions. They were the leaders of the American-Jewish home front in 1948, and their actions can be understood with reference to the massive home front campaigns of the recently ended World War. (There is also a strong parallel to Irish Americans funneling money and arms to the Irish Republican Army during the Anglo-Irish and Irish civil wars.) The Sonneborn activists did not indulge in Walter Mitty fantasies of derring-do so much as engage in a civilian parallel to the armed struggle for domination of Palestine. Clearly, they basked in a vicarious heroism, as in the recollections of Al Robison, a textile merchant from New Jersey and one of the major figures behind the operation: "Here was an opportunity that happened maybe once in a lifetime, maybe not even once in a lifetime. That we could be cloak-and-dagger people, that we could live dangerously and feel highly virtuous about it, that we could actually make history."[46] Another member of the group expressed his feelings even more viscerally: "Haganah is the biggest romance; it is the greatest thing certain Jews had had happen to them in this country. I have known Jews all my life who were waiting for the day that they could point to another Jew that carried a gun and say, 'he represents me.' Meaning not to a gangster but a hero, and in the last few weeks the papers have come forth and they mention Haganah with respect."[47] As in the old joke that a Zionist is someone who raises money for another Jew to send yet another Jew to Palestine, here a Zionist is an unarmed Jew who raises money to arm another Jew, and derives emotional satisfaction from it.

The Sonneborn group's activities were curtailed by secrecy, competition with public Zionist fund-raising, and the lack of tax-deductible status for donations. Moreover, much of the arms and equipment purchased in the United States was confiscated by the authorities, was lost or pilfered en route, or arrived too late to be of use (e.g., fighter airplanes as opposed to transport planes, which did make it and played a major role). Yet this network of Jewish businessmen and Haganah agents certainly accomplished more than its Etzel counterparts, who managed to raise only several hundred thousand dollars.[48]

The businessmen were also more generous and effective than the Jewish gangsters whose donations, both in cash and in kind (e.g., guns), are the subject of many tales of dubious accuracy. Yehuda Arazi, head of the Haganah's arms acquisition operation, claims that Meyer Lansky and an Italian named "Tough Tony" Anastasia with influence on the New York docks ensured that weapons headed to Arab lands would not get shipped or would meet with accidents. It is not possible to verify this assertion. More likely is the connection between the Miami-based gangster Sam Kay and the president of Panama, Henrique Adolfo Jimenez, who agreed to let the Israeli arms ships fly under the Panamanian flag. As to fund-raising, Reuven Dafni of the Haganah claims to have met Bugsy Siegel, who arranged to go weekly to a restaurant on La Cienega Boulevard in Los Angeles and pick up suitcases stuffed with cash. Dafni claims the total amount raised was $50,000. Murray Greenfield of the Haganah's agency for illegal immigration, Ha-Mosad le-Aliyah Bet, claimed to have received $90,000 in an evening from a group of Jewish gangsters in Baltimore. Irgun activist Yitzhak Ben-Ami, who visited the United States under the aegis of the American League for a Free Palestine, claims that he received some $120,000 from gangster Mickey Cohen and other hoodlums, who extorted businessmen, Gentile and Jewish, to come up with the cash. Even if these stories are true, the totals are paltry in comparison with the funds raised by the Sonneborn group. What's more, Jewish gangsters did not always display a sentimental attachment to Israel; in 1951 two Detroit Jews, Arthur Leebove and Sam Stein, were convicted of trying to smuggle twenty-one U.S. warplanes from Newark to Egypt during the 1948 war.[49]

The contributions of not only the Jewish gangsters, but even the more civilized members of the Sonneborn group, paled in comparison with the massive United Jewish Appeal (UJA) fund-raising drive of 1948. From the start, relations between the Haganah arms acquisition operation and the Sonneborn group, on the one hand, and official (and legal) American Zionist organizations, on the other, were complicated. Several professional Zionist functionaries attended the 1 July 1945 meeting, which was facilitated by UJA director Henry Montor. Yet the meeting was kept secret from the American Zionist Emergency Council and American Jewish Agency Executive.[50] Nonetheless, in 1946 the Haganah's arms acquisitions initiative received a $400,000 loan from the UJA, with subsequent separate loans of $1 million and $2 million.[51] Over time, Abba Hillel Silver, president of the Zionist Organization of America, and other mainstream American Zionist officials grew worried about exposures of illegal activity (like dynamite spilling onto the New York docks) and the negative consequences this could have on Zionist activity as a whole within the United States. Silver's Revisionist Zionist sympathies may have also turned him against blanket American Zionist support for an operation run by and for the Haganah. In early 1948 the Jewish Agency declared its desire to take public responsibility for the arms acquisition project by focusing on the entirely legal goal of raising money to be sent to Israel, with the understanding that much of it would go to buying arms abroad.

In 1948 the United Jewish Appeal set itself the astronomical figure of $250 million as its annual campaign goal. The campaign did reach $150 million, which exceeded previous years' tallies by five- or even tenfold. Whereas in previous years only some 20 to 35 percent of the total campaign receipts were allocated to the United Palestine Appeal, in 1948 the UPA received 45.5 percent, or almost $70 million, of which $41 million was dedicated specifically to arms purchases for Israel. In addition, $15 million from the American Jewish Joint Distribution Committee's UJA allocation that year went to civilian needs in Israel, and millions more came in to Israel from more than a hundred different American-Jewish organizations.[52] The UJA's stunning tally was four times greater than the American Red Cross' entire annual campaign, and twelve times greater than that of the American Cancer Society.[53] The campaign's success was at least in part a product of Golda Meir's charismatic speechmaking and negotiations with the UJA over the percentages of receipts to be allocated to the Jewish Agency in general and arms purchase in particular.[54] Meir helped whip up a veritable frenzy of Jewish giving to Zionist causes, which, one scholar has estimated, amounted to approximately 2.5 percent of American Jewry's aggregate net disposable income.[55]

Total arms costs for Israel in 1948 were $78 million. Between the funds raised in the United States and another $15 million raised in Europe, 86 percent of the cost of Israel's arms purchased abroad in 1948 was borne by foreign sources. These funds paid for heavy arms and equipment purchased in France, Italy, and eventually Czechoslovakia. (The last of these receives the most historical attention, but it was the purchase in the spring of 1948 of western European armor that allowed Israel to withstand, although just barely, the first Arab assault of May and June.)[56] The funds also paid for more modest purchases such as machinery for the manufacture of small arms and munitions, which proved to be of immense benefit to Israel since the Arab states began the war with superior weaponry but soon ran out of spare parts and ammunition.

For hundreds of thousands of Jews the world over, Israel in 1948 was a personal affair. The sums they contributed ranged from vast to paltry. Most were bystanders, yet a few thousand trekked to the battlefields in Palestine, and some held positions of command. This story has been documented by scholars, journalists, and participants, but it is not part of the popular story of 1948 that is disseminated in Jewish schools, organized trips to Israel, and publications aimed at a popular audience. Why? At the time it was largely clandestine, but the story has long been known, and often told. More salient might be fear on the part of American Jews of accusations of dual loyalty, that Jews act not only for what they perceive as their collective interests but also, at least in theory, against those of their land of residence.

It is for this reason, I believe, that biographical sketches of Mickey Marcus usually refer to him as the only American who died fighting for a foreign power yet was buried with full military honors at West Point.

The subliminal message behind this phrasing is that Israel's foreignness is illusory, that it is linked in some unique, intimate, even existential way with the United States, that the Jewish world war of 1948 was at heart an American war as well, and by extension that Israel's future battles will share a common purpose with those of its strongest, perhaps only, protector in the world today. Marcus' life story conjures up the specter of dual loyalty, only to drive it away as the fight for Israel becomes identical, as Marcus himself imagined it, with the struggle for liberty and democracy.

But this version of Marcus' life, and even more so of his death, overlooks some simple facts: Marcus did nothing illegal by going to Palestine in early 1948 as a private citizen advising a militia that was not at war with the United States. After May 15, when Israel won de facto recognition from the United States as a sovereign country, Marcus, like any Machal fighter, was technically violating U.S. law against fighting for foreign powers, laws that might well have been enforced had Israel been at war with a U.S. treaty ally such as the United Kingdom, but the British had conveniently left the field to the Israelis and Arab states to battle it out. More important, Marcus, like any West Point graduate, had cemetery privileges at the academy, and the funerary pomp was entirely to be expected for a highly decorated colonel who had had combat experience and carried out prominent administrative functions in wartime and afterward. Marcus' funeral dossier at West Point contains drab, bureaucratic details about drill, ceremony, and the erection of a tombstone, and detailed, at times anxious, letters from Marcus' widow Emma concerning the funeral, the maintenance of the grave site, and, eventually, her own burial alongside her beloved spouse.[57] Mickey Marcus may have died as a Jew, but he was buried as an American officer. Jews remember Marcus as they wish, but in the bureaucratic rationality of West Point there are no Jewish wars, only American ones.

The disparity between action and awareness, or between awareness in real time and the transmission of memory through institutionalized narratives, becomes all the more apparent as we consider what information about events on the ground in 1947 through 1949 was available to American Jews, and how those events were presented. The results are, to say the least, surprising.

## 1948: The View from America

In the summer of 1947 the Labour Zionist leadership in Palestine was engaged in both an international diplomatic struggle for the establishment of a Jewish state and an internecine struggle with the Revisionists. In order to promote unrestricted Jewish immigration to Palestine under the auspices of Labour, a consortium of American-Jewish organizations founded the Americans for Haganah on 8 July 1947. The new organization was headed up by Abe Feinberg, a wealthy New York City businessman and prominent Zionist activist who would go on to become a confidant of several American presidents on Israel issues.[58] The organization's executive director, David Wahl, had previously served as secretary to the American Jewish Conference, which advocated for displaced persons and the cause of immigration to Palestine before world governments. Americans for Haganah enjoyed the support of not only American Labor Zionist organizations but also nonpartisan Zionist bodies such as Hadassah, the Zionist Organization of America, and Young Judea. Its Labor colorings made it appealing as well to the American Trade Union Council, and its solid association with Jewish self-defense won it the support of the American Jewish War Veterans.[59] Its national council included luminaries with close ties to Jewish and Zionist causes such as Herbert Lehman, former governor of New York, New York's mayor, William O'Dwyer (whose brother was involved in weapons purchase operations for the Jewish Agency), Senator Robert Wagner, and the actors Eddie Cantor and Edward G. Robinson. Also on the council were the presidents of the Congress of Industrial Organizations and the Farmers' Union.[60]

The broad spectrum of support for the Americans for Haganah makes its biweekly newspaper (first called *Americans for Haganah*, then *Haganah Speaks!* and then *Israel Speaks!*) of particular interest. Its articles about the situation in Palestine were written largely by Haganah apparatchiks and destined for a committed but not necessarily expert American audience. These articles contained detailed and highly critical assessments of Arab military preparedness, assessments not at all in keeping with what would become American-Jewish collective memory of the 1948 war and that surprisingly foreshadow the findings of Israel's "new history" of the 1980s and 1990s. In October of 1947, a lead article claimed that the

> Arab states can collectively muster about 150,000 soldiers—for the most part ill-trained, poorly equipped, badly disciplined and under-nourished. They have few modern weapons and fewer men trained to use them. An air force is practically non-existent, as is a navy. There are no arms factories and no replacements for equipment.[61]

The article goes on to note the one exception, the "splendidly equipped and excellently trained armies" of Transjordan, some twenty-five thousand strong. But in general, the Arab world is too riven by internal rivalries, too busy putting down revolts at home, to defeat a nascent Jewish state. To be sure, within Palestine the Arab Higher Committee and other groups will "successfully incite sporadic but violent clashes and revolts."[62] The Haganah, however, is more than a match for the Palestinians, most of whom would vastly prefer to live in peace with the Jews rather than fight them.

After the United Nations' passage of the partition resolution and the outbreak of Jewish-Arab violence in Palestine, *Americans for Haganah* continued to avow the Palestinians' overall indifference to fighting and the incompetence of those few who did take up arms.[63] This newspaper, produced by staunch Zionists in real time, made claims about the passivity of the Palestinian civilian population that have been made again recently in a tendentious form by two scholars with opposed political agendas, the anti-Zionist Ilan Pappe and the hawkish Ephraim Karsh, and with greater subtlety and substance by Hillel Cohen.[64] Of course, one might write off the newspaper's dismissive accounts of Arab military ability as morale-boosting propaganda. This argument is refuted by the newspaper's increasingly dark and anxious tone as the war intensified in the winter of 1948 and the relatively well-trained and well-equipped pan-Arab force known as the Arab Liberation Army established a base of operations in the northern West Bank.[65] The Haganah's offensive of March and April 1948 was a source of great relief, although the newspaper continued to assert categorically that the Arab forces did not have the means to "prevent the establishment of the Jewish state."[66] On this issue the newspaper made good use of the powerful rhetoric of Michael

Comay, a South African Jew who had fought for the British in North Africa during World War II and then settled in Palestine, where he worked for the Jewish Agency in fund-raising and lobbying ventures among American Jewry. (Comay went on to become Israel's ambassador to Canada, the United Nations, and the United Kingdom.)

To be sure, there was more than a bit of deceptive rhetoric in a claim, made at the end of May, that "the frontiers of the Jewish state as demarcated by the United Nations have not been dented at a single point." What's more, the Etzion bloc of settlements in the Hebron hills and Beit Ha-Aravah, just north of the Dead Sea, both lay within the designated territory of the Arab state, and both had recently fallen.[67] But the newspaper's detailed assessment of the Arab states' military capacities, made on 15 May, the day after Israel's declaration of independence, is entirely in keeping with the arguments and evidence offered by Benny Morris in his now-standard histories of the 1948 war: Except for the Arab Legion, the Arab armies had no general staff or effective logistic structure. The Arab states lacked an armaments industry to supply their armies. The Syrian and Egyptian armies were needed at home to quell or deter internal dissent and so could not be fully deployed abroad. The newspaper described in vivid detail the suffering of Jerusalem's residents under Transjordan's siege but also noted, correctly, that by the eve of the first United Nations–imposed truce, Israel had taken the battle "into enemy territory," expanding its borders beyond those accorded to it by the United Nations.[68]

My narrative of a narrative—the Americans for Haganah's tale of Israel's heroic battles in 1947 and 1948—demonstrates that information available to American Jews at the time of the war contradicted stories that American Jews would manufacture later, as the dust of battle settled and Israel's victory came increasingly to be seen as a miracle rather than the product of rational and knowable factors. Just as the newspaper reported frankly on Israel's military strengths vis-à-vis the Arabs, it did not shy away from reporting on the fate of the Palestinian refugees. "Where Are the Arabs?" ran the headline of an article in September of 1948.[69] According to the article, some 400,000 Arabs were displaced from their homes over the course of the war, and only about 100,000 remained within the borders of the state of Israel. These figures are far too low; moreover, the article claims falsely that all Arabs who pledged to remain in their towns and villages and live amicably with the Jews were allowed to stay and "were accorded the same privileges as Jewish citizens." Yet the article does acknowledge, albeit via tortuously indirect language, that substantial numbers of Arabs were expelled from their homes:

> In the Palestine area assigned to the Arabs, 40 villages were completely evacuated. The cities of Jaffa and Acre were almost completely abandoned, and Jenin was left without a single inhabitant. Ramleh and Lydda, captured Arab strongholds on the Jerusalem road, were partially evacuated.

"Evacuated" here is a euphemism for "expelled." The article might be faulted for its deceptive language, but one might still wonder why the issue of "evacuation" was even raised in the first place.

More direct is the article's assessment of the main reason for Palestinian flight: "lack of faith in their own strength and leadership," "a fear psychosis at every point occupied or approached by Israeli forces," and "mortal terror, fearing that the Jews might do to them half of what the Arabs would have done to the Jews if they had been the victors." Aside from the egregiously nasty tone of the final phrase, these arguments hold up in scholarship on the subject, even more than sixty years after the fact. There is no claim here, as there would be in years following the war, that Arabs were ordered by their leaders to leave the battlefield so as to avoid being caught in the cross fire and were promised the spoils of Jewish property after the Arabs' victory. This article substantiates the argument of Anita Shapira, the doyenne of Israeli historians, that in the immediate aftermath of the war Israelis knew full well about large-scale expulsions of Palestinians, and that myths of orchestrated Arab flight only began to circulate in the mid-1950s.[70]

The producers of the periodical were no doubt careful about anything they put into writing. There was no reportage on American-Jewish volunteer fighters until 1949. There were only two articles after that, and one was about a former U.S. marine who went to Palestine in March of 1948, before Israel's declaration of statehood.[71] Clearly, the issue of the American volunteers was a touchy one given the illegality of American citizens being recruited to fight under foreign flags. Similarly cagey was the reportage of the death of Mickey Marcus. As we noted earlier, the colonel was killed at Abu Ghosh by a Haganah sentry as he approached the encampment late at night and, unable to speak or understand Hebrew, did not respond to the sentry's command that he identify himself. The newspaper describes Marcus as having been killed in action and even supplies an eyewitness who alleges to have been with Marcus on that fateful night, fighting together for the terrain that would become the site of the Burma Road, the improvised route to Jerusalem that broke the Jordanian siege of the city.[72] A year later, the newspaper still referred to Marcus as having "met his death in action," although the real circumstances of his death were by then common knowledge.[73] (Similarly, Berkman's biography of Marcus is subtitled *The Story of Mickey Marcus Who Died to Save Jerusalem*, a formulation that nicely elides the actual cause of his death.)

It is difficult to determine how widely the Americans for Haganah's newspaper was read, but its monthly circulation ranged between 30,000 and 100,000,[74] and it was no doubt distributed to its corporate and individual sponsors, who included most of American Jewry's mainstream leadership. As is well known to students of the dissemination of news about the Holocaust, there is a vast difference between the availability of information and its consumption, and between a partial or glancing awareness of an event and a fully processed understanding of its scope and import. My point is a modest one: that during the 1948 war, in the United States, representations of the fighting, made with a Jewish audience in mind, presented the situation in a radically different way than American Jews would come to perceive it, and in great measure still do to this day.

▪ ▪ ▪

Just as American Jews in World War II fought an American war with a particular Jewish impetus to destroy Hitler, the Amalek of the twentieth century, so in 1948 did they fight a Jewish war that was justified in terms of American values and President Harry S. Truman's support for the Jewish state's establishment. In the name of that state many American Jews bent and even broke the law, and after the fact they expressed nothing but pride in their actions, without which the Jewish state could not have survived its birth. The men of the Machal and the Sonneborn group had not yet made the clear distinction, which would become common after 1948, between what is called in Hebrew *dam* and *damim*, blood and money. During Israel's War of Independence, diaspora Jews donated their bodies as well as funds. Afterward, Jews abroad distanced themselves from the battlefield and contented themselves to give money in a legal and orderly fashion.

For two decades after Israel's creation, diaspora Jewry failed to maintain the level of financial commitment it had displayed in 1948. In the early 1950s, American-Jewish contributions to Israel plummeted, and even the Suez crisis prompted only a modest increase in UJA receipts from $60 million in 1955 to $85 million in the following year. Only in 1967, as Israel faced the threat of a multifront Arab attack and then won a spectacular victory, did UJA receipts exceed 1948 levels, and they did so by a vast margin—$240 million versus the $150 million garnered during Israel's War of Independence.[75] Israel fought the 1967 war, and all its wars thereafter, without significant volunteer combat or support troops from abroad. Diaspora Jewish financial support for Israel, however, has continued to spike during periods of military conflict.

In the recent past other ethnic groups in North America have aided their homeland communities in times of war. During the Yugoslav wars of the 1990s, Croatian-Americans sent money and volunteers to the Balkans, and Tamil Canadians had a long and checkered history of financial support for the Tamil Tigers prior to their decisive defeat by the Sri Lankan government in 2009. Unlike the civil wars in Sri Lanka and the Balkans, however, the Israeli-Palestinian conflict shows no sign of ending. Currently, the prospects of a nuclear-armed Iran and of Islamicist regimes along Israel's borders have strengthened a long-standing mentality among many Jews the world over that they live in a constant state of emergency. So long as Jews believe that the enemies of Israel and of the diaspora are one and the same and that the present situation is analogous to, even a continuation of, the war for Jewish survival that was waged in Europe and Palestine almost seventy years ago, all of Israel's wars will continue to be Jewish world wars.

# Epilogue

In April of 2008, Israel's prime minister Ehud Olmert told an American journalist:

> Jews are not safer in Israel than they are in other parts of the world, but there is only one place that Jews can fight for their lives as Jews, and that is here. They can fight as Americans, they can fight as Australians—but as individuals. Jews were persecuted, Jews were attacked, Jews were suppressed. But they could never defend themselves as Jews.[1]

Strikingly, Olmert admits that the Zionist goal of creating a safe haven for persecuted Jewry has been a failure. Yet he maintains the classic Zionist claim that diaspora Jewish life is inauthentic and incomplete. If Jews can only live as Jews in Israel, they can only fight and die as Jews in Israel. This book has argued against this simplistic and tendentious claim. Over the century and a half from the French revolutionary wars to World War II Jews in military service were carriers of multiple, overlapping, and at times clashing identities. They often felt a sincere, profound attachment to their homeland and fought with no sense of qualitative difference from their countrymen. Believing that their homeland epitomized toleration and respect for human dignity, Jews in western Europe and North America defined their countries' wars as Jewish wars. The fear of fratricide hung heavy over the battlefield, and the candor with which Jews expressed that fear testified to the vitality of their clashing identities. Jews celebrated their men in uniform not only for their virility and bravery, not only for fulfilling their patriotic duty, but also for boldly asserting their religious particularism. The Jewish soldier at a Sabbath service in the field or a synagogue at home brought glory to his community not simply because he donned his uniform and decorations but because he did so while occupying a manifestly Jewish space.

Since World War II, Jews in North America have lost the thrill induced by gazing at their menfolk in uniform. The voices of Jewish soldiers have grown ever fainter. The decline of overt antisemitism and the lifting of barriers to desirable workplaces, universities, neighborhoods, and social clubs reduced the pressure on Jews to produce apologetic literature, including documentation of the Jews' historic contribution to the military.[2] The state of Israel became the main source of Jewish martial pride. The only aspect of the modern Jewish diaspora's fighting heritage that continued to be remembered was heroism during the Holocaust. The ghetto rebel and partisan became pillars of Holocaust memory, which was the cornerstone of Jewish civil religion in the United States and Canada.[3]

The omnipresent commemoration of Holocaust heroism in contemporary North America has been accompanied by a widespread failure to honor the Jews who fought for the Allied Powers in World War II. In 1954, the Jewish War Veterans of the United States of America purchased a modest building off the Mall in Washington, D.C., and four years later received a congressional charter to establish a museum of American-Jewish military history. The museum attracts a few thousand visitors per year, mostly veterans or the families of veterans, or groups of Jewish day-school students from the Washington area. Nearby, the United States Holocaust Memorial Museum receives some two million visitors per year. In Toronto, in recent years vast sums of money have flowed into a new Holocaust museum and education center, while far more modest plans to construct a monument honoring Canadian-Jewish soldiers of World War II were shelved owing to a lack of funds.[4]

The constant, ritualistic invocation of Jewish heroism during the Holocaust is a refutation of the accusation that Jews went to their deaths like lambs to the slaughter. Ironically, this accusation originated among Jews themselves, as rage over their mass destruction turned inward in a spasm of self-recrimination. Three generations after the end of World War II, the monologue of self-accusation and self-exculpation continues. Both are obsessive gestures that reveal but cannot heal the underlying trauma induced by the genocide. Many Jews take comfort in Israel's military prowess, which, they believe, will protect it from those who seek to destroy it. Yet Israel's military is in fact of limited therapeutic benefit, as no display of force, no matter how vast, can retroactively prevent the Holocaust.

While diaspora Jews dwell on the heroism of ghetto fighters and of Israeli soldiers, over the past decade there have been quiet signs of a blossoming of military activity among American Jews. At the height of American military involvement in Iraq and Afghanistan at the end of the 2000s, about 4,700 self-identified Jews served in the combined U.S. military forces. There may have been as many as ten thousand more who chose not to register as Jews out of concerns for their relationships with their Christian fellow soldiers and, if they were sent overseas, local Muslim populations. Over this period, 1 to 2 percent of West Point's cadets and midshipmen at the U.S. Naval Academy were Jews.[5] Jewish officer trainees were somewhat underrepresented in terms of the Jews' overall percentage of the American population, and in the armed forces as a whole Jews were decidedly underrepresented. This is not surprising. In our age, all-volunteer armies tend not to be attractive to affluent sectors of the population or to immigrant communities that strive to send their children into high-income professions. (For example, the Canadian armed forces hold little appeal for Chinese-Canadians.)[6]

American Jews and the U. S. military are still not a natural fit. At the U.S. Air Force Academy in Colorado Springs, proselytizing and intimidation of Jewish cadets have received widespread media attention. Complete recognition of Judaism as a denomination of equal stature to Protestantism and Catholicism came belatedly to West Point and Annapolis, with Jewish chapels completed only in 1984 and 2005 respectively.

Jews in the United States' military, however, have decidedly outnumbered the American Jews who choose to go to Israel in order to join the Israel Defense Force. Today, the Machal of 1948 fame attract only about two hundred volunteers per year.[7] In 2010 some five hundred American men and women served in the IDF as "lone soldiers," that is, new arrivals who had come without families and for whom army service was usually a major motivation behind the decision to immigrate.[8] The reality that American Jews are more likely to join their own country's military than Israel's continues to clash with the emotional appeal of the IDF as a repository of sovereign Jewish power. In many synagogues in the United States, as throughout the Jewish world, prayers are said every Sabbath for the well-being of Israel's troops, and *yizkor* prayers for fallen

IDF soldiers appear in the holiday liturgies. There is no *yizkor* for the 50 American-Jewish soldiers who fell in Iraq and Afghanistan, or the 269 who died in Vietnam, not to mention the 11,000 who perished in World War II.[9]

Until the 1990s, the world's second-largest diaspora community was the Soviet Union, where Jews developed sharply different views about military service than did their American counterparts. Despite the centrality of the draft-dodging motif in family narratives of North American Jews, two-thirds of Russia's Jews stayed within the empire, and after 1917 hundreds of thousands of Jews became loyal soldiers in the Red Army. After the Second World War, Jewish Red Army veterans recalled the military as a liberating force that defeated the Nazi menace and offered Jews positions of honor and influence as commanding officers. In the 1990s, as part of the mass immigration of Jews from the former Soviet Union to Israel, elderly Soviet Jewish veterans came with their war memories and medals. On V-E Day, they donned their old uniforms and marched in parades celebrating their courage, heroism, and sacrifice, much to the surprise of Israelis whose education has made little room for heroism within the framework of a diaspora army.[10]

Israeli society has belatedly acknowledged diaspora Jewish valor of the 1940s. In June of 2012, a memorial to the Red Army in World War II was dedicated in Netanya. The dedication ceremony was a grand event, featuring Russia's president, Vladimir Putin, Israel's president, Shimon Peres, and Jewish leaders from Russia and throughout the globe.[11] The Machal have also received their due. Already during the late 1960s and 1970s the Israeli government expressed gratitude for the Machal fighters' contributions to the founding of the state, but large-scale public recognition has come only recently, with the opening in April 2012 of an exhibition at Tel Aviv's Diaspora Museum (Beit Hatefutsot) devoted to the foreign volunteers who manned the ships that brought illegal immigrants to Palestine and who fought in Israel's War of Independence.[12] Over the past several years, Beit Hatefutsot has been preparing for a major renovation of its permanent exhibition that will present the diaspora and the land of Israel as equal partners in the history of Jewish civilization. The commemoration of the Machal at what is now called "the museum of the Jewish people" is but one of many ways in which classic Zionist deprecation of the diaspora has gradually given way among Israel's political and cultural elites to an appreciation of diaspora Jewry's vitality, creativity, philanthropic innovation and generosity, and political clout.

This book has been about the diaspora, not Israel, yet from the start Israel has hovered over it, an alleged exception to general patterns of modern Jewish political behavior. When viewed in the context of this book, however, Israel does not appear to be an exception at all, but rather yet another example of modern Jews' contingent and flexible responses to conscription and militant patriotism. Where Jews had incentives to identify with the state, they were no more likely than their countrymen to dodge military service. When and where the military was both prestigious and open to Jews, they sought it out. One could object that the most striking cases of Jews volunteering to fight or embracing military careers occurred in countries such as France and Italy where Jews were highly acculturated and likely to have strayed from strict observance. By this logic, an attachment to the military followed or accompanied the abandonment of a strong Jewish identity. Yet as we saw from French-Jewish army officers whose fathers were rabbis and kosher butchers and who married Jewish women from good families, acculturation and the adoption of a military life were not tantamount to assimilation. Besides, in Israel Jews are not just allowed but are effectively compelled to maintain a distinct collective identity. The state enforces rabbinic law in swaths of everyday life and vigorously promotes religious learning and ritual observance. Yet the military is the country's most prestigious institution.

The international Zionist movement and the new Zionist Yishuv were led by Ashkenazic Jews who took it for granted that military service was a requirement for membership in the body politic. Israel's founders were veterans of world wars and revolutions who conceived of political, cultural, and military mobilization of the populace as fully interdependent and intertwined. Their visceral rejection of conscientious objection, the mobilized voluntarism of the Yishuv's militias, and the sense during Israel's formative decades of living under constant threat ensured that pacifist movements would have negligible appeal.[13] If Jews were usually willing to serve in the military of any country that treated them with a modicum of toleration and respect, how much more so would they accept being drafted into the IDF. Israel's first prime minister David

Ben-Gurion was well aware of the connection between patriotism and good citizenship in the diaspora, and martial valor in the newly founded Jewish state. In December of 1948 he commented that the IDF's archive should

> gather material on not only the IDF and its predecessors in the land (the defense of Jewish settlements from the founding of Petakh Tikvah, Hashomer, the Jewish Legion, the Haganah in all its branches, etc.) but also Jewish self-defense throughout the diaspora and Jewish participation in wars of national and international liberation and the role of Jews in the development of military practice and technology.

This comment, scribbled on a letter sent to Ben-Gurion by the archive's director, adorns a pillar at the entrance to the archive. The letter is reproduced on the Web site of the archive's separate Division of the Jewish Fighter, which in the 1970s began to gather material as per Ben-Gurion's dictate.

Military service in Israel represented as much a continuity as a rupture with the challenges and opportunities that faced Jews in modern armies. Ben-Gurion thought in terms of the discipline and esprit de corps that an army could instill into anyone, whether in the diaspora or in the land of Israel. Many Orthodox Zionists shared Ben-Gurion's veneration of the army and ensured that religion would dwell comfortably within the soldier's tent. There was a dovish, antimilitaristic streak in the religious Zionism of the early twentieth century, but Palestine's first Ashkenazic chief rabbi, Abraham Isaac Kook (1865–1935), paved the way toward the synthesis of Orthodoxy and the use of armed force. During World War I, Kook wrote that the sovereign had the capacity to declare war as an exceptional situation in which religious laws against self-endangerment need not apply.[14]

Kook's conception of war as a state of exception made it possible for Orthodox Zionist authorities to accept as legitimate discretionary wars fought in and for the land of Israel. Kook himself believed that the Jewish commonwealth, as a pure and holy entity, would arise without bloodshed. The destruction necessary to make possible the commonwealth's establishment would be carried out by, and against, others. Yet Kook's ideas would form the basis for the thought of later, explicitly hawkish

Israeli rabbis such as Shaul Yisraeli (1910–95) who argued that the laws of warfare are universal, and that when in the field the IDF is not subject to any specifically Jewish ethical norms.[15] Shlomo Goren, who served as chief rabbi of the IDF before becoming the chief Ashkenazic rabbi of the state of Israel, took a somewhat different tack and strove to create a modern halakha of war. Its purpose would be not to constrain war but to direct it toward what Goren believed were its sacred purposes. Upon Israel's conquest of the Sinai in 1956, Goren extolled "the combination of the Bible and the sword, the cannon and the Torah. The spirit of Judaism and the machine gun that depend upon one another."[16]

Eastern European Jewry's long-standing distrust of the army as a tool of assimilation did not disappear in the Jewish state. To be sure, the IDF has historically consisted overwhelmingly of Jews and has accommodated the needs of religious soldiers regarding diet, prayer, and ritual observance. Yet it is fundamentally a secular institution, with a historic majority of nonobservant soldiers. Israeli rabbis, like their ancestors in nineteenth-century Europe, have written exhaustive tracts on how observant soldiers can successfully overcome the challenges to their way of life while in military service, particularly in combat situations, and how to get by with their nonobservant fellows.[17]

Over time, concerns about accommodating Orthodox soldiers are likely to fade, as the IDF's officer corps and elite combat units are increasingly drawn from the national-religious camp. The fundamental challenge facing observant Jews in diaspora armies was how to balance commitments to faith and country or, in other words, between the particularity of ethnoreligious attachment and the homogeneous brotherhood of the barracks. In Israel, military service poses ever fewer obstacles for soldiers who adhere to a rigorously Orthodox way of life. The preservation of liberal values—for instance, nondiscrimination against female soldiers—has proven much more difficult to maintain.

In the diaspora, even the most fervently Orthodox Jewish authorities accepted the principle of obligatory military service, although in practice they did not shy from helping young Jewish men avoid the draft. In the Yishuv and then the state of Israel, however, ultra-Orthodox Jews have overwhelmingly shunned military service. They do not object in principle to the use of force; they would defend themselves if attacked and are quite capable of violent behavior. Rather, they have considered the secular state of Israel to be a blasphemous creation that can be redeemed only through the sanctity of those who devote their lives to the study of Torah and the performance of ritual commandments. Tellingly, Israel's most extreme ultra-Orthodox community, the Neturei Karta of Jerusalem, originated out of a protest against the Yishuv leadership's imposition in 1938 of a tax to support the Yishuv's official militia, the Haganah, which carried out training exercises on the Sabbath and on Jewish holidays.[18]

The conscription of haredim in Israel is the subject of clamorous debate and an array of legislative proposals, none of which has proven effective. Secular and Orthodox-Zionist Israeli Jews accuse haredim of benefiting from the protection of the state and watching from the sidelines as their countrymen risk their lives on the front lines. This rhetoric unwittingly rehashes antisemitic accusations throughout modern history that Jews shirked the draft and lacked patriotic spirit. Haredi leaders have tried to turn the tables on their accusers by alleging that secular, affluent Israelis in north Tel Aviv are sunk in hedonistic depravity and shirk the draft in droves. The response from Tel Aviv has been a barrage of statistics demonstrating that graduates from secular high schools in affluent neighborhoods beat the national average for recruitment into the IDF, especially into its combat units.[19] The old rhetorical battles of the nineteenth- and twentieth-century diaspora are being replayed on Israel's soil. The irony of the situation is striking given that one of Zionism's principal goals was to remove Jews from the vicious circle of hostility, accusation, and apologetic defense regarding their patriotism and courage that had bedeviled them throughout modern history.

In the years to come increasing numbers of haredim are likely to engage in military service. They will do so because of not only legislative fiat from without but also pressures from within. With limited government funds to support them and a burgeoning population, haredim cannot forever retain their current status as a society of Torah scholars, two-thirds of whose adult males do not have gainful employment. Just as haredim are gradually entering the workforce, so will more of them carry out some sort of national service as a transition from full-time religious education to Torah study as a part-time avocation. Most haredim will probably choose civilian service, but some will become soldiers, augmenting the approximately 1,500 who currently serve as support personnel and in a haredi-only combat unit. Haredim have the potential to become more engaged with the military institutions of the state, although they may go the way of those Orthodox Zionists who view the army not as the defender of the state of Israel so much as an instrument for maintaining, extending, and perpetuating Jewish settlement in the West Bank, the heartland of the biblical land of Israel.

The primacy of the army in Israeli society is in part a logical response to the country's daunting security concerns. It is also a product of the Jews' heritage of collective cohesiveness and of trauma induced by persecution, particularly the genocide of European Jewry. Last but not least, Israel has continued along the path of those modern Jews who claimed the military uniform as a natural part of their raiment, thereby subverting the biblical motif of the timid patriarch Jacob furtively donning the animal skins worn by his elder brother, the hunter Esau. In the centuries before Israel's creation, some Jews lustily wielded military power, others fantasized about it, but few condemned it altogether. In Israel, Jews completed the process of integration into the army and into the collective exercise of armed force that had begun in Europe a century and a half previously. In military affairs, as in so many other respects, Israel represents a continuation of the diaspora via other means.

# NOTES

## Introduction

1. Yehuda Slutsky and Mordechai Kaplan, *Hayalim yehudim be-tsiv'ot eyropa* (Tel Aviv: Ministry of Defense, 1967); Michael Stanislawski, *Tsar Nicholas and the Jews: The Transformation of Jewish Society in Russia, 1825–1855* (Philadelphia: Jewish Publication Society, 1983); Olga Litvak, *Conscription and the Search for Modern Russian Jewry* (Bloomington: Indiana University Press, 2008); Yohanan Petrovsky-Shtern, *Jews in the Russian Army, 1827–1917: Drafted into Modernity* (New York: Cambridge University Press, 2009); Erwin Schmidl, *Juden in der k. (u.) k. Armee 1788–1918 / Jews in the Habsburg Armed Forces* (Eisenstadt: Österreichisches Jüdisches Museum, 1989); Istvan Deak, *Beyond Nationalism: A Social and Political History of the Habsburg Officer Corps, 1848–1918* (New York: Oxford University Press, 1990), esp. 171–77; idem, "Pacesetters of Integration: Jewish Officers in the Habsburg Monarchy," *Eastern European Politics and Societies* 3, no. 1 (1989): 22–50; Marsha Rozenblit, *Reconstructing a National Identity: The Jews of Habsburg Austria during World War I* (New York: Oxford University Press, 2001); Horst Fischer, *Judentum, Staat und Heer in Preussen im frühen 19. Jahrhundert* (Tübingen: Mohr, 1968); *Deutsche Jüdische Soldaten. Von der Epoche der Emanzipation bis zum Zeitalter der Weltkriege* (Hamburg: E. S. Mittler, 1996); Christine Krüger, *"Sind wir denn nicht Brüder?" Deutsche Juden im nationalen Krieg 1870/71* (Paderborn: Ferdinand Schöningh, 2006); Yaakov Rosenthal, *Epizodah shel "rish'ut"? "Sfirat ha-yehudim" be-milhemet ha-'olam ha-rishonah* (Tel Aviv / Jerusalem: Ha-kibbutz Hame'uhad / Leo Baeck Institute, 2005); Pierre Birnbaum, *The Jews of the Republic: A History of State Jews in France from Gambetta to Vichy* (Stanford, Calif.: Stanford University Press, 1996), 45–53, 179–96; Philippe Landau, *Les Juifs de France et la Grande Guerre: Un patriotisme républicain, 1914–1941* (Paris: CNRS, 1999); Alberto Rovighi, *I militari di origine ebraica nel primo secolo di vita dello Stato italiano* (Rome: Stato maggiore dell'esercito, 1999); Meir Michaelis, "Gli ufficiali superiori ebrei nell 'esercito italiano dal Risorgimento all Marcia su Roma," *La Rassegna Mensile de Israel* 30, no. 4 (1964): 156–71; Christopher Sterba, *Good Americans: Italian and Jewish Immigrants during the First World War* (New York: Oxford University

Press, 2003); Deborah Dash Moore, *G. I. Jews: How World War II Changed a Generation* (Cambridge, Mass.: Harvard University Press, 2004). Outside these works, material in recent scholarship on the Jewish experience of war as soldiers, rather than as civilians, is scarce. For example, of the seventeen essays in Jonathan Sarna and Adam Mendlsohn, eds., *Jews and the Civil War: A Reader* (New York: New York University Press, 2010), only three are about soldiers, and two of these were culled from Jewish periodical literature of the mid-twentieth century.

2. The notion that the Jew cannot be a patriot because of a sense of innate superiority and self-imposed isolation goes back to debates over Jewish "civil improvement" in late eighteenth-century Germany. It was reproduced in a particularly nasty form by the twentieth-century philosopher Carl Schmitt, who wrote in 1938 that the Jews "watch as the peoples of the world kill one another; for them this mutual slaughter and carnage is lawful and kosher. Thus they eat the flesh of the slaughtered peoples and live upon it." Carl Schmitt, *Der Leviathan in der Staatslehre des Thomas Hobbes* (Cologne: Hohenheim, 1982), 18.

3. Karen Hagemann, *"Mannlicher Muth und Teutsche Ehre": Nation, Militär und Geschlecht zur Zeit der Antinapoleonischen Kriege Preußens* (Paderborn: F. Schöningh, 2002).

4. Stefan Dudink and Karen Hagemann, "Masculinity in Politics and War in the Age of Democratic Revolutions, 1750–1859," in *Masculinities in Politics and War: Gendering Modern History*, ed. Stefan Dudink, Karen Hagemann, and John Tosh (Manchester, UK: Manchester University Press), 2004, 11.

5. For an excellent account of Jewish women's peace activism, and more broadly of the development of an antimilitarist definition of citizenship, see Melissa Klapper, "'Those by Whose Side We Have Laboured': American Jewish Women and the Peace Movement between the Wars," *Journal of American History* 97 (2010): 636–58.

6. Jean Quataert, *Staging Philanthropy: Patriotic Women and the National Imagination in Dynastic Germany, 1813–1916* (Ann Arbor: University of Michigan Press), 2001, 5–6.

7. David A. Bell, *The First Total War: Napoleon's Europe and the Birth of Warfare as We Know It* (New York: Houghton Mifflin, 2007), 15.

8. E.g., Alan Forrest, *Conscripts and Deserters: The Army and French Society during the Revolution and Empire* (New York: Oxford University Press, 1989); idem, *The Legacy of the French Revolutionary Wars: The Nation-in-Arms in French Republican Memory* (New York: Cambridge University Press, 2009); Ute Frevert, *A Nation in Barracks: Modern Germany, Military Conscription and Civil Society* (New York: Berg, 2004); James Sheehan, *Where Have All the Soldiers Gone? The Transformation of Modern Europe* (New York: Houghton Mifflin, 2008); Alan Forrest, Karen Hagemann, and Jane Rendall, eds., *Soldiers, Citizens and Civilians: Experiences and Perceptions of the Revolutionary and Napoleonic Wars, 1790–1820* (Basingstoke: Palgrave Macmillan, 2008).

9. For readers in the United States, the example that comes first to mind is that of African-Americans. On their attempts in the twentieth century to parlay military service into improved status, see Ronald R. Krebs, *Fighting for Rights: Military Service and the Politics of Citizenship* (Ithaca, N.Y.: Cornell University Press, 2006). Another case is that of Japanese Hawaiians in the United States armed forces during World War II. See Takashi Fujitani, *Race for Empire: Koreans as Japanese and Japanese as Americans during World War II* (Berkeley and Los Angeles: University of California Press, 2011). In modern Europe, there were many similarities between the experience of Jews in the military and that of Mennonites. See the pioneering monograph by Mark Jantzen, *Mennonite German Soldiers: Nation, Religion and Family in the Prussian East, 1772–1880* (South Bend, Ind.: Notre Dame University Press, 2010).

10. Anita Shapira, *Land and Power: The Zionist Resort to Force, 1881–1948* (New York: Oxford University Press, 1992); Michael Berkowitz, *Zionist Culture and West European Jewry before the First World War* (Cambridge: Cambridge University Press, 1993); John Efron, *Defenders of the Race: Jewish Doctors and Race Science in Fin-de-Siècle Europe* (New Haven, Conn., and London: Yale University Press, 1994); Daniel Boyarin, *Unheroic Conduct: The Rise of Heterosexuality and the Invention of the Jewish Man* (Berkeley and Los Angeles: University of California Press, 1997), chapter 7; Moshe Zimmerman, "Muscle Jews versus Nervous Jews," and Gideon Reuveni, "Sports and the Militarization of Jewish Society," both in *Emancipation through Muscles: Jews and Sports in Europe*, ed. Michael Brenner and Gideon Reuveni (Lincoln: University of Nebraska Press, 2006), 13–26 and 44–61; Todd Presner, *Muscular Judaism: The Jewish Body and the Politics of Regeneration* (London: Routledge, 2007), chapter 6.

11. Educational and popular literature written in the Yishuv before the details of the Holocaust were fully known tended to be more celebratory of diaspora Jewish valor than books written after World War II. For the former type, see Yaakov Poleskin, *Sefer ha-tsava ha-ʿivri mi-tekufat ha-tanakh ʿad yemeinu eleh* (Tel Aviv: Holmim ve-lohmim, 1941); and Yosef Klarsfeld, *Sarei tsava me-yisraʾel: Parashat gevuratam u-gedulatam shel ketsinim yehudim be-maʾarakhot ha-ʿolam* (Jerusalem: Reuven Mas, 1941). For the latter, in which diaspora soldiering is either marginalized or ignored altogether, see Adir Cohen, *Heylot yisraʾel u-milhamoteihem ba-avar u-va-hoveh* (Tel Aviv: Shimon, 1957); idem, *Gevurat yisraʾel be-hazon ha-dorot* (Tel Aviv: A. Zelkowitz, 1968); Shraga Gafni, *Ha-kravot ha-mefursamim be-toldot yisraʾel* (Tel Aviv: M. Mizrahi, 1962). For a work produced in the United States with a similar Palestinocentric approach, see Monroe Rosenthal and Isaac Mozeson, *Wars of the Jews: A Military History from Biblical to Modern Times* (New York: Hippocrene, 1990).

12. Israel Halperin, *Sefer ha-gevurah: antologyah historit-sifrutit* (Tel Aviv: Am Oved, 1949/50–1950/51); also Ben-Tsion Dinur's magisterial opening prefatory essay to the official history of the Haganah, *Sefer toldot ha-haganah*, ed. Ben-Tsion

Dinur et al. (Tel Aviv: Ma'arakhot, 1954–72); Slutsky and Kaplan, *Hayalim yehudim be-tsiv'ot eyropa*. According to Israel Bartal, the purpose of *Sefer ha-gevurah* was to counter earlier literature that presented Jews as passive victims throughout history. Yet as Bartal notes, "It is of great significance that among the selected texts [in Halperin's work], not a single one deals with the courage of Jewish fighters who took part in other people's wars of national liberation, or who distinguished themselves as soldiers in the armies of various European countries." See Israel Bartal, "The Ingathering of Traditions: Zionism's Anthology Projects," *Prooftexts* 17 (1997): 77–93, esp. 85–87 and 92 n. 24. In their book *Poles and Jews: A Failed Brotherhood* (Hanover, N.H.: Brandeis University Press, 1992), 117–19, Magdalena Opalski and Israel Bartal write of the Polish Zionist author Abraham Kabak, whose 1944 Hebrew novel *Under the Hanging Tree* narrates the tale of a Polish Jew's involvement in the 1863 uprising in order to demonstrate the futility of Jewish participation in wars or revolts on behalf of Gentiles.

13. A major conference held in Tel Aviv in 1974 and published in book form three years later, on the subject of "violence and defense in the Jewish experience," offered detailed attention to biblical and rabbinic laws and discussions of warfare, but the sessions on medieval and modern history focused almost entirely on Jews as victims of antisemitism. The overwhelming emphasis was on halakhic norms, not actual Jewish behavior or lived sensibilities. Salo Baron and George S. Wise, eds., *Violence and Defense in the Jewish Experience* (Philadelphia: Jewish Publication Society, 1977). A similar imbalance characterizes a recent Israeli work on the subject, an edited volume whose essays are mostly about literary and religious texts. Only one deals with Jewish military service in diaspora armies, and its focus is on rabbinic authority in Russian communities faced with the crisis of conscription, not on the conscripts themselves. Mordechai Zalkin, "Bein 'benei elohim' li-'venei adam': rabanim, bahurei yeshivot, veha-giyus la-tsava ha-rusi ba-meah ha-tesha esreh," in *Shalom u-milhamah ba-tarbut ha-yehudit*, ed. Avriel Bar-Levav, (Jerusalem: Zalman Shazar Center, 2006), 165–222.

14. Shapira, *Land and Power*, 235.

15. Ehud Luz, *Wrestling with an Angel: Power, Morality, and Jewish Identity* (New Haven, Conn.: Yale University Press, 2003; 1998 Hebrew original), 34.

16. Mark Meyerson, *A Jewish Renaissance in Fifteenth-Century Spain* (Princeton, N.J.: Princeton University Press, 2004); Elliott Horowitz, *Reckless Rites: Purim and the Legacy of Jewish Violence* (Princeton, N.J.: Princeton University Press, 2006); Yisrael Yuval, *Two Nations in Your Womb: Perceptions of Jews and Christians in Late Antiquity and the Middle Ages* (Berkeley and Los Angeles: University of California Press, 2006).

17. Daniel Boyarin, *Unheroic Conduct: The Rise of Heterosexuality and the Invention of the Jewish Man* (Berkeley and Los Angeles: University of California Press, 1997). Habibi's lines from 1986 are cited in Idith Zertal, *Israel's Holocaust and the Politics of Nationhood* (Cambridge: Cambridge University Press, 2005), 127. Habibi's inclusion of Brecht into his pantheon appears to assume that any German

communist intellectual or artist of stature during the Weimar era must have been Jewish.

18. Hannah Arendt, *On Violence* (New York: Harcourt, Brace, 1969), 45.

19. Ibid., 56. See also 53–55.

20. Shai Agnon, *'Ir u-melo'ah* (Jerusalem: Shocken, 1973), 461.

21. Yoram Peri, *Between Battles and Ballots: Israeli Military in Politics* (New York: Cambridge University Press, 1983); idem, *Generals in the Cabinet Room: How the Military Shapes Israeli Policy* (Washington, D.C.: United States Institute of Peace, 2006); Shapira, *Land and Power*; Stuart Cohen, *The Scroll or the Sword? Dilemmas of Religion and Military Service in Israel* (Amsterdam: Hardwood, 1997); Uri Ben-Eliezer, *The Making of Israeli Militarism* (Bloomington: Indiana University Press, 1998); Martin van Crefeld, *The Sword and the Olive: A Critical History of the Israel Defense Force* (New York: Public Affairs, 1998); Yagil Levy, *Israel's Materialist Militarism* (Lanham, Md.: Lexington, 2007); idem, *Mi-tseva ha-'am li-tseva ha-periferiyot* (Jerusalem: Karmel, 2007); idem, *Mi sholet al ha-tsava? ben pikuah 'al ha-tsava li-shelitah bi-tseva'iyut* (Jerusalem: Magnes, 2010); Neve Gordon, *Israel's Occupation* (Berkeley and Los Angeles: University of California Press, 2008); Gabriel Sheffer and Oren Barak, eds., *Militarism and Israeli Society* (Bloomington: Indiana University Press, 2010).

22. In addition to the sources cited in notes 3 through 9 above, see Linda Colley, *Britons: Forging the Nation, 1707–1837* (New Haven, Conn.: Yale University Press, 1992); Bell, *The First Total War*; and Karen Hagemann, Gisela Mettele, and Jane Rendall, eds., *Gender, War and Politics: Transatlantic Perspectives, 1775–1830* (Basingstoke, and New York: Palgrave Macmillan, 2010).

## Chapter One

1. See Winter's insightful critique of the misuse and abuse of the term "collective memory," as well as a discussion of how it has far exceeded the specific definition assigned to it by its inventor, Maurice Halbwachs, in the introductory chapters to Winter's *Remembering War: The Great War between History and Memory in the Twentieth Century* (New Haven, Conn.: Yale University Press, 2006); also see Jay Winter and Emmanuel Sivan, eds., *War and Remembrance in the Twentieth Century* (Cambridge: Cambridge University Press, 1999), 1.

2. Kenneth Stow, *Alienated Minority: The Jews of Medieval Latin Europe* (Cambridge, Mass.: Harvard University Press), 1993.

3. Here I have been influenced by, yet have modified, Amos Funkenstein's concept of "passive messianism," which Funkenstein defined as the normative Jewish stance of patiently awaiting divine deliverance and not attempting to hasten the advent of the messianic era. Funkenstein distinguished passive and active messianism, on the one hand, and true passivity, on the other. Traditional Judaism, he argued, was not at all passive; it was respectful but not slavishly deferential to the state, and the rabbinic concept that "the law of the land is law" commanded

obedience only to state laws that Jewish authorities considered just. Amos Funkenstein, *Maimonides: Nature, History and Messianic Beliefs* (Tel Aviv: Ministry of Defense, 1997), 70–75. I share Funkenstein's sentiment but believe he stretched his argument too far. Throughout history, Jews wielded various forms of power within and outside their communities, and at times they took up arms in self-defense. Yet the rabbinic tradition urges the utmost caution in dealing with Gentile authority. To be sure, Jews in the Middle Ages and early modern period at times enjoyed considerable economic and administrative power (e.g., as lessees in the Polish-Lithuanian commonwealth), but they invariably depended upon a Gentile protector and at times came to an unfortunate end, thus providing a cautionary rather than positive model for their Jewish peers. What's more, until late modern times, Jews engaged in armed conflict only in isolated or extreme situations. Thus I prefer the more expansive term "theological passivity" over "passive messianism," as the former connotes a sense of divinely sanctioned wariness toward the Gentile world. Clearly, though, even this more capacious term has little in common with pacifism, which is part of neither the Judaic tradition nor of lived Jewish reality.

4. Even anti-Zionist Orthodoxy, which has historically shunned the military, has in recent years embraced a zealous militancy toward the Occupied Territories and a greater sense of connection with the Israeli armed forces. See Nurit Stadler's illuminating article, "Playing with Sacred/Corporeal Identities: Yeshiva Students' Fantasies of Military Participation," *Jewish Social Studies* 13 (2007): 155–78.

5. I am indebted to Robert Eisen, *The Peace and Violence of Judaism: An Exploration in Jewish Ethics from the Bible to Modern Zionism* (New York: Oxford University Press, 2011); and Reuven Firestone, *The Death and Resurrection of Jewish Holy War: A Study of a Religious Notion* (New York: Oxford University Press, 2012). Thanks to both Professors Eisen and Firestone for permitting me to read their manuscripts prior to publication.

6. Jeffrey L. Rubinstein, *The Culture of the Babylonian Talmud* (Baltimore: Johns Hopkins University Press, 2003), 54–64.

7. See Geoffrey B. Levy, "Judaism and the Obligation to Die for the State," *Association for Jewish Studies Review* 12, no. 2 (1987): 175–203; Efraim Inbar, "War in Jewish Tradition," *Jerusalem Journal of International Relations* 9 (1987): 83–99; Reuven Kimelman, "War," in *Frontiers of Jewish Thought*, ed. Steven Katz (New York: Basic Books, 1992), 307–32; Aviezer Ravitsky, "Prohibited Wars in the Jewish Tradition," in *The Ethics of War and Peace: Religious and Secular Perspectives*, ed. Terry Nardin (Princeton, N.J.: Princeton University Press, 1998), 15–27; Shalom Carmy, "The Origin of Nations and the Shadow of Violence: Theological Perspectives on Canaan and Amalek," in *War and Peace in the Jewish Tradition*, ed. Lawrence Shiffman and Joel B. Wolowelsky (New York: Yeshiva University Press, 2007), 163–200; Martin Goodman, *Rome and Jerusalem: The Clash of Ancient Civilizations* (London: Allen Lane, 2007), 339–47; Eisen, *The Peace and Violence of Judaism*, part 2.

8. Michael J. Broyde, "Just Wars, Just Battles and Just Conduct in Jewish

Law: Jewish Law Is Not a Suicide Pact!" in *War and Peace in the Jewish Tradition*, ed. Shiffman and Wolowelsky, 10; Stuart Cohen, "The Quest for a Corpus of Jewish Military Ethics in Modern Israel," *Journal of Israeli History* 26, no. 1 (2007): 54.

9. Haim Hillel Ben-Sasson, "Yihud am yisra'el le-da'at benei ha-me'ah ha-shteim esreh," *Perakim* 2 (1969–74): 217.

10. Steven Bowman, "'Yossipon' and Jewish Nationalism,'" *Proceedings of the Academy for Jewish Research* 61 (1995): 23–51. See also Yisrael Yuval, *Two Nations in Your Womb: Perceptions of Jews and Christians in Late Antiquity and the Middle Ages* (Berkeley and Los Angeles: University of California Press, 2006); Elliott Horowitz, *Reckless Rites: Purim and the Legacy of Jewish Violence* (Princeton, N.J.: Princeton University Press, 2006).

11. So argues Judith Bleich, "Military Service: Ambivalence and Contradictions," in *War and Peace in the Jewish Tradition*, ed. Shiffman and Wolowelsky, 415–76.

12. Jacob L. Wright, "Surviving in an Imperial Context: Foreign Military Service and Judean Identity," in *Judah and the Judeans in the Achaemenid Period: Negotiating Identity in an International Context*, ed. Oded Lipschits, Gary N. Knoppers, and Manfred Oeming (Winona Lake, Ind.: Eisenbrauns, 2011), 505–28.

13. Reproduced in Jacob Marcus, ed., *The Jew in the Medieval World: A Source Book, 315–1791*, rev. ed. (Cincinnati: Hebrew Union College Press)ß, 1999, 128.

14. Jacob Katz, *Exclusiveness and Tolerance: Studies in Jewish-Gentile Relations in Medieval and Modern Times* (New York: Oxford University Press, 1961), 6. Robert Chazan notes that the Jews' armed self-defense against the mob was a desperate act of last resort: *European Jewry and the First Crusade* (Berkeley and Los Angeles: University of California Press, 1996), 98.

15. David Biale, *Power and Powerlessness in Jewish History* (New York: Shocken, 1986), 72–73.

16. Haim Hillel Ben-Sasson, *A History of the Jewish People* (Cambridge, Mass.: Harvard University Press, 1976), 411–18.

17. Thanks to Joseph Schatzmiller for sharing this information with me from his current research, to be published by Princeton University Press under the title *Jews and Christian Art: Collaboration and Exchange in the Medieval Marketplace*.

18. See Yosef Haim Yerushalmi, *Haggadah and History: A Panorama in Facsimile of Five Centuries of the Printed Haggadah from the Collections of Harvard University and the Jewish Theological Seminary of America* (New York: Jewish Publication Society, 1997), plates 11 and 60; and http://www.bl.uk/onlinegallery/onlineex/ expfaith/judmanu/barchagg/largeimage73984.html; http://www.jewishagency.org/ JewishAgency/English/Jewish+Education/Compelling+Content/Jewish+Time/ Festivals+and+Memorial+Days/Pesach/Haggadot/The+Prague+Haggadah.htm, accessed 5 February 2010.

19. The wicked son as soldier prefigured a theme in modern Jewish literature, found in the writings of Karl Emil Franzos, Abraham Cahan, and Joseph Roth,

where a physically powerful, somewhat wild young Jewish man is attracted to soldiering ways and assimilates, often with tragic results.

20. See Gershon David Hundert's splendid overview, *Jews in Poland-Lithuania in the Eighteenth Century: A Genealogy of Modernity* (Berkeley and Los Angeles: University of California Press, 2004).

21. Cited in Moshe Verbin, *Ha-yehudim 'im neshek bi-yedeihem. Perek be-helkam shel ha-yehudim be-milhamot polin be-me'ot 16–17* (Lod: Haberman, 2000), 12.

22. Witold Maisel, *Sądownictwo miasta Poznania do końca XVI wieku* (Poznan, 1961), 241. Many thanks to Magdalena Teter for this reference.

23. Responsum 37.

24. The 1453 Privilege to Polish Jewry affirmed that Jews who came into possession of hereditary property (i.e., that of nobles, used as security for debts) would not assume the military obligations, personal or financial, that would normally be expected of the holder of the land. http://www.earlymoern.org/workshops/2004/telller/text01.english.php?tid=50, accessed 9 February 2010.

25. Maurycy Horn, "Swiadczenia Zydow na rzecz obronnosci kraju i miast rodzinnych w dawnej Polsce," *Biuletyn ZIH* 98, no. 2 (1976): 3–17.

26. Maurycy Horn, "Obrona miast jako umocnionych punktow—glowne swiadczenie wojenne Zydow w Rzeczypospolitej w XVI i XVII wieku," *Biuletyn ZIH* 100, no. 4 (1976): 19–33; idem, "Udzial Zydow w wojnach z Tatarami i Turcja w XVII wieku," *Biuletyn ZIH* 102, no. 2 (1977): 5–15.

27. Cited in Paul Rieger, "Das Gutachten Abraham Geigers über die Militärpflichtigkeit der Juden," *Im Deutschen Reich*, August–September 1915, 166–75. See also *The Jewish Encyclopedia*, q.v., "Berachah 'The Hero.'"

28. Israel Halperin, *Pinkas Va'ad Arba' Aratsot* (1945 ed.), Latin/Polish section, document 17, XVIII; Magdalena Teter, *Jews and Heretics in Catholic Poland: A Beleaguered Church in the Post-Reformation Era* (New York: Cambridge University Press, 2006), 58.

29. Shaul Stampfer, "What Actually Happened to the Jews of Ukraine in 1648?" *Jewish History* 17 (2003): 207–27; Adam Teller, "Jewish Literary Responses to the Events of 1648–1649 and the Creation of a Polish-Jewish Consciousness," in *Culture Front: Representing Jews in Eastern Europe*, ed. Benjamin Nathans and Gabriella Safran (Philadelphia: University of Pennsylvania Press, 2008), 17–45; Edward Fram, "Creating a Tale of Martyrdom in Tulczyn, 1648," in *Jewish History and Jewish Memory: Essays in Honor of Yosef Haim Yerushalmi* (Hanover, N.H.: University Press of New England, 1998), 89–112.

30. Cited in Nachum Gelber, "Yehudim be-tsava Polin," in *Hayalim yehudim be-tsiv'ot europa*, ed. Yehuda Slutsky and Mordechai Kaplan (Tel Aviv: Ministry of Defense, 1967), 85. See also the English translation of the chronicle, *Abyss of Despair* (New Brunswick, N.J.: Transaction, 1995).

31. Jonathan Gribetz, "Popularizing Massacres: An Analysis of the Yiddish *Yeven Metsulah*," unpublished essay, 2003. Many thanks to Dr. Gribetz for sharing this essay, originally written for a graduate course at Columbia University.

32. Johann Christoph Wagenseil, *Exercitationes Sex Varii Arumenti.* Altdorf, 1698, 150. The text features the Hebrew original and a Latin translation.

33. Simon Neuberg, ed., *Das Schwedesch Lid. Ein westjiddischer Bericht über die Ereignisse in Prag im Jahre 1648* (Hamburg: Helmut Buske Verlag, 2000). Stanzas 29/30 (22). Many thanks to Rachel Greenblatt for this reference.

34. Teller, "Jewish Literary Responses."

35. Arnold Wiznitzer, "Jewish Soldiers in Dutch Brazil, 1630–1654," *PAJHS* 46, no. 1 (1956): 40–50.

36. Lengthy excerpts from the writings of Dutch scholars of this subject, Hendrik Jacob Koenen and Nicholas Godfried Van Kampen, are provided in Simon Wolf, *The American Jew as Patriot, Soldier and Citizen* (Cranbury, N.J.: Scholars' Bookshelf, 2006; 1895 original), 454–71. Although Wolf's book is a highly romanticized and inaccurate apologetic, his arguments about the Nassys' activities are compatible with those of his sources, and also with the current research of Natalie Zemon Davis on this subject.

37. In 1748, one Jacob Levy owned two corsairs, and a decade later, the Jews of Saint-Esprit owned one collectively. Abraham Gradis' corsair, fitted with twenty-four cannons and boasting a crew of over two hundred, engaged British ships on 8 April 1757. Zosa Szajkowski, "Jews in the French Armed Forces," typescript ms., Archive of the Israel Defense Force, Tel Ha-Shomer, Israel (hereafter AIDF), 86/1511/1998, 3.

38. Joseph Roth, *Job* (Woodstock, N.Y.: Overlook, 1982), esp. 28, 34, 68, 72, 135.

39. The pioneer of this field was Michael Stanislawski, in *Tsar Nicholas I and the Jews: The Transformation of Jewish Society in Russia, 1825–1855* (Philadelphia: Jewish Publication Society, 1983); idem, *Psalms for the Tsar: A Minute-Book of a Psalms Society in the Russian Army, 1864–1867* (New York: Ktav, 1988).

40. Yohanan Petrosky-Shtern, *Jews in the Russian Army, 1827–1917: Drafted into Modernity* (New York: Cambridge University Press, 2009), 91.

41. Ibid., 97. Similar arguments underlie Olga Litvak, *Conscription and the Search for Modern Russian Jewry* (Bloomington: Indiana University Press), 2006.

42. Reproduced in the *JC*, 9 February 1855, 63. See also 12 May 1854, 283.

43. Ibid., 14 September 1855, 307. According to Petrovsky-Shtern, the poem may be based on a legend about a Jewish guard who offended Tsar Nicholas by refusing to pronounce a benediction for the Savior, thus infuriating the tsar, who ordered all Jews in guard units into the navy.

44. Petrovsky-Shtern, *Jews in the Russian Army*, 163–64, 195–96.

45. Michal Kopczysnski, "The Physical Stature of Jewish Men in Poland in the Second Half of the 19th Century," *Economics and Human Biology* 9 (2011): 203–10.

46. Petrovsky-Shtern, *Jews in the Russian Army*, 134–35.

47. Ibid., 139–42.

48. See the important monograph by Eugene Avrutin, *Jews and the Imperial State: Identification Politics in Tsarist Russia* (Ithaca, N.Y.: Cornell University Press, 2010), 61–72.

49. *AZdJ*, 7 August 1854, 404–5.

50. Anita Shapira, *Brenner: sipur hayim* (Tel Aviv, 2008), 54; Shlomo Lambroza, "The Pogroms of 1903–1906," in *Pogroms: Anti-Jewish Violence in Modern Russian History*, ed. John D. Klier and Shlomo Lambroza (Cambridge: Cambridge University Press, 2004), 215.

51. *Ha-Melitz*, 8 July 1880, 290–95; 3 April 1903, 1; 4 May 1903, 1.

52. Zalkin, "Bein 'benei elohim' li-'venei adam.'"

53. Yisrael Meir ben Ari Zev Ha-Kohen, *Sefer mahaneh yisra'el* (Vilna, 1881). A reception history of this work across time and space, as well as a study of the textual variations among the editions, would be fascinating. Just to provide one example of the work's lasting popularity, in his memoirs, Meyer Birnbaum, a strictly Orthodox lieutenant in the U.S. Army in World War II, studied the book with a rabbi during the week before he reported for service. Birnbaum's mother had urged him to dodge the draft, but the young man's longtime *rosh yeshiva* declared that doing so would be an act of desecration of God's name, *hilul ha-shem*. See Meyer Birnbaum and Yonason Rosenblum, *Lieutenant Birnbaum: A Soldier's Story; Growing Up Jewish in America, Liberating the D.P. Camps, and a New Life in Jerusalem* (New York: Artscroll, Mesorah Publications, 1993), 46–50. For historical contextualization of the book, see Michael Stanislawski, "Reflections on the Russian Rabbinate," *Jewish Religious Leadership: Image and Reality*, vol. 2, ed. Jack Wertheimer (New York: Jewish Theological Seminary, 2004), 442–45. A propos of our discussion of Joseph Roth's novel *Job* above, the Chofetz Chaim preferred that Jews stay in Russia, difficult though army service often was, rather than immigrate to the New World and uproot themselves from the traditional authority structures that have maintained observance and inhibited assimilation.

54. *Sefer mahaneh yisra'el*, 92.

55. Litvak, *Conscription*, 78.

56. *Ha-Melitz*, 8 November 1878, 359–65. Jewish veterans were not, however, granted unfettered access to the interior. See Benjamin Nathans, *Beyond the Pale: The Jewish Encounter with Late Imperial Russia* (Berkeley and Los Angeles: University of California Press, 2004), 181–83.

57. E.g., *Ha-Tsefirah*, 23 November 1875, 365; see also 8 January 1880, 12.

58. Yohanan Petrovsky-Shtern, "The Guardians of Faith, or Jewish Self-Governing Societies in the Russian Army," in *The Military and Society in Russia, 1450–1917*, ed. Eric Lohr and Marshall Poe (Leiden: Brill, 2002), 432, 436.

59. Yohanan Petrovsky-Shtern, "Dual Identity Revisited: The Case of Russian-Jewish Soldiers," *Jews in Russia and Eastern Europe* 1 (2004): 135.

60. Ruth Rubin, *Voices of a People: The Story of Yiddish Folksong* (New York: McGraw Hill, 1973), 214.

61. A good example of this type was Zeev (Wolf) Trumpeldor, a cantonist who served a full twenty-five-year term without giving up his faith and became a *felsher*

(barber-surgeon) in the Jewish hospital in Rostow-on-the-Don. Trumpeldor is best known for fathering the Russian and Zionist military hero Joseph Trumpeldor.

62. Although they were only granted full citizenship in 1879, Rumania's Jews became liable for conscription in 1864, and in the late 1860s and early '70s were given the right to be promoted through the ranks. The first Jews to be offered citizenship were some nine hundred veterans of the Russo-Turkish War. During the 1890s, there were ongoing legislative efforts to keep Jews out of the Rumanian army altogether, and they were deprived the right of promotion through the ranks, though by the eve of World War I their position had somewhat improved. Z. Phillip, "Yehudim be-tsava ha-rumani," in *Hayalim yehudim bi-tsiv'ot eyropa*, ed. Slutsky and Kaplan, 168–72.

## Chapter Two

1. There is a sizable literature on the relationship between state building, nationalism, and citizenship in modern Europe, e.g., Alan Forrest, *Conscripts and Deserters: The Army and French Society during the Revolution and Empire* (New York: Oxford University Press, 1989); idem, *The Legacy of the French Revolutionary Wars: The Nation-in-Arms in French Republican Memory* (New York: Cambridge University Press, 2009); Ute Frevert, *A Nation in Barracks: Modern Germany, Military Conscription and Civil Society* (New York: Berg, 2004); Ronald R. Krebs, *Fighting for Rights: Military Service and the Politics of Citizenship* (Ithaca, N.Y.: Cornell University Press, 2006); James Sheehan, *Where Have All the Soldiers Gone? The Transformation of Modern Europe* (New York: Houghton Mifflin, 2008); Alan Forrest, Karen Hagemann, and Jane Rendall, eds., *Soldiers, Citizens and Civilians: Experiences and Perceptions of the Revolutionary and Napoleonic Wars, 1790–1820* (Basingstoke: Palgrave Macmillan, 2008).

2. Sheehan, *Where Have All the Soldiers Gone?* 17.

3. Israel Bartal has laid out the typological distinction between the Jewish conscript and volunteer in his pithy entry on Jews and the military in *Zman yehudi hadash: tarbut yehudit be-'idan hiloni. Mabat entsiklopedi* (Jerusalem: Keter, 2007), 1:298–302. Bartal's approach is oriented toward eastern Europe, as he associates the conscript with the reluctant soldier in the army of an absolutist state, whereas in fact conscription was seen as a matter of honor for Jews in Germany, Italy, France, and much of the Dual Monarchy. Moreover, although I agree with Bartal about the significance of the Jewish volunteer with the civil guards of revolutionary France and cities throughout Europe in 1848, this type was not unique to revolutionary situations, as seen by the hundreds of Jewish volunteers for Prussia in its war of liberation against Napoleonic France, or in the Ottoman Empire during the Russo-Turkish War of 1877–78.

4. Jacques Basnage, *Histoire des juifs* (1716 ed.), 8:13, 400–401, 403; 9:1, 290–91; 9:3, 950; 9:3, 965–66.

5. *Dissertatio iuris publici de iudaeo milite* (Halle, 1723; Scholem Collection, Hebrew and National University Library, Jerusalem).

6. *Dissertatio philosophica de militia judaeorum* (Copenhagen, 1737). Thanks to the Royal Danish Library, Copenhagen, for sending me an electronic version of what is apparently the only extant library copy of this text.

7. Gad Freudenthal, "Aaron Solomon Gumperz, Gotthold Ephraim Lessing and the First Call for the Improvement of the Civil Rights of Jews in Germany," *Association for Jewish Studies Review* 29, no. 2 (2005): 299–353.

8. Christian Wilhelm von Dohm, *Über die Bürgerliche Verbesserung der Juden* (Hildesheim: Georg Olms, 1973), 1:136.

9. Ibid., 2:222–46. See also 1:135–48.

10. Michael Silber has nicely analyzed Dohm's position in a preconscription political order in "From Tolerated Aliens to Citizen-Soldiers: Jewish Military Service in the Era of Joseph II," in *Constructing Nationalities in East Central Europe*, ed. Peter M. Judson and Marsha L. Rozenblit (New York: Berghahn, 2004), 22–23. See also Michael Hochelinger, "'Verbesserung' und 'Nutzbarmachung'? Zur Einführung der Militärdienstpflicht für Juden in der Habsburgermonarchive 1788–89," in *Militär und Religiosität in der Frühen Neuzeit*, ed. Michael Kaiser and Stefan Kroll (Münster: LIT, 2004), 97–120.

11. Michaelis' rejoinder to Dohm was published in Dohm, *Über die Bürgerliche Verbesserung der Juden*, 2:31–71.

12. Cited in Ronald Schechter, *Obstinate Hebrews: Representations of Jews in France, 1715–1815* (Berkeley and Los Angeles: University of California Press, 2002), 92. See also Alyssa Goldstein Sepinwall, *The Abbé Grégoire and the French Revolution: The Making of Modern Universalism* (Berkeley: University of California Press, 2005).

13. Silber, "From Tolerated Aliens to Citizen-Soldiers," 24–26.

14. Erwin Schmidl, *Juden in der k. (u.) k. Armee 1788–1918 / Jews in the Habsburg Armed Forces* (Eisenstadt: Österreichisches Jüdisches Museum, 1989), 112.

15. Saul Ascher, *Bemerkungen über die bürgerliche Verbesserung der Juden veranlasst be der Frage, Soll der Jude Soldat werden?* (Berlin, 1788), 4–10, 32–40.

16. Ibid., 79, 83–84.

17. Stefan Dudink and Karen Hagemann, "Masculinity in Politics and War in the Age of Democratic Revolutions," in *Masculinities in Politics and War*, ed. Stefan Dudink, Karen Hagemann, and John Tosh (Manchester, UK: Manchester University Press, 2004), 5.

18. Ruth Kestenberg-Gladstein, *Neuere Geschichte der Juden in den böhmischen Ländern. Erster Teil: Das Zeitalter der Aufklärung 1780–1839* (Tübingen: Mohr, 1969), 74–75.

19. *Ha-Me'asef*, 5549 [1789], 252.

20. The speech is reproduced in Kestenberg-Gladstein, *Neuere Geschichte der Juden in den böhmischen Ländern*, 70–72. In another version of the speech, Landau concludes with further verses from Psalm 91: "For he shall send his angels to thee, who will protect thee; they will keep thee in thy ways. Yet pay heed that thy foot not stumble (that you not willingly violate the religious laws). Even if thy enemy rage like a tiger or approacheth as poisonous as a serpent, thou willst trample upon him." See Alexander Kisch, *Zur Geschichte der israelitischen Militärfürsorge in Deutschland und Österreich* (Prague: Selbstverlag, 1917), 2–3. Kisch reproduced this version from a 1903 Hebrew biography of Landau, which in turn reproduced it from a 1902 article in *Der Jüdische Volkblatt*.

21. Kestenberg-Gladstein, *Neuere Geschichte der Juden in den böhmischen Ländern*, 339–40.

22. Bleich, "Military Service: Ambivalence and Contradictions," in *War and Peace in the Jewish Tradition*, ed. Lawrence Shiffman and Joel B. Wolowelsky (New York: Yeshiva University Press, 2007), 422.

23. Schmidl, *Juden in der k. (u.) k. Armee 1788–1918*, 106. See also the intriguing responsa of 1841 and 1842 by the Hungarian rabbi Meir Asch. In the first responsum, he rules that a Jew, presumably well-to-do or a scholar, may hire another Jew to serve in his place, claiming that it is possible to maintain ritual observance in the army. In the second, he reverses himself and argues that Jews who go off to the military abandon observance and become Gentiles in all but name. See *She'elot u-Teshuvot Imrei Esh* (Brooklyn, 1954; Jerusalem, 1981), 39r–v, Yoreh De'eah, and 15r, Even ha-Ezer. Thanks to Matt Goldish for this reference.

24. The Hatam Sofer was aware of this practice and prohibited communities from handing over social undesirables, not only paupers but "even . . . . adulterers or Sabbath violators," to the army. Gerald Bildstein, "The State and the Legitimate Use of Force and Coercion in Modern Halakhic Thought," *Jews and Violence: Studies in Contemporary Jewry XVIII* (2003): 8.

25. Mark Jantzen, *German Mennonite Soldiers: Nation, Religion and Family in the Prussian East, 1772–1880* (South Bend, Ind.: Notre Dame University Press, 2010).

26. So, for example, although rabbis fretted about the inability of Jewish recruits to observe the Sabbath while in service, they did not see a halakhic problem in Jews *fighting* on the Sabbath, as talmudic discussion makes room for violating commandments if necessary for self-defense or as a result of an unexpected threatening situation. Bohemian and German rabbis made similar concessions during the Napoleonic wars. Silber, "From Tolerated Aliens to Citizen-Soldiers," 28; Shmuel Feiner, *The Jewish Enlightenment* (Philadelphia: University of Pennsylvania Press, 2002), 269; Erik Lindner, *Patriotismus deutscher Juden von der napoleonischen Ära bis zum Kaiserreich: Zwischen korporativem Loyalismus und individueller deutsch-jüdischer Identität* (Frankfurt am Main: Peter Lang, 1997), 61–62, 190.

27. Silber, "From Tolerated Aliens to Citizen-Soldiers," 28.

28. Sheehan, *Where Have All the Soldiers Gone?* 7–14.

29. Frevert, *A Nation in Barracks*, 14, 50–51, 101; Ute Planert, *Der Mythos vom Befreiungskrieg: Frankreichs Krieg und der deutsche Süden: Alltag—Wahrnehmung—Deutung 1792–1841* (Paderborn: Ferdinand Schöning Verlag, 2007).

30. On the struggle of the French revolutionary government to establish a viable draft and to combat desertion during the 1790s, see Forrest, *Conscripts and Deserters*. The ongoing debate over the course of the nineteenth century about conscription, and its relationship to citizenship, is treated in Forrest, *The Legacy of the French Revolutionary Wars*, and in Eugen Weber, *Peasants into Frenchmen: The Modernization of Rural France, 1870–1914* (Stanford, Calif.: Stanford University Press, 1976), 292–300; On endemic and chronic desertion in Italy, see Sheehan, *Where Have All the Soldiers Gone?* 13.

31. *Militär-Statistisches Jahrbuch des K. u. k. Reichs-Kriegs-Ministeriums*. The entire run of this source is available at the U.S. Library of Congress. No-show rates are usually provided in the first few pages of each volume, with detailed break-downs by kingdom, province, and military district. Until the 1880s, no-shows were divided into "excused" and "unexcused" categories, with the former accounting for about a fifth of the total.

32. This subject has been explored impressionistically and through literature, e.g., Agnon, *'Ir u-melo'ah*, and Karl Emil Franzos, *Moschko von Parma* (Berlin: Ruetten and Loening, 1984; original 1880), but it deserves careful study, particularly in comparison with the situation in Rumania and the Russian Empire.

33. Schmidl, *Juden in der k. (u.) k. Armee 1788–1918*, 120.

34. Ibid.; I also consulted the document cited by Schmidl, a report of 3 May 1870 by Josef Heinold to the L'viv district general command, Kaiserliches u. königliches Kriegsarchiv, Vienna, KM Präs 1870 26-9:1.

35. *Ha-Tzefirah*, 5 March 1885, 76.

36. Frevert, *A Nation in Barracks*, 159–60; Michal Kopczynski, "The Physical Stature of Jewish Men in Poland in the Second Half of the 19th century," *Economics and Human Biology* 9 (2010): 203–10.

37. Sheehan, *Where Have All the Soldiers Gone?* 12.

38. Cited in David A. Bell, *The First Total War: Napoleon's Europe and the Birth of Warfare as We Know It* (New York: Houghton Mifflin, 2007), 79.

39. Ibid., 80; Linda Colley, *Britons: Forging the Nation, 1707–1837* (New Haven, Conn.: Yale University Press, 1992), chapter 1.

40. Marc Saperstein, "War and Patriotism in Sermons to Central European Jews, 1756–1815," *Leo Baeck Institute Year Book XXXVIII* (1993): 3–14.

41. Cited in Shmuel Feiner, *Moses Mendelssohn* (New Haven, Conn.: Yale University Press, 2010), 58.

42. Joseph Michman, "Jewish Soldiers in the Batavian Republic and under French Rule," *Dutch Jewish History* 3 (1993): 295–307.

43. Léon Kahn, *Les professions manuelles et les institutions de patronage* (Paris, 1885), 15–16.

44. Ibid., 17; Frances Malino, *A Jew in the French Revolution: The Life of Zalkind Hourwitz* (New York: Oxford University Press, 1997, 92.

45. Zosa Szajkowski, "Jews in the French Armed Forces," typescript ms., Archive of the Israel Defense Force (AIDF), F86/1511/1998, 4–14. Much but not all of the material on the eighteenth century in this manuscript was published in 1957 in an article titled "French Jews in the Armed Forces during the Revolution of 1789," reproduced in *Jews and the French Revolutions of 1789, 1830, and 1848* (New York: Ktav, 1970), 554–75.

46. Horst Fischer, *Judentum, Staat und Heer im Preussen im frühen 19. Jahrhundert* (Tübingen: Morh Siebeck, 1968), 41; Lindner, *Patriotismus deutscher Juden*, 70, 98; Deborah Hertz, *How Jews Became Germans: The History of Conversion and Assimilation in Berlin* (New Haven, Conn.: Yale University Press, 2007), 112–15.

47. Reproduced in Moritz Stern, *Aus der Zeit der deutschen Befreiungskriege, 1813–1815* (Berlin: Verlag Hausfriend, 1918), 11.

48. Michael Brenner, "From Subject to Citizen," in *German-Jewish History in Modern Times, Volume 2: Emancipation and Acculturation, 1780–1871*, general ed. Michael Meyer (New York: Columbia University Press, 1997), 257; Amos Elon, *The Pity of It All: A History of the Jews in Germany, 1743–1933* (New York: Metropolitan / Henry Holt, 2002), 95. Cohen's memoirs were published in 1993, in an edition edited by Erik Lindner.

49. Cited in Lindner, *Patriotismus deutscher Juden*, 61. Rabbis in France were more restrictive than their German counterparts about authorizing nonobservance of Jewish commandments while serving in the military. The French version of the Great Sanhedrin's responses to Napoleon asserts that exemptions from ritual practice are allowed throughout one's military service, but the Hebrew version distinguishes wartime, when the exemptions do apply, from peacetime, when they do not. Gil Graff, *Separation of Church and State: Dina de-Malkhuta Dina in Jewish Law, 1750–1848* (Tuscaloosa: University of Alabama Press, 1985), 93.

50. Dror Wahrman, *The Making of the Modern Self: Identity and Culture in Eighteenth-Century England* (New Haven, Conn.: Yale University Press, 2006), 21–30; David Hopkin, "The World Turned Upside Down: Female Soldiers in the French Armies of the Revolutionary and Napoleonic Wars," in *Soldiers, Citizens and Civilians: Experiences and Perceptions of the Revolutionary and Napoleonic Wars, 1790–1820*, ed. Alan Forest, Karen Hagemann, and Jane Rendall (London: Palgrave Macmillan, 2009), 77–95.

51. Hertz, *How Jews Became Germans*, 120–21.

52. Jean Quataert, *Staging Philanthropy: Patriotic Women and the National Imagination in Dynastic Germany, 1813–1916* (Ann Arbor: University of Michigan Press, 2001). See also the excellent article by Karen Hagemann, "Female Patriots: Women, War and the Nation in the Period of the Prussian-German Anti-Napoleonic Wars," *Gender and History* 16 (2004): 397–424. Despite her Germanic focus, Hagemann also draws on examples from Britain and France.

53. Chana C. Schuetz, "Deutsche jüdische Soldaten," in *Judenemanzipation und Antisemitismus in Deutschland im 19. u. 20. Jahrhundert*, ed. Wolfgang Michalka and Martin Vogt (Eggingen: Isele, 2003), 40.

54. Rieger, "Das Gutachten Abraham Geigers." The memorandum is largely reproduced in Ludwig Geiger, *Die deutschen Juden und der Krieg* (Berlin: A. Schwetschke, 1915). Quote is from page 43.

55. Orthodox rabbis in the heavily Polish province of Posen were no less keen than Geiger to endorse Jewish military service, though they described a collective duty of the Jewish "nation" to fight for king and country, while Geiger spoke of Jews fighting as individual Germans. Lindner, *Patriotismus deutscher Juden*, 189.

56. Fischer, *Judentum, Staat und Heer*, 151–76.

57. Christina Bettin, "Italian Jewry and the Construction of a European Jewish Identity," forthcoming in *The European Legacy: Journal of the Society for the Study of European Ideas* 17 (2012), n. 25.

58. On Jewish involvement in the Polish rebellions see most recently Antony Polonsky, *The Jews in Poland and Russia* (Oxford and Portland: Litman Library, 2010), 1:199–200, 298–99, 309–11, 314.

59. Marjan Kukiel, "Czy istniał pułk Berka?" in *Album pamiątkowy ku czci Berka Joselewicza pułkownika wojsk polskich w 125-letnią rocznicę jego bohaterskiej śmierci 1809–1934*, ed. Majer Bałaban (Warsaw: Wydawnictwo Komitetu Wileńskiego ku uczczeniu pamięci Berka Joselewicza Pułkownika Wojsk Polskich, 1934), 61–65.

60. Ernest Łuniński, "Berek Joselewicz (Szkic historyczny)," and Majer Bałaban, "Prawdziwe imię Berka I przebieg jego służby wojskowej," in *Album*, ed. Bałaban, 45–60 and 79–90.

61. The proposal, in German, is reproduced in Emil Kipa, "Berka Joselewicza projekt legjonu ochotniczego w roku 1796," in *Album*, ed. Bałaban, 71–75. Thanks to Francois Guesnet and Michael Silber for bringing this document to my attention.

62. Francois Guesnet, "The Turkish Cavalry in Swazedz; or, Jewish Political Culture at the Borderlines of Modern History," *Jahrbuch des Simon-Dubnow-Instituts* 6 (2007): 227–48.

63. Israel Bartal, "Giborim o-mogei lev? Yehudim be-tsiv'ot shel Polin (1794–1863)," in *Kiyum ve-shever. Yehudei polin le-doroteihem*, ed. Israel Bartal and Israel Gutman (Jerusalem: Merkaz Zalman Shazar, 1997), 353–67.

64. *AZdJ*, 7 May 1849, 255; *Der Orient*, 12 May 1849, 95. In 1848, the Habsburg navy, the overwhelming majority of whose sailors and officers were Italian, lost most of its ships to revolutionary Italian forces and its principal berth in Venice. In March of 1849, the newly appointed imperial naval commander von Dahlerup launched a concerted drive to acquire new ships, thus presumably motivating Vienna's Jews to make their bold offer.

65. *Der Orient*, 10 June 1848, 188; 8 September 1849, 163–66.

66. *Der Orient*, 8 April 1848, 114; Robert Wistrich, *The Jews of Vienna in the Age of Franz Joseph* (Oxford: Oxford University Press, 1989), 28–29.

67. *Der Orient*, 24 June 1848, 204–6.

68. Critina Bettin, *Italian Jews from Emancipation to the Racial Laws* (London: Palgrave Macmillan, 2010), 48.

69. *Der Orient*, 6 August 1848, 273–74. Hermann Jellinek was later executed by Habsburg authorities.

70. Elon, *The Pity of It All*, 163.

71. *AZdJ*, 17 April 1848, 252.

72. Something similar happened in the United States at the outbreak of the Civil War, where Jews on both sides quickly formed separate Jewish companies, which the army gratefully accepted in its search for anyone with the resources to raise and outfit a unit, especially cavalry, as horses were costly to acquire and maintain. See Bertram W. Korn, *American Jewry and the Civil War* (Philadelphia: Jewish Publication Society, 1961), 116–19.

73. *AZdJ*, 10 April 1848, 241.

74. Michael Miller, "Die Nationalgarde 1848: Grenzen der Emanzipation." *XXVI Mikulovske Sympozium 2000*, Brno 2003, 151–59; also in idem, *Rabbis and Revolution: The Jews of Moravia in the Age of Emancipation* (Stanford Calif.: Stanford University Press, 2010), 252–58.

75. *AZdJ*, 8 May 1848, 286–87; 15 May 1848, 288–90, 311.

76. On Jewish self-defense in 1848 see Jacob Toury, *Mehumah u-mevukhah be-mahapekhat 1848* (Tel Aviv: Moreshet, 1968), 89–98, and the primary sources anthologized in Israel Halperin, *Sefer ha-gevurah. Antologyah historit-sifrutit* (Tel Aviv: Am Oved, 1977), 2:11–21.

77. Frevert, *A Nation in Barracks*, 61, 101, 137.

78. Dudink and Hagemann, "Masculinities in Politics and War," 17–18. A principled critique of militarism and warfare did, however, continue to come from the German left. See Nicholas Stargardt, *The German Idea of Militarism: Radical and Socialist Critics, 1866–1914* (New York: Cambridge University Press, 1994).

79. *Ha-Maggid*, 26 February 1903, 83.

80. *Ha-Tsefirah*, 4 Adar 5622 [4 February 1862], 1.

81. The story first appeared in *Les Archives Israélites*, 10 October 1855, and was then picked up by the *Allgemeine Zeitung des Jundentums* and London's *Jewish Chronicle* on 26 November and 7 December respectively.

82. *AI*, 1878, 20–104; 17 March 1881, 82–3; 30 March 1882, 100–101; 26 February 1885, 67. There were also generous Passover leave policies in Holland, though the time period was shorter as the distances traveled between base and home were so much less. *Ha-Maggid*, 21 May 1903, 209.

83. *AI*, 1 November 1883, 359.

84. Ismar Schorsch, "Art as Social History: Moritz Oppenheim and the German-Jewish Vision of Emancipation," in *From Text to Context: The Turn to History in Modern Judaism* (Hanover, N.H.: Brandeis University Press/University Press of

New England, 1994), 108–10; Richard I. Cohen, *Jewish Icons: Art and Society in Modern Europe* (Berkeley and Los Angeles: University of California Press, 1998), 169–71; Lindner, *Patriotismus deutscher Juden*, 320; Christine G. Krüger, *"Sind wir denn nicht Brüder?" Deutsche Juden im nationalen Krieg 1870/71* (Paderborn: Ferdinand Schöningh, 2006), 117–19, 286–87.

85. See the interesting discussion on appropriate Jewish military pastoral care in the *AZdJ*, 3 July 1866, 429.

86. Kisch, *Zur Geschichte der israelitischen Militärfürsorge*, 6, 13.

87. *Jüdisches Lexicon*, q.v. "Militärdienst der Juden."

88. *AZdJ*, 13 December 1870, 979; 17 January 1871, 48–49; Krüger, *"Sind wir denn nicht Brüder?"* 123–24.

89. *AI*, 1 August 1873, 464–65; *UI*, 1 February 1874, 351; 15 February 1874, 356–58; 1 June 1874, 595–96.

90. Sharman Kadish, *A Good Jew and a Good Englishman: The Jewish Lads' and Girls' Brigade, 1895–1995* (London: Vallentine, Mitchell, 1995), 58.

91. Bertram W. Korn, "Jewish Welfare Activities for the Military during the Spanish-American War," *Publications of the American Jewish Historical Society* 41, nos. 1–4 (1951–52): 359–65.

92. Julia Phillips Cohen, "Fashioning Imperial Citizens: Sephardi Jews and the Ottoman State, 1856–1912," Ph.D. dissertation, Stanford University, 2008.

93. Michelle U. Campos, *Ottoman Brothers: Muslims, Christians and Jews in Early Twentieth-Century Palestine* (Stanford, Calif.: Stanford University Press, 2011), 148–58; Reeva Simon, "Iraqi Jews in the Turkish Military during World War I," unpublished paper delivered at a conference on "Jews, the Military and Collective Belonging," Emory University, 8 May 2012.

94. Personal communication from Reeva Simon, 26 March 2009.

95. Jacob L. Wright, "Surviving in an Imperial Context: Foreign Military Service and Judean Identity," in *Judah and the Judeans in the Achaemenid Period: Negotiating Identity in an International Context*, ed. Oded Lipschits, Gary N. Knoppers, and Manfred Oeming (Winona Lake, Ind.: Eisenbrauns, 2011), 512–14.

96. Cited in Stern, *Aus der Zeit der deutschen Befreiungskriege*, 26.

97. Heinrich Graetz, *The Structure of Jewish History and Other Essays* (New York: Ktav, 1975), 89.

98. *Der Orient*, 23 December 1848, 412.

99. Krüger, *"Sind wir denn nicht Brüder?* 102.

100. Bartal, "Giborim o-mogei lev?" 363.

101. Rieger, "Das Gutachten Abraham Geigers über die Militärpflichtigkeit der Juden," *Im Deutschen Reich*, August–September 1915, 165–74. The quote is from 168.

102. *UI*, July 1859, 543–50; *AZdJ*, 6 June 1859, 341–44; 10 July 1866, 444; M. Maurice Bloch, "Les vertus militaires des juifs," *Revue des études juives* 34 (1897): xviii–liii. Today, one would expect such an apologetic narrative to highlight Samuel ibn Naghrela (Shmuel Ha-Nagid, 993–1056), who served as deputy vizier and com-

mander of the armed forces of the king of Granada. But he is not singled out in the mid-nineteenth-century sources, perhaps because his war poetry was not published until the 1930s.

103. The call was issued in the *AZdJ*'s issue of 27 December 1870, with further requests and updates provided regularly until June of 1871, when the memorial volume *Gedenkbuch an den deutsch-französischen Krieg von 1870–1871 für den deutschen Israeliten* was published.

104. *Ha-Maggid*, 29 June 1859, 99.

105. Ibid., 20 July 1881, 233; 22 January 1885, 30; 12 May 1898, 147; *Ha-Melitz*, 13 October 1878, 5023–25.

106. Solomon was in fact an important resource for the revolutionary government, although Wolf and other Jewish propagandists considerably exaggerated his significance and selflessness. Contrary to legend, Solomon did not lend money with no expectation of return, and although he died in debt, this was so only because his assets were tied up in unredeemed government paper. See Beth Wenger, *History Lessons: The Creation of American Jewish Heritage* (Princeton, N.J.: Princeton University Press, 2010), 179–85.

107. Simon Wolf, *The American Jew as Patriot, Soldier and Citizen* (1895, pub. 1941; Cranbury, N.J.: Scholars' Bookshelf, 2006), 430. A similar blending of finance and fighting characterizes Leon Huehner, "Jews in the War of 1812," *Publications of the American Jewish Historical Society* 26 (1918): 173–200.

108. The story of the warships (known as the "Laird Rams" after the Laird Shipyards in Birkenhead where they were built), their intended use, and seizure is well known. The confiscation of the ships did involve the fronting of ten million dollars in United States bearer bonds, and the legend of a mysterious benefactor was perpetrated by L. E. Chittenden, register of the Treasury at the time. Wolf embellished the legend even further. In fact, the funds were provided by John Murray Forbes, a railway magnate from Boston, and the businessman W. H. Aspinwall.

109. "Army" and "War," www.jewishencyclopedia.com, accessed 17 January 2010.

110. Jewish reference works produced after World War II, including the 1971 and 2007 editions of the American *Encyclopedia Judaica*, feature far fewer entries about Jewish officers. *The Universal Jewish Encyclopedia*, published in the United States in 1943, features a forty-page entry under "Soldier, Jew as." The entry in the *Encyclopedia Judaica* is less than half that length.

111. Yohanan Petrovsky-Shtern, *Jews in the Russian Army, 1827–1917: Drafted into Modernity* (New York: Cambridge University Press, 2009), 157, 163–64.

112. Olga Litvak, *Haskalah: The Romantic Movement in Judaism* (New Brunswick, N.J.: Rutgers University Press, 2012). Many thanks to Professor Litvak for letting me read the draft book manuscript. In order to maximize its political bite, Mendele's novella is set back in the early 1850s, when the *khappers* were painfully visible signs of the Jewish communities' moral corruption, and the term and conditions of army service were particularly harsh.

113. Dan Bitan, "'Or sagi poreah': Mitosim shel gevurah lohemet be-reshit ha-tsiyonut (1880–1903)," in *Mitos ve-zikaron. Gilguleihah shel ha-toda'ah ha-yisre'elit*, ed. David Ohana and Robert S. Wistrich (Jerusalem: Van Leer Institute and Hakibutz Hameuhad, 1996), 169–88.

114. Shmuel Feiner, "Conflict and Tolerance: The Beginnings of the Jewish Kulturkampf in the 18th and 19th Centuries," in *Die Dritte Joseph Carlebach-Konferenz: Toleranz im Verhältnis von Religion und Gesellschaft*, ed. Miriam Gillis-Carlebach and Barbara Vogel (Hamburg: Doelling and Galitz, 1997), 47–48.

115. Theodor Friedgut, "Jews, Violence and the Russian Revolutionary Movement," *Studies in Contemporary Jewry XVIII* (2003): 43–58. On Novomesky, see Ilan Troen, "The Price of Partition, 1948: The Dissolution of the Palestine Potash Company," *The Journal of Israeli History* 15 (1994): 53–81; for Shochat, Shabtai Teveth, *Ben-Gurion: The Burning Ground, 1886–1948* (New York: Random House, 1987), 56; for Rutenberg, Eli Shaltiel, *Pinhas Rutenberg: 'aliyato u-nefilato shel "ish hazak" be-Erets-Yiśra'el, 1879–1942* (Tel Aviv: Am Oved, 1990), 28.

116. In his poem Bialik deliberately ignored acts of Jewish bravery and resistance, as he wished to present the situation of diaspora Jewry as utterly abject and unredeemable. See the special issue of *Prooftexts* (25, 2005), edited by Alan Mintz, on Bialik's poem and the Kishinev pogrom.

117. Shlomo Lambroza, "Jewish Self-Defense during the Russian Pogroms of 1903–1906," *Jewish Journal of Sociology* 23, no. 2 (1981): 123–34; Iris Milner, "'In the City of the Slaughter': The Hidden Voice of the Pogrom Victims," *Prooftexts* 25 (2005): 60–72; Gerald D. Surh, "Russia's 1905 Era Pogroms Reexamined," *Canadian-American Slavic Studies* 44 (2010): 253–95.

118. Petrovsky-Shtern, *Jews in the Russian Army*, 264. By 1929, Jews were 10.3 percent of the army's senior officers though only 1.7 percent of the total population. *Jüdisches Lexikon*, q.v. "Militärdienst der Juden."

119. Israel Zwi Tanner, *Joseph Trumpeldor. Ein Jüdischer Held*, 3rd ed. (Vienna: Joseph Belf, 1936), 151–61.

120. The European Jewish press also took great satisfaction in the Spanish-American War. For example, *Ha-Maggid* noted with pride that a Jewish officer was appointed to be the U.S. Army's representative to the commission investigating sinking of the *Maine*. Satisfied that the country that had expelled its Jews would be judged by a Jew, the newspaper wrote, "This is mere coincidence, yet the Spanish, who know in their heart of the terrible wrong that they did to our Jewish ancestors, now truly fear the American Jews, and in the way of all those who hate us they inflate and worship the Jews' power and they spread terrifying rumours" (that rich American Jews in New York pushed war on the American government as vengeance against Spain for 1492). *Ha-Maggid*, 12 May 1898, 147.

121. Korn, "Jewish Welfare Activities."

122. The economist John A. Hobson and a number of government officials and journalists believed that Jewish mining interests stood to gain if Britain overthrew the Transvaal Republic and replaced it with a sympathetic British administration.

Richard Mendelsohn, "The Jewish War: Anglo-Jewry and the South African War," in Greg Cuthberstson, Albert Grundling, and Mary-Lynn Suttie, eds., *Writing a Wider War: Rethinking Gender, Race and Identity in the South African War, 1899–1902* (Athens: Ohio University Press, 2002), 247–65.

123. According to Shira Schnitzer, exact figures are not available, because many volunteers did not indicate their religion when signing up. "'No Conflicts of Principle': The Patriotic Rhetoric of Anglo-Jewish Sermons during the Boer War," *Journal of Modern Jewish Studies* 3, no. 3 (2004): 289–305. Cecil Roth claimed that some three to four thousand Jews volunteered in the war. "Jews in the Defence of Britain," *Transactions of the Jewish Historical Society of England* 15 (1946). Estimates provided shortly after the war were more modest; in 1903, the speaker at the annual Hanukkah event honoring British Jews in uniform provided the figure of 1,197. *Ha-Maggid*, 8 January 1903, 16.

124. Ibid.

125. *Ha-Maggid*, 8 January 1903, 16.

126. *JC*, 20 October 1899, 10; 11 May 1900, 10; 18 May 1900, 11.

127. E.g., 19 October 1900, 10.

128. *JC*, 15 December 1899, 5; 8 June 1900, 3.

129. *JC*, 29 June 1900, 18; see also 11 October 1901, 10.

130. *JC*, 25 April 1902, 9; 30 May 1902, 9, 15.

131. Kadish, *A Good Jew and a Good Englishman*, 36ff.

132. *JC*, 13 July 1900, 17.

133. *AZdJ*, 22 July 1904, supplement, 1; 30 September 1904, supplement, 2.

## Chapter Three

1. Hannah Arendt, *The Origins of Totalitarianism* (New York: Harvest, 1994; orig. 1950), part 1, chapters 2 and 4.

2. Pierre Birnbaum, *The Jews of the Republic: A History of State Jews from Gambetta to Vichy* (Stanford, Calif.: Stanford University Press, 1996).

3. E.g, E. Rubin, *140 Jewish Marshals, Generals and Admirals* (London: De Vero, 1952); J. Ben Hirsch, *Jewish General Officers* (Military Historical Society of Australia, 1967); Alfred Posselt, *Jüdische Generale unter Fremden Fahnen* (Vienna: Verlag des Vereines zur Förderung und Pflege des Reform-Judentums in Österreich, 1985).

4. Joseph Roth, *The Radetzky March* (New York: Overlook, 2002), 70.

5. Sharman Kadish, *A Good Jew and a Good Englishman: The Jewish Lads' and Girls' Brigade, 1895–1995* (London: Vallentine, Mitchell, 1995), 48.

6. *Encyclopedia Judaica*, q.v. "Military Service" (9:1573).

7. C. B. Otley, "The Social Origins of British Army Officers," *Sociological Review* 18 (1970): 213–39; Edward Spiers, *The Army and Society, 1815–1914* (London: Longman, 1980), 1–29; idem, *The Late Victorian Army, 1868–1902* (Manchester, UK: Manchester University Press, 1992), 94–105; David French, *Military Identities:*

*The Regimental System, the British Army, and the British People, c. 1870–2000* (Oxford: Oxford University Press, 2005).

8. Cecil Roth, "Jews in the Defence of Britain," *Transactions of the Jewish Historical Society of England* 15 (1946): 15–19, 21–24; Kadish, *The Jewish Lads' and Girls' Brigade*, 58.

9. Paul Nathan, ed., *Der Jude als Soldat* (Berlin: Comité zur Abwehr antisemitischer Begriffe, 1896), 132–33; Roth, "Jews in the Defence of Britain," 26 n. 1.

10. "Adolph Moses," *Jewish Encyclopedia*. The entire text of this 1901–6 work is available online; for this entry see http://www.jewishencyclopedia.com/articles/11060-moses-adolph, accessed 8 November 2011.

11. David Koffman, "The Jews' Indian: Culture and Commerce between Jews and Native Americans, 1824–1924," Ph.D. dissertation, New York University, 2011, chapter 2.

12. Rubin, *140 Jewish Marshals, Generals and Admirals*, 261.

13. Joseph Bendersky, *The "Jewish Threat": Antisemitic Politics of the U.S. Army* (New York: Basic Books, 2001).

14. Biographical sketches of all three of these figures may be found in Hirsch, *Jewish General Officers*.

15. Werner T. Angress, "Die jüdische Offizier in der neuren deutschen Geschichte, 1813–1918," in *Willensmenschen: Über deutsche Offiziere*, ed. Ursula Breymayer, Bernd Ulrich, and Karin Wieland (Frankfurt am Main: Fischer Verlag, 1999), 69.

16. Werner Angress, "Prussia's Army and the Jewish Reserve Officer Controversy before World War I," *Leo Baeck Institute Year Book XVII* (1972): 19–42; Ursula Breymayer, "'Mein Kampf': Das Phantom des Offiziers. Zur Autobiographie eines jüdischen Wilhelminers," in *Willensmenschen*, ed. Breymayer et al., 79–93.

17. Wolfgang Schmidt, "Die Juden in der Bayerischen Armee," in *Deutsche Jüdische Soldaten. Von der Epoche der Emanzipation bis zum Zeitalter der Weltkriege*, ed. Frank Nägler (Hamburg: E. S. Mittler, 1996), 63–86.

18. See Ludwig Geiger's introduction to Meno Burg, *Geschichte meines Dienstlebens*, 3rd ed. (Leipzig: M. M. Kaufmann, 1916), xv. For another example of the lionization of Burg in German-Jewish apologetics, see Michael Frankel, *Der Anteil der jüdischen Freiwilligen an dem Befreiungskriege 1813–1814* (Breslau, 1922).

19. Renatus Rieger, *Major Meno Burg: Ein preussischer Offizier jüdischen Glaubens (1789–1853)* (Duisburg: Universität-Gesamthochschule-Duisburg, 1990).

20. Cited by Geiger in Burg, *Geschichte meines Dienstlebens*, xiii–xv.

21. Istvan Deak, "Pacesetters of Integration: Jewish Officers in the Habsburg Monarchy," *Eastern European Politics and Societies* 3, no. 1 (1989): 22–50; idem, *Beyond Nationalism: A Social and Political History of the Habsburg Officers Corps, 1848–1918* (New York: Oxford University Press, 1990), 133, 171–77, 196.

22. Erwin Schmidl, *Juden in der k. (u.) k. Armee 1788–1918 / Jews in the Habsburg Armed Forces* (Eisenstadt: Österreichisches Jüdisches Museum, 1989), 136.

23. Roth, *Radetzky March*, 72, 79, 102.

24. Alberto Rovighi, *I Militari di Origine Ebraica nel Primo Secolo di Vita dello Stato Italiano* (Rome: Stato Maggiore dell'Esercito Ufficio Storico, 1999), 18.

25. Ibid., 3, 4, 8.

26. Ibid., 17.

27. Ibid., 52–53.

28. Meir Michaelis, "Gli ufficiali superiori ebrei nell'esercito italiano dal Risorgimento alla marcia su Roma," *La rassegna mensile d'Israel* 30, no. 4 (1964): 157–58.

29. Ulrich Wyrwa, "Antisemitism in Europe and the Italian Jewish Response: The Coverage of the Journal *Il Vessillo Israelitico* (1879–1914)," *Studia Judaica* 15 (2007): 196–209.

30. Michaelis, "Ufficiali superiori," 159–62.

31. Abraham Berliner, *Geschichte der Juden in Rom von der ältesten Zeit bis zur Gegenwart* (Frankfurt am Main: J. Kaufmann, 1893), vol. 2, n.p. Many thanks to Kenneth Stow for this reference.

32. In 1892, Captain André Crémieu-Foa estimated that there were some 300 Jewish career officers in the French army (Serge William Serman, "Le corps des officiers français sous la Deuxième République et le Second Empire," Doctorat d'état, Paris IV, 1976, 2:1099). According to the 1901–6 *Jewish Encyclopedia*, by 1895 the number had climbed to 350, of whom 280 were lieutenants or captains (q.v. "Army"). In 1896, the German publication *Der Jude als Soldat* listed some 800 Jewish officers, but whoever compiled the list appears to have included reserve officers and to have chosen people based on names that indicated Jewish origin, and such evidence is suggestive more than definitive. A check of the dossiers of officers with some of the more ambiguous names (e.g., Lambert, Lippmann) in the French military archives revealed some of them to be Christians. If we use the lower figure of 350 as a base, one has to take into account the constant flow of retirees out of the service and of young men into the officer pool as graduates of the military academies or as volunteers who were promoted through the ranks.

33. Philippe Landau, *L'Opinion juive et l'affaire Dreyfus* (Paris: Albin Michel, 1995), 95; Pierre Birnbaum, "L'armée française était-elle antisemite?" in *L'Affaire Dreyfus*, ed. Michel Winock (Paris: Seuil, 1998), 73.

34. Statistics on the number of officers in each corps are listed in the *Annuaire de l'armée française pour 1894* (Paris: Berger Levrault).

35. See the lists headlined "Israel chez nous" in *L'Antijuif*, 11 September 1898, 3–4; 25 September 1898, 3; 2 October 1898, 4; 16 October 1898, 3.

36. Robert Nye, *Masculinity and Male Codes of Honor in Modern France* (Berkeley and Los Angeles: University of California Press, 1993), 205–10. In a breach of dueling etiquette, Captain Crémieu-Foa's brother Ernest published an illicit transcript of the duel between his brother and Lamase, and this faux pas became a much greater scandal than the duels themselves.

37. See the lengthy obituary for Armand and description of his funeral service in *AI*, 30 June 1892, 201–6; also Michael Marrus, *The Politics of Assimilation: The*

*French Jewish Community at the Time of the Dreyfus Affair* (Oxford: Clarendon Press of Oxford University Press, 1971), 197–99.

38. Vincent Duclert, *Alfred Dreyfus. L'honneur d'un patriote* (Paris: Fayard, 2006), 62, 69.

39. The Dreyfus Affair is arguably the most closely studied political scandal in modern history. The classic account is Jean-Denis Bredin, *The Affair: The Case of Alfred Dreyfus* (Paris: Georges Braziller, 1986). Also invaluable are Michael Burns, *Dreyfus: A Family Affair, 1789–1945* (New York: HarperCollins, 1991); and most recently, Ruth Harris, *Dreyfus: Politics, Emotion, and the Scandal of the Century* (New York: Metropolitan, 2010).

40. William Serman, *Les officiers français dans la nation 1848–1914* (Paris: Aubier Montaigne, 1982), 108.

41. Landau, *L'Opinion juive et l'affaire Dreyfus*, 95; Birnbaum, "L'armée française," 75–78.

42. Birnbaum, "L'armée française," 74; Paul-Marie de la Gorge, *The French Army: A Military-Political History* (London: Weidenfeld and Nicolson, 1963), 41, 56, 59.

43. On French-Jewish commanders during World War I, see Sylvain Halff, "Participation of the Jews of France in the Great War," *American Jewish Yearbook* 21 (1919–20): 31–97.

44. Spiers, *The Army and Society*, 3.

45. Serman, *Les officiers français*, 16; de la Gorge, *The French Army*, 35, 48–50.

46. Serman, *Les officiers français*, 145–48.

47. In his pocket history of the Jews written for British servicemen in World War I, Paul Goodman goes so far as to claim that Dreyfus had been framed in order to get all Jews out of France's officer corps. Paul Goodman, *A History of the Jews: Soldiers' and Sailors' Edition* (London and Toronto: J. M. Dent & Sons, 1917).

48. Compte de Chesnel, *Encyclopédie militaire et maritime*, 5th ed. (Paris: Armand Le Chevalier, 1868), 503–5; André Corvisier, *Dictionnaire d'art et d'histoire militaires* (Paris: Presses Universitaires, 1988), 287; idem, *Histoire militaire de la France* (Paris: Presses Universitaires de France, 1992), 2:430–31; André Bach, *L'armée de Dreyfus. Une histoire politique de l'armée française de Charles X à "L'Affaire"* (Paris: Tallandier, 2004, 477), 488, 499.

49. The *Annuaire de l'armée française pour 1883*, 80, lists Samuel as of 30 December 1881 as "chef d'état major de la 6e division d'infantrie." In October of 1886, the *Allgemeine Zeitung des Judentums* referred to "the recently deceased Oberst Abraham Auguste Samuel of the General Staff" in an article on Jewish officers in European armies (680–82).

50. E.g., Captain Moise-Menahem Ferdinand Valabregues (Ninth Brigade infantry), Captain Armand-Bernard Lipman (Thirtieth Regiment artillery), Captain Lucien Levy (Thirty-fourth Division infantry / Seventeenth Corps army), Leopold-Adrian Levy (état-major particulier adjoint à la direction de Versailles). *Annuaire de l'armée française pour 1894*, 114, 16–17, 120. On the transformation of the General Staff and Dreyfus' position in it, see Duclert, *Dreyfus*, 69, 74, 80–90.

51. Bach, *L'armée de Dreyfus*, 538.

52. Ibid., 511–12; Duclert, *Dreyfus*, 44–45, 69, 74, 92.

53. See Cerfbeer's birth certificate, service record, and the letter from his father to the war minister, dated 26 July 1810, in Service historique de l'armée territoriale, Vincennes (hereafter SHA), 3Yf 75715.

54. Hinsten's career dossier includes his marriage contract, witnessed by his brothers, Charles, "lieutenant de vaisseau," and Napoleon, a civil engineer. SHA, 9Yd 146.

55. SHA, 5Yf 83888.

56. SHA, 6Yf 65196.

57. SHA, 5Yf 85209.

58. SHA, 13 Yd 124.

59. Archives de la Marine, Vincennes, CC7 4e Moderne C.464 D.9.

60. Serman, *Les officers français*, 188, 191, 221–222.

61. Ibid., 153, 160, 165. 167, 170, 176, 178; idem, "Le corps des officiers français," 2:973–83.

62. SHA, 5Yf 41489.

63. See the wedding contract, dated 13 March 1869, and a letter dated 23 February 1869 from the Paris Prefecture of Police in SHA, 7Yd 1615.

64. SHA, 9M 597.

65. SHA, 9Yd 386.

66. SHA, 10Yd 1119.

67. SHA, 9Yd 471.

68. See, for example, Bernard Avraham, who in 1858 married the daughter of a respectable cloth manufacturer from Lorraine, and who brought 50,000 francs (SHA, 10Yd 88); Jules Levy Moch, who in 1858 married the daughter of a rabbi and obtained a dowry of 34,000 francs (SHA, 5Yf 29311); Hippolyte Solomon Weill, who married a French Jewish woman domiciled in Algeria with an income of 1,700 francs per year (SHA, 5Yf 85209); and Samuel Weil, the son of a peddler who joined up in 1875 and in 1906 married a woman with only 300 francs per year in income (SHA, 6Yf 65196).

69. Serman, "Le corps des officiers français," 2:1097.

70. Between 1848 and 1870, only 6 percent of officers were shorter than 1.6 meters. Most were between 1.6 and 1.8 meters, and only 3 percent were 1.8 meters or taller. Serman, "Le corps des officiers français," 1:650.

71. SHA, 5Ye 55415.

72. SHA, B5Ye 56181.

73. Reports of 1890 and 1891, in SHA, 3Ye 6886.

74. SHA, 3Ye 8798.

75. SHA, 6Yf 73371.

76. See the negative evaluations of Cerbeer's request for a staff position of 8 and 22 June 1821, and his commanding officers' recommendations for decoration and promotion, dated 9 July 1823 and 10 May 1832, in SHA, 3Yf 75715.

77. From his career table in SHA, 9Yd 386.

78. SHA, 6Yf 78853.

79. See the letter of 4 July 1892 from the Naval Ministry to the mayor of Paris' tenth arrondissement, asking that the officer's brother-in-law be informed; also the letter of 13 September 1892 (infantry staff to Naval Ministry) in SHA 3Ye 6886.

80. *AI*, 1 December 1892, 378–79.

81. Jean-Denis Bredin, *Bernard Lazare: de l'anarchiste au prophète* (Paris: Editions de Fallois), 1992.

82. Archives Nationales, Correspondence du Capitaine Fernand Bernard avec ses parents, son frère et son fils, AB XIX 4283. Deepest thanks to Eric Jennings for alerting me to the presence of this collection and to Caroline Piketty, former director of private archives at the AN, for facilitating my access to the letters.

83. Letter of 27 February 1897.

84. E.g, letters of 16 January 1897, 14 and 27 February 1897, 26 April 1898.

85. Fernand Bernard, *L'Indo-Chine: erreurs et dangers—un programme* (Paris: Charpentier, 1901).

86. Andrew Hardy, "The Economics of French Rule in Indochina: A Biography of Paul Barnard (1892–1960)," *Modern Asian Studies* 32, no. 4 (1998): 243; M. Meuleau, *Des pionniers en Extreme-Orient. Histoire de la Banque d'Indochine, 1875–1975* (Paris, 1990), 353, 457.

87. Henry Frenay, *La nuit finira* (Paris: Mundi, 1973), 75, 99–100; Bredin, *Bernard Lazare*, 19.

88. Letter of 26 April 1898; see also letter of 9 September 1898.

89. Letter of 1 May 1898; see also the letter to his brother Armand, dated 7 March 1898.

90. Letters of 16 January and 7 March 1898.

91. Letter of 9 September 1898.

92. For the actress' biography, see Sylvie Chevalley, *Rachel* (Paris: Calmann-Levy, 1989); Rachel M. Brownstein, *Tragic Muse: Rachel of the Comedie-Francaise* (New York: Knopf, 1993).

93. Archive de la Marine, CC 7—Alpha—864.

94. My account of Mayer's life is taken from the materials (including Mayer's memoirs) assembled in Vincent Duclert, ed., *Le colonel Mayer: de l'affaire Dreyfus à de Gaulle* (Paris: Armand Collin, 2007). The quote is from 157.

95. Ibid., 380–81.

96. On the prominence of Jews in the Saint-Simonian movement see Michael Graetz, *The Jews in Nineteenth-Century France: From the French Revolution to the Alliance Israelite Universelle* (Stanford, Calif.: Stanford University Press, 1996), 110–42, 152–63.

97. Duclert, *Le colonel Mayer*, 194.

98. Ibid.

## Chapter Four

1. Cited in Jonathan Gribetz, "Muslims, Christians, and Jews in the 'Arab-Zionist' Encounter: A Study of Mutual Perceptions in Late Ottoman Palestine," Ph.D. dissertation, Columbia University, 2010, 198–99.

2. A few years before Zaidan, the secular Arab nationalist Najib Azuri and the influential Islamic reformer Rashid Ridha also described Jews as a nation: Derek J. Penslar, "Antisemites on Zionism: From Indifference to Obsession," in *Israel in History: The Jewish State in Comparative Perspective* (London: Routledge, 2006), 125.

3. For an analysis of this same topic from a different perspective, emphasizing Jewish patriotism at the expense of confessional solidarity, see David Aberbach, "Zionist Patriotism in Europe, 1897–1942: Ambiguities in Jewish Nationalism," *International History Review* 31 (2009): 268–98.

4. In the midst of the war, Labour Zionists in America acknowledged that Poles, Ukrainians, Serbs, and Armenians all faced a similar fate of fighting on rival sides. *The Jews and the War: Memorandum of the Jewish Socialist Labour Confederation Poale-Zion* (New York, 1916), 38, cited in Suzanne Schneider, "The Great War and the Politics of Transformation: Reading the World War I Jewish Experience," M.A. thesis, Department of Middle East and Asian Languages and Cultures, Columbia University, 2008, 44–45.

5. Many thanks to Piotr Wrobel for this observation.

6. John Keegan, *A History of Warfare* (New York: Knopf, 1993), 34, 44.

7. Moshe Verbin, *Ha-yehudim 'im neshek bi-yedeihem. Perek be-helkam shel ha-yehudim be-milhamot polin be-me'ot tet-zayin-yod-zayin* (Lod: Merkaz Haberman le-mehkarei sifrut, 1990).

8. Barry Schwartz, "*Hanoten Teshua*: The Origin of the Traditional Jewish Prayer for the Government," *Hebrew Union College Annual* 57 (1986): 113–20.

9. Samuel ben Nathan Ha-Levi Loew, *Mahatsit Ha-shekel*, 284:7. Many thanks to Rachel Greenblatt for this reference. As Jonathan Sarna has pointed out, the pioneering American rabbi Jacob Leeser dropped this part of the prayer from his 1848 prayer book, nor does it appear in the popular prayer book of Philip Birnbaum, first published in 1949. See Jonathan D. Sarna, "Jewish Prayers for the U.S. Government: A Study in the Liturgy of Politics and the Politics of Liturgy," in *Moral Problems in American Life*, ed. Karen Halttunen and Lewis Perry (Ithaca, N.Y.: Cornell University Press, 1998), 201–21. For a general history of the prayer, see Schwartz, "*Hanoten Teshua*, 113–20; and idem, "Ha-tefilah li-shlom ha-malkhut ve-ha-medinah," in *Pirkei mehkar le-yom ha-atsma'ut* (Ramat Gan: Bar Ilan University, 1998), 176–200.

10. Marc Saperstein, *Jewish Preaching in Times of War, 1800–2001* (Oxford: Littman Library, 2008), 85.

11. Ibid., 86.

12. *Transactions of the Parisian Sanhedrin or Acts of the Assembly of Israelitish [sic] Deputies of France and Italy*, ed. Diogene Tama, trans. F. D. Kirwan (Cincin-

nati: Hebrew Union College–Jewish Institute of Religion, 1956), 24. (Sitting of the Assembly of Notables of 7 August 1806.)

13. Gregory Caplan, "Germanising the Jewish Male: Military Masculinity as the Last Stage of Acculturation," in *Towards Normality? Acculturation and Modern German Jewry*, ed. Rainer Liedtke and David Rechter (Tübingen: Mohr Siebeck, 2003), 159–84.

14. Marc Saperstein, "British Jewish Preachers in Time of War (1800–1918)," *Journal of Modern Jewish Studies* 4, no. 3 (2005): 255–71.

15. David A. Bell, *The First Total War: Napoleon's Europe and the Birth of Warfare as We Know It* (New York: Houghton Mifflin, 2007), 287.

16. Ben Baader, *Gender, Judaism, and Bourgeois Culture in Germany, 1800–1870* (Bloomington: Indiana University Press, 2006), 80. See also Till van Rahden, "Jews and the Ambivalences of Civil Society in Germany, 1800–1933: Assessment and Reassessment," *Journal of Modern History* 77 (2005): 1024–47.

17. *AZdJ*, 1 May 1848, 269–72.

18. "Die Verbindung unter den Juden," *AZdJ*, 26 March 1849, 165–68.

19. *AZdJ*, 21 May 1849, 275.

20. *AZdJ*, 23 October 1848, 633–34.

21. *AZdJ*, 3 July 1866, 427–28.

22. See the references to the *JC* of 29 July and 9 September 1870 in Saperstein, *Jewish Preaching in Times of War*, 237; also *AZdJ*, 30 August 1870, 689–90.

23. *JC*, 2 March 1900, 17; 20 April 1900, 12–13, 15.

24. *AI*, 2 November 1899, 351.

25. *Ha-Tzefirah*, 28 February 1878, 76–77.

26. *Ha-Melitz*, 18 October 1901, 1–2.

27. Samuel Spitzer, *Das Heer- und Wehrgesetz der alten Israeliten im Vergleiche zu den in Ungarn-Österreich bestehenden diesfälligen Bestimmmungen* (Pest, 1869), 1.

28. Adolph Ehrentheil, *Mot Yesharim (Ehrentod der Braven). Rede, gehalten zur Seelensgedächtnissfeier für die im jüngsten Kriege gefallenen Soldaten israelitischer Religion am 11. November 1866 in der Synagoge zu Horic* (Prague, 1866), 9.

29. Adolph Jellinek, *Gedächtnissrede auf die im letzten Kriege gefallenen Soldaten israelitischer Religion am 13. November 1866 gehalten* (Vienna, 1867).

30. Paul Nathan, ed., *Die Juden als Soldaten* (Berlin, 1896).

31. Armand Bloch, *L'esprit militaire des juifs. Conférence fait à Bruxelles, le 1er jour de Hanouca 5664 (13 Decembre 1903)* (Brussels: Michel van Dantzig, 1904), 30.

32. Cited in Meir Michaelis, "Gli ufficiale superiori ebrei nell'esercito italiano dal Risorgimento alla marcia su Roma," *La rassegna mensile d'Israel* 30, no. 4 (1964): 162–63. Pacifici was a prominent Jewish activist who advocated a blend of Orthodoxy, Zionism, and diaspora Jewish cultural renewal.

33. *UI*, 1870, 592.

34. Saperstein, *Jewish Preaching in Times of War*, 252.

35. Kruger, *Sind wir denn nicht Bruder?* 157–59, 189–203.

36. *Ha-Tzefirah*, 13 March 1884, 34–35.

37. *Ha-Maggid*, 1 June 1899, 163–64.

38. Abraham Duker, "Jewish Volunteers in the Ottoman-Polish Cossack Units during the Crimean War," *Jewish Social Studies* 16, no. 3 (1954): 203–18, 351–76.

39. Ibid., 355.

40. *UI*, 1859, 531–36.

41. *AI*, 17 October 1901; *JC*, 17 August 1900, 7, 11 October 1901, 10.

42. A series of opposing letters to the editor on "The Jew and the Military Spirit" appeared in the *JC* on 1, 8, and 15 November 1901, 7–8, 9–10, and 7 respectively. See also the *JC* of 6 December 1901, 11, for a letter to the editor accusing the Boers of lacking humanity.

43. *JC*, 21 April 1854, 248.

44. Saperstein, *Jewish Preaching in Time of War*, 21; see also *AZdJ*, 10 May 1864, 309.

45. Esdra Pontremoli, "Importanza della lingua sacra per la nazionalità religiosa israelitica," *L'Educatore Israelita* 5 (1857): 3–6, 47–51, 65–69.

46. Ibid., 50.

47. Ibid., 50–51.

48. These themes are thoroughly developed in Krüger, *Sind wir denn nicht Brüder?*

49. "Le Vainqueur," *UI*, 1871, 49.

50. See Bell, *The First Total War*, 35, on the development of medieval jousting and dueling into warfare via the institution of single combat.

51. Martii Koskenniemi, *The Gentle Civilizer of Nations: The Rise and Fall of International Law, 1870–1960* (Cambridge: Cambridge University Press, 2001), 29, 269–74.

52. Lisa Leff, *Sacred Bonds of Solidarity: The Rise of Jewish Internationalism in Nineteenth-Century France* (Stanford, Calif.: Stanford University Press, 2006); Benedict Anderson, *The Spectre of Comparisons: Nationalism, Southeast Asia and the World* (London: Verso, 1998), 30–45.

53. Cited in Vicki Caron, *Between France and Germany: The Jews of Alsace-Lorraine, 1871–1918* (Stanford, Calif.: Stanford University Press, 1988), 35. See also Birnbaum, *The Jews of the Republic*, 179–85.

54. Koskenniemi, *The Gentle Civilizer of Nations*, 36, 39, 84; *AI* 31 (1870): 515, 32; (1871): 8–10, 42–49.

55. *Die Israelitische Wochenschrift* (1871): 273–74, 281–82. *L'Univers Israelite* consistently misidentifies the place of publication as Stettin.

56. Krüger, *"Sind wir denn nicht Brüder?"* 218–19.

57. "La guerre actuelle et les juifs," *UI*, 1871, 78–80.

58. *AZdJ*, 4 October 1870, 789; 11 October 1870, 805–6.

59. *AZdJ*, 25 October 1870, 844–45.

60. *AI*, 1 March 1873, 154–55.

61. Julia Phillips Cohen, "Fashioning Imperial Citizens: Sephardi Jews and the Ottoman State, 1856–1912," Ph.D. dissertation, Stanford University, 2008.

62. Thanks to Yithzak Lewis for preparing a literal yet vibrant translation of the poem.

63. During the revolutionary and Napoleonic wars, almost a quarter of France's Jews were involved in military purveying, with an elite of Jewish financiers sitting atop a network of local Jewish merchants who dealt in produce and livestock. After 1815, the French government instituted its own supply corps. Zosa Szjakowski, "French Jews in the Armed Forces during the Revolution of 1789," in *Jews and the French Revolutions of 1789, 1830 and 1848* (New York: Ktav, 1970), 567–75; Michael Graetz, "Aliyato u-shkia'to shel sapak ha-tsava ha-yehudi: kalkalah yehudit be-i'itot milhamah," *Tsiyon* 56, no. 3 (1991): 255–74.

64. For a colorful story of Jewish military contracting in mid-nineteenth-century Britain and the short-lived Confederate States of America, see Adam Mendelsohn, "Samuel and Saul Isaac: International Jewish Arms Dealers, Blockade Runners, and Civil War Profiteers," forthcoming in *Southern Jewish History*.

65. Pauline Wengeroff, *Rememberings: The World of a Russian-Jewish Woman in the Nineteenth Century*, tr. Henry Wenkart, ed. Bernard D. Cooperman (College Park: University of Maryland Press, 2000), 8–9, 199–200. During the Balkan War of 1877–78, military provisioning was handled entirely by a private consortium known as the Partnership, four of whose six shareholders were Jewish, which did business with hundreds of Jewish subcontractors. The Partnership struggled valiantly but unsuccessfully to provision the army in Rumania across a vast supply line in inhospitable terrain, and its efforts were repaid by the Military Commissariat with charges of corruption and demands for the return of disbursed funds. Yohanan Petrovsky-Shtern, *Jews in the Russian Army, 1827–1917: Drafted into Modernity* (New York: Cambridge University Press, 2009), 168–74.

66. Benjamin Ginsberg, *The Fatal Embrace: Jews and the State* (Chicago: University of Chicago Press, 1999), 64–65.

67. A. J. Sherman, "German-Jewish Bankers in World Politics: The Financing of the Russo-Japanese War," *Leo Baeck Institute Year Book XXVIII* (1983): 59–73; Jonathan Frankel, "The Paradoxical Politics of Marginality: Thoughts on the Jewish Situation during the Years 1914–1921," *Studies in Contemporary Jewry IV* (1988): 12; Naomi W. Cohen, *Jacob H. Schiff: A Study in American Jewish Leadership* (Hanover, N.H.: Brandeis University Press, 1999), 33, 135; Ginsberg, *Fatal Embrace*, 70–72.

68. Cohen, *Schiff*, 191–200.

69. On Bleichröder, see Fritz Stern's classic study *Gold and Iron: Bismarck, Bleichröder, and the Building of the German Empire* (New York: Vintage, 1977). On Warburg, Rothschild, and Bloch see Niall Ferguson, *The Pity of War: Explaining World War I* (New York: Basic Books, 1999), 139, 189. For a thorough biographical sketch of Bloch, see B. Friedberg, "Jüdische Vorkämpfer für das Menschenreich der Zukunft," *Ost und West*, July–August 1919, 180–98. Biographical information on

Bloch is also available through the Web site of the Jan Bloch Foundation, http://www.bloch.org.pl/en/, accessed 8 November 2011. Several of Bloch's essays, which summarize arguments from his massive tome, are available online from the U.S. Army Command and General Staff College at www.cgsc.army,mil/carl/resources/csi/Bloch/BLOCH.asp.

70. Holger H. Herwig, "Germany and the 'Short-War' Illusion: Toward a New Interpretation?" *Journal of Military History* 66 (2002): 681–94.

71. Ferguson, *Pity of War*, 193.

72. Ibid.; also 191–97 passim and 257; idem, *War of the World: Twentieth-Century Conflict and the Descent of the West* (New York: Penguin, 2006), 80–90; Peter Pulzer, *Jews and the German State* (New York: Blackwell, 1992), 194–207; see also Pulzer's contribution to Michael Meyer, general ed., *German-Jewish History in Modern Times* (New York: Columbia University Press, 1998), 3:182–83, 374–76.

73. The essay, "Hear O Israel," is widely available in print and online, e.g., http://germanhistorydocs.ghi-dc.org/sub_document.cfm?document_id=717, accessed 8 November 2011. Many scholars have written en passant on Rathenau's tortured Jewish identity as part of a general overview of German Jewry at the fin de siècle. For a more rigorous analysis, see Rudolf Kallner, *Herzl und Rathenau. Wege Jüdischer Existenz an der Wende des 20. Jahrhunderts* (Stuttgart: Ernst Klett, 1976). Rathenau's books include *Criticism of the Age, The Mechanism of the Mind, In Days to Come*, and *The New Economy*, all written between 1912 and 1918.

74. Cited in Harry Kessler, *Walther Rathenau: His Life and Work* (New York: Harcourt, Brace, 1930), 243. For recent biographies of Rathenau, see Christian Schölzel's comprehensive study, *Walther Rathenau: Eine Biographie* (Paderborn: Ferdinand Schöningh, 2006); and Shulamit Volkov's elegant and insightful *Walther Rathenau: Weimar's Fallen Statesman* (New Haven, Conn.: Yale University Press, 2012).

75. Cited in Kessler, *Walther Rathenau*, 166.

76. Gerald Feldman, *Army, Industry and Labour in Germany, 1914–1918* (Princeton, N.J.: Princeton University Press, 1966), 46, 48–51.

77. Jordan Schwartz, *The Speculator: Bernard M. Baruch in Washington, 1917–1965* (Chapel Hill: University of North Carolina Press, 1981), 50–108. One of the seven other members of the board was a Jew—the gold magnate Eugene Meyer, the board's adviser on nonferrous metals, who would go on to become chair of the Federal Reserve Bank, owner of the *Washington Post*, and the first director of the World Bank.

78. M. Adler, *Prayer Book for Jewish Members of H. M. Forces* (H. M. Stationery Office, 1918; 1st ed. 1914).

79. Reproduced in Rolf Vogel, ed., *Ein Stück von Uns. Deutsche Juden in deutschen Armeen 1813-1976. Eine Dokumentation* (Mainz: v. Hase & Koehler, 1977), 126–27.

80. Amos Elon, *The Pity of It All: A History of the Jews in Germany, 1743–1933* (New York: Metropolitan / Henry Holt, 2002), 320.

81. Michael Stanislawski, *Autobiographical Jews: Essays in Jewish Self-Fashioning* (Seattle: University of Washington Press, 2004), 110.

82. Elisabeth Albanis, "Ostracised for Loyalty: Ernst Lissauer's Propaganda Writing and its Reception," *Leo Baeck Institute Year Book XLIII* (1998): 195–224.

83. Cited in Benjamin Pollock, "From Nation State to World Empire: Franz Rosenzweig's Redemptive Imperialism," *Jewish Studies Quarterly* 11 (2004): 9.

84. Peter Pulzer, "The First World War," in *German-Jewish History in Modern Times*, ed. Michael Meyer (New York: Columbia University Press, 1996–99), 3:364.

85. *L'Univers Israélite*, 18 February 1916, 604. This subject is thoughtfully treated in Philippe E. Landau, *Les Juifs de France et la Grande Guerre: Un patriotisme républicain, 1914–1941* (Paris: CNRS, 1999), 135–39.

86. Rudolf Stern, "Fritz Haber: Personal Reflections," *Leo Baeck Institute Year Book VIII* (1963): 70–113.

87. Feldman, *Army, Industry and Labour in Germany*, 46–51; Schölzel, *Walther Rathenau*.

88. Ulrich Sieg, *Jüdische Intellektuelle im Ersten Weltkrieg* (Berlin: Akademie Verlag, 2001); Peter Pulzer, *Jews and the German State: The Political History of a Minority, 1848–1933* (London: Blackwell, 1992), 206; Rivka Horwitz, "Voices of Opposition to the First World War among Jewish Thinkers," *Leo Baeck Institute Year Book XXXIII* (1988): 233–59.

89. David Cesarani, "An Embattled Minority: The Jews in Britain during the First World War," *Immigrants and Minorities* 8 (1989): 61–81; Mark Levine, "Against the Grain: Two Jewish Diaries of War and Anti-War, 1914–1918," in *Forging Modern Jewish Identities: Public Faces and Private Struggles*, ed. Michael Berkowitz, Susan L. Tananbaum, and Sam W. Bloom (London: Vallentine Mitchell, 2003), 81–114.

90. Cited in Zosa Zsjakowski, *Jews and the French Foreign Legion* (New York: Ktav, 1975), 24. See also Landau, *Les Juifs de France et la Grande Guerre*, 58–59, 61.

91. Murray Polner and Naomi Goodman, eds., *The Challenge of Shalom: The Jewish Tradition of Peace and Justice* (Philadelphia: New Society, 1994), 88. Many thanks to Jonathan Crane for our conversations on this subject.

92. Marcy McCune, "*The Whole Wide World Without Limits*": International Relief, Gender Politics, and American Jewish Women, 1893–1930 (Detroit: Wayne State University Press, 2005), 55.

93. Joseph Rappaport, *Hands across the Sea: Jewish Immigrants and World War I* (New York: Hamilton Books, 2005), esp. 107–26, 139–57.

94. Christopher M. Sterba, *Good Americans: Italian and Jewish Immigrants during the First World War* (New York: Oxford University Press, 2003).

95. Evelyn Wolcock, *Pacifism and the Jews* (Landsdown, UK: Hawthorn Press, 1994); Polner and Goodman, *The Challenge of Shalom*. Recently Melissa Klapper has undertaken a serious scholarly study of pacifism within a broader framework of American Jewish women's activism in the interwar period; see, for example, " 'Those by Whose Side We Have Laboured': American Jewish Women and the Peace Movement between the Wars," *Journal of American History* 97 (2010): 636–58.

96. Jürgen Matthäus, "Deutschtum und Judentum under Fire: The Impact of the First World War on the Strategies of the Centralverein and the Zionistische Vereinigung," *Leo Baeck Institute Year Book XXXIII* (1988): 133.

97. "Vaterlandsliebe, kein Chauvinismus!" *IF*, 18 February 1915, 2.

98. Alon Rahamimov, *POWs and the Great War: Captivity on the Eastern Front* (New York: Berg, 2001), 50, also 151.

99. See the Hebrew typescript history of this organization in the Central Archive for the History of the Jewish People, Jerusalem, 149/2; also Trude Maurer, "'Sehr wichtig sind Bücher von der Jüdischen Geschichte': Zu den Lebensverhältnissen und Lektüreninteressen jüdischer Kriegsgefangener aus dem Russischen Reich (1917/18)," *Tel Aviv Jahrbuch für deutsche Geschichte* 20 (1991): 259–86. Surveys of the Jewish POWs' reading requests revealed that about one-fifth were able and wanted to read Hebrew books. Almost a third asked for historical literature, and almost a fifth asked specifically for the work of Heinrich Graetz.

100. *JC*, 3 September 1915, 9–11; 20 October 1916, 9; *Im deutschen Reich*, September 1916, 225.

101. S. Ansky, *The Enemy at His Pleasure: A Journey through the Jewish Pale of Settlement during World War I* (New York: Holt, 2004), 23–24.

102. Judith Bleich, "Military Service: Ambivalence and Contradictions," in *War and Peace in the Jewish Tradition*, ed. Lawrence Shiffman and Joel B. Wolowelsky (New York: Yeshiva University Press, 2007), 451.

103. *JC*, 2 July 1915, 12.

104. Michael Keren and Shlomit Keren, *We Are Coming, Unafraid: The Jewish Legions and the Promised Land in the First World War* (London: Rowman & Littlefield, 2010), 69.

105. Vogel, *Ein Stück*, 183–84.

106. Ibid., 187–88.

107. Robert Soucy, "France: Veterans' Politics between the Wars," in *The War Generation: Veterans of the First World War*, ed. Stephen R. Ward (Port Washington, N.Y.: National University Publications, 1975), 61–66.

108. *Der Schild*, 15 June 1925, 224.

109. *Drei Jahre Bund Jüdischer Frontsoldaten Österreichs*, Vienna, 1935, front matter.

110. *Der Schild*, 9 October 1925, 374–75; see also the piece by British military chaplain Michael Adler reproduced in *Der Schild* on 22 October 1931, 155–56.

111. *Die Jüdische Front*, 15 November 1935, 3. Also *The Jewish Ex-Serviceman*, December 1935, 21.

112. *The Jewish Ex-Serviceman*, March/April 1936, 17, May/June 1936, 1.

113. Ibid., April 1935, 14.

114. Ibid., August–September 1935, 24.

115. S. A. Henderson, "The Symbol," *AJEX Bulletin*, February 1935, 8–9.

## Chapter Five

1. Felix Theilhaber, *Jüdische Flieger im Weltkrieg* (Berlin: Der Schild, 1924), 48–50.

2. Antoine Prost, *In the Wake of War: "Les Anciens Combattants" and French Society, 1914–1939* (Oxford: Berg, 1992), 12.

3. See the classic work of Shalom Spiegel, originally published in Hebrew in 1950 and in English in 1967: *The Last Trial: On the Legends and Lore of the Command to Abraham to Offer Isaac as a Sacrifice* (New York: Jewish Lights, 1993).

4. During World War I, the Isaac motif was invoked on occasion by Jews in France, perhaps reflecting the country's Catholic culture with its greater emphasis on passive suffering. See Ivan Strenski, *Contesting Sacrifice: Religion, Nationalism and Social Thought in France* (Chicago: University of Chicago Press, 2002), 84–87. The Isaac story became a powerful motif in Zionist consciousness and Israeli literature, but its valence was far from uniformly positive. See Yael Feldman, *Glory and Agony: Isaac's Sacrifice and National Narrative* (Stanford, Calif.: Stanford University Press, 2010).

5. See the important monograph of Benjamin Ziemann, *War Experience in Rural Germany, 1914–1923* (New York: Berg, 2007).

6. Maurice Vanikoff, *La commémoration des engagements voluntaires des juifs d'origine étrangere 1914–1918* (Paris: Le Voluntaire Juif, 1932), 8, 15; Philippe E. Landau, *Les Juifs de France et la Grande Guerre: Un patriotisme républicain, 1914–41* (Paris: CNRS, 1999), 22, 26, 58–59; Zosa Szajkowski, *Jews and the French Foreign Legion* (New York: Ktav, 1975).

7. *Le livre d'or du judaisme algérien* (Algiers: Comité Algérien d'Études Sociales, 1919); Landau, *Le Juifs de France et la Grande Guerre*, 89–90, 131–35.

8. David Cesarani, "An Embattled Minority: The Jews in Britain during the First World War," *Immigrants and Minorities* 8 (1989): 61–81.

9. Harold Shukman, *War or Revolution: Russian Jews and Conscription in Britain, 1917* (London: Vallenitne, Mitchell, 2006), 83.

10. Marsha Rozenblit, *Reconstructing a National Identity: The Jews of Habsburg Austria During World War I* (New York: Oxford University Press, 2001), 82–105.

11. *Im deutschen Reich* 10, no. 9 (September 1914): 1.

12. Arnold Tänzer, "Feldrabbiner," *Jüdisches Lexicon* IV/1 (Berlin, 1930), 184.

13. The text, from Italiener's *Von Heimat und Glauben. Kriegsbetrachtungen* (Darmstadt: H. L. Schlapp Buchhandlung, 1916), 1–46, is reproduced in Rolf Vogel, ed., *Ein Stück von Uns. Deutsche Juden in deutschen Armeen 1813–1976. Eine Dokumentation* (Mainz: v. Hase & Koehler, 1977), 122–23. Vogel incorrectly attributes this sermon to Rabbi Martin Salomonsky. Many thanks to Dr. Peter Appelbaum for this correction.

14. Gregory Caplan, "Wicked Sons, German Heroes: Jewish Soldiers, Veterans and Memories of World War I in Germany," Ph.D. dissertation, Georgetown University, 2001, 70. Orthodox rabbinical reactions to the war ranged from jingoism

to pacifism, but in general the rabbinate supported the war as a battle against oppressive tsarist Russia and called upon Orthodox male youth to do their patriotic duty for their country. Mordechai Breuer, *Modernity within Tradition: The Social History of Orthodox Jewry in Imperial Germany* (New York: Columbia University Press, 1992), 318, 385–87.

15. Reinhold Lewin, *Der Krieg als jüdisches Erlebniss: Ein Vortrag* (Berlin: Jüdisches Verlag, 1919).

16. David Fine's monograph *Jewish Integration in the German Army in the First World War* (Berlin: De Gruyter, 2012), was published after I completed this manuscript.

17. E.g., George Mosse, *The Jews and the German War Experience, 1914–1918*, Leo Baeck Memorial Lecture 21 (New York: Leo Baeck Institute, 1977); Steven Aschheim, *Brothers and Strangers: The East European Jew in German and German Jewish Consciousness, 1800–1923* (Madison: University of Wisconsin Press, 1982), chapter 7; Clemens Picht, "Zwischen Vaterland und Volk: Das deutsche Judentum im Ersten Weltkrieg," in *Der Erste Weltkrieg: Wirkung, Wahrnehmung, Analyse*, ed. Wolfgang Michalka (Munich: Piper, 1994), 736–55; Paul Mendes-Flohr, "The *Kriegserlebnis* and Jewish Consciousness," in *Jüdisches Leben in der Weimarer Republik/Jews in the Weimar Republic*, ed. Wolfgang Benz, Arnold Paucker, and Peter Pulzer (Tübingen: Mohr, Siebeck, 1998), 225–37.

18. To be sure, the war experience can desensitize soldiers to violence and predispose them upon their return to civilian life to a politics fueled by rage and distrust. This is especially likely if the country for which they fought lost the war or won an ambivalent victory. Predisposition, however, is just that; and the vast majority of soldiers did not undergo a psycho-political sea change as a result of their war experience. During World War I, the German government attempted to instill an ethos of blind obedience and hatred of the enemy into its soldiers, but it did so precisely because of fading morale as what had appeared at first to be a defensive war was now revealed to be one bent on conquest and annexation. Anne Lipp, *Meinungslenkung im Krieg: Kriegserfahrungen deutscher Soldaten und ihre Deutung 1914–1918* (Göttingen: Vandenhooeck & Ruprecht, 2003). See also Ziemann, *War Experience in Rural Germany*; and Jay Winter, *Sites of Memory, Sites of Mourning: The Great War in European Cultural History* (New York: Cambridge University Press, 1998).

19. Caplan, *Wicked Sons, German Heroes*, chapter 2 passim, also 87, 159. See also the ongoing research of Judith Gerson (Rutgers University) on German-Jewish refugees' memoirs, including the writings of veterans of World War I.

20. The two most commonly cited texts on the census' effects on German Jewry are Ernst Simon, "Unser Kriegserlebnis" (1919), in *Brücken: Gesammelte Aufsätze.* (Heidelberg: Verlag Lambert Schneider, 1965), 17–23; and Lewin, *Der Krieg als jüdisches Erlebnis.* There is a vast scholarly literature on the census, from the pioneering work of Egmont Zechlin and Hans Joachim Bieber, *Die deutsche Politik und die Juden im Ersten Weltkrieg* (Göttingen: Vandenhoeck & Ruprecht, 1969), 516–43, to, most recently, Jacob Rosenthal, *Epizodah shel "rish'ut"? "Sefirat ha-yehudim"*

*be-milhemet ha-ʿolam ha-rishonah* (Jerusalem: Ha-Kibbutz Ha-Meuhad and the Leo Baeck Institute, 2005).

21. Sabine Hank and Hermann Simon, *Feldpostbriefe Jüdischer Soldaten 1914–1918. Briefe ehemaliger Zöglinge an Sigmund Feist, Direktor des Reichenheimschen Waisenhauses in Berlin*, 2 vols. (Teetz: Hentrich & Hentrich, 2002).

22. The prominent Hungarian rabbi Jekutiel Judah Greenwald wrote a decidedly lachrymose narrative of his war service; its account of humiliating and brutal antisemitism foreshadows Avigdor Hameiri's novel *The Great Madness* (1929), which was based on his own experience in the Hungarian army: *Sefer ha-zikhronot: kolel et kol ha-telaʾot ve-ha-tiltulim asher metsaʾuni be-meshekh ha-milhamah ha-gedolah be-ʿomdi mezuyan mul ha-oyev* (Budapest, 1922).

23. Landau, *Juifs de France et la Grande Guerre*, 68–69, 161–64.

24. Anne Lloyd, "Jews Under Fire: The Jewish Community and Military Service in World War I Britain," Ph.D. dissertation, University of Southampton, 2009.

25. *The Jewish Ex-Serviceman*, November 1934, 17.

26. Much of this information is available in memorial volumes published in various German and Austrian cities during and after the war. For example, the memorial book published by the Munich chapter of the Reichsbund jüdischer Frontsoldaten provides the location and cause of death for every fallen Jew. One hundred twenty-eight died on the western front, thirty-seven in the east, five in Italy, one in the Ottoman Empire, and twelve in noncombatant situations. Ortsgruppe München des RjF, *Unseren Gefallenen Kameraden. Gedenkbuch für die im Weltkrieg gefallenen Münchener Juden* (Munich: b. Heller, 1928).

27. Archives of the Leo Baeck Institute: Center for Jewish History, New York (hereafter ALBINY), B1887.

28. E.g., Hans Senft's letter of 5 November 1916: "It is forbidden for us to send home detailed reports. In the trenches one is not in the mood to write reports, where death looms over one at every moment. For you in Berlin cannot imagine an artillery barrage such as what is now here." Hank and Simon, *Feldpostbriefe*, 2:560–62.

29. E.g., the diary entry of 4 June 1915 of Paul Schoenfeld, killed at Ypres on 24 April 1915. AIDF, 133/2005/I.

30. ALBINY, MM41.

31. DIGB to Centralstelle für Auslandsdienst, 5 November 1914, and subsequent correspondence up to and including 10 February 1915, Deutsch-Israelitische Gemeindebund Archive, Stiftung Neue Synagoge Berlin–Centrum Judaicum (hereafter DIGB Archive), Ge I 1, 75 C Ge 1, Nr. 963 (10853).

32. Pappenheim to DIGB directorate, 4 October 1914, DIGB Archive, Ge I 1, 75 C Ge 1, Nr. 956 (10845).

33. *Die Jüdischen Gefallenen des deutschen Heeres, der deutschen Marine und der Deutschen Schutztruppen 1914–1918. Ein Gedenkbuch* (Berlin: Verlag "Der Schild," 1932).

34. *1914–1918: Les Israélites dans l'armée Francaise* (Angers: Imprimerie Frederic Gaultier, 1921); Michael Adler, ed., *British Jewry Book of Honor* (London: Caxton, 1922).

35. Daniel Sherman, "Bodies and Name: The Emergence of Commemoration in Interwar France," *American Historical Review* 102, no. 2 (1998): 443–66.

36. Protocol of meeting of 30 May 1916, DIGB Archive, 75 C Ve 1, Nr. 223 (Film 12846). This file, along with Nr. 222 (Film 12845), contains the protocols of all the meetings referred to here. On the origins of the Committee, see *Im Deutschen Reich*, October 1918, 3; and Jacob Segall, "Aus den Ergebnissen der jüdischen Kriegsteilnehmerstatistik," *Zeitschrift für Demographie und Statistik der Juden* 15 (1919): 113–20.

37. See Derek Penslar, *Shylock's Children: Economics and Jewish Identity in Modern Europe* (Berkeley and Los Angeles: University of California Press, 2001), 216–22.

38. In the many publications of the Committee for War Statistics, I found data about wounded Jewish soldiers in only one essay on the Jewish communities of East Prussia (e.g., Königsberg, Tilsit, Memel): Segall, "Aus dem Ergebnissen der jüdischen Kriegsteilnehmerstatistik," 119.

39. Thanks to Sabine Hank, archivist of the Centrum Judaicum, Berlin, for this information.

40. David A. Gerber, ed., *Disabled Veterans in History* (Ann Arbor: University of Michigan Press), 2000.

41. Deborah Cohen, *The War Come Home: Disabled Veterans in Britain and Germany, 1914–1939* (Berkeley and Los Angeles: University of California Press, 2001), 101–2. Robert Weldon Whalen, *Bitter Wounds: German Victims of the Great War, 1914–1939* (Ithaca, N.Y.: Cornell University Press, 1984), 125.

42. Tim Grady, *The German-Jewish Soldiers of the First World War in History and Memory* (Liverpool: Liverpool University Press, 2011), 95.

43. For France, see Prost, *In the Wake of War*; and for the United Kingdom, see Graham Wooton, *The History of the British Legion* (London: Macdonald and Evans, 1956).

44. Wahlen, *Bitter Wounds*, 121–28; James Diehl, *Thanks of the Fatherland: German Veterans after the Second World War* (Chapel Hill: University of North Carolina Press, 1993), 6; Young-Sun Hong, *Welfare, Modernity and the Weimar State, 1919–1933* (Princeton, N.J.: Princeton University Press, 1998), 92–97.

45. Ernestine Eschelbacher, "Die Arbeit der jüdischen Frauen in Deutschland Während des Krieges," *Ost und West*, May–June 1919, 137–50; *IF*, 21 January 1915, 20.

46. Penslar, *Shylock's Children*, chapter 5. On German-Jewish welfare services for war victims, see Sharon Gillerman, *Germans into Jews: Remaking the Jewish Social Body in the Weimar Republic* (Stanford, Calif.: Stanford University Press, 2009), esp. chapter 6.

47. DIGB flyer of 24 August 1914; Greifswald community to DIGB, 9 September 1914, in DIGB Archive, Ge I 1, 75 C Ge 1, Nr. 956 (10845).

48. Otto Eichelbaum, Insterburg, to DIGB, 26 June 1916; Zentral für private Fürsorge to DIGB, DIGB Archive, Ge I 1, 75 C Ge 1, Nr. 956 (10845). There were also sundry local initiatives to visit wounded soldiers in hospital and read to the blind. Eschelbacher, "Die Arbeit der jüdischen Frauen"; *Im Deutschen Reich*, February 1918, 84, and July 1918, 308.

49. *Im Deutschen Reich*, September 1916, 205–8.

50. In 1917, the directorial board of the Berlin community, responding to a query from the Reich Committee for the Care of War Wounded, opined that sanitoriums under the supervision of the German Red Cross could accommodate observant Jews. Moreover, "For the Jewish participants in war as for the German-Jewish community in general, it is politically and socially of very high importance that Jewish and Christian war participants receive welfare in the same manner and that these welfare services be distributed in common for all concerned." *Im Deutschen Reich*, May 1917, 224. See also discussion of a separate institution for Jewish war blind in *Im Deutschen Reich*, February 1919, 91.

51. Gillerman, *Germans into Jews*; also Penslar, *Shylock's Children*, 219–22.

52. Carl J. Rheins, "German Jewish Patriotism 1918–1935: A Study of the Attitudes and Actions of the 'Reichsbund Jüdischer Frontsoldaten,' the 'Schwarzes Fähnlein,' 'Jungenschaft,' and the 'Deutscher Vortrupp,' 'Gefolgschaft Deutscher Juden' 1918–1935," Ph.D. dissertation, State University of New York at Stony Brook, 1978, 43–46. A small estate near Cottbus was purchased in 1930 and, the following year, settled by a small group of would-be Jewish farmers.

53. *Der Schild*, 9 August 1926, 249, also 11 April 1927, 108. Around this same time, an international congress of disabled Jewish veterans met in Danzig to protest inadequate assistance from state governments. *Der Schild*, 19 July and 9 August 1926, 226 and 250.

54. *Der Schild*, 11 February 1932, 22.

55. Walter Callman, "Der Reichsbund jüdischer Frontsoldaten," typed ms. dated October 1956, Yad Vashem Archives, Jerusalem, 3-K.

56. *JC*, 2 August 1918, 13–14; 9 August 1918, 4; 16 August 1918, 4, 9; 23 August 1918, 7; 30 August 1918, 9; 6 September 1918, 27; 27 September 1918, 17. See also *JC*, 9 October 1914, 13–18; 20 November 1914, 14–15; 19 March 1915, 26–29; 23 April 1915, 18–19; 21 May 1915, 7–8; 20 August 1915, 17–18; 29 October 1915, 13, 15–18; 28 January 1916, 17, 25–27; 19 January 1917, 15–17; 12 April 1918, 15–16; 21 February 1919, 7; 5 May 1922, 21.

57. Michael Adler, *The Jews of the Empire and the Great War* (London, 1919), 3; Vivian D. Lipman, *A Century of Social Service 1859–1959: The History of the Jewish Board of Guardians* (London: Routledge and Kegan Paul, 1959), 163, 167. By 1922, 474 loans had been granted, with a total worth of 15,730 British pounds. Extract from the Executive Committee Meeting of 8 May 1922, Harley Library Archives, Southampton University: MS 173—Archives of Jewish Care, 1757–1989, 1/2/3.

58. Adler, *The Jews of the Empire and the Great War*, 5; *AI*, 16 March 1916, 42; *Jews in the World War: A Study in Jewish Patriotism and Heroism* (New York: Jewish War Veterans of the United Sates, 1938). This entire pamphlet was reprinted in *The Jewish Veteran* in November of 1938.

59. *The Jewish Veteran*, convention issue, August 1934, unpaginated; see also the convention issue of August 1939, 14–15.

60. At AJEX's National Remembrance Service and Re-Union Tea in November of 1934, the AJEX honorary president, Lord Melchett, urged the assembled not to engage in vigilante actions against the Blackshirts: "We have always been an orderly people, and let us remain so." *The Jewish Ex-Serviceman*, December 1934, 8–9. The marble-tossing incident is mentioned in an interview with Flight Lieutenant Mark Kosky of the 617th Dambuster Squadron, in *Jewish War Heroes of the British Armed Forces*, a video documentary produced and directed by Jeremy Wootliff for the Association of Jewish Ex-Servicemen, 2007.

61. Paul Lerner, *Hysterical Men: War, Psychiatry and the Politics of Trauma in Germany, 1890–1930* (Ithaca, N.Y.: Cornell University Press, 2003).

62. *Im Deutschen Reich*, January 1915, 229. The original report came from *Das Israelitische Familienblatt*.

63. *Der Schild*, 30 August, 6 September, and 13 September 1926.

64. For a similar argument, see Meyer Friedeberg, "Der Krieg und die Nerven der Juden," *IF*, 28 January 1915.

65. On commemoration of the dead as a means of diverting attention from the maimed bodies of the surviving wounded veterans, see Seth Koven, "Remembering and Dismemberment: Crippled Children, Wounded Soldiers, and the Great War in Great Britain," *American Historical Review* 99, no. 4 (1994): 1169.

66. *Die Jüdische Front*, 15 November 1935, 3.

67. Benedict Anderson, "The Goodness of Nations," in *The Spectre of Comparisons: Nationalism, Southeast Asia, and the World* (New York: Verso, 1997), 363.

68. Thomas Laqueur, "Memory and Naming in the Great War," in *Commemorations: The Politics of National Identity*, ed. John Gillis (Princeton, N.J.: Princeton University Press, 1994), 150–68.

69. *Unseren Gefallenen Kameraden*, 9.

70. On this point see Joanna Bourke, *Dismembering the Male: Men's Bodies, Britain and the Great War* (Chicago: University of Chicago Press, 1996), 56–70.

71. *Der Schild*, 15 April 1925, 161, also 1 June 1925, 211.

72. Cited in Caplan, *Wicked Sons, German Heroes*, 171. On the homoerotic elements in German-Jewish imagery of war, see Todd Presner, *Muscular Judaism: The Jewish Body and the Politics of Regeneration* (London: Routledge, 2007), 196–97.

73. Rheins, "German Jewish Patriotism," 47.

74. Cited in Presner, *Muscular Judaism*, 200. See also Gideon Reuveni, "Sports and the Militarization of Jewish Society," in *Emancipation through Muscles: Jews and Sports in Europe*, ed. Michael Brenner and Gideon Reuveni (Lincoln: University of Nebraska Press, 2006), 44–61.

75. Avraham Barkai, "Political Orientations and Crisis Consciousness," in *German-Jewish History in Modern Times,* ed. Michael Meyer (New York: Columbia University Press, 1998), 4:121–23; David Rechter, *The Jews of Vienna during the First World War* (London: Littman Library, 2001), 173–77.

76. Simon memoirs, in a typescript ms. dated 17 December 1979, Archive of the Israel Defense Force, Jewish Fighter's Collection (hereafter AIDF), 45/1511/1998. Simon went on to become a champion German athlete, a physical education teacher in Palestine, and a director of sport in the Israeli government between 1948 and 1953. His account of Einstein's travels and whereabouts in November of 1923 matches up with the information in standard biographies of the scientist, e.g., Thomas Levenson, *Einstein in Berlin* (New York: Random House, 2004), 302–3.

77. Cited in Caplan, *Wicked Sons, German Heroes,* 230.

78. ALBINY, MM42.

79. *Der Schild,* 15 May 1925, 186; 7 June 1926, 178.

80. Hugo Rudberg received his decoration on 5 February 1935: AIDF, 45/1511/1998. The banker Friedrich Simon from Karlsruhe received his on 14 February 1935: Personal communication from Ernest Simon, 16 February 2010.

81. The documents are in AIDF, 1511/1998/120.

82. Caplan, *Wicked Sons, German Heroes,* chapter 6; Grady, *German-Jewish Soldiers,* 135–38.

83. Brian E. Crim makes a similar argument in " 'Was It All Just a Dream?' German-Jewish Veterans and the Confrontation with Völkisch Nationalism in the Interwar Period," in *Sacrifice and National Belonging in Twentieth-Century Germany,* ed. Greg Eghigian and Matthew Paul Berg (Arlington: University of Texas Press, 2002), 82. But I disagree with his characterization of the RjF as wedded to the principles of republicanism and liberal concepts of citizenship.

84. *The Jewish Veteran,* August 1939, 29.

85. The two groups were the Union of Jewish Veterans of the Wars of Liberation and Brit Hayal.

86. Landau, *Les juifs de France et la Grande Guerre,* 175–187, 211–12.

87. *The Jewish Ex-Serviceman,* December 1934, 6.

88. Marion Kaplan, *Between Dignity and Despair: Jewish Life in Nazi Germany* (New York: Oxford University Press, 1998), 22; Martin Senekowitsch, *Gleichberechtigt in einer grossen Armee: zur Geschichte des Bundes Jüdischer Frontsoldaten Österreichs, 1932–1938* (Vienna: Militärkommando Wien, 1994), 11.

89. Alfred Meyer, "My Attitudes Towards Germany," ALBINY, AR25075.

90. Grady, *German-Jewish Soldiers,* 141–45.

91. Victor Klemperer, *I Will Bear Witness: A Diary of the Nazi Years, 1942–1945* (New York: Modern Library, 2001), entries for 16 March, 8 May, 26 July, 30 December 1942; 27 January 1943; 12 March and 21 June 1944. On this point see the dissertation in progress of Anna Hajkova (University of Toronto) on the concentration camp society of Terezin, where men found courage to face their current suffering by recalling the ordeals of the trenches.

92. Edwin Halle, "Kriegserinnerungen mit Auszügen aus meinem Tagebuch 1914–1916," ALBINY, MM31.

93. Letter to Frank Mecklenberg, dated June, 1986 [sic], ALBINY, MM44.

94. Tim Grady, "Dying for the Fatherland: The Remembrance of the Fallen German-Jewish Soldiers of the First World War, 1914–1978," D.Phil. dissertation, University of Southampton, 2006, 164.

95. Fritz Heymann, *Der Chevalier von Geldern. Eine Chronik der Abenteuer der Juden* (Cologne: Joseph Melzer, 1963), xii. See also Franz Kobler, "Fritz Heyman und seine Chronik vom Abenteuer der Juden," *Bulletin des Leo Baeck Instituts* 13 (1961): 44–55; Julius Schoeps, "'Jeder Stein ist besudelt.' Der Weg des Journalisten Fritz Heymann aus Nazi-Deutschland in das Amsterdamer Exil," in *Deutsche Publizistik im Exil 1933–1945*, ed. Markus Behmer (Münster: LIT, 2000), 83–94.

96. Heymann, *Der Chevalier von Geldern*, 19.

97. Ibid., 14.

98. In 1840 Jews in Damascus were accused of the ritual murder of a Christian monk in Damascus. The affair catalyzed international Jewish intervention and is seen as a point of departure in the history of modern Jewish politics. See Jonathan Frankel, *The Damascus Affair: 'Ritual Murder,' Politics, and the Jews in 1840* (New York: Cambridge University Press, 1997).

99. Heymann, *Der Chevalier von Geldern*, 12.

100. "Die jüdische Armee—Der Beginn einer jüdischen Politik?" (14 November 1941), repr. in Hannah Arendt, *Vor Antisemitismus ist man nur noch auf dem Monde sicher: Beiträge für die deutsch-jüdische Emigrantenzeitung "Aufbau," 1941–1945*, ed. Mari Luise Knott (Munich and Zurich: Piper, 2000), 23, emphasis in original.

101. Ibid., 165 (article of 6 October 1944).

102. Ibid., 163 (article of 8 September 1944).

## Chapter Six

1. There is a vast literature on the Jewish Legion, much of it written by participants, most famously Zeʾev Jabotinsky's *Megilat ha-gedud: sipurei ha-gedudim ha-ʿivrim be-milhemet ha-ʿolam ha-rishonah* (Tel Aviv: Ministry of Defense, 1991; orig. 1946); also Elias Gilner, *War and Hope: A History of the Jewish Legion* (New York: Herzl Press, 1969). Among more scholarly works, Haim Hillel Ben-Sasson's long chapter on the legion in the official history of the Haganah, *Sefer toldot ha-haganah*, remains valuable, as is Martin Watts, *The Jewish Legion and the First World War* (New York: Palgrave Macmillan, 2004). The most thorough and analytically rich work on the subject is Yigal Elam, *Ha-gedudim ha-ʿivrim be-milhemet ha-ʿolam ha-rishonah* (Tel Aviv: Maʿarakhot, 1973).

2. Elam, *Ha-gedudim ha-ʿivrim*, 103, 201, 239; Watts, *The Jewish Legion*, 123, 136.

3. Elam, *Ha-gedudim ha-ʿivrim*, 189–190.

4. Michael Keren and Shlomit Keren, *We Are Coming, Unafraid: The Jewish Legions and the Promised Land in the First World War* (London: Rowman & Littlefield, 2010).

5. Elam, *Ha-gedudim ha-'ivrim*, 171–77; Anita Shapira, *Land and Power: The Zionist Resort to Force, 1881–1948* (New York: Oxford University Press, 1992), 86–98.

6. Elam, *Ha-gedudim ha-'ivrim*, 174, 221–23.

7. Elias Gilner, *War and Hope: A History of the Jewish Legion* (New York: Herzl Press, 1969), 60.

8. Salaman's *Letters from a Jewish Officer in Palestine during the Great War* (1920) was serialized in *The Jewish Ex-Serviceman* in 1934 and 1935. The quotations are from the issues of February and March of 1935.

9. M. Krel, *Zikhroynes fun Yidishn legion: tsum tsvantsik yerikn aniversar* (Montevideo: Y. Blekhman, 1938), chapter 6.

10. For examples of the new Hebrew military commands, see *AI*, 20 June 1918, 104. On Avihail, see *The Jewish Ex-Serviceman*, December 1935, 10–11.

11. Israel Zwi Kanner, *Josef Trumpeldor: Ein jüdischer Held*, 3rd ed. (Vienna: Josef Belf, 1936), 151–61; Shulamit Laskov, *Trumpeldor: sipur hayav* (Haifa: Shikmona, 1972), 155–56.

12. Oleg Budnitskii, *Russian Jews between the Reds and the Whites, 1917–1920* (Philadelphia: University of Pennsylvania Press, 2012), 369–83; idem, "The 'Jewish Battalions' in the Red Army," in *Revolution, Repression, and Revival: The Soviet Jewish Experience*, ed. Zvi Gitelman and Yaacov Roi (Lanham, Md.: Rowman & Littlefield, 2007), 15–36.

13. David Diamant, *Yidn in shpanishn krig, 1936–1939* (Warsaw: Bukh, 1967), 98, 113, 378.

14. *50ème anniversaire de le création des brigades internationals, 1936–1986*, pamphlet without publication information, in AIDF, 1511/98/71.

15. Arno Lustiger, *Schalom, Libertad! Juden im Spanischen Bürgerkrieg* (Cologne: Kiepenheuer & Witsch, 1991); 32; Albert Prago, "Jews in the International Brigades in Spain," reprint from *Jewish Currents*, February and March 1979, in AIDF, 1511/98/70. (Prago served in the Abraham Lincoln Brigade and later became a professor of labor studies at Cornell.) Martin Sugarman, "Against Fascism: Jews Who Served in the International Brigade in the Spanish Civil War," http://www.jewishvirtuallibrary.org/jsource/History/spanjews.pdf, accessed 6 September 2009.

16. Interview with Pierre Scharf in Alain Brossat and Sylvia Linberg, *Le yiddishland révolutionnaire* (Paris: Balland, 1983), 132.

17. Myron Momryk, "Jewish Volunteers from Canada in the Spanish Civil War, 1936–39," in AIDF, 1511/98/71.

18. Myron Momryk, National Archives of Canada, to E. Kaplansky, 10 August 1995, in AIDF, 1511/98/71.

19. Gerald Tulchinsky, *Branching Out: The Transformation of the Canadian Jewish Community* (Toronto: Stoddart, 1998), 132–40.

20. Moshe Bachar, "'Hanita Is Preferable to Madrid': The Reaction of the Yishuv in Palestine to the Civil War in Spain," M.A. thesis, Tel Aviv University, 1998, xvi.

21. Estimates about the number of volunteers from the Yishuv vary widely, as noted by Raanan Rein, "Belated Inclusion: Jewish Volunteers in the Spanish Civil War and Their Place in the Israeli National Narrative," *Israel Studies* 17 (2012): 24–49. The most definitive count has been made by Dan Yahav, *Gam eleh ba-giborim. Lohmim mitnadvim erets-yisre'elim ba-"brigadot ha-beinle'umiyot" bi-Sefarad (1936–1938)* (Tel Aviv: Tcherikover, 2008). On the harsh treatment of David Dagan, David Karon, and Yeshiyahu Vind Bachar by their kibbutzim, see Bachar, "'Hanita,'" 19; also the interview with David Karon, dated 5 July 1965, in the archives of the Institute for Contemporary Jewry, Hebrew University of Jerusalem, Mt. Scopus campus.

22. Cited in Bachar, "'Hanita,'" 15; see also Diamant, *Yidn*, 103, and Gerben Zaagsma, "Jewish Volunteers in the Spanish Civil War: A Case Study of the Botwin Company," M.A. thesis, School of Oriental and African Studies, London, 2001, 9.

23. Newspaper clippings from March and April of 1972, mostly authored by Levy Yitzhak Yerushalmi, in AIDF, 1511/1998/74.

24. Lustiger, *Schalom, Libertad!* 302–3.

25. Zaagsma, "Jewish Volunteers," 12; Lustiger, *Schalom, Libertad!* 302–7; Joshua Rothenberg, "The Jewish Naftali Botwin Company," *Jewish Frontier*, April 1980, 14–19.

26. Compare the diverging accounts in Prago, "Jews in the International Brigades," Zaagsma, "Jewish Volunteers," 16, and Diamant, *Yidn*, 199.

27. Cited in Diamant, *Yidn*, 317.

28. Zaagsma, "Jewish Volunteers"; see also Zvi Loker, "Balkan Jewish Volunteers in the Spanish Civil War," in AIDF, 1511/1998/74.

29. Lustiger, *Schalom, Libertad!* 326–27.

30. Reproduced in Diamant, *Yidn*, 534.

31. Cited in Prago, "Jews in the International Brigades," 15.

32. Cited in Lustiger, *Schalom, Libertad!* 322.

33. Rothenberg, "Botwin," 17.

34. Ibid., 18.

35. Ibid.

36. *The Complete Black Book of Soviet Jewry* (New Brunswick, N.J.: Transaction Books, 2003).

37. From Luigi Longo's introduction to Gina Birenzweig Medem, *Los Judios voluntarios de la libertad: un año de lucha en las Brigadas Internacionales*, cited in Lustiger, *Schalom, Libertad!* 304.

38. Diamant, *Yidn*, 98; also 49, 112.

39. Ibid., 120, 165, 170–72, 194, 246–47.

40. Ibid., 353–58, 372; Zaagsma, "Jewish Volunteers," 19.

41. Lustiger *Schalom, Libertad!* 52–53.

42. Letter of Mikhail Taliakotzu to the editor of *Ha-Aretz*, 8 August 1986, AIDF, 1511/98/70.

43. B. Balti, "Let Us Prove to the Fascists That We Can Fight," journal clipping, produced on the occasion of 1972 international convention of the Jewish brigadistas in Tel Aviv, in AIDF, 1511/98/70.

44. Loker, "Balkan Jewish Volunteers"; Lustiger, *Schalom, Libertad!* 173–75, 180.

45. Although there is a vast literature on the Holocaust, Jewish partisans, and ghetto rebels, there is no general history of Jewish soldiers in Allied armies during the Second World War. For country-specific studies, see Martin Sugarman, *Fighting Back: Anglo-Jewry's Contribution to the Second World War* (London: Vallentine Mitchell, 2009); Yitzhak Arad, *Be-tsel ha-degel ha-adom. Yehudei berit-ha-mo'atsot ba-lehimah neged Germanyah ha-Natsit* (Jerusalem: Ministry of Defense / Yad Vashem, 2008); Deborah Dash Moore, *GI Jews: How World War II Changed a Generation* (Cambridge, Mass.: Harvard University Press, 2004).

46. David Engel, "Ha-berihah ha-hafganatit shel hayalim yehudim me-ha-tsava ha-polani be-anligyah bi-shnat 1944: parashah 'bein anglim, polanim, ve-yehudim bi-tekufat milhemet ha-'olam ha-shniyah,'" *Yahadut Zemaneinu* 2 (1985): 177–207.

47. A. Hank, "Yehudim be-tsava tchekoslovakia," in *Hayalim yehudim be-tsiv'ot eyropa*, ed. Yehuda Slutsky and Mordechai Kaplan (Tel Aviv: Ministry of Defense, 1967), 160–63.

48. Lucien Steinberg, "Les juifs de France dans la resistance exterieure et interieure," typescript ms. dated September 1965, in AIDF, 86/1511/1998.

49. Zvi Gitelman, "Why They Fought: What Soviet Jewish Solders Saw and How It Is Remembered," NCEER Working Paper, 21 September 2011, http://www.ucis.pitt.edu/nceeer/2011_824-03g_Gitelman.pdf, accessed 14 December 2011.

50. A. Tiomr, "Yehudim be-'tsava ha-adom,'" in *Hayalim yehudim be-tsiv'ot eyropa*, ed. Slutsky and Kaplan, 133; A. Guri, "Yehudim be-'tsava ha-adom' be-milhemet ha-'olam ha-2," ibid., 142; for a general history of Soviet Jewish heroism during the war, see Oz Almog, *Dem Morgenrot Entgegen. Helden der Sowjetunion* (Vienna: Jüdisches Museum, 2002).

51. J. George Fredman and Louis A. Falk, *Jews in American Wars* (Hoboken, N.J.: Terminal, 1942), 81.

52. Tulchinsky, *Branching Out*, 210–13.

53. See Michael Young's analysis of Jewish pacifists in World War II in Murray Polner and Naomi Goodman, *The Challenge of Shalom: The Jewish Tradition of Peace and Justice* (Philadelphia: New Society, 1994), 156–67.

54. These ratios are extrapolated from data in Evelyn Wilcock, *Pacifism and the Jews* (Landsdown, UK: Hawthorn Press, 1994), 142; and Nicholas Krebiehl, *General Lewis B. Hershey and Conscientious Objection During World War II* (Columbia, Mo.: University of Missouri Press, 2012), 10.

55. Moore, *GI Jews*.

56. My late stepfather, the composer and pianist Joe Harnell, was a recruit training in the American South during the war, and ran afoul of an antisemitic drill sergeant who, in the kitchen one day, deliberately poured scalding water over the

young musician's hands. For a detailed and level-headed first-person account of antisemitic encounters with American officers and men, both stateside and in Europe, see Seymour Lionel Rosenberg, *The Smile Belongs to the Dream: A Memoir* (Kingston, Ontario: Harbinger House Press, 2002). For a scholarly analysis of antisemitic influences on military policy, see Joseph Bendersky, *The 'Jewish Threat': Anti-Semitic Politics of the U.S. Army* (New York: Basic Books, 2000).

57. Greg Palmer and Mark S. Zaid, eds., *The GI's Rabbi: World War II Letters of David Max Eichorn* (Lawrence: University Press of Kansas, 2004), 14.

58. Mac Davis, *Jews Fight Too!* (New York: Hebrew Publishing Company, 1945), 13.

59. Ibid., 96–97.

60. Ibid., 9.

61. "Pensioners of Haym Salomon: Revolutionary Soldiers Whom He Aided," *The Jewish Veteran*, July 1938.

62. *The Jewish Veteran*, December 1941, 8.

63. Cecil Roth, "Jews in the Defence of Britain," *Transactions of the Jewish Historical Society of England* 15 (1946). This piece originated as an address at Magdalen College, Oxford, in October of 1940.

64. The comic books are in the Judaica collection of Harvard's Widener Library.

65. Daniel S. Levy, *Two-Gun Cohen* (New York: St. Martin's, 1997).

66. American and Canadian Jewish celebrations of their contributions to the war had parallels in the Soviet Union, where a series of wartime Yiddish pamphlets on Jewish heroes of the Soviet Union glorified the likes of Chaim Diskin, Leyzer Papernik, Yosef Makovsky, and Israel Fisanovich (the last of whom shows up as well in the Canadian comics). Originally published in 1943 and 1944, some were reprinted later in Russian translation with references to the individuals' Jewish background, identity, or motivations carefully deleted. See Mordechai Altschuler, "Jewish Warfare and the Participation of Jews in Combat in the Soviet Union as Reflected in Soviet and Western Historiography," in *The Historiography of the Holocaust Period: Proceedings of the Fifth Yad Vashem International Historical Conference*, ed. Yisrael Gutman and Gideon Greif (Jerusalem: Yad Vashem, 1988), 217–38.

67. Abba Hillel Silver, "We Have Taken Up the Challenge," in *United Palestine Appeal 1941 Yearbook Published on the Occasion of "Night of Stars,"* 7, 82.

68. Abraham Revusky, "Palestine Jews Fight for Home and Freedom," ibid., 13.

69. Yoav Gelber, *Ha-hitnadvut le-tsava ha-briti be-milhemet ha-ʿolam ha-sheniyah* (Jerusalem: Merkaz Hahasbarah, 1995).

70. Revusky, "Palestine Jews," 66.

71. Boris Smolar, "Canadian Jews and the World War," *The Jewish Veteran*, November 1940, 6.

72. Tulchinsky, *Branching Out*, 204–11.

73. Thanks to David Engel for this information.

74. Rufus Learsi, *The Jew in Battle* (New York: American Zionist Youth Commission, 1944), 20.

75. My narrative on Revisionist Zionism in the United States during World War II draws largely upon Judith Tydor Baumel, *The "Bergson Boys" and the Origins of*

*Contemporary Zionist Militancy* (Syracuse, N.Y.: Syracuse University Press, 2005). I have also made use of Rafael Medoff, *Militant Zionism in America: The Rise and Impact of the Jabotinsky Movement in the United States, 1926–1948* (Tuscaloosa: University of Alabama Press, 2002).

76. Baumel, *The "Bergson Boys,"* 97.

77. Ibid., 98–100.

78. Ibid., 84.

79. See the section "Jewish Army" in Ben-Gurion's Statement of Zionist Policy, hand-dated 15 October 1941, in Central Zionist Archive, Jerusalem (CZA), Z4/14632, as well as his Memorandum on the Defense of Palestine and the Jews, sent to Moshe Shertok (Sharett) and dated 8 July 1942, CZA, 74/14632.

80. Gelber, *Hitnadvut*.

81. Baumel, *The "Bergson Boys,"* 133.

82. Medoff, *Militant Zionism in America*, 83.

83. Ibid., 85, 153–55.

84. Baumel, *The "Bergson Boys,"* 220.

85. Ibid., 132, 220.

86. See appendix 4 to Samuel Halperin, *The Political World of American Zionism* (Detroit: Wayne State University Press, 1961).

87. Medoff, *Militant Zionism in America*, 179–80.

88. Douglas Century, *Barney Ross: The Life of a Jewish Fighter* (New York: Shocken, 2006), 151–56.

89. Medoff, *Militant Zionism in America*, 180.

## Chapter Seven

1. For an overview of the historiographical debates of the 1980s and 1990s about the 1948 war, see Derek J. Penslar, *Israel in History: The Jewish State in Comparative Perspective* (London: Routledge, 2006), chapters 1 and 2. The most authoritative and up-to-date history of the war is Benny Morris, *1948: A History of the First Arab-Israeli War* (New Haven, Conn.: Yale University Press, 2008).

2. Anita Shapira, *Yigal Alon, Native Son: A Biography* (Philadelphia: University of Pennsylvania Press, 2008), 83, 99, 104.

3. Broadsheet dated 6 April 1939, in AIDF, 4/1511/1998. The biographical information on Avisar is provided by an unsigned Hebrew manuscript, most likely prepared by an archivist, in the file.

4. The Haganah Archive in Tel Aviv contains Reihan's brief undated memoir (52.87/44.35), two short descriptions, dated 1942 [*sic*] and 28 July 1954, of his work with the Haganah Field Units in the Haifa region (57.18/43/58), and an interview with Reihan, dated 14 December 1970 (178.26/24/2).

5. Yoav Gelber, *Ha-hitnadvut le-tsava ha-briti be-milhemet ha-ʻolam ha-sheniyah* (Jerusalem: Merkaz Hahasbarah, 1995).

6. *Ha-hayal ha-ʻivri*, no. 1, 10 January 1943, 1–2.

7. "Al Ha-Shoah," ibid., 4.

8. The information in this paragraph is taken from Yaakov Markovitsky, "Hagahal: giyus huts-la-arets be-milhemet ha-atsma'ut," in *Milhemet ha-atsma'ut tasha'h-tasha't: diyun mehudash*, ed. Alon Kadish (Tel Aviv: Ministry of Defense, 2004, 525–37). This article summarizes material from Markovitsky's book *Gahelet Lohemet. Giyus hutz la-aretz be-milhemet ha-atsma'ut* (Tel Aviv: Ministry of Defense, 1995).

9. Ricky-Dale Calhoun tartly terms the operation "a highly effective criminal conspiracy" in his article "Arming David: The Haganah's Illegal Arms Procurement Network in the United States, 1945–1949," *Journal of Palestine Studies* 36 (2007): 31.

10. There is a vast body of writing on the Machal, much of it the memoirs of participants or celebratory accounts by amateur historians, e.g., Henry Katzer, *South Africa's 800: The Story of South African Volunteers in Israel's War of Birth*, rev. ed. (Israel [n.p.]: Machal Museum, 2003). For a reliable overview, see Yaakov Markovitzky, *Machal: Overseas Volunteers in Israel's War of Independence* (Jerusalem: Old City Press, 2003). For a more thorough account that is both scholarly and riveting, see David Bercuson, *The Secret Army* (New York: Stein and Day, 1983). The most important recent work on Machal is Benny Gshur's doctoral dissertation (Hebrew University, 2009), "Mitnadvim mi-tsafon amerika be-milhemet ha-shihrur." Many thanks to Dr. Gshur for providing me with a copy of the dissertation.

11. Maud Mandel, "Transnationalism and Its Discontents during the 1948 Arab-Israeli War," *Diaspora* 12, no. 3 (2003): 329–60.

12. See the sober analysis of the limited role of air power in the 1948 war in Amitzur Ilan, *The Origin of the Arab-Israeli Arms Race: Arms, Embargo, Military Power and Decision in the 1948 Palestine War* (New York: New York University Press, 1996), 5–6, 107–8, 172.

13. J. Wandres, *The Ablest Navigator: Lieutenant. Paul N. Shulman USN, Israel's Volunteer Admiral* (Annapolis: U.S. Naval Institute Press, 2010).

14. Morris, *1948*, 227–29.

15. Ted Berkman, *Cast a Giant Shadow: The Story of Mickey Marcus Who Died to Save Jerusalem* (New York: Pocket Books, 1962).

16. Melville Shavelsohn's film *Cast a Giant Shadow* presents an even more heroic image of Marcus. In the film, Kirk Douglas' character embodies classic Israeli characteristics—he is angry, rebellious, moody, and distant, loved by women but all but unable to love them back. He is courageous, strong, and powerfully sexy, much more so than the film's Israeli characters, who are scrappy and solid but never brilliant in the field and do not exude erotic power, not even Yul Brenner's character, Asher. The love interest, Magda (based on Marcus' Israeli secretary, Irene Broza), tells Marcus that her Holocaust survivor husband Andre cannot satisfy her in bed and invites Marcus to make a pass at her. After they get together, Marcus says of Magda that she "always has her motor on." Thus in this film Marcus is able to subdue, then satisfy a stereotypically fierce and beautiful sabra warrior in a way that Israelis cannot. What's more, in the film, Ben-Gurion is reduced to a whiny Jew-

ish grandfather, capable of speechifying but little else. He speaks only of defense, avoiding civilian casualties, and striving for peace with the Arabs, while Marcus urges going on the offensive, unifying the Palmach, Haganah, Irgun, and Lechi, as if Ben-Gurion never thought of it, and as if the Haganah did not decide on its own to go on the offensive in April of 1948. Military, political, and sexual power are all linked in this fantasy, which is more about American than Jewish power, as the film was packaged for a mainstream American audience.

17. Berkman, *Cast a Giant Shadow*, 9.

18. Ibid., 67.

19. Ibid., 198.

20. Uri Milstein, *History of Israel's War of Independence* (Lanham, Md.: University Press of America, 1996), 1:322–34.

21. Tom Segev, *1949: The First Israelis* (New York: Free Press, 1986), 272–79.

22. Bercuson, *The Secret Army*, 146–47, 215.

23. The information here draws from Benjamin Dunkelman, *Dual Allegiance* (Halifax: Goodread, 1984).

24. Ibid., 266, emphasis in original.

25. Uri Avneri, "Kakh nitslah Natsrat," *Ha-Olam Ha-Zeh*, 9 July 1980, 34–35. The article reproduces the page from the draft autobiography. It appears that the text was made available to the newspaper by Dunkelman's ghostwriter, Peretz Kidron.

26. Dunkleman, *Dual Allegiance*, 318.

27. Gshur, "Mitnadvim," chapter 2 (I was provided an unpaginated draft of this dissertation).

28. See the quotations from Machal fighters in obituaries published in the spring 2011 newsletter of the American Veterans of Israel Legacy Corporation.

29. Leonard Slater, *The Pledge* (New York: Simon and Schuster, 1970), 230–31.

30. Antoine Prost, *In the Wake of War: "Les Anciens Combattants" and French Society 1914–1939* (Oxford: Berg, 1992), 12.

31. Gshur, "Mitnadvim," chapter 1.

32. Ibid., chapter 3.

33. Ibid.

34. Moshe Naor, "Israel's 1948 War of Independence as a Total War," *Journal of Contemporary History* 43, no. 2 (2008): 241–257. Thanks to both Dr. Naor and David Tal for their insights on these issues.

35. Yitzhak Greenberg, "Financing the War of Independence," *Studies in Zionism* 9, no. 1 (1988): 63–80; Haim Barkai, "Ha-'alut ha-realit shel milhemet ha-'atsma'ut," in *Milhemet ha-atsma'ut 1948-1949*, ed. Kadish, 2:759–91; Moshe Naor, "From Voluntary Funds to National Loans: The Financing of Israel's 1948 War Effort," *Israel Studies* 11 (2006): 62–82.

36. Rafael Rosenzweig, *The Economic Consequences of Zionism* (Leiden: Brill, 1997), 135–36.

37. For conflicting accounts about the Sonneborn Institute's key players, see Bernard Postal and Henry W. Levy, *And the Hills Shouted for Joy: The Day Israel Was Born* (Philadelphia: Jewish Publication Society, 1973), 134–44; and Robert St. John,

*Ben-Gurion* (London: Jarrolds, 1959), 92. The archival document with the actual list of attendees at the meeting is reproduced in appendix B of Doron Almog, *Ha-rekhesh ba-artsot ha-berit 1945–1949* (Tel Aviv: Ministry of Defense, 1987).

38. Travis' handwritten memoir, dated April 1994, is preserved in the William Breman Jewish Heritage Museum in Atlanta. The memoir, which breathlessly narrates the founding and activities of the Sonneborn group, is particularly interesting for its description of a host of secondary Zionist activists in the southeastern United States who raised money and acquired munitions and equipment to be sent to Palestine. On Shapiro, see the online *Encyclopedia of Cleveland History*, http://ech.cwru.edu/ech-cgi/article.pl?id=SEZ, accessed 21 March 2010.

39. For Sonneborn, see his father's and his obituaries in the *New York Times*, 20 September 1940 and 4 June 1986 respectively, and Gilbert Sandler, *Jewish Baltimore: A Family Album* (Baltimore: Johns Hopkins University Press, 2000), 84, 169. For Rosenbloom, see the oral history by Alex Lowenthal, transcribed in 1978 by Selma Berkman, Pittsburgh Jewish Federation archives (many thanks to Professor Barbara Burstin of the University of Pittsburgh for this information); the *Pittsburgh Post-Gazette*, 19 May 1970; and Rosenbloom's obituaries in the *Pittsburgh Jewish Chronicle*, 5 April 1973, 1, 21, 31, and the *New York Times*, 2 April 1973. For Sylk, see Murray Friedman, ed., *Philadelphia Jewish Life, 1940–1985* (Ardmore, Pa.: Seth Press, 1986, 68); For Lowenthal and Lown, see their obituaries in the *New York Times*, 12 January 1990 and 3 November 1976 respectively. Fliegelman is mentioned briefly in *Time*, 17 August 1953, in an article on the founding of the Brandeis Camp Institute. For Broad, see his obituary in the *Miami Herald*, 9 November 2001, and Deborah Dash Moore, *To the Golden Cities: Pursuing the American Jewish Dream in Miami and Los Angeles* (New York: Free Press, 1994), 45, 52, 159–61.

40. The first book-length study of the Sonneborn group's activity was Leonard Slater's journalistic, riveting, and, if read judiciously, useful account, *The Pledge*. Doron Almog's *Ha-rekhesh ba-artsot ha-berit, 1945–1949* (Tel Aviv: Ministry of Defense, 1987) is slim but packed with information about the relation between the Sonneborn group and the Haganah's American operatives, as is Ilan, *Origin of the Arab-Israeli Arms Race*. The most important recent monograph on the subject is Doron Rozen, *Be-ikhvot ha-otsar ha-amerika'i: pe'ilut ha-haganah ba-artsot ha-berit 1945–1949* (Tel Aviv: Ministry of Defense, 2008). The statistic about Jewish involvement in the United States trucking industry appears in Slater, *The Pledge*, 187, and in Almog, *Rekhesh*, 46.

41. Almog, *Rekhesh*, 37–38, 41; Rozen, *Be-ikhvot ha-otsar ha-amerika'i*, 131, 135, 137, 343–44, 351.

42. Rozen, *Be-ikhvot ha-otsar ha-amerika'i*, 138.

43. Rozen, *Be-ikhvot ha-otsar ha-amerika'i*, 75–76, 90, 99–109, 344–46, 351–53.

44. Almog, *Rekhesh*, 106–7. Schwimmer stayed in Israel after the war and founded Israel Aircraft Industries, which became the pillar of Israel's military and civilian aerospace industry. See Anthony David, *Ha-shamayim hem ha-gvul. Al Shvimmer, mekayem ha-ta'asiyah ha-avirit* (Tel Aviv: Schocken, 2008).

45. Slater, *The Pledge*, 71, 181, 192, 319–21; Almog, *Rekhesh*, 102, 114.

46. Interviewed by Slater in *The Pledge*, 321.

47. Slater (ibid., 123–24) attributes this quotation to a "gentleman from Philadelphia," speaking at a meeting of Sonneborn activists at the Waldorf Astoria hotel in New York in October of 1947.

48. Almog, *Rekhesh*, 56.

49. Robert Rockaway, *But He Was Good to His Mother: The Lives and Crimes of Jewish Gangsters* (Jerusalem and New York: Geffen, 2001), 246–53.

50. Ilan, *Origin of the Arab-Israeli Arms Race*, 89.

51. Rozen, *Be-ikhvot ha-otsar ha-amerika'i*, 133, 138.

52. Ibid., 309; Samuel Halperin, *The Political World of American Zionism* (Detroit: Wayne State University Press), 1961, appendix 4.

53. Samuel Halperin, "Ideology or Philanthropy? The Politics of Zionist Fund-Raising," *The Western Political Quarterly* 13, no. 4 (1960): 969–70.

54. Deborah Dash Moore, "Bonding Images: Miami Jews and the Campaign for Israel Bonds," in *Envisioning Israel: The Changing Ideals and Images of American Jews*, ed. Alon Gal (Jerusalem: Magnes / Detroit: Wayne State University Press, 1996, 258; Rozen, *Be-ikhvot ha-otsar ha-amerika'i*, 309, 314, 322–23.

55. This estimate is offered in Haim Barkai, "Ha-'alut ha-realit shel milhemet ha-'atsma'ut," in *Milhemet Ha-Atsma'ut 1948–1949*, ed. Kadish, 2:779. Barkai came up with this sum by calculating the net disposable income of the United States' entire population, assumed 4 percent of that sum represented American Jewry, and then divided the Jews' alleged collective income by the total amount of money contributed to Palestine/Israel in 1948. This is admittedly a highly imperfect calculation, as aggregate Jewish income may have been greater or less than the mean, giving patterns among Jews varied greatly, and not all funds for Palestine in 1948 necessarily came from Jews. For example, in 1946 John D. Rockefeller gave $100,000 to the UJA, and similar large gifts may well have come from non-Jews in 1948 (Halperin, "Ideology or Philanthropy?" 969). However, since American Jews in the late 1940s were not a particularly affluent community, it may well be that the total percentage of Jews' disposable income that went to Palestine was greater than 2.5 percent. In past campaigns, a small percentage of Jews had contributed the bulk of annual campaigns; for example, in the New York City Federation Drive of 1940, 900 individuals, less than 2 percent of all donors, provided 51.5 percent of the total receipts (ibid., 966n). But it is difficult to imagine 2 percent of American Jewry providing half—that is, $75 million—of the funds raised by the UJA in 1948. The giving must have been more widely distributed.

56. Greenberg, "Financing," 74; Ilan, *Origin of the Arab-Israeli Arms Race*, 153, 181ff, 224; Rozen, *Be-ikhvot ha-otsar ha-amerika'i*, 322.

57. Many thanks to Alicia Mauldin from the West Point archive for sending me a pdf of Marcus' funeral/gravesite dossier.

58. On Feinberg's colorful life and political influence under the administrations of Presidents Truman, Kennedy, and Johnston, see Tom Segev, *1967: Israel, the War*

*and the Year That Transformed the Middle East* (New York: Metropolitan, 2007), 110–16, 573–74.

59. *Americans for Haganah* 1, no. 1 (15 August 1947): 4.

60. *Americans for Haganah* 1, no. 7 (15 December 1947): 1.

61. *Americans for Haganah* 1, no. 4 (15 October 1947): 1–2.

62. See also the issue of 25 November 1947, page 7, for a dismissive assessment of the Egyptian military threat.

63. *Americans for Haganah* 1, no. 7 (15 December 1947): 2–3.

64. Ilan Pappe, *The Ethnic Cleansing of Palestine* (London: Oneworld, 2007); Hillel Cohen, *Army of Shadows: Palestinian Collaboration with Zionism, 1917–1948* (Berkeley and Los Angeles: University of California Press, 2008); Ephraim Karsh, *Palestine Betrayed* (New Haven, Conn.: Yale University Press, 2010).

65. *Haganah Speaks!* 2, no. 2 (16 February 1948): 2.

66. *Haganah Speaks!* 2, no. 7 (1 May 1948): 2; see also 2, no. 1 (30 January 1948): 3, 5.

67. *Haganah Speaks!* 2, no. 9 (31 May 1948): 4.

68. *Haganah Speaks!* 2, no. 8 (15 May 1948): 8; 2, no. 10 (14 June 1948): 6.

69. *Haganah Speaks!* 2, no. 16 (17 September 1948): 2.

70. Anita Shapira, "Hirbet Hizah: Between Remembrance and Forgetting," *Jewish Social Studies* 7 (2000): 1–62.

71. *Israel Speaks!* 3, no. 1 (7 January 1949): 2, 7; 3, no. 5 (8 April 1949): 3.

72. *Haganah Speaks!* 2, no. 10 (16 June 1948): 1, 7; 2, no. 11 (2 July 1948): 1, 3.

73. *Israel Speaks!* 3, no. 10 (24 June 1949): 4.

74. Rozen, *Be-ikhvot ha-otsar ha-amerika'i*, 177.

75. Menahem Kaufman, "Envisaging Israel: The Case of the United Jewish Appeal," in *Envisioning Israel: The Changing Ideals and Images of North American Jews*, ed. Allon Gal (Jerusalem: Magnes Press, 1996).

## Epilogue

1. Ehud Olmert interview with Jeffrey Goldberg in *The Atlantic*, http://www.theatlantic.com/doc/print/200805/israel, accessed 21 April 2008.

2. In the late 1940s several American-Jewish authors published best-selling war novels, but these were neither celebratory nor apologetic. Instead, they laid bare the horrors of war, the torments of antisemitism, and the internal identity struggles of the books' Jewish characters. Leah Garrett, "Young Lions: Jewish American War Fiction of 1948," *Jewish Social Studies*, forthcoming.

3. Peter Novick, *The Holocaust in American Life* (New York: Houghton, Mifflin, 2000). Hasia Diner has offered a partial corrective to Novick in her book *We Remember with Reverence and Love: American Jews and the Myth of Silence after the Holocaust, 1945–1962* (New York: New York University Press, 2009). Diner argues convincingly that the Holocaust was widely discussed in synagogues and Jewish schools and summer camps during the late 1940s and 1950s, but there is an impor-

tant difference between presence and dominance, between reverent remembrance and an all-encompassing civil religion—the latter being, as Novick argues, a product of the 1970s.

4. *Toronto Star*, 7 November 2006; *Canadian Jewish News*, 14 January 2009, http://www.urbantoronto.ca/archive/index.php/t-648.html, accessed 16 January 2010. The envisioned memorial, to be designed by Daniel Liebeskind and placed in a park near a Toronto Jewish Community Center, was to consist of a fifteen-meter-high shield pierced by an arrowlike structure. The shield was to be illuminated by eight lights, and the arrow tipped by an eternal flame, recalling the branches of the nine-branched candelabra lit for the holiday of Hanukkah, a celebration of an ancient Jewish military victory. The memorial was also to include a theater surrounded by walls engraved with the names of Jewish veterans and festooned with the flags of the nations for whom the soldiers fought. Only one-tenth of the budget of seven million dollars was raised. While fund-raising for this project limped along, a single donor, Chaim Neuberger, donated ten million dollars for the building of a Holocaust education center at the Jewish Community Center. http://www.jewishtoronto.net/page.aspx?id=177963, accessed 15 January 2010.

5. *Forward*, 23 October 2009, 1, 10; http://www.jta.org/news/article/2011/1290822/west-points-jewish-choir-sings-for-the-president-and-diversity, accessed 16 July 2012; personal communication from the Friends of the Jewish Chapel at the U.S. Naval Academy, 16 July 2012.

6. Chinese Canadians "make up four per cent of Canada's population but .4 per cent of its military's regular force and 1.2 per cent of its primary reserves." *Toronto Globe and Mail*, 14 July 2011, A4.

7. Newsletter of the American Veterans of Israel Legacy Corporation, Winter 2012, 2.

8. http://www.haaretz.com/print-edition/news/why-do-so-many-diaspora-jews-want-to-join-the-idf-1.283800, accessed 5 April 2010.

9. *Forward*, 18 February 2011, 6–8, 10; 14 September 2012, 1, 8–10.

10. Sveta Roberman, "From Exclusion to Inclusion: Jewish WWII Soldiers in the Israeli National Narrative," *Israel Studies* 14, no. 2 (2009): 50–71.

11. The memorial was paid for mainly by donations from Russian-Jewish plutocrats. http://www.jpost.com/DiplomacyAndPolitics/Article.aspx?id=275225, accessed 30 November 2012.

12. Newsletter of the American Veterans of Israel Legacy Corporation, Winter 2012, 2–3; http://www.haaretz.com/weekend/anglo-file/not-home-alone-foreigners-came-to-israel-s-rescue-in-1948.premium-1.436650, accessed 16 June 2012.

13. Tamar Hermann, "Pacifism and Anti-Militarism in the Period Surrounding the Birth of the State of Israel," *Israel Studies* 15 (2010): 127–48.

14. See Abraham Kook, *Mishpat Kohen* (Jerusalem: Mosad Ha-Rav Kook, 1937), responsum no. 143, and the analyses of Nahum Rakover, *Mesirut nefesh: hakravat ha-yehid le-hatsalat ha-rabim* (Jerusalem: Justice Ministry, 2000), 118–23; and Elie Holzer, "Attitudes Towards the Use of Military Force in Ideological Currents of Re-

ligious Zionism," in *War and Peace in the Jewish Tradition*, ed. Lawrence Shiffman and Joel B. Wolowelsky (New York: Yeshiva University Press, 2007), 346–56.

15. R. Yisraeli's intellectual predecessors include R. Avraham Dov Shapiro, whose 1905 book *Davar Avraham* justified state control over territory through conquest alone, and R. Naftali Zvi Yehuda Berlin (the Netsiv, 1816–1893), who judged that killing in wartime does not constitute a violation of the Noahide commandment against murder. Gerald Bildstein, "The State and the Legitimate Use of Force and Coercion in Modern Halakhic Thought," *Jews and Violence: Studies in Contemporary Jewry XVIII* (2003): 3–22; Arye Edrei, "Divine Spirit and Physical Power: Rabbi Shlomo Goren and the Military Ethic of the Israel Defense Forces," *Theoretical Inquiries in Law* 7 (2005): 255–97; idem, "Law, Interpretation, and Ideology: The Renewal of the Jewish Laws of War in the State of Israel," *Cardozo Law Review* 28 (2006): 187–227.

16. Cited in Yona Hadari-Ramage, "War and Religiosity: The Sinai Campaign in Public Thought," in *Israel: The First Decade of Independence*, ed. S. Ilan Troen and Noah Lucas (Albany: State University of New York Press, 1995), 364.

17. Stuart Cohen, "The Quest for a Corpus of Military Ethics in Modern Israel," *Journal of Israeli History* 26, no. 1 (2007): 35–66; idem, "The Re-Discovery of Orthodox Jewish Laws Relating to the Military and War (*Hilkhot Tzavah u-Milchamah*) in Contemporary Israel: Trends and Implications," *Israel Studies* 12, no. 2 (2007): 1–28; idem, "Dilemmas of Military Service in Israel: The Religious Dimension," in *War and Peace in the Jewish Tradition*, ed. Shiffman and Wolowelsky, 313–40.

18. See the proclamation by the Neturei Karta Committee of Haredi Jewry in Eran Kaplan and Derek J. Penslar, *The Origins of Israel, 1882–1948: A Documentary History* (Madison: University of Wisconsin Press, 2011), 161–64.

19. http://www.haaretz.com/opinion/which-draft-dodgers-from-north-tel-aviv.premium-1.450824, accessed 13 July 2012.

# BIBLIOGRAPHY

## Archives

Archive de la Marine, Vincennes
Archive of the Israel Defense Force (AIDF), Tel Ha-Shomer, Israel
Archives Nationales, Paris
Archives of the Institute for Contemporary Jewry, Hebrew University of Jerusalem
Archives of the Leo Baeck Institute: Center for Jewish History, New York (ALBINY)
Central Archive for the History of the Jewish People, Jerusalem
Central Zionist Archive (CZA), Jerusalem
Deutsch-Israelitische Gemeindebund (DIGB) Archive, Stiftung Neue Synagoge Berlin–
    Centrum Judaicum, Berlin
Haganah Archive, Tel Aviv
Harley Library Archives, University of Southampton
Kaiserliches u. königliches Kriegsarchiv, Vienna
Service historique de l'armée territoriale (SHA), Vincennes
Yad Vashem Archives, Jerusalem

## Primary Source Periodicals

### (INDIVIDUAL ARTICLES NOT CITED SEPARATELY)

*Die Allgemeine Zeitung des Judentums (AZdJ)*
*Americans for Haganah*
*Annuaire de l'armée française*
*L'Antijuif*
*Les Archives Israélites (AI)*
*Ha-Aretz*
*Canadian Jewish News*
*L'Educatore Israelita*
*Haganah Speaks!*
*Ha-hayal ha-ivri*
*Im Deutschen Reich*
*Israel Speaks!*
*Israelitisches Familienblatt (IF)*

*Die Israelitische Wochenschrift*
*The Jewish Chronicle (JC)*
*Jewish Currents*
*The Jewish Ex-Serviceman*
*Jewish Frontier*
*The Jewish Veteran*
*Die Jüdische Front*
*Das Jüdische Volksblatt*
*Ha-Maggid*
*Ha-Me'asef*
*Ha-Melitz*
*Miami Herald*
*Militär-Statistisches Jahrbuch des K. u. k. Reichs-Kriegs-Ministeriums*
*New York Times*
*Der Orient*
*Ost und West*
*Pittsburgh Jewish Chronicle*
*Pittsburgh Post-Gazette*
*Revue des études juives*
*Der Schild*
*Time*
*Toronto Star*
*Ha-Tsefirah*
*L'Univers Israélite (UI)*
*Zeitschrift für Demographie und Statistik der Juden*

## Books and Articles

Aberbach, David. "Zionist Patriotism in Europe, 1897–1942: Ambiguities in Jewish Nationalism." *International History Review* 31 (2009): 268–98.

Adler, M. *Prayer Book for Jewish Members of H. M. Forces.* H. M. Stationery Office, 1918.

Adler, Michael, ed. *British Jewry Book of Honor.* London, 1922.

———. *The Jews of the Empire and the Great War.* London, 1919.

Agnon, Shai. *Ir u-melo'ah.* Jerusalem, 1973.

Albanis, Elisabeth. "Ostracised for Loyalty: Ernst Lissauer's Propaganda Writing and Reception." *Leo Baeck Institute Year Book XLIII* (1998): 195–224.

Almog, Doron. *Ha-rekhesh ba-artsot ha-berit 1945–1949.* Tel Aviv, 1987.

Almog, Oz. *Dem Morgenrot Entgegen. Helden der Sowjetunion.* Vienna, 2002.

Altschuler, Mordechai. "Jewish Warfare and the Participation of Jews in Combat in the Soviet Union as Reflected in Soviet and Western Historiography." In *The Historiography of the Holocaust Period: Proceedings of the Fifth Yad Vashem International Historical Conference,* ed. Yisrael Gutman and Gideon Greif. Jerusalem, 1987, 217–38.

Amitzur, Ilan. *The Origin of the Arab-Israeli Arms Race: Arms, Embargo, Military Power and Decision in the 1948 Palestine War.* New York, 1996.

Anderson, Benedict. *The Spectre of Comparisons: Nationalism, Southeast Asia and the World.* London, 1998.

Angress, Werner T. "Die jüdische Offizier in der neuren deutschen Geschichte, 1813–1918." In *Willensmenschen: Über deutsche Offiziere*, ed. Ursula Breymayer, Bernd Ulrich, and Karin Wieland. Frankfurt am Main, 1999, 67–78.

———. "Prussia's Army and the Jewish Reserve Officer Controversy before World War I." *Leo Baeck Institute Year Book XVII* (1972): 19–42.

Ansky, S. *The Enemy and His Pleasure: A Journey through the Jewish Pale of Settlement during World War I.* New York, 2004.

Arad, Yitzhak. *Be-tsel ha-degel ha-adom. Yehudei berit-ha-mo'atsot ba-lehimah neged germanyah ha-natsit.* Jerusalem, 2008.

Arendt, Hannah. *On Violence.* New York, 1969.

———. *The Origins of Totalitarianism.* New York, 1994.

Ascher, Saul. *Bemerkungen über die bürgerliche Verbesserung der Juden veranlasst be der Frage, Soll der Jude Soldat werden?* Berlin, 1788.

Aschheim, Steven. *Brothers and Strangers: The East European Jew in German and German Jewish Consciousness, 1800–1923.* Madison, Wisc., 1982.

Baader, Benjamin Maria. *Gender, Judaism, and Bourgeois Culture in Germany, 1800–1870.* Bloomington, Ind., 2006.

Baader, Benjamin Maria, Sharon Gillerman, and Paul Lerner, eds. *Jewish Masculinities: German Jews, Gender, and History.* Bloomington, Ind., 2012.

Bach, André. *L'armée de Dreyfus. Une histoire politique de l'armée française de Charles X à "L'Affaire."* Paris, 2004.

Bachar, Moshe. "Hanitah adifah 'al Madrid: teguvat ha-Yishuv be-Erets-Yisrael le-milhemet ha-ezrahim bi-Sefarad." M.A. thesis, Tel Aviv University, 1998.

Balaban, Majer, ed. *Album pamiątkowy ku czci Berka Joselewicza pułkownika wojsk polskich w 125-letnią rocznicę jego bohaterskiej śmierci 1809–1934.* Warsaw, 1934.

Barkai, Haim. "Ha-'alut ha-realit shel milhemet ha-'atsma'ut." In *Milhemet ha-atsma'ut 1948–1949: diyun mehudash*, ed. Alon Kadish. Tel Aviv, 2004, 759–91.

Baron, Salo, and George S. Wise, eds. *Violence and Defense in the Jewish Experience.* Philadelphia, 1977.

Bartal, Israel. "Giborim o-mogei lev? Yehudim be-tsiv'ot shel Polin (1794–1863)." In *Kiyum ve-shever. Yehudei polin le-doroteihem*, ed. Israel Bartal and Israel Gutman. Jerusalem, 1997, 353–67.

———. "The Ingathering of Traditions: Zionism's Anthology Projects." *Prooftexts* 17 (1997): 77–93.

———. "Ha-yehudim veha-tsava." In *Zman yehudi hadash: tarbut yehudit be-'idan hiloni. Mabat entsiklopedi*, chief ed. Yirmiyahu Yovel. Jerusalem, 2007, 1:298–302.

Baumel, Judith Tydor. *The "Bergson Boys" and the Origins of Contemporary Zionist Militancy.* Syracuse, N.Y., 2005.

Bell, David A. *The First Total War: Napoleon's Europe and the Birth of Warfare as We Know It.* New York, 2007.

Bendersky, Joseph. *The "Jewish Threat": Anti-Semitic Politics of the U.S. Army.* New York, 2000.

Ben-Sasson, Haim Hillel. *A History of the Jewish People.* Cambridge, Mass., 1976.

———. "Yihud 'am yisra'el le-da'at benei ha-me'ah ha-shteim esreh." *Perakim* 2 (1969–74), 145–218.

Bercuson, David. *The Secret Army.* New York, 1983.

Berkman, Ted. *Cast a Giant Shadow: The Story of Mickey Marcus Who Died to Save Jerusalem.* New York, 1962.

Berkowitz, Michael. *Zionist Culture and West European Jewry before the First World War.* Cambridge, UK, 1993.

Berliner, Abraham. *Geschichte der Juden in Rom von der ältesten Zeit bis zur Gegenwart.* Frankfurt am Main, 1893.

Bernard, Fernand. *L'Indo-Chine: erreurs et dangers—un programme.* Paris, 1901.

Bernfeld, Simon. *Sefer ha-demaʾot: meʾorot ha-gezerot ve-ha-redifot ve-hashmadot.* Berlin, 1923–26.

Bettin, Christina. *Italian Jews from Emancipation to the Racial Laws.* London, 2010.

Biale, David. *Power and Powerlessness in Jewish History.* New York, 1986.

Bildstein, Gerald. "The State and the Legitimate Use of Force and Coercion in Modern Halakhic Thought." *Jews and Violence: Studies in Contemporary Jewry XVIII* (2003): 3–22.

Birnbaum, Meyer, and Yonason Rosenblum. *Lieutenant Birnbaum: A Soldier's Story; Growing Up Jewish in America, Liberating the D.P. Camps, and a New Life in Jerusalem.* New York, 1993.

Birnbaum, Pierre. "L'armée française était-elle antisemite?" In *L'Affaire Dreyfus*, ed. Michel Winock. Paris, 1998.

———. *The Jews of the Republic: A History of State Jews in France from Gambetta to Vichy.* Stanford, Calif., 1996.

Bitan, Dan. "'Or sagi poreah': Mitosim shel gevurah lohemet be-reshit ha-tsiyonut (1880–1903)." In *Mitos ve-zikaron. Gilguleihah shel ha-todaʾah ha-yisreʾelit*, ed. David Ohana and Robert S. Wistrich. Jerusalem, 1996, 169–88.

Bleich, Judith. "Military Service: Ambivalence and Contradictions." In *War and Peace in the Jewish Tradition*, ed. Lawrence Schiffman and Joel B. Wolowelsky. New York, 2007, 415–76.

Bloch, Armand. *L'esprit militaire des juifs. Conférence fait à Bruxelles, le 1er jour de Hanouca 5664 (13 Decembre 1903).* Brussels, 1904.

Bourke, Joanna. *Dismembering the Male: Men's Bodies, Britain and the Great War.* Chicago, 1996.

Bowman, Steven. "'Yossipon' and Jewish Nationalism." *Proceedings of the Academy for Jewish Research* 61 (1995): 23–51.

Boyarin, Daniel. *Unheroic Conduct: The Rise of Heterosexuality and the Invention of the Jewish Man.* Berkeley and Los Angeles, 1997.

Bredin, Jean-Denis. *The Affair: The Case of Alfred Dreyfus.* Paris, 1986.

———. *Bernard Lazare: de l'anarche au prophète.* Paris, 1992.

Breuer, Mordechai. *Modernity within Tradition: The Social History of Orthodox Jewry in Imperial Germany.* New York, 1992.

Breymayer, Ursula. "'Mein Kampf': Das Phantom des Offiziers. Zur Autobiographie eines jüdischen Wilhelminers." In *Willensmenschen: Über deutsche Offiziere*, ed. Ursula Breymayer, Bernd Ulrich, and Karin Wieland. Frankfurt am Main, 1999, 79–93.

Brownstein, Rachel M. *Tragic Muse: Rachel of the Comédie-Française.* New York, 1993.

Broyde, Michael J. "Just Wars, Just Battles and Just Conduct in Jewish Law: Jewish Law Is not a Suicide Pact!" In *War and Peace in the Jewish Tradition*, ed. Lawrence Schiffman and Joel B. Wolowelsky. New York, 2007, 1–44.

Brubaker, Rogers. *Nationalism Reframed: Nationhood and the National Question in the New Europe.* New York, 1996.

Budnitsky, Oleg. "The 'Jewish Battalions' in the Red Army." In *Revolution, Repression, and Revival: The Soviet Jewish Experience*, ed. Zvi Titelman and Yaacov Roi. Lanham, Md., 2007, 15–36.

———. *Russian Jews between the Reds and the Whites, 1917–1920*. Philadelphia, 2012.

Burg, Meno. *Geschichte meines Dienstlebens*, 3rd ed. Leipzig, 1916.

Burns, Michael. *Dreyfus: A Family Affair, 1789–1945*. New York, 1991.

Calhoun, Ricky-Dale. "Arming David: The Haganah's Illegal Arms Procurement Network in the United States, 1945–1949." *Journal of Palestine Studies* 36 (2007): 22–32.

Campos, Michelle U. *Ottoman Brothers: Muslims, Christians and Jews in Early Twentieth-Century Palestine*. Stanford, Calif., 2011.

Caplan, Gregory. "Germanising the Jewish Male: Military Masculinity as the Last Stage of Acculturation." In *Towards Normality? Acculturation and Modern German Jewry*, ed. Rainer Liedtke and David Rechter. Tübingen, 2003, 159–84.

———. "Wicked Sons, German Heroes: Jewish Soldiers, Veterans and Memories of World War I in Germany." Ph.D. dissertation, Georgetown University, 2001.

Carmy, Shalom. "The Origins of Nations and the Shadow of Violence: Theological Perspectives on Canaan and Amalek." In *War and Peace in the Jewish Tradition*, ed. Lawrence Schiffman and Joel B. Wolowelsky. New York, 2007, 163–200.

Caron, Vicki. *Between France and Germany: The Jews of Alsace-Lorraine, 1871–1918*. Stanford, Calif., 1988.

Century, Douglas. *Barney Ross: The Life of a Jewish Fighter*. New York, 2006.

Cesarani, David. "An Embattled Minority: The Jews in Britain during the First World War." *Immigrants and Minorities* 8 (1989): 61–81.

Chazan, Robert. *European Jewry and the First Crusade*. Berkeley and Los Angeles, 1996.

Chesnel, Compte de. *Encyclopédie militaire et maritime*, 5th ed. Paris, 1868.

Chevalley, Sylvie. *Rachel*. Paris, 1994.

Cohen, Adir. *Gevurat yisra'el be-hazon ha-dorot*. Tel Aviv, 1968.

———. *Heylot yisra'el u-milhamoteihem ba-avar u-va-hoveh*. Tel Aviv, 1957.

Cohen, Deborah. *The War Come Home: Disabled Veterans in Britain and Germany, 1914–1939*. Berkeley and Los Angeles, 2001.

Cohen, Hillel. *Army of Shadows: Palestinian Collaboration with Zionism, 1917–1948*. Berkeley and Los Angeles, 2008.

Cohen, Jeremy. *Sanctifying the Name of God: Jewish Martyrs and Jewish Memories of the First Crusade*. Philadelphia, 2006.

Cohen, Julia Phillips. "Fashioning Imperial Citizens: Sephardi Jews and the Ottoman State, 1856–1912." Ph.D. dissertation, Stanford University, 2008.

Cohen, Naomi W. *Jacob H. Schiff: A Study of American Jewish Leadership*. Hanover, N.H., 1999.

Cohen, Richard I. *Jewish Icons: Art and Society in Modern Europe*. Berkeley and Los Angeles, 1998.

Cohen, Stuart A. "Dilemmas of Military Service in Israel: The Religious Dimension." In *War and Peace in the Jewish Tradition*, ed. Lawrence Schiffman and Joel B. Wolowelsky. New York, 2007, 313–40.

———. "The Quest for a Corpus of Jewish Military Ethics in Modern Israel." *Journal of Israeli History* 26, no. 1 (2007): 35–66.

——. "The Rediscovery of Orthodox Jewish Laws Relating to the Military and War (*Hilkhot Tzavah U-Milchama*) in Contemporary Israel: Trends and Implications." *Israel Studies* 12 (2007): 1–28.

——. "Reversing the Tide of Jewish History: Culture and the Creation of Israel's "People's Army." In *The New Citizen Armies: Israel's Armed Forces in Comparative Perspective*, ed. Stuart A. Cohen. London, 2011, 56–73.

Corvisier, André. *Dictionnaire d'art et d'histoire militaries*. Paris, 1988.

——. *Histoire militaire de la France*. Paris, 1992.

Crim, Brian E. "'Was It All Just a Dream?' German-Jewish Veterans and the Confrontation with Völkisch Nationalism in the Interwar Period." In *Sacrifice and National Belonging in Twentieth-Century Germany*, ed. Greg Eghigian and Matthew Paul Berg. Arlington, Tex., 2002, 64–89.

Dash Moore, Deborah. "Bonding Images: Miami Jews and the Campaign for Israel Bonds." In *Envisioning Israel: The Changing Ideals and Images of American Jews*, ed. Alon Gal. Jerusalem, 1996, 254–69.

——. *G.I. Jews. How World War II Changed a Generation*. Cambridge, Mass., 2004.

——. *To the Golden Cities: Pursuing the American Jewish Dream in Miami and Los Angeles*. New York, 1994.

David, Anthony. *Ha-shamayim hem ha-gvul. Al Shvimmer, mekayem ha-ta'asiyah ha-avirit*. Tel Aviv, 2008.

Davis, Mac. *Jews Fight Too!* New York, 1945.

Deak, Istvan. *Beyond Nationalism: A Social and Political History of the Hapsburg Officer Corps, 1848–1918*. New York, 1990.

——. "Pacesetters of Integration: Jewish Officers in the Habsburg Monarchy." *Eastern European Politics and Societies* 3 (1989): 22–50.

Diamant, David. *Yidn in shpanishn krig, 1936–1939*. Warsaw, 1967.

Diehl, James. *Thanks of the Fatherland: German Veterans after the Second World War*. Chapel Hill, N.C., 1993.

Dinur, Ben-Tsion, et al., eds. *Sefer toldot ha-haganah*. Tel Aviv, 1954–72.

Dohm, Christian Wilhelm von. *Über die Bürgerliche Verbesserung der Juden*. Hildesheim, 1973.

Duclert, Vincent. *Alfred Dreyfus. L'honneur d'un patriote*. Paris, 2006.

——, ed. *Le colonel Mayer: de l'affaire Dreyfus à de Gaulle*. Paris, 2007.

Duker, Abraham. "Jewish Volunteers in the Ottoman-Polish Cossack Units during the Crimean War." *Jewish Social Studies* 16, no.4 (1954): 351–76.

——. "Mickiewicz and the Jewish Problem." In *Adam Mickiewicz, Poet of Poland: A Symposium*, ed. Manfred Kirdl. New York, 1951, 108–25.

Dunkelman, Benjamin. *Dual Allegiance*. Halifax, 1984.

Edrei, Arye. "Divine Spirit and Physical Power: Rabbi Shlomo Goren and the Military Ethic of the Israel Defense Forces." *Theoretical Inquiries in Law* 7 (2005): 255–97.

——. "Law, Interpretation, and Ideology: The Renewal of the Jewish Laws of War in the State of Israel." *Cardozo Law Review* 28 (2006): 187–227.

Efron, John. *Defenders of the Race: Jewish Doctors and Race Science in Fin-de-Siècle Europe*. New Haven, Conn., and London, 1994.

Ehrentheil, Adolf. *Mot Yesharim (Ehrentod der Braven). Rede, gehalten zur Seelensgedächtnissfeier für die im jüngsten Kriege gefallenen Soldaten israelitischer Religion am 11. November 1866 in der Synagoge zu Horic*. Prague, 1866.

Eisen, Robert. *The Peace and Violence of Judaism: An Exploration in Jewish Ethics from the Bible to Modern Zionism*. New York, 2011.

Elam, Yigal. *Ha-gedudim ha-ʿivrim be-milhemet ha-ʿolam ha-rishonah*. Tel Aviv, 1973.

Elon, Amos. *The Pity of It All: A History of the Jews in Germany, 1743–1933*. New York, 2002.

Engel, David. "Ha-berihah ha-hafganatit shel hayalim yehudim meha-tsava ha-polani be-angliyah bi-shnat 1944: parashah bein anglim, polanim, ve-yehudim bi-tekufat milhemet ha-ʿolam ha-shniyah." *Yahadut Zemaneinu* 2 (1985): 177–207.

Falk, Hans. *Die Juden in den Kriegsgesellschaften. Nach Amtlichen Material*. Berlin, 1920.

Feiner, Shmuel. *The Jewish Enlightenment*. Philadelphia, 2002.

———. *Moses Mendelssohn*. New Haven, Conn., 20.

Feldman, Gerald D. *Army, Industry and Labor in Germany, 1914–1918*. Princeton, N.J., 1966.

Feldman, Yael. *Glory and Agony: Isaac's Sacrifice and National Narrative*. Stanford, Calif., 2010.

Ferguson, Niall. *The Pity of War: Explaining World War I*. New York, 1999.

———. *War of the World: Twentieth-Century Conflict and the Descent of the West*. New York, 2006.

Fine, David. *Jewish Integration in the German Army in the First World War*. Berlin, 2012.

Firestone, Reuven. *The Death and Resurrection of Jewish Holy War: The History of a Religious Notion*. New York, 2012.

Fischer, Horst. *Judentum, Staat und Heer in Preussen im frühen 19. Jahrhundert*. Tübingen, 1968.

Forrest, Alan. *Conscripts and Deserters: The Army and French Society during the Revolution and Empire*. New York, 1989.

———. *The Legacy of the French Revolutionary Wars: The Nation-in-Arms in French Republican Memory*. New York, 2009.

Forrest, Alan, Karen Hagemann, and Jane Rendall, eds. *Soldiers, Citizens and Civilians: Experiences and Perceptions of the Revolutionary and Napoleonic Wars, 1790–1820*. Basingstoke, 2008.

Fram, Edward. "Creating a Tale of Martyrdom in Tulczyn, 1648." In *Jewish History and Jewish Memory: Essays in Honor of Yosef Haim Yerushalmi*. Hanover, N.H., 1998, 89–112.

Frankel, Jonathan. *The Damascus Affair: "Ritual Murder," Politics, and the Jews in 1840*. New York, 1997.

———. "The Paradoxical Politics of Marginality: Thoughts on the Jewish Situation during the Years 1914–1921." In idem, *Crisis, Revolution and Russian Jews*. New York, 2009, 131–54.

Frankel, Michael. *Der Anteil der jüdischen Freiwilligen an dem Befreiungskriege 1813–1814*. Breslau, 1922.

Franzos, Karl Emil. *Moschko von Parma (1880)*. Berlin, 1984.

Fredman, J. George, and Louis A. Falk. *Jews in American Wars*. Hoboken, N.J., 1942.

Frenay, Henry. *La nuit finira*. Paris, 1973.

French, David. *Military Identities: The Regimental System, the British Army, and the British People, c. 1870–2000*. Oxford, 2005.

Freudenthal, Gad. "Aaron Solomon Gumperz, Gotthold Ephraim Lessing and the First Call for the Improvement of the Civil Rights of Jews in Germany." *Association for Jewish Studies Review* 29 (2005): 299–353.

Frevert, Ute. *A Nation in Barracks: Modern Germany, Military Conscription and Civil Society.* Oxford, 2004.

Friedgut, Theodore. "Jews, Violence and the Russian Revolutionary Movement." *Studies in Contemporary Jewry XVIII* (2003): 43–58.

Friedman, Murray, ed. *Philadelphia Jewish Life, 1940–1985.* Ardmore, Pa., 1986.

Fujitani, Takashi. *Race for Empire: Koreans as Japanese and Japanese as Americans during World War II.* Berkeley and Los Angeles, 2011.

Funkenstein, Amos. *Maimonides: Nature, History and Messianic Beliefs.* Tel Aviv, 1997.

Gafni, Shraga. *Ha-kravot ha-mefursamim be-toldot yisra'el.* Tel Aviv, 1962.

Gartner, Lloyd. *The Jewish Immigrant in England, 1870–1914.* London, 1960.

Geiger, Ludwig. *Die deutschen Juden und der Krieg.* Berlin, 1915.

Gelber, Yoav. *Ha-hitnadvut le-tsava ha-briti be-milhemet ha-'olam ha-sheniyah.* Jerusalem, 1995.

Gerber, David A., ed. *Disabled Veterans in History.* Ann Arbor, Mich., 2000.

Gillerman, Sharon. *Germans into Jews: Remaking the Jewish Social Body in the Weimar Republic.* Sanford, Calif., 2009.

Gilner, Elias. *War and Hope: A History of the Jewish Legion.* New York, 1969.

Ginsberg, Benjamin. *The Fatal Embrace: Jews and the State.* Chicago, 1999.

Goldstein Sepinwall, Alyssa. *The Abbé Grégoire and the French Revolution: The Making of Modern Universalism.* Berkeley and Los Angeles, 2005.

Goodman, Martin. *Rome and Jerusalem: The Clash of Ancient Civilizations.* London, 2007.

Goremberg, Gershon. *The Unmaking of Israel.* New York, 2011.

Grady, Tim. *The German-Jewish Soldiers of the First World War in History and Memory.* Liverpool, 2011.

Graetz, Heinrich. *The Structure of Jewish History and Other Essays.* New York, 1975.

Graetz, Michael. "Aliyato u-shkia'to shel sapak ha-tsava ha-yehudi: kalkalah yehudit be-i'itot milhamah." *Tsiyon* 53 (1991): 255–74.

———. *The Jews in Nineteenth-Century France: From the French Revolution to the Alliance Israelite Universelle.* Stanford, Calif., 1996.

Graff, Gil. *Separation of Church and State: Dina de-Malkhuta Dina in Jewish Law, 1750–1848.* Tuscaloosa, Ala., 1985.

Greenberg, Yitzhak. "Financing the War of Independence." *Studies in Zionism* 9, no.1 (1988): 63–80.

Greenwald, Jekutiel Judah. *Sefer ha-zikhronot: kolel et kol ha-tela'ot ve-ha-tiltulim asher metsa'uni be-meshekh ha-milhamah ha-gedolah be-'omdi mezuyan mul ha-oyev.* Budapest, 1922.

Gribetz, Jonathan. "Defining Neighbors: Religion, Race, and the Early Zionist-Arab Encounter." Ph.D. dissertation, Colombia University, 2010.

Gshur, Benny. "Mitnadvim mi-tsafon amerika be-milhemet ha-shihrur." Ph.D. dissertation, Hebrew University, 2009.

Guesnet, Francois. "The Turkish Cavalry in Swazedz; or, Jewish Political Culture at the Borderlines of Modern History." *Jahrbuch des Simon-Dubnow-Instituts* 6 (2007): 227–48.

Hadari-Ramage, Yona. "War and Religiosity: The Sinai Campaign in Public Thought." In *Israel: The First Decade of Independence,* ed. S. Ilan Troen and Noah Lucas. Albany, N.Y., 1995, 355–74.

Ha-Kohen, Yisrael Meir ben Ari Zev. *Sefer Mahaneh Yisrael*. Vilna, 1881.

Halff, Sylvain. "Participation of the Jews of France in the Great War." *American Jewish Yearbook* 21 (1919–20): 31–97.

Halperin, Israel. *Sefer ha-gevurah: antologyah historit-sifrutit*. Tel Aviv, 1949/50–1950/51.

Halperin, Samuel. "Ideology or Philanthropy? The Politics of Zionist Fund-Raising." *Western Political Quarterly* 13, no. 4 (1960): 950–73.

———. *The Political World of American Zionism*. Detroit, 1961.

Hameiri, Avigdor. *The Great Madness*. New York, 1929.

Hank, Sabine, and Hermann Simon. *Feldpostbriefe Jüdischer Soldaten 1914–1918. Briefe ehemaliger Zöglinge an Sigmund Feist, Direktor des Reichenheimschen Waisenhauses in Berlin*. Teetz, 2002.

Hardy, Andrew. "The Economics of French Rule in Indochina: A Biography of Paul Bernard (1892–1960)." *Modern Asian Studies* 32 (1998): 807–48.

Harris, Ruth. *Dreyfus: Politics, Emotion, and the Scandal of the Century*. New York, 2010.

Hengel, Martin. *Judentum und Hellenismus*, 3rd ed. Tübingen, 1988.

*Herev pipiyot be-yadayim. Aktivizm tseva'i ba-machshavah shel ha-tsiyonut ha-datit*. Jerusalem, 2009.

Hertz, Deborah. *How Jews Became Germans: The History of Conversion and Assimilation in Berlin*. New Haven, Conn., 2007.

Heymann, Fritz. *Der Chevalier von Geldern. Eine Chronik der Abenteuer der Juden*. Cologne, 1963.

Hirsh, J. Ben. *Jewish General Officers: A Biographical Dictionary*. Melbourne, 1967.

Holzer, Elie. "Attitudes Towards the Use of Military Force in Ideological Currents of Religious Zionism." In *War and Peace in the Jewish Tradition*, ed. Lawrence Schiffman and Joel B. Wolowelsky. New York, 2007, 341–414.

———. "The Use of Military Force in the Religious Zionist Ideology of Rabbi Yitzhak Yaakov Reines and His Successors." *Jews and Violence: Studies in Contemporary Jewry* XVIII (2003): 74–94.

Hong, Young-Sun. *Welfare, Modernity and the Weimar State, 1919–1933*. Princeton, N.J., 1998.

Horn, Maurycy. "Obrona miast jako umocnionych punktow—glowne swiadczenie wojenne Zydow w Rzeczypospolitej w XVI i XVII wieku." *Biuletyn ZIH* 100, no. 4 (1976): 19–33.

———. "Swiadczenia Zydow na rzecz obronnosci kraju i miast rodzinnych w dawnej Polsce." *Biuletyn ZIH* 98, no. 2 (1976): 3–17.

———. "Udzial Zydow w wojnach z Tatarami i Turcja w XVII wieku." *Biuletyn ZIH* 102, no. 2 (1977): 5–15.

Horowitz, Elliot. *Reckless Rites: Purim and the Legacy of Jewish Violence*. Princeton, N.J., 2006.

Horwitz, Rivka. "Voices of Opposition to the First World War among Jewish Thinkers." *Leo Baeck Institute Year Book* XXXIII (1988): 233–59.

Huehner, Leon. "Jews in the War of 1812." *Publications of the American Jewish Historical Society* 26 (1918): 173–200.

Hundert, Gershon David. *Jews in Poland-Lithuania in the Eighteenth Century: Genealogy of Modernity*. Berkeley and Los Angeles, 2004.

Inbar, Efraim. "War in Jewish Tradition." *Jerusalem Journal of International Relations* 9 (1987): 83–99.

Jabotinsky, Ze'ev. *Megilat ha-gedud: sipurei ha-gedudim ha-'ivrim be-milhemet ha-'olam ha-rishonah.* Tel Aviv, 1991.

Jantzen, Mark. *Mennonite German Soldiers: Nation, Religion and Family in the Prussian East, 1772–1880.* South Bend, Ind., 2010.

Kadish, Sharman. *A Good Jew and a Good Englishman: The Jewish Lads' and Girls' Brigade, 1895–1995.* London, 1995.

Kahn, Léon. *Les professions manuelles et les institutions de patronage.* Paris, 1885.

Kallner, Rudolph. *Herzl und Rathenau. Wege Jüdischer Existenz an der Wende des 20. Jahrhunderts.* Stuttgart, 1976.

Kaplan, Marion, ed. *Between Dignity and Despair: Jewish Life in Nazi Germany.* New York, 1998.

———. *Jewish Daily Life in Germany, 1618–1945.* New York, 2005.

Karp, Jonathan. *The Politics of Jewish Commerce: Economic Thought and Emancipation in Europe, 1638–1848.* New York, 2008.

Katzer, Henry. *South Africa's 800: The Story of South African Volunteers in Israel's War of Birth,* rev. ed. N.p. (Machal Museum), 2003.

Kaufman, Menahem. *An Ambiguous Partnership: Non-Zionists and Zionists in America, 1939–1948.* Jerusalem, 1991.

Keegan, John. *A History of Warfare.* New York, 1993.

Keren, Michael, and Shlomit Keren. *We Are Coming, Unafraid: The Jewish Legions and the Promised Land in the First World War.* London, 2010.

Kessler, Harry. *Walter Rathenau: His Life and Work.* New York, 1930.

Kestenberg-Gladstein, Ruth. *Neuere Geschichte der Juden in den böhmischen Ländern. Erster Teil: Das Zeitalter der Aufklärung 1780–1839.* Tübingen, 1969.

Kimelman, Reuven. "War." In *Frontiers of Jewish Thought,* ed. Steven Katz. New York, 1992, 307–32.

Kisch, Alexander. *Zur Geschichte der israelitischen Militärsorge in Deutschland und Österreich.* Prague, 1917.

Klapper, Melissa. "'Those by Whose Side We Have Labored': American Jewish Women and the Peace Movement between the Wars." *Journal of American History* 97 (2010): 636–58.

Klemperer, Victor. *I Will Bear Witness: A Diary of the Nazi Years, 1942–1945,* 3 vols. New York, 2001.

Kobler, Franz. "Fritz Heymann und seine Chronik vom Abenteuer der Juden." *BLBI* 13 (1961): 44–55.

Koffman, David. "The Jews' Indian: Culture and Commerce between Jews and Native Americans, 1824–1924." Ph.D. dissertation, New York University, 2011.

Kook, Abraham Isaac. *Mishpat Kohen.* Jerusalem, 1937.

Kopczysnski, Michal. "The Physical Stature of Jewish Men in Poland in the Second Half the 19th Century." *Economics and Human Biology* 9, no. 2 (2011): 203–10.

Korn, Bertram W. *American Jewry and the Civil War.* Philadelphia, 1961.

Koskenniemi, Martii. *The Gentle Civilizer of Nations: The Rise and Fall of International Law, 1870–1960.* Cambridge, UK, 2001.

Koven, Seth. "Remembering and Dismemberment: Crippled Children, Wounded Soldiers, and the Great War in Great Britain." *American Historical Review* 99, no. 4 (1994): 1167–1202.

Krebs, Ronald R. *Fighting for Rights: Military Service and the Politics of Citizenship.* Ithaca, N.Y., 2006.

Krel, M. *Zikhroynes fun Yidishn legion: tsum tsvantsik yerikn aniversar.* Montevideo, 1938.

Krüger, Christine. *"Sind wir denn nicht Brüder?" Deutsche Juden im nationalen Krieg 1870/71.* Paderborn, 2006.

La Gorge, Paul-Marie de. *The French Army: A Military-Political History.* London, 1963.

Lambroza, Shlomo. "Jewish Self-Defense during the Russian Pogroms of 1903–1906." *Jewish Journal of Sociology* 23 (1981):123–34.

———. "The Pogroms of 1903–1906." In *Pogroms: Anti-Jewish Violence in Modern Russian History,* ed. John D. Klier and Shlomo Lambroza. Cambridge, UK, 2004, 195–247.

Landau, Philippe. *Les Juifs de France et la Grande Guerre: Un patriotisme républicain, 1914–1941.* Paris, 1999.

———. *L'Opinion juive et l'affaire Dreyfus.* Paris, 1995.

Laor, Dan. "Kishinev Revisited: A Place in Jewish Historical Memory." *Prooftexts* 25, (2005): 30–38.

Laqueur, Thomas. "Memory and Naming in the Great War." In *Commemorations: The Politics of National Identity,* ed. John Gillis. Princeton, N.J., 1994.

Laskov, Shulamit. *Trumpeldor: Biografiya.* Jerusalem, 1995.

Learsi, Rufus. *The Jew in Battle.* New York, 1944.

Leff, Lisa. *Sacred Bonds of Solidarity: The Rise of Jewish Internationalism in Nineteenth-Century France.* Stanford, Calif., 2006.

Lerner, Paul. *Hysterical Men: War, Psychiatry and the Politics of Trauma in Germany, 1890–1930.* Ithaca, N.Y., 2003.

Levenson, Thomas. *Einstein in Berlin.* New York, 2004.

Levine, Mark. "Against the Grain: Two Jewish Diaries of War and Anti-War, 1914–1918." In *Forging Modern Jewish Identities: Public Faces and Private Struggles,* ed. Michael Berkowitz, Susan L. Tananbaum, and Saw W. Bloom. London, 2003, 81–114.

Levy, Daniel S. *Two-Gun Cohen.* New York, 1997.

Levy, Geoffrey B. "Judaism and the Obligation to Die for the State." *Association for Jewish Studies Review* 12 (1987): 175–203.

Lewin, Reinhold. *Der Krieg als jüdisches Erlebnis: Ein Vortrag.* Berlin, 1919.

Lindner, Erik. *Patriotismus deutscher Juden von der napoleonischen Ära bis zum Kaiserreich: Zwischen korporativem Loyalismus und individueller deutsch-jüdischer Identität.* Frankfurt am Main, 1997.

Lipman, Vivian D. *A Century of Social Service, 1859–1959: The History of the Jewish Board of Guardians.* London, 1959.

Lipp, Anne. *Meinungslenkung im Krieg: Kriegserfahrungen deutscher Soldaten und ihre Deutung 1914–1918.* Göttingen, 2003.

Litvak, Olga. *Conscription and the Search for Modern Russian Jewry.* Bloomington, Ind., 2008.

Lloyd, Anne. "Jews Under Fire: The Jewish Community and Military Service in World War I Britain." Ph.D. dissertation, University of Southampton, 2009.

Lustiger, Arno. *Schalom, Libertad! Juden im Spanischen Bürgerkrieg.* Cologne, 1991.

Luz, Ehud. *Wrestling with an Angel: Power, Morality and Jewish Identity.* New Haven, Conn., 2003.

Maisel, Witold. *Sądownictwo miasta Poznania do końca XVI wieku*. Poznan, 1961.

Malino, Frances. *A Jew in the French Revolution: The Life of Zalkind Hourwitz*. New York, 1997.

Mandel, Maud. "Transnationalism and Its Discontents during the 1948 Arab-Israeli War." *Diaspora* 12 (2003): 329–60.

Markovitsky, Yaakov. "Ha-gahal: giyus huts-la-arets be-milhemet ha-atsma'ut." In *Milhemet ha-atsma'ut tasha"h-tasha"t: diyun mehudash*, ed. Alon Kadish. Tel Aviv, 2004, 525–37.

———. *Gahelet lohemet. giyus hutz la-aretz be-milhemet ha-atsma'ut*. Tel Aviv, 1995.

———. *Machal: Overseas Volunteers in Israel's War of Independence*. Jerusalem, 2003.

Marrus, Michael. *The Politics of Assimilation: The French Jewish Community at the Time of the Dreyfus Affair*. Oxford, 1971.

Mattäus, Jürgen. "Deutschtum und Judentum under Fire: The Impact of the First World War on the Strategies of the Centralverein and the Zionistische Vereinigung." *Leo Baeck Institute Year Book XXXIII* (1988): 129–47.

Maurer, Trude. "'Sehr wichtig sind Bücher von der Jüdischen Geschichte': Zu den Lebensverhältnissen und Lektüreninteressen jüdscher Kriegsgefangener aus dem Russischen Reich (1917/18)." *Tel Aviv Jahrbuch für deutsche Geschichte* 20 (1991): 259–86.

McCune, Marcy. *"The Whole Wide World Without Limits": International Relief, Gender Politics, and American Jewish Women, 1893–1930*. Detroit, 2005.

Medoff, Rafael. *Militant Zionism in America: The Rise and Impact of the Jabotinsky Movement in the United States, 1926–1948*. Tuscaloosa, Ala., 2002.

Mendelsohn, Richard. "The Jewish War: Anglo-Jewry and the South African War." In *Writing a Wider War: Rethinking Gender, Race and Identity in the South African War, 1899–1902*, ed. Greg Cuthberton, Albert Grundling, and Mary-Lynn Suttle. Athens, Ohio, 2002, 247–65.

Mendes-Flohr, Paul. "The *Kriegserlebnis* and Jewish Consciousness." In *Jüdisches Leben in der Weimarer Republik/Jews in the Weimar Republic*, ed. Wolfgang Benz, Arnold Paucker, and Peter Pulzer. Tübingen, 1998, 225–37.

Meuleau, M. *Des pionniers en Extreme-Orient. Histoire de la Banque d'Indochine, 1875–1975*. Paris, 1990.

Meyer, Michael, general ed. *German-Jewish History in Modern Times*, 4 vols. New York, 1996–1998.

Meyerson, Mark. *A Jewish Renaissance in Fifteenth-Century Spain*. Princeton, N.J., 2004.

Michaelis, Meir. "Gli ufficiali superiori ebrei nell' esercito italiano dal Risorgimento all Marcia su Roma." *La Rassegna Mensile de Israel* 30, no. 4 (1964): 156–71.

Michman, Joseph. "Jewish Soldiers in the Batavian Republic and under French Rule." *Dutch Jewish History* 3 (1993): 295–307.

Miller, Michael. *Rabbis and Revolution: The Jews of Moravia in the Age of Emancipation*. Stanford, Calif., 2010.

Milner, Iris. "In the City of Slaughter: The Hidden Voices of Pogrom Victims." *Prooftexts* 25 (2005): 60–72.

Milstein, Uri. *History of Israel's War of Independence*, vol. 1. Lanham, Md., 1996.

Mintz, Alan. "Kishinev and the Twentieth Century: Introduction." *Prooftexts* 25, (2005): 1–7.

Morris, Benny. *1948: A History of the First Arab-Israeli War*. New Haven, Conn., 2008.

Mosse, George. *The Jews and the German War Experience, 1914–1918*. Leo Baeck Memorial Lecture 21. New York, 1977.

Naor, Moshe. "From Voluntary Funds to National Loans: The Financing of Israel's 1948 War Effort." *Israel Studies* 11 (2006): 62–82.

———. "Israel's 1948 War of Independence as a Total War." *Journal of Contemporary History* 43 (2008): 241–57.

Nathan, Paul, ed. *Der Jude als Soldat*. Berlin, 1896.

Nathans, Benjamin. *Beyond the Pale: The Jewish Encounter with Late Imperial Russia*. Berkeley and Los Angeles, 2004.

Neuberg, Simon, ed. *Das Schwedesch Lid. Ein westjiddischer Bericht über die Ereignisse in Prag im Jahre 1648*. Hamburg, 2000.

Novak, David. *The Image of the Non-Jew in Judaism: An Historical and Constructive Study of the Noahide Laws*. Lewiston, N.Y., 1984.

Nye, Robert. *Masculinity and Male Codes of Honor in Modern France*. Berkeley and Los Angeles, 1993.

Opalski, Magdalena, and Israel Bartal. *Poles and Jews: A Failed Brotherhood*. Hanover, N.H., 1992.

Otley, C. B. "The Social Origins of British Army Officers." *Sociological Review* 18 (1970): 213–39.

Palmer, Greg, and Mark S. Zaid, eds. *The GI's Rabbi: World War II Letters of David Max Eichorn*. Lawrence, Kans., 2004.

Pappe, Ilan. *The Ethnic Cleansing of Palestine*. Oxford, 2007.

Penslar, Derek J. "Antisemites on Zionism: From Indifference to Obsession." In *Israel in History: The Jewish State in Comparative Perspective*. London, 2006, 112–29.

———. *Shylock's Children: Economics and Jewish Identity in Modern Europe*. Berkeley and Los Angeles, 2001.

———. "An Unlikely Internationalism: The Jewish Experience of Warfare in Modern Western Europe." *Journal of Modern Jewish Studies* 7 (2008): 309–24.

Petrovsky-Shtern, Yohanan. "Dual Identity Revisited: The Case of Russian-Jewish Soldiers." *Jews in Russia and Eastern Europe* 1 (2004): 130–44.

———. "The Guardians of Faith, or Jewish Self -Governing Societies in the Russian Army." In *The Military and Society in Russia, 1450–1917*, ed. Eric Lohr and Marshall Poe. Leiden, 2002, 412–39.

———. *Jews in the Russian Army, 1827–1917: Drafted into Modernity*. New York, 2009.

Picht, Clemens. "Zwischen Vaterland und Volk: Das deutsche Judentum im Ersten Weltkrieg." In *Der Erste Weltkrieg: Wirkung, Wahrnehmung, Analyse*, ed. Wolfgang Michalka. Munich, 1994.

Planert, Ute. *Der Mythos vom Befreiungskrieg: Frankreichs Krieg und der deutsche Süden: Alltag—Wahrnehmung—Deutung 1792-1841*. Paderborn, 2007.

Pollock, Benjamin. "From Nation State to World Empire: Franz Rosenzweig's Redemptive Imperialism." *Jewish Studies Quarterly* 11 (2004): 332–53.

Polner, Murray, and Naomi Goodman, eds. *The Challenge of Shalom: The Jewish Tradition of Peace and Justice*. Philadelphia, 1994.

Polonsky, Antony. *The Jews in Poland and Russia*, 3 vols. London, 2009–12.

Posselt, Alfred. *Jüdische Generale unter Fremden Fahnen*. Vienna, 1985.

Postal, Bernard, and Henry W. Levy. *And the Hills Shouted for Joy: The Day Israel Was Born*. Philadelphia, 1973.

Presner, Todd. *Muscular Judaism: The Jewish Body and the Politics of Regeneration*. London, 2007.

Prost, Antoine. *In the Wake of War: "Les Anciens Combattants" and French Society, 1914–1939*. Oxford, 1992.

Pulzer, Peter. *Jews and the German State: The Political History of a Minority, 1848–1933*. London, 1992.

Quataert, Jean. *Stanging Philanthropy: Patriotic Women and the National Imagination in Dynastic Germany, 1813–1916*. Ann Arbor, Mich., 2001.

Rahamimov, Alon. *POWs and the Great War: Captivity on the Eastern Front*. New York, 2001.

Rakover, Nahum. *Mesirut nefesh: hakravat ha-yehid le-hatsalat ha-rabim*. Jerusalem, 2000.

Rappaport, Joseph. *Hands across the Sea: Jewish Immigrants and World War I*. New York, 2005.

Ravitsky, Aviezer. "Prohibited Wars in the Jewish Tradition." In *The Ethics of War and Peace: Religious and Secular Perspectives*, ed. Terry Nardin. Princeton, N.J., 1998, 15–27.

Rechter, David. *The Jews of Vienna during the First World War*. London, 2001.

Reuveni, Gideon. "Sports and the Militarization of Jewish Society." In *Emancipation Through Muscles: Jews and Sports in Europe*, ed. Michael Brenner and Gideon Reuveni. Lincoln, Neb., 2006, 44–61.

Rheins, Carl J. "German Jewish Patriotism, 1918–1935: A Study of the Attitudes and Actions of the 'Reichsbund Jüdischer Frontsoldaten,' the 'Schwarzes Fähnlein,' 'Jungenschaft,' and the 'Deutscher Vortrupp,' 'Gefolgschaft Deutscher Juden' 1918–1935." Ph.D. dissertation, State University of New York at Stony Brook, 1978.

Rieger, Rentaus. *Major Meno Burg: Ein preussischer Offizier jüdischen Glaubens (1789–1853)*. Duisburg, 1990.

Rigg, Brian. *Hitler's Jewish Soldiers*. Lawrence, Kans., 2002.

Roberman, Sveta. "From Exclusion to Inclusion: Jewish WWII Soldiers in the Israeli National Narrative." *Israel Studies* 14 (2009): 50–71.

Rockaway, Robert. *But He Was Good to His Mother: The Lives and Crimes of Jewish Gangsters*. Jerusalem and New York, 2001.

Rosenberg, Seymour Lionel. *The Smile Belongs to the Dream: A Memoir*. Kingston, Ontario, 2002.

Rosenthal, Jacob. *Epizodah shel "rish'ut"? "Sefirat ha-yehudim" be-milhemet ha-'olam ha-rishonah*. Jerusalem, 2005.

Rosenthal, Monroe, and Isaac Mozeson. *War of the Jews: A Military History from Biblical to Modern Times*. New York, 1990.

Roth, Cecil. "Jews in the Defence of Britain." *Transactions of the Jewish Historical Society of England* 15 (1946).

Roth, Joseph. *Job*. Woodstock, N.Y., 1982.

———. *The Radetzky March*. New York, 2002.

Rovighi, Alberto. *I militari di origine ebraica nel primo secolo di vita dello Stato italiano*. Rome, 1999.

Rozen, Doron. *Be-ikhvot ha-otsar ha-amerika'i: pe'ilut ha-haganah ba-artsot ha-berit 1949–1949.* Tel Aviv, 2008.

Rozenblit, Marsha. *Reconstructing a National Identity: The Jews of Hapsburg Austria during World War I.* New York, 2001.

Rubin, E. *140 Jewish Marshals, Generals and Admirals.* London, 1952.

Rubin, Ruth. *Voices of a People: The Story of Yiddish Folksong.* New York, 1973.

Rubinstein, Jeffrey L. *The Culture of the Babylonian Talmud.* Baltimore, 2003.

Rubinstein, Joshua. *Tangled Loyalties: The Life and Times of Ilya Ehrenburg.* Toronto, 1996.

Sandler, Gilbert. *Jewish Baltimore: A Family Album.* Baltimore, 2000.

Saperstein, Marc. "British Jewish Preachers in Time of War (1800–1918)." *Journal of Modern Jewish Studies* 4, no. 3 (2005): 255–71.

———. *Jewish Preaching in Times of War, 1800–2001.* Oxford, 2008.

———. "War and Patriotism in Sermons to Central European Jews, 1756–1815." *Leo Baeck Institute Year Book XXXVIII* (1993): 3–14.

Sarna, Jonathan D. "Jewish Prayers for the U.S. Government: A Study in the Liturgy of Politics and the Politics of Liturgy." In *Moral Problems in American Life*, ed. Karen Halttunen and Lewis Perry. Ithaca, N.Y., 1998, 201–21.

Schechter, Ronald. *Obstinate Hebrews: Representations of Jews in France, 1715–1815.* Berkeley and Los Angeles, 2002.

Schmidl, Erwin. *Juden in der k. (u.) k. Armee 1788–1918 / Jews in the Habsburg Armed Forces.* Eisenstadt, 1989.

Schmidt, Wolfgang. "Die Juden in der Bayerischen Armee." In *Deutsche Jüdische Soldaten. Von der Epoche der Emanzipation bis zum Zeitalter der Weltkriege*, ed. Frank Nägler. Hamburg, 1996, 63–86.

Schnitzer, Shira. "'No Conflict of Principle': The Patriotic Rhetoric of Anglo-Jewish Sermons During the Boer War." *Journal of Modern Jewish Studies* 3 (2004): 289–305.

Schoeps, Julius. "'Jeder Stein ist besudelt.' Der Weg des Journalisten Fritz Heymann aus Nazi-Deutschland in das Amsterdamer Exil." In *Deutsche Publizistik im Exil 1933–1945*, ed. Markus Behmer. Münster, 2000.

Schölzel, Christian. *Walter Rathenau: Eine Biographie.* Paderborn, 2006.

Schorsch, Ismar. "Art as Social History: Moritz Openheim and the German-Jewish Vision of Emancipation." In *From Text to Context: The Turn to History in Modern Judaism.* Hanover, N.H., 1994, 93–117.

Schuetz, Chana C. "Deutsche jüdische Soldaten." In *Juden, Emanzipation und Antisemitismus in Deutschland im 19. u. 20. Jahrhundert*, ed. Wolfgang Michalka and Martin Vogt. Eggingen, 2003, 39–44.

Schwartz, Barry. "*Hanoten Teshua*: The Origin of Traditional Jewish Prayer for the Government." *Hebrew Union College Annual* 57 (1986): 113–20.

———. "Ha-tefilah li-shlom ha-malkhut ve-ha-medinah." *Pirkei mehkar le-yom ha-atsma'ut.* Ramat Gan, 1998, 176–200.

Schwartz, Jordan A. *The Speculator: Bernard M. Baruch in Washington, 1917–1965.* Chapel Hill, N.C., 1981.

Segev, Tom. *1949: The First Israelis.* New York, 1986.

———. *1967: Israel, the War and the Year That Transformed the Middle East.* New York, 2007.

Senekowitsch, Martin. *Gleichberechtigt in einer grossen Armee: zur Geschichte des Bundes Jüdischer Frontsoldaten Österreichs, 1932–1938.* Vienna, 1994.

Serman, William. "Le corps des officiers français sous la Deuxième République et le Second Empire." Doctorat d'état, University of Paris, 4 vols., 1976.

———. *Les officiers français dans la nation, 1848–1914.* Paris, 1982.

Shaltiel, Eli. *Pinhas Rutenberg: 'aliyato u-nefilato shel "ish hazak" be-Erets-Yisra'el, 1879–1942,* vol. 1. Tel Aviv, 1990.

Shapira, Anita. *Brenner: sipur hayim.* Tel Aviv, 2008.

———. "Hirbet Hizah: Between Remembrance and Forgetting." *Jewish Social Studies* 7 (2001): 1–62.

———. " 'In the City of Slaughter' versus 'He Told Her.' " *Prooftexts* 25, (2005): 86–102.

———. *Land and Power: The Zionist Resort to Force, 1881–1948.* New York, 1992.

———. *Yigal Alon, Native Son: A Biography.* Philadelphia, 2008.

Sheehan, James. *Where Have All the Soldiers Gone? The Transformation of Modern Europe.* New York, 2008.

Sherman, A. J. "German-Jewish Bankers in World Politics: The Financing of the Russo-Japanese War." *Leo Baeck Institute Year Book XXVIII* (1983): 59–73.

Sherman, Daniel. "Bodies and Names: The Emergence of Commemoration in Interwar France." *American Historical Review* 102 (1998): 443–66.

Shukman, Harold. *War or Revolution: Russian Jews and Conscription in Britain, 1917.* London, 2006.

Sieg, Ulrich. *Jüdische Intellektuelle im Ersten Weltkrieg.* Berlin, 2001.

———. "Nothing More German than the German Jews? On the Integration of a Minority in a Society at War." In *Towards Normality? Acculturation and Modern German Jewry,* ed. Rainer Liedtke and David Rechter. Tübingen, 2003, 201–16.

Silber, Michael. "From Tolerated Aliens to Citizen-Soldiers: Jewish Military Service in the Era of Joseph II." In *Constructing Nationalities in East Central Europe,* ed. Peter M. Judson and Marsha L. Rozenblit. New York, 2004, 19–36.

Simon, Ernst. *Brücken: Gesammelte Aufsätze.* Heidelberg, 1965.

Simonsohn, Shlomo. *A Documentary History of the Jews of Italy: The Jews in Sicily; Volume Eight, 1490–1497.* Leiden, 2006.

Slater, Leonard. *The Pledge.* New York, 1970.

Slutsky, Yehuda, and Mordechai Kaplan. *Hayalim yehudim be-tsiv'ot eyropa.* Tel Aviv, 1967.

Sokel, Anthony. *The Imperial Royal Austro-Hungarian Navy.* Annapolis, Md., 1968.

Spiegel, Shalom. *The Last Trial: On the Legends and Lore of the Command to Abraham to Offer Isaac as a Sacrifice.* New York, 1993.

Spiers, Edward. *The Army and Society, 1815–1914.* London, 1980.

———. *The Late Victorian Army, 1868–1902.* Manchester, UK, 1992.

Spitzer, Samuel. *Das Heer- und Wehrgesetz der alten Israeliten im Vergleiche zu den in Ungarn-Österreich bestehenden diesfälligen Bestimmmungen.* Pest, 1869.

St. John, Robert. *Ben-Gurion.* London, 1959.

Stadler, Nurit. "Playing with Sacred/Corporeal Identities: Yeshiva Students' Fantasies of Military Participation." *Jewish Social Studies* 13 (2007), 155–78.

Stampfer, Shaul. "The Geographic Background of East European Jewish Migration to the United States before World War I." In *Migration across Time and Nations: Popula-*

*tion Mobility in Historical Contexts*, ed. Ira A. Glazier and Luigi de Rosa. New York, 1986, 220–30.

——. "What Actually Happened to the Jews of Ukraine in 1648?" *Jewish History* 17 (2003): 207–27.

Stanislawski, Michael. *Autobiographical Jews: Essays in Jewish Self-Fashioning.* Seattle, 2004.

——. *Psalms for the Tsar: A Minute-Book of a Psalms Society in the Russian Army, 1864–1867.* New York, 1988.

——. "Reflections on the Russian Rabbinate." In *Jewish Religious Leadership: Image and Reality*, ed. Jack Wetheimer. New York, 2004, 2:429–46.

——. *Tsar Nicholas and the Jews: The Transformation of Jewish Society in Russia, 1825–1855.* Philadelphia, 1983.

Stargardt, Nicholas. *The German Idea of Militarism: Radical and Socialist Critics, 1866–1914.* New York, 1994.

Sterba, Christopher. *Good Americans: Italian and Jewish Immigrants during the First World War.* New York, 2003.

Stern, Fritz. *Gold and Iron: Bismarck, Bleichröder, and the Building of the German Empire.* New York, 1977.

Stern, Moritz. *Aus der Zeit der deutschen Befreiungskriege, 1813–1815.* Berlin, 1918.

Stern, Rudolf. "Fritz Haber: Personal Reflections." *Leo Baeck Institute Year Book VIII* (1963): 70–113.

Stow, Kenneth. *Alienated Minority: The Jews of Medieval Latin Europe.* Cambridge, UK, 1993.

Strenski, Ivan. *Contesting Sacrifice: Religion, Nationalism and Social Thought in France.* Chicago, 2002.

Sugarman, Martin. *Fighting Back: Anglo-Jewry's Contribution to the Second World War.* London, 2009.

Surh, Gerald D. "Russia's 1905 Era Pogroms Reexamined." *Canadian-American Slavic Studies* 44 (2010): 253–95.

Szajkowski, Zosa. *Jews and the French Foreign Legion.* New York, 1975.

——. *Jews and the French Revolutions of 1789, 1830, and 1848.* New York, 1970.

Tama, Diogene, ed. *Transactions of the Parisian Sanhedrin, or Acts of the Assembly of Israelitish [sic] Deputies of France and Italy.* Trans. F. D. Kirwan. Cincinnati, 1956.

Tanner, Israel Zwi. *Joseph Trumpeldor. Ein Jüdischer Held*, 3rd ed. Vienna, 1936.

Teller, Adam. "Jewish Literary Responses to the Events of 1648–1649 and the Creation of a Polish-Jewish Consciousness." In *Culture Front: Representing Jews in Eastern Europe*, ed. Benjamin Nathans and Gabriella Safran. Philadelphia, 2008, 17–45.

Teter, Magdalena. *Jews and Heretics in Catholic Poland: A Beleaguered Church in the Post-Reformation Era.* New York, 2006.

Teveth, Shabtai. *Ben-Gurion: The Burning Ground, 1886–1948.* New York, 1987.

Theilhaber, Felix. *Jüdische Flieger im Weltkrieg.* Berlin, 1924.

Toury, Jacob. *Mehumah u-mevukhah be-mahapekhat 1848.* Tel Aviv, 1968.

Troen, Ilan. "The Price of Partition, 1948: The Dissolution of the Palestine Potash Company." *Journal of Israeli History* 15 (1994):53–81.

Tulchinsky, Gerald. *Branching Out: The Transformation of the Canadian Jewish Community.* Toronto, 1998.

van Rahden, Till. "Jews and the Ambivalences of Civil Society in Germany, 1800–1933: Assessment and Reassessment." *Journal of Modern History* 77 (2005): 1024–47.

Vanikoff, Maurice. *La commémoration des engagements voluntaires des juifs d'origine étrangère, 1914–1918.* Paris, 1932.

Verbin, Moshe. *Ha-yehudim 'im neshek bi-yedeihem. Perek be-helkam shel ha-yehudim be-milhamot polin be-me'ot 16–17.* Lod, 2000.

Vogel, Rolf. *Ein Stück von Uns. Deutsche Juden in deutschen Armeen 1813–1976. Eine Dokumentation.* Mainz, 1977.

Wagenseil, Johann Christoph. *Exercitationes Sex Varii Arumenti.* Altdorf, 1698.

Wahrman, Dror. *The Making of the Modern Self: Identity and Culture in Eighteenth-Century England.* New Haven, Conn., 2004.

Wandres, J. *The Ablest Navigator: Lieutenant. Paul N. Shulman USN, Israel's Volunteer Admiral.* Annapolis, Md., 2010.

Ward, Stephen, ed. *The War Generation: Veterans of the First World War.* Port Washington, N.Y., 1975.

Watts, Martin. *The Jewish Legion and the First World War.* New York, 2004.

Weber, Eugen. *Peasants into Frenchmen: The Modernization of Rural France, 1870–1914.* Stanford, Calif., 1976.

Wenger, Beth. *History Lessons: The Creation of American Jewish Heritage.* Princeton, N.J., 2010.

Wengeroff, Pauline. *Rememberings: The World of a Russian-Jewish Woman in the Nineteenth Century,* trans. Henry Wenkart, ed. Bernard D. Cooperman. College Park, Md., 2008.

Westman, Robert S., and David Biale, eds. *Thinking Impossibilities: The Intellectual Legacy of Amos Funkenstein.* Toronto, 2008.

Whalen, Robert Weldon. *Bitter Wounds: German Victims of the Great War, 1914–1939.* Ithaca, N.Y., 1984.

Wilcock, Evelyn. *Pacifism and the Jews.* Landsdown, 1994.

Winter, Jay. *Remembering War: The Great War between History and Memory in the Twentieth Century.* New Haven, Conn., 2006.

———. *Sites of Memory, Sites of Mourning: The Great War in European Cultural History.* New York, 1998.

Winter, Jay, and Emmanuel Sivan, eds. *War and Remembrance in the Twentieth Century.* Cambridge, UK, 1999.

Wistrich, Robert. *The Jews of Vienna in the Age of Franz Joseph.* Oxford, 1989.

Wiznitzer, Arnold. "Jewish Soldiers in Dutch Brazil, 1630–1654." *Proceedings of the American Jewish Historical Society* 46 (1956): 40–50.

Wolf, Simon. *The American Jew as Patriot, Soldier and Citizen.* Cranbury, N.J., 2006.

Wooton, Graham. *The History of the British Legion.* London, 1956.

Wright, Jacob L. "Surviving in an Imperial Context: Foreign Military Service and Judean Identity." In *Judah and the Judeans in the Achaemenid Period: Negotiating Identity in an International Context,* ed. Oded Lipschits, Gary N. Knoppers, and Manfred Oeming. Winona Lake, Ind., 2011, 505–28.

Wyrwa, Ulrich. "Antisemitism in Europe and the Italian Jewish Response: The Coverage of the Journal *Il Vessillo Israelitico* (1879–1914)." *Studia Judaica* 15 (2007): 196–209.

Yahav, Dan. *Gam eleh ba-giborim. Lohmim mitnadvim erets-yisre'elim ba-"brigadot ha-beinle'umiyot" bi-Sefarad (1936–1938)*. Tel Aviv, 2008.

Yerushalmi, Yosef Haim. *Haggadah and History: A Panorama in Facsimile of Five Centuries of the Printed Haggadah from the Collections of Harvard University and the Jewish Theological Seminary of America*. New York, 1997.

———. *Zakhor, Jewish History and Memory*. Seattle, 1982.

Yuval, Yisrael. *Two Nations in Your Womb: Perceptions of Jews and Christians in Late Antiquity and the Middle Ages*. Berkeley and Los Angeles, 2006.

Zaagsma, Gerben. "Jewish Volunteers in the Spanish Civil War: A Case Study of the Botwin Company." M.A. thesis, School of Oriental and African Studies, London, 2001.

Zalkin, Mordechai. "Bein 'benei elohim' li-'venei adam': rabanim, bahurei yeshivot, veha-giyus la-tsava ha-rusi ba-meah ha-tesha esreh." In *Shalom u-milhamah ba-tarbut ha-yehudit*, ed. Avriel Bar-Levav. Jerusalem, 2006, 165–222.

Zechlin, Egmont, Hans Joachim Bieber. *Die deutsche Poliitk und die Juden im ersten Weltkrieg*. Göttingen, 1969.

Zertal, Idith. *Israel's Holocaust and the Politics of Nationhood*. Cambridge, UK, 2005.

Ziemann, Benjamin. *War Experience in Rural Germany, 1914–1923*. New York, 2007.

Zimmerman, Moshe. "Muscle Jews versus Nervous Jews." In *Emancipation through Muscles: Jews and Sports in Europe*, ed. Michael Brenner and Gideon Reuveni. Lincoln, Neb., 2006, 13–26.

# INDEX